EXPORTING FREEDOM

EXPORTING FREEDOM

Religious Liberty and American Power

ANNA SU

Harvard University Press
CAMBRIDGE, MASSACHUSETTS
LONDON, ENGLAND
2016

Second printing

Library of Congress Cataloging-in-Publication Data

Su, Anna, 1980– author.
Exporting freedom : religious liberty and American power / Anna Su.
pages cm
Includes bibliographical references and index.
ISBN 978-0-674-28602-3 (hardcover : alk. paper)
1. Freedom of religion—United States—History. 2. Freedom of religion—History.
3. United States—Foreign relations. 4. Religion and international relations—United States—History. I. Title.
KF4783.S8 2015
323.44'20973—dc23
2015003577

In memory of my father, Su Hun Tiat

Contents

EXPORTING FREEDOM

Introduction

In 1906, the American legation in Bolivia wrote to Elihu Root, then U.S. secretary of state, with the happy news that the Bolivian Congress voted to reform its constitution and allow for freedom of religions other than the established Roman Catholic Church.[1] Seven years earlier, Root's predecessor, John Hay, had asked U.S. diplomatic officials in Bolivia and other South American republics to examine the legal conditions pertaining to the ability of foreigners to engage in the public exercise of religion, including the recognition of non-Catholic marriages, and to make the necessary entreaties to the Bolivian government accordingly.[2] What started out as a diplomatic effort to protect the rights and liberties of U.S. citizens traveling abroad ended with a constitutional provision guaranteeing religious freedom for all inside Bolivia.

But at that time, the Bolivian episode was simply one in many such attempts by the United States to promote religious freedom abroad. Often at the behest of American missionaries, the U.S. government advocated for the religious freedom of Christians in China and the protection of Jews within the Ottoman Empire, and it protested the treatment of Jews in Romania without being a party to any relevant treaty.[3] As an illustration of how strongly the United States felt about the issue of religious freedom abroad, in 1911, it abrogated an 1832 treaty on mutual freedom of commerce and travel with Russia over the latter's relentless persecution of Jews within its territory, especially sojourning American Jews.[4] There could be no clearer act of diplomatic rebuke.

Religious freedom in the United States has an illustrious history. That narrative often begins with the seventeenth-century European persecutions that drove English colonists to found settlements in the New World, moves on to the great constitutional experiment of designing a government without an established religion during the Founding period, and continues with the contemporary struggles over the meanings of this freedom in American public life.[5] Unfettered by a national church, now as then, it is commonplace to hear that "religious freedom is what makes America great."[6] As the abovementioned episodes show, American conflation of its national identity with the principle of religious liberty did not mean that they were only concerned with religious liberty at home but also with religious freedom abroad. From the early years of the Republic, religious Americans traveled as missionaries to distant lands and preached the Gospel. At first, they appealed both to the U.S. government to protect their own efforts to evangelize among foreign peoples, but in time, such petitions encompassed promoting the religious freedom of those among whom they lived. In the latter half of the nineteenth century, Americans also participated in a transnational civilizational discourse with Europe that saw it as a duty of civilized, if mostly Christian, nations to bring religious liberty to the less enlightened parts of the world. Finally, the influx of immigrants of various religious and ethnic affiliations also meant that these new Americans remained concerned with the welfare of their coreligionists living overseas, viewing themselves as faith communities that transcended national borders.

Thus, when Congress enacted the 1998 International Religious Freedom Act incorporating the promotion of religious freedom as part of U.S. foreign policy, it was not doing anything new.[7] In fact, it was reviving and institutionalizing an old American tradition. What is different in the twenty-first century is the world in which such promotion efforts are now undertaken. No longer appealing to notions of religious liberty as natural law or principle of civilization, today, the right to religious liberty as law is enshrined in almost all national constitutions and in the foundational documents of international law as a basic human right. And when the United States government promotes religious freedom abroad, it does so by appealing to these legal documents, which are supported by a variety of domestic and international mechanisms for monitoring, if not enforcement.

The task of historians, it has been said, is not only to remember what others have forgotten or wished to forget but also to stand back from contemporary events and see it in a broader context and a longer perspective.[8] It is striking that prevailing narratives of either American foreign policy or religious freedom do not include these efforts to promote religious freedom abroad[9] and that current histories of the international law on religious freedom do not recognize its American origins.[10] To be sure, other imperial powers, most notably Great Britain, were also concerned with religious freedom abroad, but American ascendancy had entirely new ramifications, in part because it took place as formal empire became increasingly illegitimate. British and French religious freedom promotion efforts occurred within the broad confines of their respective empires as religious liberty largely facilitated the civilizing mission either to transform recalcitrant natives into loyal imperial subjects or to protect beleaguered Jews and Christians in extraterritorial extensions within other empires.[11] As those empires crumbled, so too did their efforts.

Through six historical episodes spanning a century of U.S. foreign policy, this book recovers the outward-looking story of American religious freedom and the transnational legal regime it generated. As American geopolitical power rose, promoting religious freedom ceased to be limited to diplomatic overtures on behalf of persecuted believers elsewhere. Instead, the U.S. government participated directly in the drafting of these international laws and national constitutions and, in some cases, their implementation. These are the very laws invoked by the U.S. government when it promotes religious freedom today. Some of these episodes might seem familiar enough. For instance, the American role in the drafting of the Japanese postwar constitution and the Universal Declaration of Human Rights has been well documented and analyzed. But others, such as President Woodrow Wilson's belief in the importance of religious freedom as international law in order to remove a source of future conflicts, or the circumstances surrounding the Jackson-Vanik amendment to the 1974 Trade Reform Act, which leveraged trade concessions to Communist economies on the observance of human rights, may not be. Casting familiar episodes alongside obscure ones in an unfamiliar light upends several existing understandings of what religious freedom is and what its promotion by a world power actually means.

One such understanding is the right to religious freedom as a human right. In a recent spate of writings, scholars have begun to question the right's claim to timelessness, universality, and neutrality.[12] As part of a broader academic turn to place human rights within historical and politically contingent contexts, this line of scholarship emphasizes religious liberty as a principle that operates in the midst of murky politics and one that protects certain spheres of autonomy inasmuch as it produces and manages them.[13] The right to religious liberty emancipates inasmuch as invoking such right also subjects. In the same vein, this emergent critical literature also revives notions of religious liberty as a tool employed by Western powers to achieve geopolitical ends as historically demonstrated by European incursions in Asia and the Middle East during the nineteenth century. The picture thus painted of religious liberty is a dramatic shift away from its competing, if more mainstream, portrayal as a hard-won freedom born from the ashes of centuries of European conflicts and as a philosophical triumph that saw the emergence of a neutral public sphere and a sacrosanct individual conscience.[14]

The cautionary and less celebratory impulse is understandable. The view of religious liberty as a culturally contingent product, if at times an outright Western imposition, is a prominent feature of contemporary human rights discourse. And as national religious freedom promotion efforts expand from that of an American monopoly to include similar present-day arrangements explicitly patterned after that of the United States by different Western institutions and governments such as Canada, Italy, and the European Union, a meaningful engagement with this critique would go a long way in ensuring some modicum of progress for these contemporary efforts.[15] Take, for instance, a frequent charge that cultural bias undermines the right's claim to neutrality. A cursory look at the jurisprudence of the European Court of Human Rights indeed reveals a continuing interpretation of religious freedom as a distinctively Christian inheritance underlying European culture.[16]

An alternative history that views the modern international law on religious freedom as birthed by American power offers at once both a complementary and a new vantage point into the genealogy of the laws governing religious freedom. This book looks at the entirety of U.S. foreign policy, from its emergence as a world power with its defeat of a crumbling Spanish empire as historical raw material to elaborate on the multifaceted aspects of religious freedom promotion. The malleability of religious freedom enabled its invocation abroad to be articulated and made salient within particular historical and institutional contexts. In this account, religious liberty has an older history than modern-day human rights. It begins instead with the promotion of religious freedom as an expression of the civilizing impulse, evident in McKinley's Instructions for the Philippines and Wilson's drafts for the Covenant of the League of Nations, which shifts to being a key ingredient for the democratization of states as shown in the American imprint on the foundational documents of the new postwar order, such as the Charter of the United Nations, and in the 1947 Japanese Constitution and finally as part of the promotion of individual human rights. But human rights and its promotion, though primarily recovered from its ancient antecedents and forged in its new contemporary shape during the Cold War, have acquired a different meaning in the post–Cold War world.[17] Consider a difference between the Jackson-Vanik amendment of the 1974 Trade Reform Act and the 1998 International Religious Freedom Act. The former was an American weapon against the Soviet Union, while the latter justifies continuing American power in the post–Cold War world.

Excavating the political, cultural, and intellectual milieu surrounding these laws and charters on religious freedom requires an acknowledgment of the imperial contexts of their drafting and codification.[18] Those who were at the receiving end of these religious freedom provisions under study here knew what that meant; otherwise, the Japanese would not describe the first instance they were presented with the American draft constitution as something like "swallowing boiling water." The religious freedom guarantees in the minority protection regime were indeed imposed by the Big Four countries during the 1919 Paris Peace Conference on Poland and Czechoslovakia. The UN Charter was no doubt largely an Anglo-American drafting affair.[19] Great Power thinking animated their origins, whether as part of an American civilizing mission or part of exporting democratic values, and was clearly manifested in the relationships and assumptions of the handful present in the respective drafting rooms.

But what does *imperial* mean? Since the end of the Cold War and hitting a peak in the aftermath of the tragic events of September 11, 2001, American power has been analyzed in a number of ways to no end. Scholars have argued around terms such as *empire, hegemony,* and *ascendancy* without arriving at a consensus about their meanings. Each remains highly contested in both academic scholarship and public discourse. In this book, *imperial* does not describe actions by a kind of political organization with a dominant center ruling over weaker territories. Instead it refers to a way of seeing the world from a position of power and acting accordingly. That is only conceivable within the particular context of unequal relationships in terms of the availability of various modes of political action.[20]

To approach the origins of various laws on international religious freedom through the lens of the imperial, of American power, allows us first and foremost to situate U.S. history as part of a wider, global narrative.[21] It broadens the frame within which we can see why particular historical actors thought and acted the way they did, and gives us a glimpse of the interconnectedness of the global and the local. It allows precisely the kind of narratives located at the intersection between domestic American religious freedom and its foreign policy.

Second, it gives a distinctive place to law as a subject of analysis. For the United States, international lawmaking was not anathema to but rather facilitated and continues to provide a framework for its global ascendancy. The U.S. government had a profound role in the creation and expansion of norms on religious freedom in international law and in the domestic constitutions of countries it has militarily occupied in the construction of an international liberal order. These norms shaped the legal spaces in other sovereign states within which the practice of religious freedom could be regulated, foreclosing as well as enabling certain types of action as much as they furthered distinct American geopolitical aims. Though not any more important than religious liberty as morality or principle of natural law, as positive law, it carries with it the machinery of state power.

Finally, it exposes the continuities in the course of projecting U.S. power abroad and avoids the unproductive question of whether the United States was or still is an empire. Such a question elides the variety of nonmilitary, ideological expressions of American power, which includes prevailing understandings of religious freedom. Moreover, a debate over these categories often only highlights the existence of concrete institutions denoting American imperial power such as overseas colonies or military installations. In reality, several mechanisms of governance employed during the U.S. experiment in formal empire at the turn of the twentieth century continue to inform its current manifestations even as most of the underlying imperial structure has fallen into disrepute and withered away.

German chancellor Otto von Bismarck once remarked that God had a special providence for fools, drunks, and the United States of America. It is a belief that Americans have taken to heart since the first Plymouth colonists arrived in the seventeenth century. An early example of American exceptionalism, the "city upon a hill" view (that is, the belief that the United States has been blessed and created to be an exemplar for the rest of the world) has greatly influenced the grand narrative, both secular and religious, of U.S. foreign relations.[22] Religious freedom promotion, first as policy and then later as law, arose from a patchwork of motives, not always wholly religious. That it became a salient feature of U.S. foreign relations depended in large part on the fact that religious liberty as an ideal and principle carried significant purchase with the American people.[23] Clearly, domestic developments mattered. The American model of church–state separation had unleashed an incredible religious energy, especially compared to the stale results produced by the established church model in Europe. Recovering the American origins of the international law on religious freedom allows the use of these laws, though intended for others or for the international community as a whole, as a "magic mirror" on which the evolving face of religious freedom in America is likewise reflected.[24]

The domestic American experience of religion and religious freedom was the font on which U.S. officials drew for their ideas on the ground abroad. It was this very experience that led Eleanor Roosevelt to reject minority and collective rights in the Universal Declaration of Human Rights, saying that, per the American situation, assimilation is the ideal situation in a heterogeneous liberal society. As historian Andrew Preston argued, the role of religion in U.S. foreign relations depended to a large extent on individual biographies, and these individuals were invariably very much a product of their own surroundings and history.[25] Consider how FDR learned his lessons from the failure of Woodrow Wilson or how L. Paul Bremer III perhaps unconsciously imbibed the proconsul mentality of General Douglas MacArthur in Japan. Was it just a coincidence that MacArthur was a lifelong admirer of General Leonard Wood, the American proconsul in Cuba and the Moro province in the Philippines at the height of the U.S. colonial enterprise?

This is not to imply that the meaning of American religious freedom remained static. To the contrary, religious freedom within the United States, for the most part, was a battleground among warring denominations and between religions. Catholics and Protestants battled over the mantle of religious freedom.[26] The same freedom was used to undermine Native American claims to self-determination.[27] From the seamless mixing of religion and government in the nineteenth century to the ascendant secularism in the twenty-first, the domestic landscape remained fluid and a site of struggle. But these contests over details were largely absent in American motivations in the drafting of religious freedom guarantees for others. The specifics might have been in debate, but everyone upheld the principle. At the same time American Catholics and Protestants were struggling over the precise meaning and implication of the principle of separation of church and state at home, U.S. officials readily prescribed it for the postwar Japanese constitution. The shift highlighted in this book concerns the ideological garb of religious freedom promotion rather than the theological vagaries of the principle itself. Thus, the decision whether to promote free exercise over its American variant, separation and disestablishment, depended on the dictates of geopolitics and prudence.

The heart of this book originated from the following question: Why did the United States seek to promote free exercise of religion and separation of church and state during its colonial project in the Philippine Islands at the turn of the twentieth century, an attempt it repeated, uncannily enough more than a century later in post–Saddam Hussein Iraq? As such, the historical inquiry is limited to American policies, the officials who drafted them, and their immediate milieu. Such focus is not meant to render the actual effects of these laws and policies on the lives of those on the ground who received them as any less important; instead, it is a means to evaluate contemporary legal institutions and arrangements, to find its pitfalls and blind spots.[28] It uses the past to think about the present and future, as a catalog of possible roads not taken. In addition, the elite-centric frame necessarily foregrounds individuals who were involved in these episodes of transnational lawmaking, again, not to resuscitate "great man history," a long discredited focus on individuals at the expense of larger historical forces and trends, but to use them as a means to illuminate precisely the kinds of conditions that imbue their actions with such consequence and importance.

Most of what we consider traditions today owes less to historical evidence than to the apparent demands of our present predicaments. Religious freedom is no exception. The inclination to ground current arrangements in distant origins makes it seem as if there were no forks in the road, no strategic choices made. But a consensus did not always exist around the idea that religious freedom as we know it today was good as a matter of positive international law. For an ideal that has such a foundational provenance—indeed, does not the modern state system itself owe its origins to the principle of religious freedom?[29]—its application was not initially meant to be universal. Powerful states saw it largely as an affront to their sovereignty. Even a charismatic and powerful figure like Woodrow Wilson, who had lobbied hard to include it as a matter of universal application in the League of Nations Covenant, could not make it so. Nonetheless, religious liberty, during crucial historical moments, shaped the purview of American national interest and security, and U.S. government officials acted accordingly.[30] Article 18 of the Universal Declaration of Human Rights protecting the right to freedom of conscience might be an expression of a timeless moral good, but there is nothing natural about its particular content and form.

It is important to remember that our contemporary transnational laws on religious freedom represent not only the emergence of one claim, with its attendant understanding and background, but also a foreclosure of others. The loss that we incur if we do not is not only measured in terms of what we forget in the past but also of what we would fail to imagine for the future. For instance, current definitions of human rights, including religious freedom, almost exclusively focus on ideas about the individual, and ideas about religious group rights, which were clearly salient in the past, have now been discredited, if not marginalized or forgotten, for good or ill. This amnesia robs us today of additional resources to use in coming to grips with the challenges posed by religious revivalism as well as religious persecution.

And yet to recognize the imperial provenance or the double-edged nature of religious liberty promotion is not a reason to leave it for dead. Even with the abovementioned emphasis on power, the themes of transformation and unintended consequences nevertheless run through the narrative that unfolds in the following pages. The intertwined story of the Jackson-Vanik amendment and U.S. leadership in the implementation of the Helsinki Accords during the Cold War and how it accidentally opened the floodgates for a transnational network of nongovernmental human rights organizations is an example. More important, there is no doubt that religious freedom presents a genuine and continuing dilemma in a variety of cultural settings.[31] Persecution on account of one's religious beliefs and community is still a grim reality in many places around the world. The Pew Research Center recently found that 33 percent of 198 countries and territories in the world currently have high levels of religious hostilities, a marked increase from previous years.[32] The 2013 International Religious Freedom Report issued by the U.S. Department of State stated that 75 percent of the world population lives in places with high levels of religious restrictions.[33] The goal of this book is not to reject altogether contemporary promotion efforts to address these problems but rather to urge some caution; it is intended to remind policymakers and all concerned, among many others, of the hidden, underlying biases in these laws through the hubris at the moment of their creation.[34] By showing the historicity and contingency of religious freedom, it also opens the space for its own transformation. But in the process, we have to take less for granted when it comes to how we think religious freedom law came about in the past and what it ought to be in our present.

The recent history of international religious freedom law—its origins an expression of American liberal ideology and a handmaiden of its rise to world power—is not a blueprint for solving the problems of global religious freedom. But an honest reckoning with that narrative is a requisite step to understand fully the panoply of laws pursuant to which transnational efforts to address these challenges are currently undertaken, and the ways by which the laws on religious freedom can transcend the aims of its forebears. First and foremost a cautionary tale, each of the following chapters illustrates the ambitions and the limits of what religious freedom promoted as law by an external power can achieve. For as long as exporting this freedom remains part of American and other Western powers' foreign policies, perhaps the most important lessons to be found are in its past wreckage, not its dreams.

1

White Man's Burden

> [W]hen that group of islands, under the impulse of the year just past, shall have become the gems and glories of those tropical seas—a land of plenty and of increasing possibilities; a people redeemed from savage indolence and habits, devoted to the arts of peace, in touch with the commerce and trade of all nations, enjoying the blessings of freedom, of civil and religious liberty, of education, and of homes, and whose children and children's children shall for ages hence bless the American republic because it emancipated and redeemed their fatherland, and set them in the pathway of the world's best civilization.
>
> —*U.S. president William F. McKinley, February 16, 1899*

Elihu Root's appointment as secretary of war came on the heels of what John Hay termed a "splendid little war" between the United States and Spain. The conflict began over American intervention in the Cuban struggle for independence, which then spilled over to the rest of the Spanish possessions in the Pacific.[1] The lopsided nature of the war was best captured in Commodore George Dewey's victory over the decrepit Spanish naval forces in the famous Battle of Manila Bay on May 1, 1898. The battle lasted for only seven hours total, including a three-hour break for breakfast,[2] with no American casualties. Although skirmishes between the two powers continued, by the end of July 1898, beleaguered Spain had sent entreaties to Washington seeking an armistice.

The aftermath of the war plunged the United States, then a fledgling global power, into a national crisis unprecedented since the Civil War. While expansion and annexation of other separate territories were not new in American history,[3] the prospect of possessing Spain's erstwhile colonies with the certainty that none of them could be incorporated as states in the union tugged at the nation's conscience. When Congress issued a joint resolution declaring war against Spain, it had sought to demonstrate benign American intentions by attaching to it the Teller amendment, which forbade the formal annexation of Cuba.[4] As President William McKinley instructed the American peace negotiators in Paris to demand all of the Philippines from Spain,[5] a divisive national debate exploded over the nature and character of the United States itself.

Colonialism clearly contradicted the self-image of a republican United States. But it also provided a means to international prestige and influence and meaningful participation in the international community. The British poet Rudyard Kipling's infamous poem "White Man's Burden," addressed to the United States as the Senate was about to vote on the ratification of the Treaty of Paris, was one such invitation into the world of empires.[6] As historian Frank Ninkovich noted, the United States, though a great industrial power by the end of the nineteenth century, exercised "little influence in shaping the political or ideological direction being taken by the industrial revolution."[7] Given this background, the common underlying national belief in American exceptionalism pointed to two opposing directions after the war. One view, espoused by the anti-imperialists, stated that the country should simply hold itself out as an example to the world.[8] To occupy the position of colonizer would repudiate longstanding American traditions and ideals. They also believed that, for immutable reasons of race and religion, American civilization could not be a matter of export. The contradictory view, however, sought to export those very ideals to what were considered "lesser" civilizations and tapped into notions of duty and obligation in order to present the case for spreading the blessings of liberty around the world. For them, the United States could be a colonizer, not in the European mold of exploiter but as a tutor and shepherd for the eventual progress and membership of these colonies into the community of nations.

Despite common domestic and international fashions of thought prevailing at the time,[9] it is important to distinguish American reasons and motivations for going to war against Spain from those in the decision to annex the Spanish possessions. Economic as well as humanitarian reasons supported the entry into war,[10] but more vague were those supporting the annexation of far-flung colonies. Although the notion of an occupied Philippines reinforced long-held American visions of an Asian gateway to the Chinese pot of gold, the majority of the arguments entertained by McKinley were a mix of ideological, religious, and geopolitical considerations.[11] The lack of clear economic or security rationales for the annexation of the Philippines provided a convenient entry for largely ideologically oriented projects. Dewey's quick victory produced seductive vistas of an overseas empire. The Philippines would be a grand experiment in the application of American constitutional principles in the spirit of tutelage, a showcase of an exceptional American empire.[12] The appointment of Root, a renowned corporate lawyer, as secretary of war when the country was about to embark on its path as a neophyte colonial power testified to a particular vision of imperialism—one that would be governed by and through law, particularly, though not quite fully as Filipinos and Puerto Ricans would later realize,[13] the U.S. Constitution.

One of these constitutional principles was the right to freedom of religion, which, in the American mind, also carried the necessary corollary of separation between church and state. While both law and religion as analytic concepts have separately been made major subjects in a reinvigorated U.S. empire literature of recent years,[14] none have as yet treated them together in reinterpreting early American visions for its newfound possessions. Moreover, there has been no account that considers McKinley's Instructions to the Second Philippine Commission, dubbed the most important document in American colonial history by Root's biographer and later distinguished international lawyer Philip C. Jessup, a central topic.[15] The lack of attention is surprising considering contemporary interest on law as a facilitator and creator of empire and subjecthood.

Looking to these two concepts together affords a unique view into the U.S. imperial mindset, especially as the constitutional right to free worship and its implementation in the Philippine Islands, among other rights, served to reconcile the seemingly paradoxical notions of self-rule and colonialism, both to the American colonizers and the Filipino colonized. Within the constitutional framework it constructed to distinguish its colonial enterprise from those of its European counterparts,[16] the U.S. government provided and promoted religious freedom in the early years of empire as it took away political independence from the Filipinos. In the Christian parts of the archipelago, disestablishment was brought about by the resolution of the friar lands controversy, which involved the sale of large tracts of land held by Spanish religious orders in the Philippines between the Holy See and the U.S. colonial government in the Philippines. This controversy was intimately tied with the growth and promotion of religious pluralism in the islands, thus ending centuries of Catholic monopoly. In the Muslim parts, on the other hand, the forcible reorganization of the political and religious structure of the area by the U.S. military government, while maintaining its adherence to free religious worship for its Muslim inhabitants, facilitated their pacification and subjugation.

Not often emphasized in previous accounts of American efforts to promote free exercise and disestablishment in the Philippines was how these efforts were as much a continuing contest and negotiation on what religious freedom meant between Catholics and Protestants in the United States as these were about the achievement of American aims in the colonies. The friar lands controversy and the civilization of the Filipino Muslims were important sites for those contests. As such, colonial policies in the Philippines were formulated even as the people responsible for these policies looked inward. Although religious liberty in the Instructions could be considered an exercise in obtaining Filipino consent, it was also an effort to reconcile the American conscience with its turn to empire. These episodes would set a similar trajectory for future American nation-building projects and partly laid the bases of enduring American visions of international order.

Writing McKinley's Instructions

What started out as an altruistic war to liberate Cubans from the tyrannical Spanish yoke quickly turned into a war against Filipino nationalists who were understandably less thrilled about the prospect of exchanging one colonial master for another.[17] Although the Philippines was not even part of the picture as a broad swath of American society clamored for U.S. intervention in Cuba,[18] the question of empire that followed thereafter took on a similar humanitarian garb. Protestant groups led the way in advocating for the imperial turn, seeing a great evangelization opportunity not only in the Philippines but in the rest of Asia, especially China. The arguments, however, were not just overtly religious. It was a reflection of American society at that time that, while church and state were formally and constitutionally separated, there was not a lot separating Christianity from the wider public culture.[19] A fusion of Christianity and progressivism, no doubt influenced by domestic intellectual developments, was the main lingua franca vis-à-vis foreign affairs. Most pro-annexation religious groups considered the Roman Catholic legacy of Spanish rule as a defective form of Christianity, no more than mere superstitions, and therefore the islands was a proper place in which to spread the Gospel anew.[20] The Philippines provided an opportunity to see the spirit of humanitarianism prevalent in the late nineteenth century in action, one more site of the moral reform movements of American Protestants.[21] It was also widely assumed that, for reasons of race, Filipinos were incapable of self-rule. The much-needed and indeed much-prescribed salve to this affliction was often a combination of Protestantism, indeed "a free Bible," and American-type law and government insofar as these structures of thought and action presupposed voluntarism and free inquiry on the part of the individual believer and citizen.

The most prominent leaders of the time, among them, William McKinley, Elihu Root, naval strategist Alfred Thayer Mahan, Henry Cabot Lodge, and Theodore Roosevelt, all subscribed to varying degrees to this view.[22] In his popular tract, *Expansion under New World Conditions,* the prominent Social Gospel adherent and Congregationalist leader Josiah Strong exhorted his fellow Americans to accept its civilizing mandate.[23] "It is time to dismiss the craven fear of being great," he wrote, "to recognize the place in the world which God has given us and to accept the responsibilities which it devolves upon us on behalf of the Christian civilization."[24] It was the same Strong who held up Romanism, a common pejorative term for the Roman Catholic religion at the time, as one of the ten perils threatening American society.[25]

Thanks to the reframing of the issue as a just cause and the fervent advocacy of it as such, the Treaty of Paris, wherein Spain ceded the Philippines to the United States in exchange for $20 million,[26] was ratified by the Senate by a 57 to 27 vote, with only one vote more than the two-thirds majority required. The outbreak of the war between the Americans and the Filipinos at the time of ratification seemingly buttressed the argument of Filipino ingratitude and incompetence. In the words of a *New York Times* editorial at the time, why else would they attack their own liberators?[27] Whereas the mission before was to save the Cubans from the Spanish, in the Philippines, it seemed, the mission was to save Filipinos from themselves.

As a long and bloody guerrilla war raged on in the Philippine countryside between the U.S. army and the Filipino insurgents, President William McKinley, in an oft-quoted account of how he arrived at the decision to keep the Islands, was telling a group of visiting Methodist ministers in the White House that he had no choice but to take them, and "to educate the Filipinos, and uplift and civilize and Christianize them," after several nights of praying to almighty God.[28] The task of determining how the uplifting and civilizing of the Filipinos would take the shape and form that it initially did fell in the lap of Elihu Root, the newly appointed secretary of war who would become the chief architect of American colonial policy.

On the eve of the Spanish-American War, Elihu Root was already one of the top corporate lawyers in New York. He was also a consummate hand in New York politics, having rubbed elbows with the likes of Chester Arthur and Theodore Roosevelt. Although he did not have any political experience beyond state-level reform efforts and as a U.S. attorney for the Southern District of New York, Root had a reputation for his keen judgment and problem-solving skills. As the *New York Times* put it, "Any person meeting Elihu Root for the first time and on occasion of no special significance would be likely to underestimate the aggressive vigor of the man's character. . . . Yet there are many men who have felt his power in legal and political controversy who are willing to concede that the new Secretary of War has the essential qualities of a fighter."[29]

Root did not initially accept McKinley's offer of appointment. He had replied that he knew "nothing about war . . . nothing about the army,"[30] and therefore it seemed like an absurd position to be in. The president's reply however, changed his mind. McKinley needed a lawyer to direct the government of these Spanish islands, and he [Root] was the lawyer he wanted. That McKinley would define the task of colonial administration as a lawyer's job was telling in itself, and it certainly appealed to Root's personal conviction in the civilizing power of the law.[31] But as the new secretary later realized while poring over his library of books on the English colonial system to familiarize himself with the workings of colonial government, the U.S. Constitution was no manual for territories not destined for statehood.[32]

The Treaty of Paris then was a place to start. While Root believed that the people of the islands had no right to be treated as citizens,[33] the U.S. government was bound by the terms of the treaty, together with the moral obligation to secure the welfare and interests of the people over whom it asserted sovereignty. But Root never contemplated wholly grafting the American system onto, much less applying the Constitution to, the Philippines, for two reasons. Judging from his remarks in the aftermath of the *Insular* cases, the limitations and accordingly the privileges provided by the Constitution were reserved for states or territories being prepared for such status. In addition, Root thought it absurd to impose common law on communities used to civil law codes.[34] Thus, the U.S. government would start with statutes that had already been adapted to "insular life and modify them only where it appears to be necessary to conform to our fundamental ideas of justice." These arguments made sense given his belief that the Filipinos were not capable of self-government. The venerable doctrine that government derives its just powers from the consent of the governed was applicable for the conditions in which Thomas Jefferson wrote it, Root declared in a speech,[35] but he reminded his audience that Jefferson did not apply it to Louisiana since the people there were as incapable of self-government as children. Even without the Constitution, however, Root nonetheless believed that there were "certain things that the U.S. government could not do because the people of the United States had declared that no government could do them—the Bill of Rights. There is a moral law which prevents the government doing certain things to any man wherever."[36] In Root's mind, the Constitution exerted only moral force outside the territorial United States. His claim, untested though it was at the time, would be validated by the Supreme Court in the *Insular* cases.

Because the Philippines existed more in the imagination rather than in reality for most Americans, McKinley appointed a commission to ascertain factual conditions in the islands and make the appropriate recommendations for a proper colonial policy. Headed by the staunch anti-imperialist and then president of Cornell University Jacob Schurman,[37] the commission arrived in the islands in the spring of 1899. Despite bitter disagreements among its members over how to deal with the ongoing Philippine rebellion that severely limited their functions—General Elwell Otis, the military-governor at that time, and Schurman never saw eye to eye on many issues—the commission collected and published an incredible amount of political, social, ethnological, and cultural facts concerning the Philippines.[38] Among their many recommendations was the establishment of a civil government.

The Schurman Commission report also painted a detailed picture of the religious situation in the Philippines. Ninety-five percent of the population in the islands belonged to the Roman Catholic religion, with the remaining 5 percent scattered among the non-Christian tribes of the northern part of the archipelago and the Muslim provinces in the south. During the annexation debates, it was the well-known assumption of various Protestant groups that it was their responsibility to Americanize, including to convert, these already Christian, if Catholic, peoples, which rankled American Catholics. Many Protestants claimed that Filipino Catholic practices were in any case a mere veneer for native superstitions. The guarantee of religious liberty in the Treaty of Paris[39] and General Otis's proclamation of religious freedom for the Filipinos on his arrival in Manila paved the way for these groups. Under Spanish rule, following an agreement with the Vatican, the islands were off-limits to missionary activity.[40] Hence, American religion entered as soon as American arms did. An American Bible Society office was opened in Manila as early as November 1899.[41] Although American official attitudes were nonpartisan with regard to religious affairs, officials largely considered the Christianizing mission as supportive of the American aims in the colonies. President McKinley, for example, appeared before an ecumenical conference in 1900 and praised his audience of missionaries for their work. The first lady, Ida McKinley, also encouraged her husband to "pursue private efforts to send Protestant missionaries to the Philippine Islands."[42] But at the same time, some officials, such as William Howard Taft and Theodore Roosevelt, also thought that the best way to uplift the Filipinos was, among others, to make them better Catholics.[43]

What Christianizing meant in the context of overwhelmingly Roman Catholic lands thus remained fluid. Early U.S. government policies affecting religion in the Philippines continued to be a site of controversy for dueling religionists on the home front for the next few years.[44] That the Filipino revolutionary movement was born primarily out of hatred for the Spanish friar class, though not necessarily against the Catholic Church, complicated the situation for the Americans. Because of the *patronato real* dating back to the sixteenth century, which granted Spanish monarchs full dominion over church and state affairs in all her colonies, the Vatican was not to enter the picture formally until the United States entered into negotiations with it. The task of completely separating what was considered to be an unholy mix of church and state that three centuries of Spanish rule had entrenched and consequently boosting American pacification efforts would fall on the deft diplomatic abilities of Elihu Root and William Howard Taft.

Armed with hundreds of pages of interviews and findings of facts, the Schurman Commission prefaced its report with an optimistic note. "The most encouraging feature in the difficult problem we have undertaken in the Philippines," the report read, "is the perfect coincidence between the theory and practice of our government, on the one hand, and ideals of the Filipinos on the other. The very thing they yearn for is what our Government will naturally desire to give them—religious liberty, fundamental personal rights and the largest practicable measure of home rule."[45] Taking into consideration the terms of the Paris treaty, as well as the recommendations of the Schurman Commission, Root proceeded to draft what is now known as McKinley's Instructions to the Second Philippine Commission. In view of the inherent cultural and racial differences between the Americans and the Filipinos,[46] the instructions would serve as the training manual for an apprenticeship in democracy.

The instructions, addressed to the Second Philippine Commission headed by the future U.S. president and Supreme Court chief justice William Howard Taft, conferred legislative powers, including the power to raise taxes and impose duties, to establish educational and civil service systems, and to organize government departments, to the commission, pursuant to McKinley's powers as commander-in-chief. Until Congress passed the Spooner Amendment in 1901[47] and subsequently the Philippine Organic Act of 1902,[48] the commission, as the civil government in the islands, exercised concurrent powers with a military governor-general. Apart from the enumerated instances of legislative power, the instructions incorporated all the guarantees present in the Bill of Rights, except for the right to trial by jury and the right to bear arms. It prohibited slavery as well. The Bureau of Insular Affairs, an office within the War Department created to oversee the colonial possessions, described the instructions in its record of accomplishments sent to Congress as a "constitution and a code of laws almost unprecedented in history . . . a nearly perfect example of organic law, jurisprudence, guarding of rights, distribution of powers, administrative provisions, checks and balances, civilization ever beheld in a single document."[49]

Root attributed the state of the Filipino, a "half-civilized Oriental,"[50] as "little advanced from pure savagery, in religion not far removed from fetishism, unable to read or write in any language, in political condition practically in a state of peonage, totally devoid of the most rudimentary idea of liberty or personal independence"[51] to the centuries-long despotism perpetuated by the church–state alliance of the Spanish colonial government. Religious liberty thus ranked high among his essential principles of government. It also helped that it was the lack of religious liberty that motivated the Filipino rebellion against Spain and thus formed one of their principal demands. In short, for the Americans, the sorry state of the Filipinos was, in some part, a result of the lack of religious freedom therein for centuries,[52] but at the same time they also recognized it was through this very principle that they would be able to secure their subjects' consent to the American civilizing project.

Through the instructions, the mandate to effect religious freedom in the islands acquired legal character vis-à-vis the U.S. colonial government.[53] It not only reproduced the text of the First Amendment: "that no law shall be made respecting an establishment of religion, or prohibiting the free exercise thereof, and that the free exercise and enjoyment of religious profession and worship without discrimination or preference shall forever be allowed" but also took pains to emphasize "that no form of religion and no minister of religion shall be forced upon any community or upon any citizen of the island, that upon the other hand no minister of religion shall be interfered with or molested in following his calling and that the separation between state and church shall be real, entire and absolute." Like its constitutional parent, these guarantees hardly spelled the end of any controversy—and to be sure, at the beginning there were many of them—but it provided a framework within which they could be resolved by the colonial authorities.

How to effect such "real, entire and absolute" separation between church and state confronted the Americans even before they arrived on Philippine shores. The peace negotiations in Paris between the United States and Spain included a representative from the Vatican who unsurprisingly kept close watch on the consequences of the peace talks on the church's interests in the Philippines, its personnel and its properties alike.[54] By September 1901, there was a new American president. Theodore Roosevelt, unlike McKinley, paid attention to Catholic concerns in the United States.[55] Dating back to his years in New York state politics, Roosevelt's religious views had been remarkably accommodating, given the prevailing anti-Catholic sentiment in American society at that time. To the contrary, he commended many American Catholics for their patriotism, appointing some of them to local office. He even became friends with Catholic priests such as Archbishop John Ireland of Minnesota, a strong supporter of Progressive social justice efforts and the Americanization of European Catholic immigrants. This proved useful when the full implications of the questions involving the Spanish friars remaining in the Philippines and their lands presented themselves. The resolution of the friar lands controversy would be instrumental in ending the ongoing rebellion.

Separating Church and State: The Friar Lands Controversy

The Americans arrived in the Philippines as a Filipino nationalist revolt was already ongoing against the Spanish colonial government. The U.S. army, led by General Otis, helped in driving out the Spanish forces, and their presence was initially thought to be friendly by the Filipino nationalists. The Benevolent Assimilation proclamation of McKinley addressed to the Filipinos arrived in the midst of a confused battlefield and was intended to assure them that the Americans had come "not as invaders or conquerors but as friends to protect the natives in their homes, in their employments and in their personal and religious rights."[56] But the phrase "American sovereignty" in the proclamation instantly created tension between the two forces. Though officials in the mainland had hoped to avoid war, General Otis was not particularly averse to another such conflict.[57] It did not take long for hostilities to break out. That American liberation was instead greeted by Filipino guerrilla warfare created much complication in the United States.[58] The Democrats based their 1900 election platform on granting immediate independence to the Filipinos,[59] a plank refuted by the Republicans on the grounds of duty and responsibility.[60] To avoid increasing the already mounting political costs of annexation, a nonmilitary solution had to be found in order to pacify and secure the islands.

Perhaps more a sign of ignorance of the colonial endeavor they were about to undertake than an outward gesture of nobility, the U.S. government found itself in a straitjacket that it created in Paris. Various articles of the treaty obligated the Americans to protect all Spanish citizens and property, including Spanish friars who wished to return to their parishes and regain control of their lands.[61] But the Filipino revolt was a revolt against the friars as much as a rebellion against Spain itself. Friars were priests who belonged to religious orders. During Spanish rule, the four largest orders in the Philippines were the Dominicans, Augustinians, Franciscans, and Recollects. The Jesuits, which were expelled from all Spanish lands in 1768 by a royal suppression decree and only allowed back in 1852, did not become as powerful (and therefore as hated) as the others. Friars, who were all Spaniards, as opposed to secular priests, who were almost always native Filipinos, led all parishes and were members of municipal governments in various capacities.[62] They helped in tax collections, formulation of policies, and generally exerted a significant influence on all aspects of Philippine society. Filipinos complained that the friars prevented the native clergy from taking parish leadership positions; charged exorbitant fees for various spiritual services, such as baptisms and weddings; and engaged in immoral behavior, such as concubinage with their parishioners.[63] The biggest and clearest symbol it seemed of friar abuse was the hundreds of thousands of acres of the best agricultural lands in the country held under their titles.[64]

The initial investigation conducted by the Schurman Commission revealed intense native hostility toward the friars for this very reason.[65] As a result, the commission recommended the purchase of the friars' lands, which were to be subsequently sold to Filipinos at affordable rates. At the time, however, no procedure for effecting such sale was suggested. Many of these lands were seized by Filipino revolutionaries during the ongoing conflict.

The constraints posed by the Treaty of Paris, as well as the U.S. Constitution's guarantee on not taking private property without due process of law, put the Americans in a bind. They pledged to protect Spanish property rights as well as the security of Spanish priests, many of whom had been held in captivity by the Filipino rebels,[66] but they needed to win Filipino support and take the air out of the insurgency.[67] Any move by the government to confiscate these properties could raise questions under the very same rubric of separation of church and state that they purported to uphold and stand for. The Filipinos were already hostile to American intentions not only to annex the country but also that they would restore the Spanish friars to their previous positions. To make the matter more difficult, the McKinley administration had to fend off criticisms by U.S. Catholics that the war in the Philippines was generally a war against the church.[68]

In the midst of grappling with the Americanist controversy, wherein the Holy See condemned as heresy the practices and ideas relating to liberalism and individualism supposedly percolating within the Roman Catholic Church in the United States, American Catholics reluctantly supported the annexation of the Philippines as a way to show their national loyalty. Nonetheless, they remained wary of the motives behind the occupation, most notably that the Philippine Islands would become fertile ground for Protestant evangelization efforts. As a result, Catholic groups and clerics kept close attention to U.S. government actions in the islands. Still, widespread nativism required a delicate hand when it came to dealing with the Vatican. Any semblance of establishing diplomatic relations with it and thus recognizing the pope as a sovereign power would spell electoral defeat for any Republican candidate. Using the services of Archbishop John Ireland, a friend of McKinley and Roosevelt and a rare Republican Catholic, Root had hoped that matters could be disposed of quickly if the Vatican would just order the withdrawal of all Spanish priests from the islands. The Vatican refused, not believing that the Filipinos wanted the friars out. U.S. Catholics believed it was a ruse to convert the islands to Protestantism.[69]

But the U.S. government also genuinely intended to proclaim religious freedom for the Filipinos. To carry out McKinley's promises in his Benevolent Assimilation proclamation, for instance, General Otis disbanded ecclesiastical monopoly by introducing the practice of civil marriage.[70] His successor, General Arthur MacArthur, reiterated this promise of religious freedom shortly after.[71] The tumult of the situation somehow obscured the object of these promises. Were they protecting the Filipinos or the Spaniards? General Otis's seemingly cordial relations with the hated Spanish archbishop of Manila, Bernardo Nozaleda, only exacerbated this confusion when he reinstated the latter to a position in a key parish. If the American intention was to align the United States with the cause of religious freedom in order to distinguish itself from the church–state entanglement identified with its colonial predecessor, the message was lost on its intended recipients. The Americans came to realize that Filipino antagonism toward the friars was political rather than religious in nature, but their abstract promises and intentions of securing religious liberty and separation of church and state had to take a more concrete form.[72]

Taking its cue from the findings of the Schurman report, the Instructions' exhortation of separation between state and church was drawn primarily in the context of the simmering issue of the friars and their lands.[73] As soon as the Taft Commission arrived in the Philippines, it held a new series of hearings in order to ascertain Filipino attitudes toward the friars and what to do with the friar properties.[74] Taft later testified before the Senate Committee on the Philippines that the friars were indeed unpopular with the natives and that it would be unwise to restore them to their parishes.[75] He affirmed the initial findings of the Schurman Commission and recommended not only the purchase of their lands but also the substitution of Spanish priests with priests of other nationalities, preferably American. This was also partly intended to show to Catholics at home that the U.S. government was not hostile toward the church.

The negotiations in Manila, however, were not proceeding as smoothly as planned. The apostolic delegate from the Vatican, Placide Chappelle of New Orleans, was as inflexible on the issue of the friars as Taft and Root were, even preventing some Spanish priests from voluntarily leaving the country.[76] By the fall of 1901, Archbishop Ireland wrote a letter to Root, at the urging of the Vatican, wherein he proposed that the McKinley administration deal with the Vatican directly. When Roosevelt became president after McKinley's assassination, he took up this suggestion and asked Root to look into the possibility of sending a delegation to Rome. The Vatican had two reasons to get involved: First, it was keen on preserving the church's interests and gains in the islands even under American sovereignty; second, its eye was turned toward Europe. Dealing with the United States, a newly minted world power, would lend necessary prestige to the church at a time when anticlericalism was on the rise in France and Spain.[77] For the United States, the concerns were more internal. Root and Taft took seriously the American responsibility of stewardship for the islands. But if any uplifting of the peoples was going to occur, order had to be restored, which would be possible only if the people's grievances against the friars were to be addressed. Even after the much-celebrated capture of the Filipino rebel leader Emilio Aguinaldo, pockets of insurgency remained. A resolution of the friar issue would greatly advance American efforts to establish a working civil government.

A White House meeting with Roosevelt, Taft, Root, and Ireland in February 1902 led to a presidential order for Taft to go to Rome, a task that spoke volumes about the amount of presidential trust in him.[78] Discreet consultations with Protestant leaders such as Homer Stuntz of the Methodists and Lyman Abbot of the Congregationalists were made before and after the meeting, and even then Taft had to assure them constantly throughout that the trip was by no means a diplomatic mission.[79] Again drafted by Root, Roosevelt's instructions to Taft were explicit about the intentions and motivations of the American mission, and it is worth quoting at length:

> It is a matter of prime importance to bring about in the Philippines as rapidly as possible conformity with the universal American practice of complete separation between church and state. The difficulties are great because under the Spanish regime the church and state were not merely united but fused in an almost inextricable tangle. *The all-important subject in securing this separation of church and state is to dispose of the friar question by acquiring the lands of the friars and securing their retirement from the islands.* Until this has been done, the religious question will cause the utmost difficulty in the Philippines. The corporations to which the friars belong are all under the final control of the authorities at Rome and it has been impossible to come to any agreement in the matter either in the Philippines or in the US. It is evident that to expedite a final settlement and to bring about in the Philippines the complete separation of state

> and church in accordance with the additional policy of this government, it will be advisable for you to negotiate as a business matter with the heads of the business corporations involved. You will therefore on your way to the Philippines stop at Rome and see whether it is possible to secure an agreement under which the ends we have in view can be achieved. You will of course remember that *it is a purely business transaction undertaken to secure a final settlement of the matter causing most difficult at present with the Philippine government* and that nothing in the nature of diplomatic relations of any kind or sort can be even contemplated.[80] (italics supplied)

But Taft's "purely business" mission to Rome was an immediate failure. Though Pope Leo XIII agreed in principle with the substance of the American proposals, the American delegation did not convince the Vatican to withdraw the friars or to have a definite agreement on the issue of the friar properties.[81] In his report to Root, Taft surmised that politics involving the monastic orders, three members of whom sat on the Vatican commission appointed by the pope to deal with the Americans, had something to do with the disappointing result.[82] He had thought the American proposals were more than generous, even offering to pay for rentals of church properties occupied by the U.S. military at that time. More than that, he had suggested that the fair market price of these properties be ascertained through arbitration. But the Vatican could only reply that a new apostolic delegate would be sent to Manila to decide the matter. As negotiations over the properties slowly continued in Manila, a bill introduced by Henry Cooper of Wisconsin (which became the Philippine Organic Act of 1902—essentially a congressional endorsement and reproduction of McKinley's Instructions[83]) authorized the Philippine Commission to purchase these lands and to issue bonds to finance such purchase.[84]

In many ways, however, the method of settling this question was probably as important as settling the question itself. From this vantage, Taft's mission to Rome was a resounding success. In recognition of the genuine American efforts for the Catholic Church in the Philippines and the lengths to which the Americans were willing to negotiate on behalf of the Filipinos, Pope Leo XIII issued an apostolic constitution, *Quae Mari Sinico,* which recognized a new autonomous Philippine church hierarchy and effectively endorsed, among others, the establishment of American colonial rule.[85] And while the Vatican never formally withdrew the Spanish friars, key church positions were gradually filled by American Catholic priests and bishops. At home, U.S. Catholics praised the Roosevelt administration's handling of the issue, and they heartily endorsed his 1904 candidacy for the presidency.[86] But more important, the mission gave Taft the necessary popularity in the Philippines to implement his envisioned reforms.[87] Indeed, he was greeted with a hero's welcome on his arrival in Manila from Rome. Root's and Taft's goals for pacification were also successful. Filipinos cooperated with the Americans in the course of the friar lands settlement, spelling an end to the nationalist movement and reconciling many to the reality and semipermanence of American rule.[88] The purchase itself of the friar lands was finally concluded in December 1903, with the Philippine Commission agreeing to pay a sum of a little over $7 million for the lands.[89]

Congressional debates on the Philippine bill closely tracked the arguments leading to the ratification of the Treaty of Paris, with Republicans bent on duty supporting it and Democrats voting against, but the Organic Act passed nonetheless and formally enacted the beginning of American civil government in the Philippines, the local insurgency all but spent. The largely nonpartisan attitude shown by U.S. officials in the friar lands affair set a template for how other religious questions in the Philippines were to be settled in light of the provisions of the Organic Act. From religious instruction in nonsectarian public schools[90] to the establishment of a breakaway Philippine Independent Church,[91] the colonial government was enmeshed in church–state affairs at the very outset to such a degree that they probably could not have anticipated. Their actions did more to promote religious pluralism in the islands than they perhaps intended, shaping it in a way not unlike the raucous religious marketplace in the United States. Taft, who famously referred to the Filipinos as his "little brown brothers," inaugurated a "Philippines for Filipinos" policy during his tenure as first civil governor of the islands, a paternalistic policy of U.S. tutelage through the art of self-government.[92] But what this really meant in practice was that the Americans allowed the Filipinos to taste the fruits of religious liberty erstwhile denied them for three centuries, on the one hand, while they constantly tested their capacity, or perhaps incapacity, for political liberty on the other.[93]

Nonetheless, the consolidation of American sovereignty over the islands was not yet complete. But the Americans were forced to think about religion anew when they confronted the Muslims of the southern Philippines.

How religious liberty also proved useful in securing their recognition of American rule took a different shape, with implications that would persist up to the present day.

Religious Liberty and the Creation of the Moro Province

In 1899, the last thing the U.S. army needed was for the Filipino Moros to join the ongoing rebellion in the northern part of the Philippines. Approximately 300,000 Moros, named as such after the Moors of the Iberian peninsula by Spanish colonizers, lived in adjacent southern islands and provinces constituting Moroland. Islam arrived in the Philippines by way of trade routes through Indonesia as early as the fourteenth century. At the time of the Americans' arrival, Moro society had the characteristics of a feudal society, with intricate social and power networks led nominally by a sultan and autonomous local chiefs called *datos,* and their authority based vaguely on syncretized Islamic law. Notwithstanding several armed clashes between the Spanish military and the Moros, Moroland had remained relatively independent throughout the period of Spanish rule. While the Moros were by no means a homogenous cultural, linguistic, and ethnic group, their common adherence to Islam and a shared history of resistance to Spain gave them a distinct and unifying sense of identity.[94]

Acting on the orders of General Otis, General John C. Bates traveled to Sulu, an island off the southwestern coast of Mindanao, the second-largest island in the Philippines, to negotiate an agreement with Sultan Jamal ul-Kiram II. Bates needed to secure Moro neutrality in the Philippine-American war but, more important, he wanted to get the Moros to acknowledge U.S. sovereignty over the islands. Perhaps diplomacy would remove the need to use force altogether. When Jacob Schurman visited Sulu a few months earlier as part of his comprehensive fact-finding investigation, he had somehow forged an understanding with the sultan that the United States would step in the same shoes that Spain previously occupied vis-à-vis the sultanate, the terms of which were spelled out in an 1878 treaty.[95] Receiving Schurman's cable, Root directed General Otis to secure the agreement in writing. But Bates did not easily accomplish his task. For one, it was unclear to the sultan how it was possible for Spain to "sell" its territory to the Americans without its knowledge or consent. The Americans proceeded to persuade the sultan in as delicate a manner as possible. The Moros might join forces with the insurgents in the north, and the army could hardly afford to fight on a new front. To indicate the importance of the matter, Secretary of State John Hay even asked the U.S. consul in Constantinople to bring up the matter of the Moros in an audience with Abdulhamid II himself. The consul communicated to Hay the satisfying news that the caliph "telegraphed to Mecca, it being the time of the annual pilgrimage, his wishes that the Moslems in the Philippines should not war with the Americans, nor side with the insurgents but should be friendly with our army. . . ."[96] In exchange, he assured the caliph that the "Americans would not interfere with their religion and would be as tolerant toward them as he (caliph) was toward the Christians in his Empire."[97]

The problem with the 1878 treaty on which the agreement with the Americans was to be based was that it meant different things to its parties. For the Spaniards, it was a recognition of their sovereignty over the sultanate, albeit providing considerable autonomy to the Moros, including the flying of the sultan's flag.[98] But for the Moros, the treaty was at best a temporary reprieve to save Jolo, Sulu's capital, from destruction. They regarded the monthly payments to the sultan simply as tribute for Moro cooperation. Thus, when General Bates sought to succeed Spain's position over the islands, he also inherited the existing mismatch of understandings. The resulting agreement, the Bates-Kiram Treaty, signed on August 20, 1899,[99] provided for, among others, the sultan's acknowledgment of U.S. sovereignty over Jolo and all its dependencies,[100] the flying of the American flag,[101] and that the rights and dignities of the sultan and all the *datos* shall be respected and that the Moros shall not be interfered with on account of their religion.[102] Except for these outward signs of sovereignty, the Americans initially intended to adopt a laissez-faire approach vis-à-vis the Moros, very much similar to the British way of indirect rule in neighboring Malaya or the Dutch in Java.[103] Although the Bates Treaty was meant to be approved by the president and confirmed by the U.S. Senate, the Senate chose to do nothing about it. Nonetheless, it remained the governing framework for U.S.-Moro relations up until its unilateral abrogation in 1904 by U.S. colonial officials.

The Senate's hesitation regarding the treaty was due to the domestic uproar over one of its provisions, which to some amounted to a recognition of the practice of slavery.[104] The provision seemed to contradict the stated raison d'être of the American colonial enterprise, which was the spread of liberty and progress. Anti-imperialists quickly pounced on the treaty to illustrate one of the many paradoxes of the American presence in the Philippines, with arresting headlines such as "Slavery and Polygamy Reestablished under the Jurisdiction of the United States."[105] A closer look at the provision reveals that the treaty allowed slaves to purchase their freedom but did not emancipate the existing ones. The nuance was lost, however, on the anti-imperialists who considered it exceptionally good fodder for their continuing opposition to American presence in the islands. The "slavery and polygamy" juxtaposition, precisely the "twin relics of barbarism"[106] that the Republican Party had pledged to root out by constitutional means in its inception, was also meant to conjure the same types of feelings it evoked against the Mormons during the latter part of the nineteenth century. While McKinley did not directly address these criticisms, he increasingly made use of antislavery rhetoric in his defense of U.S. colonial administration to counter these charges.[107] He also insisted on a reservation to the notorious Article X, stating that this in no way expresses the consent of the U.S. government to the existence of slavery in the archipelago.[108]

The promise of Moro autonomy encapsulated in the Bates Treaty, including its guarantee of religious freedom, tested the limits of what the Americans were prepared to consider as markers of civilization. The Moros considered the practice of slavery as allowed, or at least tolerated, by their religion.[109] Indeed, the lucrative slave trade was a major factor in explaining the level of affluence of the sultanate in the early eighteenth to the early nineteenth century, and its decline coincided with the joint British, Dutch, and Spanish efforts to patrol the Pacific and clamp down on the trade.[110] Honoring the terms of the Bates Treaty meant that, for the time being, U.S. officials would have to allow the continuation of slavery as such. In addition, in one of the many analogies to be made subsequently between the Moros and the North American Indians, Root cited the U.S. Supreme Court decision in *Cherokee Nation v. State of Georgia*[111] in describing the relationship between the United States and the Moro "tribes" as one between a guardian and a ward.[112] This understanding undergirded McKinley's Instructions with regard to the non-Christian population of the islands, including the Muslims in the south. Contrary to the treatment of the Christian population, the instructions generally mandated that there was to be no undue interference with the non-Christians' way of life, although some effort should be made to introduce "civilized customs."[113] To get a glimpse of how these two competing impulses would be reconciled, one need only look at the record of the federal government in its dealings with the Indian tribes. Many army officers, such as Generals George W. Davis,

John Pershing, and Leonard Wood, who held leadership positions in Moroland, were in fact veterans of federal military campaigns against the Indians and conducted their work with the Moros analogously.[114]

Given the notoriety of the Bates Treaty in the United States, Root sought to reassure the Americans back home that the popular understanding of the treaty was wrong. Putting the terms of the Bates Treaty for the Moros on the one hand, and the instructions for the entire archipelago on the other as part of a single U.S. policy continuum, Root portrayed the treaty as securing not only "peace and the suppression of piracy but open[ing] the door, under the Instructions given by the President, to the extinction of slavery and the civilizing and Christianizing of the islands."[115] The irony, of course, was not only that religious liberty was again exchanged for the Moros' political independence similar to the Filipinos in the north, but that insofar as letting the Moros practice freely their religion (within limits as they were to find out later), it would also be the same avenue through which their society would be irrevocably changed. Root's view was in accord with the general European colonial practice of encouraging the spread of Christianity without interfering with existing forms of religion, the customs of which were not in contravention with the accepted ideas of civilization and morals.[116] Because civilization and Christianity were deemed inextricable from each other, it led Schurman to conclude that contact with Christian civilization would eventually lead to the emancipation of slaves and the eradication of this institution.[117] At any rate, Root, and later Taft, further described Moro slavery as one of "mild character" different from the one abhorred in the United States because relations between the *datos* and their slaves were harmonious, they lived with and were treated as members of the family of their masters, and the slaves could purchase their freedom if they wanted to.[118] But the extent to which the U.S. army could maintain its hands-off approach in Moro affairs, as exemplified by the Bates Treaty, would be challenged by the arrival of Leonard Wood in 1903.

Born and raised in Massachusetts, where his ancestors had lived since the arrival of the Mayflower in 1620, Wood arrived in the Philippines with a sterling military résumé—a West Point graduate and a Medal of Honor recipient from his participation in the Apache campaigns, which included chasing Geronimo himself. He was also a renowned army surgeon; head of the famed unit, the Rough Riders, which included Theodore Roosevelt; and had a stint as the military governor of Cuba. His iron-fisted approach to colonial governance impressed Roosevelt, and he was sent to the Philippines, particularly to the Moroland, because the area needed a military presence that understood tribal guerilla warfare as well as an administrator who could fashion and helm a centralized government and bring order out of chaos.

The treaty did succeed in keeping the Moros neutral in the Philippine-American war. But as the Organic Act established a civil government to govern the rest of the Philippines, American military gaze turned toward the Moros, who were exempt from the coverage of the act. Roosevelt, through Root, sent Wood to govern the Moro Province, a geopolitical entity headed by a combined civil-military government created through Act Number 787 of the Philippine Commission.[119] The Moro Province was essentially a "military colony separated from the rest of the country"[120] and consisting of executive and legislative branches populated by army officers. The governor of the province, endowed with both civil and military powers, was in no uncertain terms an imperial proconsul. Though Wood was not particularly inclined to engage in civil affairs again, similar to what he did as military governor of Cuba, he was persuaded to do so by Roosevelt and he thought this assignment was an essential stepping-stone to head the prestigious Philippines Division of the army.[121] In preparation for his new assignment, he toured the major colonial locations of other imperial powers such as Cairo, Hong Kong, and the Dutch East Indies.

From the very beginning of his stint as governor, Wood found nothing to admire in Moro society. To Wood and other U.S. colonial officials, race and religion compounded the otherness of the Moro. Indeed, the creation of the Moro Province itself was justified by the distinguishing characteristics of the Moro, most notably their "warlike" character.[122] On the national level, a Bureau of Non-Christian Tribes was established in 1901 to ascertain the local customs of all tribes, including the Moros, and determine the best possible means to advance their civilization.[123] In the meantime, the creation of the Moro Province inaugurated a shift of American policy insofar as the Moros were concerned. Indirect rule was proving to be woefully inadequate to accomplish American aims. President Roosevelt himself characterized the Moro civilizing mission as one meant to protect Christian Filipinos.[124]

Although they had repeatedly assured the Moros in various ways that there would be no interference with their religion and local customs, army officials belatedly realized that all the practices they found objectionable, foremost among them slavery, were somehow related to Islam or at least

Islam as understood and practiced in Moro society. Any effort to civilize the Moros was thus bound to end in conflict.[125] Whereas Adna Chaffee, the head military official in the Philippines until 1902, previously believed that some accommodation must be made for the religion and customs of the Moros,[126] Wood believed the exact opposite. He regarded most Moro laws and customs as rubbish; in fact, nothing was worth codification.[127] U.S. officials in any case considered the Islam practiced by the Moros as a deficient version, an unruly amalgam of local customs and Islamic rules, which was also similar to how they felt about the Catholicism of the Christian Filipinos. Although Wood believed in religious freedom, it was freedom that came in a particular shape and size. He praised Jesuit missionary work in the Moro Province, for example, because he considered the principles of the Christian religion conducive to the observance of law and order and respect for authority.[128]

Thus, when Wood unsurprisingly recommended the abrogation of the Bates Treaty a mere three months after his arrival in Mindanao, he struck at Islam as the heart of these abominable Moro practices.[129] His predecessor George Davis had also urged its abrogation before he left. "The people of this island are Mohammedans," Wood wrote, "their faith teaches them that it is no sin to kill Christians and they are taught by the priests to believe it is commendable."[130] In the same memo, addressed to Taft, numbering fifty-five pages, and proposing to discard the treaty, he also singled out the practice of *juramentados,* from the Spanish word *juramentar* ("to make an oath"): a man who has "gone through a form of religious preparation and has taken an oath to die killing Christians. He must necessarily have the consent of his *dato* and his preparation is made under the direction of the priest, who practically preaches a holy war so far as he is concerned and encourages him with hope of future reward and happiness to commit murder and self-sacrifice."[131]

In Wood's view, the British approach in Malaya of ruling through the local chiefs was inapplicable to the Moro situation, a view with which Roosevelt concurred.[132] The United States could not countenance a government run by what he deemed to be a corrupt and cruel class of men. The solution therefore was to introduce liberalism.[133] In practice, that invariably meant destroying the traditional power and social relations existing at that time. The *datu* or local chief would remain a political figure but would be divested of any divine rights. The sultan, ironically, would remain a religious head but would no longer possess any political authority. Slowly but surely, the Moro government was being turned into a secularized bureaucracy.

The ensuing transformation of the political and justice systems of Moro society almost always began with American invocations of religious freedom and the principle of separation of church and state. Initially, the Moros welcomed them because, curiously enough, no government official tried to convert or baptize anybody as the Spanish had always done. Indeed, the Americans set up nonsectarian schools and set aside time for religious instruction, taught English alongside Arabic and the local language, and took to heart the advice of Lord Cromer from Egypt by encouraging trade, even establishing handicraft exchanges for the women.[134] In Zamboanga, for example, one of the provinces within Moroland, the district military governor had labored to clarify in his various public meetings the guarantee of the separation of church and state,[135] and that in pursuance thereof, they would be left alone with their practices and customs. This greatly facilitated local cooperation in the creation and running of the Moro trade exchange.

But Wood was also set on eradicating what he considered to be barbaric features of Moro society, such as slavery and the application of severe criminal penalties based on the Qur'an. It was inevitable then that he would have to discard some Moro practices and customs. He set up secular courts and disbanded religious ones,[136] adopted Western-style codes of procedure, and aligned the provisions of the Moro criminal code with the general Philippine one.[137] Wood was especially appalled at the unequal treatment of crimes against Moros (payment of small fines) and crimes against Christians (stiff prison sentences).[138] As part of the drive to liberalize Moro society, private land ownership was also instituted, with each Moro family initially given forty acres. Given all these sweeping changes, it was only a matter of time before the Moros started expressing their resentment toward American incursions to reshape their culture. The enactment of laws prohibiting slavery and polygamy and the efforts to levy taxes on the Moros in the form of a poll tax (*cedula*) in order to generate revenue for the province finally sparked widespread armed resistance against the Americans, a war that Wood did not seem particularly averse to engage in.[139] He was convinced that Moros only understood the language of force, and thus for every offense against the law, "he [the Moro] is going to be followed, taken and punished."[140] Moros regarded the poll tax as payment of a tribute to a foreign sovereign, which was not how they understood the terms of the Bates Treaty. The armed resistance would last for a decade and later became known as the Moro Wars.[141]

Taft accepted Wood's recommendations, and President Roosevelt formally approved the abrogation of the Bates Treaty in early 1904. The sultan, who was informed of the decision by Wood in person, thereafter wrote a letter addressed to Luke Wright, who had succeeded Taft as governor-general of the Philippines.[142] He had begged to be left with his rights as religious head of the Moros, to which Wood had acquiesced. But his other requests, such as not to make the Moros pay the poll tax and to continue with practices sanctioned by their religion, went unheeded. Throughout the years of the Moro Province, U.S. officials genuinely believed they were respecting Islam as their various pronouncements on religious freedom could attest, even as they went about introducing American-style reforms in the region. The American encounter with the Filipino Moros showed that U.S. policy was unable to comprehend that religious freedom in other contexts could not always follow the same trajectory, one characterized by a separation between religion and state, that it did at home. The repercussions of such understanding, incipient in this imperial episode, would be felt by many as the United States set full sail on the new century ahead.

* * *

The dawn of the twentieth century saw the emergence of the United States as a new imperial power. A conflicted and divided American society bemoaned the moral implications that the annexation of the Philippines, foremost among all Spanish possessions that the United States acquired, acutely presented. By taking up the white man's burden in the archipelago, the United States sought to settle its jarred national conscience. Promoting the religious liberty of the Filipinos achieved several aims: First, it became an avenue through which it could cast itself to the world as a benevolent apostle of liberty and progress, unlike its European counterparts; second, it proved useful for its domestic proponents to reconcile the paradox between the inherently coercive nature of the colonial enterprise and its own republican, freedom-loving self-image; and third, and more significant, it became a practical necessity during the early days of empire in order to secure Filipino consent to the American civilizing project. Each of these aims also featured in internal debates between warring religious factions inside the United States. But for America's first and newest colony, even though the guarantees of religious liberty were deployed in different ways for its Catholic and Muslim inhabitants, its grant was always accompanied by the withholding of political independence, a target that would continually move according to the whims and caprices of American domestic politics for the next thirty years. In the northern parts of the country, religious liberty was initially promised in exchange for an end to the nationalist revolt, while in the southern part of the Philippines, this freedom was guaranteed to keep the Moros at bay as their society was shaped in accordance with a distinctly American vision of progress and civilization.

Two hundred years removed from the beginning of the lively American experiment of religious liberty and separation of church and state,[143] these principles, for the first time, were exported into the organic act of a foreign territory that was, in all respects, a nation in the making. It would take a world war started from the other side of the globe, however, before the Americans could catapult the ideal of religious liberty into a transnational legal principle.

2

Removing the Fertile Sources of War

> "It had been our privilege to formulate the principles which were accepted as the basis of the peace, but they had been accepted, not because we had come in to hasten and assure the victory and insisted upon them, but because they were readily acceded to as the principles to which honorable and enlightened minds everywhere had been bred. They spoke the conscience of the world as well as the conscience of America."
>
> —*U.S. president Woodrow Wilson, July 10, 1919*

In the summer of 1919, Woodrow Wilson brought home his dream of a better world. "Dare we reject it and break the heart of the world?" the president exhorted his audience before an open session of the United States Senate, the first time a president presented a treaty in person on Capitol Hill.[1] The treaty in question was the Peace Treaty of Versailles, and its centerpiece was the Covenant of the League of Nations. By and large a product of six months of Great Power discussions in Paris, among Wilson and three other leaders (David Lloyd George of Great Britain, Georges Clemençeau of France, and Vittorio Orlando of Italy), the covenant offered a vision way ahead of its time: a world bound together by the promise of collective security and buoyed by the principle of self-determination. Vowing never again to the carnage brought about by the recent war, Wilson touted the proposed League of Nations as a "definite guarantee of peace."[2] Republican senators saw otherwise, however. After a long and bitter domestic treaty fight, the Senate rejected Wilson's dream when it refused to ratify the treaty by seven votes.

The exclusion of the United States as a founding member was not the only challenge to be faced by the moribund League of Nations.[3] The failure to include Russia and Germany had also dogged it from the outset. Within ten years from the signing of the treaty, the apparatus of collective security instituted by the League fell apart. Japan withdrew from the League in 1931 after occupying the Chinese territory of Manchuria. Germany followed shortly thereafter. A few years later, Italy violated the covenant's nonaggression principle when it invaded Abyssinia, now modern-day Ethiopia. In addition, various peoples within the new nations created in the wake of the collapse of the Austro-Hungarian Empire harbored their own reasons to dislike, if not to reject, the Versailles settlement. Eastern European Jews felt the League did not go far enough in protecting their group and individual rights. Ethnic Germans in Poland and Czechoslovakia felt betrayed by what seemed to be a denial of their own right to self-determination. And Polish leaders felt resentful toward the Polish Treaty, which recognized Poland as an independent state and imposed obligations in favor of its minority population, as unwarranted interference with their national sovereignty.

Existing accounts on the Paris Peace Conference and the subsequent fragile world settlement it produced focus almost exclusively on the catastrophic road leading to the Second World War. But that is only part of the story. The realization of Wilson's dream of a new world order would indeed wait until the end of another war. His efforts in Paris were not completely in vain, however, even with the eventual failure of the League of Nations. Wilson's lesser-known attempts to remove religious strife and intolerance as sources of war in fact brought about the modern international legal regime on religious freedom. Although his proposal to make religious liberty a universal guarantee applicable to all members of the international community did not make it to the covenant, its inclusion as an enforceable guarantee for peoples under the rule of a Mandatory Power, and as a precondition for the recognition of new states set forth in the minority protection treaties, finally made the issue of religious freedom protection a matter of international law.

Before the League Covenant, the prevailing transnational regime on religious freedom was found in the 1878 Treaty of Berlin.[4] Drafted in the aftermath of the Russo-Turkish war, the resulting treaty concluded at the Congress of Berlin recognized the creation of the new states of Serbia, Montenegro, Bulgaria, and Romania, which were all carved out of the Ottoman Empire. The Berlin Treaty conditioned the independence of these states on their guarantee of religious freedom and political equality among others, to various minority groups within their populations. However, the application of the treaty was limited to its few signatories. More important, it did not contain any provisions for enforcement or sanctions in case of violations, one of the many gaping holes from which the Great War would arise.

Wilson's efforts on behalf of international religious freedom languished in obscurity for a long time. This could be attributed to many reasons. There was scarcely any mention of religion or religious freedom in the League Covenant or the Treaty of Versailles, save for Article 22 protecting the freedom of conscience and religion for peoples in territories under the rule and tutelage of a Mandatory Power;[5] in the annex to Article 50 of the Treaty giving control to a commission governing the administration of the former German territory of Saar Basin;[6] in Article 86, in which Czechoslovakia undertakes to embody in a separate treaty that it will protect the interests of its inhabitants who differ from the majority in terms of race, language, and religion;[7] and last, in Article 93, in which Poland undertakes similar obligations toward the minorities in its territory.[8] Unlike in the Congress of Berlin, religious freedom was nowhere in the main agenda of the peace conference. Wilson himself was obsessed with the creation of the League first and foremost, ahead of seemingly more pressing issues of the day, such as war reparations and colonial possessions, while his European counterparts focused on disassembled empires and the territorial borders that were about to change drastically. Even in his much-celebrated Fourteen Points Speech, the basis of the American peace policy and under the terms of which Germany agreed to an armistice, religion did not make an appearance except for a passing reference to the well-being of "other nationalities under Turkish rule,"[9] referring to the Armenian situation.

And yet playing a larger-than-life role in the peace conference by being the only head of state to attend, Wilson personally drafted the provisions on religious liberty protections, which he intended to be enforced by the authority of an international body—the League of Nations. Recognizing religious intolerance and discrimination as "fertile sources of war," he drew on the language of the First Amendment of the U.S. Constitution, seeking to guarantee the right to exercise one's religious beliefs freely and subject only to the limitations of public order and morals.[10] But even Wilson's soaring idealism—at one point, Clemençeau exclaimed that speaking with the American president felt like he was talking to Jesus Christ[11]—could not conquer the sordid reality of the European situation. For instance, the mandate system established by the covenant was attacked by many as a mere reincarnation of nineteenth-century European imperial designs. Indeed, on his way to Paris, Wilson already had a sense of foreboding. He told Joseph Tumulty, his private secretary, that "this trip will either be the greatest success or the supremest tragedy in all history. . . ."[12]

No doubt there were more than enough tragedies to go around by the time the peace treaty was signed. But notwithstanding the later breakdown of the minority protection regime inaugurated by the covenant, it crystallized the idea of an international rights regime that became the crucial precursor of its postwar version in more ways than one. As he looked to the religious patchwork that was the United States as his model, credit should be given to Woodrow Wilson, who saw religious freedom protection in international law as an integral part of his grand vision of a world made safe for democracy.

The American Prophet in Paris

The first sitting American president to set foot on European soil, Woodrow Wilson carried the hopes of millions as he sailed for France in December 1918.[13] One year earlier, during his second inaugural address, the president laid out his vision of a new international order and made a plea to his constituents for the United States to take its necessary and rightful place within it. "We are provincials no more," Wilson declared. The burdens of achieving and maintaining a peaceful and politically stable world were to be shared by all nations. His vision eschewed the traditional balance-of-power system then prevailing in Europe and contained the core elements of what is to be known today as the liberal paradigm of international relations, which includes, among others, the equality of nations, freedom of the seas, and governments that derive their legitimacy and just powers from the consent of the governed.[14] The cheering crowds and adulation that greeted him upon his arrival in Europe testified to how this vision resonated powerfully with its war-weary peoples.

Horrified by the slaughter that had taken place in the supposed civilized territories of Europe, Wilson's self-appointed mission in Paris went beyond mere peacemaking. He would change the mind of humankind and banish war forever. That mission began with his emphasis on the exceptional nature of American participation both during the war, as exemplified by his decision to fight the war as an Associate rather than as a member of the Allies, and during the peace conference. Beginning with his declaration of war against Imperial Germany, Wilson took pains to stress that the United States had no selfish ends for her belligerency, "no indemnities for ourselves, no material compensation for the sacrifices we shall freely make."[15] He repeated the same at the peace conference, noting that, unlike other nations, the United States did not want "territory, tribute or even revenge."[16]

American exceptionalist themes had long characterized Wilson's foreign policy. He supported the annexation of the Philippines and other former Spanish colonies in 1898 as part of the American obligation to spread freedom and end tyranny abroad. Repeated U.S. military interventions in Mexico during his first term in office continued this paradox. "I am going to teach the South American republics to elect good men," was how Wilson bluntly described his Mexican policy.[17] He also threw his wholehearted support behind the century-old Monroe Doctrine, which effectively secured all of Latin America against any form of European incursion and turned the region into an American sphere of influence. Wilson saw the Monroe Doctrine differently: Instead of American overreach, the doctrine secured for all people within its coverage the freedom to determine their national fate. Through the proposed League of Nations, he could extend the same animating principles behind the doctrine to Europe and the rest of the world.[18] The law and morality represented by the League of Nations and the substantive rights to be guaranteed in the League Covenant would replace the brute force of European Old World diplomacy.

Wilson projected American values as universal values. In his famous 1917 Peace Without Victory speech before the U.S. Senate, he stressed the indispensable role of the United States to show how its ideals and practice of government would point the way to liberty for the rest of the world.[19] He considered these values to be "shared by forward-looking men and women everywhere of every modern nation of every enlightened community." Later, during a nationwide domestic campaign for the treaty's acceptance before the Senate vote, he proclaimed triumphantly to a crowd in Ohio that "we say now that all these people have the right to live their own lives under governments which they themselves chose to set up. That is the American principle."[20] The conflation of American values with universal values partly explains the resulting confusion surrounding his famous rhetoric of national self-determination, a phrase that appeared nowhere in his major policy speeches.[21] Far from being a self-evident concept, the principle of self-determination was viewed differently from each side of the Atlantic. Wilson equated self-determination with the Anglo-American civic ideal of self-government, that is, the participation by the constituents of a polity to determine its political affairs. The focus was on political liberties, not political independence. He never believed that each racial, ethnic, or language group was entitled to its own nation-state.[22] This was in stark contrast to the ethnic nationalism in the mind of those that were seeking to break free from the precarious Ottoman and Austro-Hungarian empires at that time. The divergent understandings of the principle provided a source of inspiration to early precursors of decolonization movements but also caused feelings of betrayal and resentment that ultimately undermined the resulting settlement.[23] As his secretary of state Robert Lansing later recounted, it was calamitous that the president ever thought of the phrase because it gave rise to impossible hopes that could never be realized and would inevitably cost lives. Indeed, it would be one of the hooks by which the president's critics would hang him for the failures at Paris.

The Covenant of the League of Nations was the principal means through which his vision would be realized: that of a community of democratic states with a central body capable of enforcing shared rules as embodied in the covenant's provisions and continuously corrected by the pressure of world public opinion. With one eye turned toward the American experience, Wilson saw the covenant as similarly forging a system of "governments joined with other governments for the pursuit of common purposes, in honorary equality and honorable subordination."[24] The choice of the name or instrument was not accidental. It reflected the president's personal religious upbringing in the tradition of Presbyterian covenant theology as well as his lifelong inclination to use compacts or covenants to comprehend the disorder surrounding him. One of the earliest known constitutions he had written was for his youth yacht club. "Covenants were a method of bringing order to chaos, of moving those emerging from the wilderness closer to God and heaven," he once explained.[25]

Despite his well-known moralizing rhetoric, Wilson rarely invoked God publicly. But while he believed in the constitutional separation between church and state, the sacred and secular could not be as neatly separated in his thought processes.[26] Religious ideas, particularly of the Presbyterian variety, deeply permeated his speeches and his core beliefs. The resulting worldview shaped his moral stubbornness, ardent patriotism, and self-confident righteousness and was a comprehensive prism with which to see the world around him. He confided to his personal physician, Cary T. Grayson, that if "[I] were not a Christian, [I think I] should go mad, but [my] faith in God holds [me] to the belief that He is in some way working out His own plans through human perversities and mistakes."[27] Elected to the presidency without any substantial foreign policy experience, his belief in Providence and American exceptionalism became the crucial interpretive keys to his actions and how he viewed the role of the United States in the world.

In this context, Wilson's aims and purposes for the League of Nations can be seen in a different light. The new world order was not to be based on legal foundations but on a new kind of global morality. International law was a mere tool to bring about that new moral order. The new Covenant was thus first and foremost a political document, not a legal one. This view distinguished him from the other American internationalists of the period such as Elihu Root, Nicholas Murray Butler, William Howard Taft, and Henry Cabot Lodge, who all sought to reconcile the advance of American power with the spread of the rule of law through the use of legal means such as the codification of international rules and the creation of international judicial tribunals.[28] For Wilson, a lawyer himself by education and training in addition to being a political scientist, the new Covenant was not only a body of formal rules but, more than anything, a facilitator of the larger processes of politics.[29] Unlike his contemporaries who saw in the law the means to preserve the status quo, Wilson recognized that a legal idea could embody a kind of a social revolution. Indeed, as Wilson was reading the entirety of the draft covenant inside the Hall of the Clock on February 14, 1919, one observer noted that it dawned on the audience that they were getting something akin to a "new declaration of independence" for the world.[30]

No wonder then that Wilson told General Tasker Bliss, one of the five U.S. delegates to the peace conference, that he did not want lawyers drafting the covenant, referring to an early draft prepared by the renowned American international lawyer James Brown Scott.[31] His purposive and organicist vision of the covenant, one that reflects and responds accordingly to the demands of the world, was found in the so-called second Paris draft. It was the third and last personal draft written by Wilson before an official drafting committee was appointed. Unsullied still from the taint and constraints of negotiation and compromise, it represented his ideal of what the League could achieve.

The draft contained an important clarification that the League was concerned about international conflict and not internal uprisings, a crucial factor for obtaining the support of Great Britain. But it also featured a lesser-known provision on religious freedom. Without any input from Bliss or his own personal confidante Colonel Edward House, Wilson included several supplementary articles that guaranteed the equal treatment of national and racial minorities as well as a universal protection for freedom of religion. In Supplementary Article VII, he laid out the motivations for such a provision, using language partially reminiscent of the First Amendment alongside a traditional international formulation: "Recognizing religious persecution and intolerance as fertile sources of war, the Powers signatory hereto agree, and the League of Nations shall exact from all new states and all states seeking admission to it the promise, that they will make no law prohibiting or interfering with the free exercise of religion, and that they will in no way discriminate, either in law or in fact, against those who practice any particular creed, religion, belief, whose practices are not inconsistent with public order or public morals."

The proposal for universal religious freedom was arguably as radical as the president's vision for an international organization such as the League. Under the Berlin Treaty, religious freedom was limited in its application against particular countries, specifically the four new states of Serbia, Montenegro, Romania, and Bulgaria, and there was no means of available enforcement. A case in point is Article 44 of the treaty, which particularly stated that non-Christians, most of whom were in reality Jews, were entitled to acquire Romanian citizenship.[32] The ink was barely dry on the treaty, however, before Romania proceeded to break its obligations and refused to grant citizenship to its Jewish inhabitants. Since the treaty did not provide for any sanctions, the continued discrimination and persecution of Romanian Jews was treated as a domestic issue by Romanian authorities. Only the United States, a nonsignatory to the Berlin Treaty, lodged an international protest against Romania in 1902, declaring that "this government cannot be a tacit party to such an international wrong. . . ."[33] Because the United States could not appeal to the treaty provisions, John Hay, the secretary of state, appealed instead to the "principles consigned therein because they are principles of international law and eternal justice."[34] The Berlin Treaty would be the negative example that cast a long shadow on all discussions on religious freedom and minority protection throughout the peace conference.

The president's thinking on religious freedom was largely animated by two issues: the plight of Eastern European Jews and the suffering of Armenian Christians within the Ottoman Empire. Both constituencies were front and center in Wilson's foreign policy, thanks to the domestic lobbying efforts of American Protestant missionaries and Jewish groups. As the Armenian genocide unfolded in the midst of the war, Wilson looked on helplessly, his options severely circumscribed by the complicated international situation and the limits of American power.[35] One of those complications was his overriding concern for the safety of American missionaries scattered in various parts of the empire. Short of formally declaring war against the Ottoman Empire, Wilson undertook other steps to help the Armenian cause. He issued a presidential proclamation in October 1916 urging the American public to contribute to Near East relief efforts led by the American Committee for Armenian and Syrian Relief. In his historic Fourteen Points Speech, Wilson advanced the cause of autonomy for Ottoman minorities, assuring them of "undoubted security of life and an absolutely unmolested opportunity for autonomous development" even as he declared that the Turkish parts of the empire should be secured in their sovereignty.[36] In retrospect, that was probably the most he could muster for Armenia at that time.

Wilson thus saw the League of Nations about to be created by the covenant as the solution that such a humanitarian catastrophe would be rendered impossible in the future. During his domestic campaign for the treaty's acceptance within the United States, he told his audience in Salt Lake City, Utah, "Armenia is one of the regions that is to be under the trust of the League of Nations . . . when they can enjoy their rights as free people that they never dreamed they would be able to exercise."[37]

But the world was not yet ready for such a vision. The other powers balked at the idea of universal religious freedom protection. The French felt it was unnecessary especially because the main purported offenders, Russia and Germany, were excluded from the League and therefore not bound by the covenant, while the British wanted the matter to be dealt with in separate treaties. Nonetheless, they sought to accommodate Wilson's wishes, however reluctantly. The provision underwent several changes. It was initially shortened to "The High Contracting Parties agree that they will make no law prohibiting or interfering with the free exercise of religion," a formulation Wilson was not particularly happy with but to which he relented. He reserved to himself the right to "clothe it with flesh and blood," however, leading Lord Robert Cecil of Great Britain to scoff disdainfully at what he characterized as the American leader's autocratic tendencies.[38]

Australia and New Zealand, both British dominions, remained adamantly opposed to the proposal. The worry was the provision would be used to get the League to pass judgment on otherwise purely domestic conflicts. Others also pointed out that when a state religion is disestablished, its adherents might consider themselves automatically persecuted.[39] These objections persisted despite Wilson's explanation that the motive of the article was to prevent religious persecutions as a source of wars in the future or his qualification that sought to assure the other states that the protection of freedom of religion would not come at the expense of the maintenance of public order or morals.[40] Even the head legal adviser of the American delegation, David Hunter Miller, thought the religious freedom clause was dangerous and could prove to be fatal to the incipient League.[41] Still, because of Wilson's stature in the peace conference and his evident desire to have it included in the covenant, the revised provision narrowly survived various rounds of negotiations until the final challenge posed by the famous Japanese racial equality proposal.

Japan's formal proposal was initially made on February 13, two days before Wilson had to return briefly to the United States, by Baron Makino Nobuaki, one of the Japanese delegates to the peace conference who would later serve as the Lord Keeper of the Privy Seal of Emperor Hirohito at the time of the Second World War. The proposal sought to amend Article 21, tying the prohibition on racial discrimination to that of religious discrimination. It read as follows: "The equality of nations being a basic principle of the League of Nations, the High Contracting Parties agree to accord as soon as possible to all alien nationals of States Members of the League, equal and just treatment in every respect, making no distinctions, either in law or in fact, on account of race or nationality."[42] Although there was no specific directive from Tokyo on how to remedy the problem, the issue of racial inequality was a long simmering Japanese concern. Makino reasonably stated that, if no person should suffer on account of his religion, so too should no person suffer because of his race. The proposal attracted the support of smaller states such as Brazil, Greece, and the Czech Republic. Even China viewed it favorably.

To the United States and Britain, however, the proposal was "unanswerable and unacceptable."[43] The British and Americans shared similar understandings of a racial hierarchy in the world, and although Japan had emerged from its victory over Russia in 1905 as a formidable world power, they were loath to give it equal status as a colonizer in the European mold. Lord Cecil claimed that while Britain realized the importance of the racial question, writing it into the covenant would be an encroachment on the sovereignty of its member states.[44] In addition, Billy Hughes, the Australian prime minister, could not be budged from his opposition. He colorfully described the precarious Australian situation as a "white drop in a coloured ocean ringed around with a thousand million of the coloured races." Makino's assurances that Japan's equality proposal did not encompass emigration were to no avail. Without the assent of all her dominions, Britain could not go ahead.

Wilson's hesitation was also largely due to domestic politics. Earlier, during the Roosevelt administration, the United States concluded a gentleman's agreement with the Japanese government in an exchange of diplomatic notes in which Japan promised not to issue passports to Japanese laborers bound for the continental United States. Nonetheless, this step did little to curb the tide of Japanese immigration. Widespread nativist anti-Asian sentiment reached its peak in the enactment of the Alien Land Registration Law in 1913, barring all aliens who were ineligible for citizenship from owning or leasing agricultural land in California.[45] These discriminatory immigration restrictions and alien land laws were motivated by suspicions that Japan would annex California through land ownership and were also tainted by negative perceptions of Japan's perceived alliance with Germany and its continuing military activities in China, persisting up to the time of the peace conference. Makino, who served as Japanese foreign minister in 1913, may have been using the principled issue of racial equality to extract American and British concessions regarding strategic Japanese interests in a disputed peninsula in the Chinese province of Shandong at the peace conference, but there was no doubt that racial equality loomed high among the Japanese themselves. Lawrence Ishii, the Japanese ambassador to the United States, clarified that what Japan wanted was sentimental, rather than substantial. "Every nation likes to feel that when its nationals travel anywhere in the world they shall not be subject to discrimination," he stated.[46]

However the Japanese delegates might have intended the proposal, the Americans saw it primarily as a claim to relax immigration restrictions, a move that would put Wilson squarely at odds with the Democrats of California, all strong defenders of states' rights.[47] His record on race already mixed at best, Wilson adopted a policy of deliberate obfuscation and simply hoped the issue would go away.[48] The Cecil–Miller draft circulating at the time he had to return to the United States was as follows: "The High Contracting Parties agree that they will not prohibit or interfere with the free exercise of any creed, religion or belief whose practices are not inconsistent with public order, or with public morals and that no person within their respective jurisdictions shall be molested in life, liberty or the pursuit of happiness by reason of his adherence to any such creed, religion or belief."[49] Attaching racial equality to religious freedom thus alienated both those who already had various reasons not to accept the implications of nonracial discrimination as well as those who thought religious freedom posed an equally delicate situation. Eleutherio Venizelos of Greece was among those who belonged to the latter. With pending territorial claims from Thrace to then Asia Minor, Greece was especially vulnerable to claims of religious and racial equality from its inhabitants, and Venizelos did not want any claim that would exacerbate an already volatile situation.

As international lawyer Malcolm Evans noted, if the racial equality provision was unacceptable and no satisfactory ground could be presented for distinguishing between racial equality and freedom of religion, then both would have to go.[50] Wilson did not push the matter further because the proposal might only raise national differences and racial prejudices outside the peace conference and therefore endanger the signing of the covenant itself. He was concerned that this could lead Britain to opt out of the covenant because it would not be able to disregard the position of its dominions. In putting off these two substantive principles of racial and religious equality from the negotiating table, Wilson put the covenant above all else, believing, and perhaps hoping, that the soon-to-be-created League would ultimately find ways to protect these freedoms.

In the end, various considerations of state sovereignty and American domestic politics prevented religious freedom from becoming a universal guarantee in the League Covenant. It was a testament to the prevailing sentiment at that time that no one except Wilson saw the importance of protecting religious freedom as an essential ingredient of the new world order that the League Covenant was about to inaugurate. In keeping with his organicist view of political development, Wilson also recognized that the covenant could draw the lines within which the repeated experiences of states could produce the necessary lessons for their own development. Following the demise of his general religious freedom proposal in the covenant, Wilson proposed the same to two other areas of the peace settlement. This time, his efforts were met with favorable results.

Religious Freedom in the Mandate System

Woodrow Wilson's historic Fourteen Points speech was nothing more than a repudiation of the old order, especially the matter of colonial possessions. Point Five stated that there should be "an impartial adjustment of all colonial claims, based upon a strict observance of the principle that in determining all such questions of sovereignty the interests of the populations concerned must have equal weight with the equitable claims of the Government whose title is to be determined." In a subsequent speech addressed to the U.S. Congress, the president clarified this point: "peoples and provinces were not to be bartered about from sovereign to sovereign as though they were mere chattels and pawns in a game."[51] "The world," he said while presenting the draft covenant to the plenary session at the Quai d'Orsay on February 14, 1919, "is done with annexations of helpless people, meant in some instances by some powers to be used merely for exploitation. . . ."[52] True enough, the biggest quarrel during the peace conference occurred over the issue of colonies and the corresponding role of the League.

The institutional framework established by the covenant to implement Wilson's promise was the mandate system. A result of Great Power thinking on the colonial question, the system eschewed direct international administration and instead assigned certain territories to mandatory states that would administer them on behalf of the League as trustees in all but name. The initial plan came from Jan Smuts, the South African premier, who, in a famous pamphlet entitled "League of Nations: A Practical Suggestion," called for the application of the principle of self-determination to states and territories belonging to Russia, Austria-Hungary, and the Ottoman Empire in accordance with their stage of development. It also featured a scheme of graded mandates under the trusteeship of the League. Smuts viewed the League as "the successor of the empires," a reversionary to whom these territories should pass with the right of ultimate disposal. In the League, Smuts saw similarities with how the British Empire functioned as a political system. It was notable that Smuts's plan did not include the German colonies in Asia and the Pacific, which meant that such areas would be open for direct annexation by British dominions, including South Africa. These areas were considered to be inhabited by barbarians incapable of development.

Wilson received Smuts's draft with enthusiasm but nonetheless incorporated the former German territories, along with those of the Ottoman Empire, as areas to be governed under the mandate system of the League of Nations. Well aware of the motives of the other Powers, a frustrated Wilson once confided to his personal physician, Dr. Cary Grayson, that the British and their dominions and the Japanese just wanted to "divide the swag" among them.[53] He also knew that Great Britain wanted the United States to take on an even bigger imperial role in supervising certain geographic regions. In keeping with his American exceptionalist rhetoric, the president clarified in his draft that the object of the mandate system was to create states that are fit and capable of self-determination with the goal of eventual independence in as short a time as possible, not to keep them in a state of perpetual annexation. The mandate system, in other words, was considered to be a significant advance in international morals. Before, these backward countries would have been generally controlled or exploited for primarily selfish purposes, but the mandatory power now accepts a kind of trusteeship not to benefit itself but for the benefit of the natives.[54]

For Wilson, this was no mere ruse. Like a true American leader of his time, he was thoroughly steeped in a sense of mission and duty. From his time as governor of New Jersey up to becoming president, he supported the American colonial occupation of the Philippine Islands. He also believed that the Ottoman Empire could benefit from learning the lessons of good government and the advantages of modern civilization from the United States.[55] A campaign speech in 1912 in which he stated his belief that the United States was a divinely chosen instrument to show the world "how they should walk the path of liberty" prefigured his administration's numerous military interventions in Latin America in the name of promoting liberty and democracy.[56]

Wilson was by no means an endorser of equality. He shared the prevailing views of his time that colored peoples were generally backward and needed tutelage from the people in more advanced states. But he also believed that, given proper instruction, these backward and helpless peoples could learn and develop the habits of self-government. Eventually, they could achieve the same level of political development as the civilized countries. He viewed freedom as something to be dispensed gradually, in accordance with the recipient's political maturity and advancement.[57] "Freedom is not giving the same government to all people, but wisely discriminating, and dispensing laws according to the advancement of a people," he said, applying the framework to the U.S. colonial enterprise in the Philippine Islands. Seeking to distinguish the American project from European practice, he emphasized that the ultimate goal must be to prepare the Filipinos for self-government, although the achievement of such a goal would require direct rule over a period of time in order to train the natives properly.[58]

In 1916, the Wilson administration passed the Jones Act, which enlarged the sphere of native responsibility for Philippine affairs and reorganized its governmental structure to resemble that of the United States with a view to formal independence, not statehood. The act's most important achievement was that it officially put on record the promise of the U.S. government to grant independence, the first act of such nature by any colonial power in history. It was the American experiment in the Philippines that guided Wilson on his views on the mandate system. The United States in the Philippines was his model for the rest of the world. "The League's duty," he proclaimed, is to ensure that the nations assigned as "tutors and advisers of these people" shall look to the interests and development of the mandate areas before the material desires of the mandatory nation.[59]

Article 22 of the League Covenant came to embody what is now known as the principle of international trusteeship. Whether or not it was a radical departure from old-fashioned colonialism in actual practice, the mandate territories were deemed to be a "sacred trust of civilization," and the mandatory powers had to act accordingly. The provision provided for a three-tiered system of administration and divided the territories in accordance with their supposed level of advancement. Class A mandates were comprised of the former Ottoman territories of Iraq, Syria, Lebanon, and Palestine and were considered to be provisionally independent nations subject only to administrative advice and assistance from the mandatory power until the time they could govern themselves independently. Class B mandates, on the other hand, were those located in formerly German Central Africa, while Southwest Africa and other Pacific Islands were put under the Class C regime. The graded classification was a direct result of Wilson's quarrel with the delegates of the British dominions, particularly Billy Hughes of Australia, who wanted outright annexation of certain African and Pacific territories. As a compromise, the mandatory powers over the C mandates would have the most extensive powers because these territories were regarded as the most backward and thus were governed under the same laws of the mandatory power as integral portions of its territory. The rest of Article 22 became akin to a binding code of conduct by which the business of trusteeship was to be conducted and evaluated. As a legitimate subject of international scrutiny, mandatory powers were obliged to file periodic reports to an international oversight body, established by the same article, called the Permanent Mandates Commission, with a right of appeal available to both the mandatory power and the mandate territories to the Permanent Court of International Justice.

The mandate system looked not only to the future development of the peoples within the mandate territories; it also sought to protect their present material and moral well-being. Pursuant to the requirements of Articles 22 and 23 of the League Covenant, and of the separate detailed agreements between the mandatory powers and the Council of the League Nations called Mandate Agreements, the goal of fashioning a people fit for self-government also meant the guarantee of particular rights such as liberty of conscience subject only to the limits of public order and morals, the prohibition of the slave trade, regulation of arms and liquor traffic, and restrictions on the military training of the natives except for police purposes and territorial defense. In this context, liberty of conscience meant religious freedom both for the local population as well as for the foreign (usually Western) missionaries coming from League members working in these territories.

The freedom of conscience guarantee was one among others that Wilson incorporated in his two Paris drafts, and he made it quite distinctive from Smuts's initial proposal.[60] Because this part of Article 22 was formulated much earlier than the religious freedom guarantees in the minority treaties, it was also less detailed. More important, because of its limited application, it was not controversial compared to his earlier proposal for the covenant. After all, for the Europeans, it simply reproduced the religious liberty provision of the 1885 Treaty of Berlin, which launched the so-called scramble for Africa in the late nineteenth century. For Wilson, however, it provided another opportunity to write it into the covenant, however circumscribed. The provision subsequently appeared in all mandate agreements. For example, in the agreement between the League Council and Britain over the African territory of Togo, this freedom was taken to mean freedom of conscience and of exercise of all forms of worship consonant with public order and morality. Going beyond the general language of Article 22, the agreement particularly emphasized the freedom of Western missionaries to travel freely, own property, and open religious schools in the territory.[61]

The Americans were not entirely selfless. Wilson objected, for example, to one of the C mandates over the Pacific island of Yap being given to Japan because it was a strategically crucial island for cable communications for the United States. The controversy was resolved only two years later in 1921, when Japan guaranteed equal commercial and cable rights to U.S. citizens, and the right of freedom of conscience and religion for American missionaries. The separate agreement reiterated the general mandate obligations under Article 22 and required Japan to provide the United States a duplicate copy of its annual report to the mandates commission.

The gradual institutionalization of religious freedom protection within the complex legal and political machinery of the League ensured international oversight and adjudication, a device that made the existence of religious freedom as a legal guarantee a prerequisite for sovereign statehood.

Religious Freedom in the Minority Protection Regime

In the aftermath of the war, more than 20 million Europeans found themselves displaced from their homes. Throughout the six months of the Paris Peace Conference, Europe remained a seething cauldron of conflict because of the issue of minorities. And it was not until May 1, 1919, a month before the conclusion of the peace conference, when the Council of Four officially considered the question, as part of "clearing up small matters."[62] During the meeting, Wilson proposed his draft guarantees for national and religious minorities in the treaty, warning that, as several million Germans were about to be incorporated into Poland, the persecution of Poland's Jewish population, as evidenced by the wave of pogroms over the past six months, "troubled the peace of the world."[63] In addition, as part of a growing opposition to the League at home, William Howard Taft also conveyed a similar concern in a letter sent to Paris, particularly over the lack of religious freedom guarantees in the circulating draft versions of the covenant. He reminded the president that those committed to the defeat of the treaty in the Senate would gladly take up this cause for themselves.[64] Similar to his earlier proposal for the covenant, Wilson's draft guaranteed the equality of racial and national minorities in the new states as well as the protection of the practice of any religion subject to the necessities of public order. Two days after his initial suggestion, the Council of Four agreed to create the blandly named Committee on New States (CNS) to consider the international obligations to be accepted by Poland and other new states about to be created by the peace treaties.

By this time, American officials and a transatlantic network of Jewish groups were already hard at work on several drafts of a proposed minority treaty. Manley Hudson, along with David Hunter Miller, was an American representative in the newly created CNS that was tasked by the Council of Four to draft the minority treaties. Hudson recounted that it was President

Wilson's interest to protect the European Jews because the American Jews in the United States demanded that they should be protected, which made the whole thing, presumably the minority treaties, possible.[65] It was an American proposition first that something be done for the protection of the minorities. Indeed, Wilson's draft reflected Jewish proposals.

No doubt Wilson genuinely had Jewish interests at heart. Historians largely attribute his interest in Jewish nationalism and minority rights to his close friendship with Louis Brandeis, a vocal Zionist and champion of progressive causes whom he had nominated to the U.S. Supreme Court in 1916. But he was also concerned about the geopolitical implications of disaffected minorities scattered around Europe. He particularly recognized the connection between Poland's aspirations and vulnerability and the American interest to have a stable order in the new Eastern Europe. The peace settlement had produced a difficult challenge. The nation-state emerged amid the hodgepodge of entities that participated in the Paris Peace Conference—empires, republics, and monarchies—as the triumphant mode of political organization and basic unit of the new international order. The redrawing of borders to reflect this new arrangement produced distinct peoples, however, who found themselves numerical minorities in the new states that had just been created. How does one preserve the new nation-state system and yet provide room for the nationalist passions stoked by the fires of Wilsonian self-determination? Given the impossibility of a one-nation, one-state formula, the fate of those who did not belong to the majority of the population in terms of race, language, and/or religion remained uncertain.

A liberal, minority rights regime provided an answer. Jewish groups, particularly from the United States and Great Britain, were among the most organized and influential advocates for the protection of their coreligionists in Eastern Europe.[66] Louis Marshall, head of the Committee of Jewish Delegations at the peace conference and a founder of the American Jewish Committee, particularly thought that institutionalizing American-style individual and minority rights provisions as a precondition for the recognition of new states offered the only politically stable solution to the existing state of affairs. This was a reflection of a long-standing commitment on the part of Anglo-American Jews to foster Jewish solidarity and facilitate their emancipation in their respective countries by their adherence to liberal humanist values as opposed to subscribing to Zionist aspirations of establishing a separate Jewish homeland.[67] In a letter to the president, Rabbi Stephen Wise of the American Jewish Congress proposed a "charter of liberty for the Jews which does not constitute mere promises but a grant self-executing, infeasible and cannot be evaded.... Such a result can be accomplished if the Peace Conference shall as a condition precedent to the creation of the new states before they come into existence be required to adopt as part of their organic laws irrepealable clauses which shall grant to all inhabitants of these new or enlarged states these fundamental rights."[68] Amid a steady stream of reports of anti-Semitic violence, economic boycotts, and regular pogroms against Jews in Poland and Czechoslovakia, Wilson assured American Jewish leaders that he would act given an opportunity to do so.[69]

The minority protection regime (MPR) inaugurated in the Polish Treaty, the first of several bilateral minority treaties to be concluded between each of the new states, on the one hand, and the Allied and Associated Powers, on the other, consisted of thirteen articles, the first eight of which, as Rabbi Wise urged, could not be repealed nor derogated. This meant that any form of changes to these articles must be submitted to the Council of the League of Nations for approval, something that Jan Paderewski, the Polish premier, deplored as an unwarranted intrusion into Polish sovereignty. The rest of the treaty dealt with other external obligations of the new Polish state. It was telling that Articles 2 to 8 of the Treaty, incorporating substantive protections as fundamental and essential parts of the Polish Constitution and referred to as its Wilsonian core, were reproductions of earlier Wilson proposals to insert religious equality rights in the League Covenant. It was not surprising, therefore, that Article 2 echoed the language of the U.S. Constitution. In its final form, Article 2 read as follows: "Poland undertakes to assure full and complete protection of life and liberty to all inhabitants of Poland without distinction of birth, nationality, language, race or religion. All inhabitants of Poland shall be entitled to the free exercise, whether public or private, of any creed, religion or belief, whose practices are not inconsistent with public order or public morals."

As explained by Clemençeau on behalf of the Council of Four in its cover note, the preconditions set forth in the Polish Treaty were not new. This has been established precedent since the 1878 Treaty of Berlin. To address the deficiencies of the Berlin Treaty, however, the MPR introduced two important innovations. The first lesson drawn from the Berlin precedent was that citizenship became automatically granted to all Polish nationals who had been habitual residents of the territory recognized as forming part of

Poland.[70] The second more significant innovation was international enforcement. Although the Berlin Treaty elevated religious freedom as a matter of international concern, it did not provide for any mechanisms of enforcement. One of the two British representatives in the CNS, James Headlam-Morley, was adamantly opposed to allowing the minorities any form of access to the League. He argued that "the League is a compact between states and only states should have immediate access to it." The French representative, Philippe Berthelot, on the other hand, wanted Poland to accept these obligations voluntarily. Manley Hudson, the American representative, held the view that minorities should be given the possibility of direct access to the yet-to-be-created Permanent Court of International Justice. He gave the example of the Supreme Court of the United States as proving the wisdom of leaving to the court itself the framing of safeguards against any exercise of its justice that might provoke political uneasiness.[71] When the issue arrived for final resolution at the Council of Four, pragmatic considerations prevailed. Although Wilson was mindful of the failures of Berlin, he expressed sympathy with the fears that it would be dangerous to give groups of individuals within each state a direct mechanism for appealing to the League. Nonetheless, David Lloyd George acknowledged that "the treaty will not make anti-Semitism disappear from Poland overnight" and there would be ceaseless incidents if Polish Jews or their representatives could address the League directly.[72]

The question of who could enforce the treaty provisions complicated matters further. Wilson was initially concerned that if enforcement was limited to the members of the League Council, it would give the appearance that a few powers would be imposing their will on how the text of the treaty was to be implemented. The other Great Powers disagreed. In their June 17, 1919, meeting, they assigned sole responsibility of treaty enforcement to the members of the League Council, subscribing to the British leader's view that it would assuage the feelings of the new states and make their signatures on the treaty more likely if any of the Great Powers would be the ones to present such questions before the League rather than "lesser" states.[73] In any case, Wilson changed his mind and agreed that it would be best to assign enforcement responsibilities to the League Council because Jews generally enjoyed greater freedoms within the countries of the Great Powers, and they should therefore enforce the minority guarantees themselves. The debates reflected the general impermeability of the fast-solidifying borders of national sovereignty as well as the persistence of imperial power thinking.

It should have been a welcome development for minority groups wishing to participate in the new international order.[74] But it was also a system that deprived them of the right to engage in the same kind of national self-determination that was afforded others and thus forever relegated them to protected status. The Berlin Treaty does not mention the term *minorities,* and understandably so, precisely because of the assortment of entities and fluidity of migration that was present in Europe at that time. The emergence and consolidation of the nation-state as the primary vehicle for implementing Wilsonian self-determination right after the war left more than a few religious and ethnic communities seeming like distinct alien communities in a sea of national homogeneity. As early as 1917, the Inquiry, the American entity established by Wilson to plan the postwar peace, was already using the language of majorities and minorities in their memoranda. In the Polish Treaty itself, American references to a "national minority" were replaced, however, by a more vague-sounding "Polish nationals who belong to racial, religious or linguistic minorities." By entrenching the category of minorities as a legitimate concern of international law, minorities were in fact produced, affecting both the new states on which they would be inflicted and, most especially, the people comprising these groups themselves.

For Poland, the minority provisions were a form of external intervention on the kind of nation-state that the Great Powers deemed suitable. One example is that the Council of Four intended the Polish Treaty to bolster the moderate position of Paderewski rather than that of the anti-Semitic Polish leader Roman Dmowski.[75] In a revealing statement, Wilson reminded his fellow council members that they were dealing with "states which until now have treated Jews in the spirit of the Middle Ages. Our goal must be to help transform that state of mind."[76] For minorities, and for the Polish Jews in particular, they became wards of the international system in need of continuous protection. Indeed, in Inquiry memoranda, the term *minorities* was used interchangeably with the phrase "weaker peoples."[77] And in the process of seeking to remove minority groups as pawns in Great Power politics and consequently as a source of war, the Great Powers inadvertently ensured that they would become an inevitable part of it.

The Polish Treaty guaranteed collective rights and cultural protections for minority groups and for the Polish Jewry in particular. While Article 2 protected religious freedom in general, and Article 7 ensured equal rights for all Polish nationals, Article 8 allowed religious minorities to set up their own schools and social institutions. Thanks to the efforts of Anglo-American Jewish groups, Article 9, though neutrally worded and eventually substantively diluted, upheld state support of the Yiddish language on the primary school level.[78] Jewish lobbyists argued that Yiddish was crucial to the preservation of Jewish freedom and identity, even as the British saw it as a dangerous signal of incipient Jewish separatism. When it became a heady subject of debate within the Council of Four, Wilson defended the article against British objections, stating that these protections would be unnecessary if the conditions for Jews in Poland were otherwise. Article 11 exempted Jews from being compelled to perform any acts during the Sabbath, except for the purpose of military service and national defense. It also stated that elections would not be held on a Saturday.

The treaty was a bitter pill for Poland to swallow. Paderewski considered it an infringement of Polish sovereignty and an unwelcome form of extraterritoriality, especially because the Great Powers—the United States, Britain, Italy, and France—did not have to sign such provisions for their own countries. It also negated the Polish government's ability to distinguish its treatment of citizens and foreigners because Jews at that time were classified as aliens. This was a direct response to erstwhile Romanian discrimination against its Jews under the provisions of the Berlin Treaty. As a last-ditch indictment of the treaty he felt compelled to sign, the Polish premier aired his complaints in a long memo about these and other treaty provisions addressed to the Council of Four.[79] Perhaps rightfully so, he was worried that constituting these minority guarantees as a matter for international supervision and enforcement would obstruct the process of assimilation in Poland as it was, for all intents and purposes, an open invitation for foreign interference with internal matters at such a critical nation-building period. Polish "citizens could not learn to be conscious of their duties towards their state, if, feeling themselves under foreign protection, they were encouraged to lodge complaints against their own state with a foreign court of appeal," he wrote.

For Wilson, though sympathetic to Polish concerns, the heart of the matter was that of liberal toleration as a means of preserving peace. In view of the failure to incorporate the same protections in the League Covenant and thus make it universally applicable, particular minority protections offered another way to extend his promise of self-determination to groups that were denied the right to form their own states. That meant not only individual rights protections but also protections for groups to maintain and preserve their collective identity. These provisions formed a template for subsequent minority treaties that featured customized group protections for the Jews in Greece and Romania, and the Muslims in Albania, Croatia, Serbia, and Slovenia. Taken together, provisions dealing with minority rights inaugurated by the Polish Treaty substantially advanced the international legal framework of collective minority protection.[80]

***

The Covenant of the League of Nations that was brought into being by the signing of the Treaty of Versailles bore little resemblance to the original Wilsonian vision for it. Prior to the peace conference, Wilson envisioned an "impartial justice in every form of the settlement and the justice that knows no favorites and knows no standards but the equal rights of the several peoples concerned."[81] By the end of the conference, many would argue against the realization of this promise and vision in the resulting covenant. Still, thanks to Wilson's persistent efforts, an international legal regime for the protection of religious freedom, however partial, had managed to emerge from the interstices between the old empire and the new world order. It was precisely due to this delicate balancing act that the origins of the international law on religious freedom did not derive from a concern for individual or collective liberty per se but rather as a means to preserve international peace. The guarantee of religious freedom came in various forms, from protecting the inhabitants of mandate territories, the missionaries in such areas, and the minorities in the new states upon which the MPR was imposed. This account not only recognizes Woodrow Wilson's little acknowledged contribution to the field but also challenges the conventional notion that the religious freedom protection intended by the covenant focused largely on collective religious rights. Although more prominent in the MPR, Wilson sought to apply this guarantee in all its possible guises and in the broadest way possible as expediency and practicality would allow.

Because of his single-minded determination to draft and finalize the covenant and protect it from further damaging alterations, however, Wilson was also rendered unable and perhaps even unwilling to compromise in many respects, which consequently resulted in the failure to endow the covenant with a responsibility to protect the religious freedom for all peoples of the world. Imperial imperatives saw to it that the covenant would sanction the Great Powers' hand in the internal affairs of the newly created states, although they would remain free within their own sovereign walls. The constitutionalist in Wilson had hoped that whatever the covenant's deficiencies, it would be elastic enough to be given life by those who exercised power in accordance with the changing circumstances of the time and be amply guided by world opinion. The covenant's failure did not mean that nothing was advanced. To the contrary, the establishment of international institutions such as the mandate system and the minority protection regime gave the nascent international law on religious freedom a reach that was previously not possible. To paraphrase Wilson's early words, the law of religious freedom in the League Covenant already represented a growth of international society as reflected in its institutions and practices.[82] It was his efforts that sowed the early seeds to make it a matter of international inquiry and enforcement.

As world leaders signed the Treaty of Versailles on June 28, 1919, few could have predicted that the world order was to change again fundamentally in a short time. The international legal protection of individual religious freedom would not emerge until after another tragic war, one that—ironically—traces its roots to the breakdown of the minority protection regime itself.

3

A God-Fearing Democracy

> Under this document we have good reason to expect the framing of an international bill of rights, acceptable to all the nations involved. That bill of rights will be as much a part of international life as our own Bill of Rights is a part of our Constitution. The Charter is dedicated to the achievement and observance of human rights and fundamental freedoms. Unless we can attain those objectives for all men and women everywhere—without regard to race, language or religion—we cannot have permanent peace and security.
>
> —*U.S. president Harry S. Truman, Closing Session of the United Nations Conference, San Francisco, California, June 26, 1945*

Dumbarton Oaks, a sprawling estate and center of Byzantine and medieval studies located in the Georgetown district of Washington, DC, was the historic site of four-power exploratory talks for the creation of a postwar international organization to succeed the defunct League of Nations. There, a familiar 1919-esque conversation took place sometime in the late summer of 1944. Sir Alexander Cadogan, the British delegate, was opposing any reference to human rights and fundamental freedoms in the document, which would become the Dumbarton Oaks Proposals. Such a provision, he argued, would give rise to the possibility that the organization might engage in unwarranted criticism of the internal organization of its member states.[1] The Soviet representative, Ambassador Andrei Gromyko, agreed, opining that a reference to human rights and basic freedom was not germane to the main tasks of an international organization.[2] The third man in the room, Edward Stettinius Jr., insisted, however. As U.S. secretary of state and the head American delegate to the Washington Conversations, he echoed the desire of President Franklin Roosevelt to include some kind of reference to human rights in the proposals.

By 1944, however, with the tide of war shifting visibly in favor of the Allied forces, an overriding concern for the impenetrable walls of state sovereignty was back again among all the Great Powers, even for the Americans who had been, according to the British description, unfortunately obsessed with "rights talk" throughout the conversations.[3] An American attempt to refer to human rights in the General Purposes of the organization was contested by both the British and the Russians. It was decided in the end to put off the matter for later consideration. Thus, in the final version of the proposals, an anemic and negligible phrasing of "promote respect for human rights and fundamental freedoms" was deeply buried under the chapter for "Arrangements for International Economic and Social Cooperation"[4]—a pitiful attempt to serve the two seemingly irreconcilable masters that are universal human rights and state sovereignty. Hundreds of nongovernmental organizations would decry this slight by the time of the drafting of the Charter of the United Nations at the San Francisco conference.

Though the League of Nations was by and large its model, the United Nations (UN) that emerged from San Francisco is, in many important respects, different from its predecessor. At the most obvious level, the UN Charter mentions the term *human rights* seven times, whereas it was nowhere to be found in the League Covenant.[5] Thanks to the efforts of various private groups in San Francisco, the charter explicitly provides that the promotion and encouragement of respect for human rights and for fundamental freedoms for all without regard to race, sex, language, or religion form part of the purposes of the UN.[6] In its stirring preamble, it included a reaffirmation of the "faith in fundamental human rights, in the dignity and worth of the human person, in the equal rights of men and women and of nations large and small. . . ."[7]

In addition, as a response to the atrocities committed during the Second World War, a preparatory commission of the UN, pursuant to Article 68 of the charter empowering the Economic and Social Council (ECOSOC) to set up a commission for the promotion of human rights, recommended to the General Assembly the creation of such a commission, whose initial task would be the formulation of an international bill of human rights. The initial fruit of those efforts, the Universal Declaration of Human Rights (UDHR), adopted by the General Assembly on December 10, 1948, remains one of the General Assembly's biggest achievements. Its authoritative catalogue of rights put the necessary flesh and blood into the broad definition of human rights articulated in the charter, and spelled out, in a more precise fashion, the human rights obligations of its member states.

One powerful driving force behind the explosion of utopian thinking during this period was the rights-oriented ideological scaffolding constructed through the wartime actions and rhetoric of President Roosevelt. His Four Freedoms Speech in January 1941 occupies a singular place in the annals of history in terms of its significance and the consequences it generated. Perhaps more important than its immediate purpose of coaxing his reluctant country to join the Allied war effort, it would become the battle cry of many human rights advocates from all over the world until the adoption of the UDHR. All of these four freedoms, in various incarnations, would find themselves enshrined both in the UN Charter and the UDHR.[8]

Most existing accounts of the four freedoms focus on the revolutionary appearance of the "freedom from want" on the global front—FDR's bold attempt to internationalize his domestic New Deal program no less.[9] Often mentioned without debate is the inclusion of religious freedom, in Roosevelt's words, "the freedom of every person to worship God in his own way everywhere in the world," as one of the indispensable freedoms in his envisioned new world order. While religious liberty took its rightful place alongside others in the pantheon of important rights enumerated in the UN Charter and the UDHR, it also performed a significant role in the diplomatic thought of FDR.[10] This chapter tells the story of how religious liberty helped in marshaling Roosevelt's arguments for the necessary American participation in the war, and its role in the creation and eventual realization of his postwar vision, an example of what legal scholar Richard Primus describes as the incarnation of wartime political commitments into positive legal language.[11] As historian Andrew Preston deftly shows, religious freedom played a key role in FDR's wartime rhetoric. Equally important, however, is the role of religious freedom in the creation of the largely American-engineered institutions of peace, eventually finding itself in the charter and the UDHR as a legally guaranteed individual human right. In the mind of FDR, however, religious liberty was not yet the contemporary human right as we know it today but a core component of a democratic order. It was crucial not only as an ideological weapon in the war against totalitarian Nazi Germany but as a pillar of enduring peace. Thus, he sought to promote this freedom in as many ways as it would serve his wartime policy and postwar vision.

The story, however, is far from triumphalist. As the episode from Dumbarton Oaks showed, despite the incalculable human suffering and the role played by human rights rhetoric during the war, concerns involving the preservation of state sovereignty would be foremost between and among the Great Powers by the war's end. In view of such constraints, group rights were discarded and individual human rights became a fitting and less dangerous alternative, if not more appealing to the public.[12] This had profound consequences on the practice of religious freedom. A draft international bill of rights, initially proposed in 1942 to become a binding annex to the UN Charter, was never again considered inside or outside the U.S. government. Attempts to refer to human rights, as vague as the term sounded, in the charter encountered numerous hurdles. By 1948, with the Cold War between the United States and the Soviet Union already well underway, the euphoria that met the historic adoption of the UDHR was undercut by the fact that it was a nonbinding declaration, which was illustrated by the stark contrast between U.S. Secretary of State George C. Marshall publicly heralding the UDHR as necessary for "free men in a free world"[13] and then-U.S. delegate to the General Assembly John Foster Dulles nervously clarifying one day before the declaration's formal adoption that it was not a legally binding document.[14] As Dulles later on mused, "[T]he fact that a UDHR has been adopted does not of course mean that from now on everyone is actually going to get all those rights. The UN does not have that power of direct action. It can proclaim with great moral authority standards of conduct and it can expect that the peoples of the world will try to make their nations live up to those standards."[15]

Notwithstanding the seeming handicap posed by their less noble origins,[16] the human rights provisions of the UN Charter and the UDHR, including that of religious liberty, have since taken on lives of their own, inspiring national constitutions and regional human rights regimes. But it was the wartime drive to protect and later export the ideal of religious liberty, as understood in Roosevelt's four freedoms, and in helping shape the contemporary human rights regime through the UN Charter and the UDHR, that would pave the way for the role of the United States as the world's arsenal of democracy.

Religious Liberty and the Road to War

Of all the four freedoms, it is the "freedom to worship God everywhere" alone that has enjoyed the longest public history in the United States, dating as it were from the very arrival of its first English colonists. Freedom of speech and expression, though part of the First Amendment to the U.S.

Constitution, gained widespread currency only during the period of the First World War and was legally applied to states only thereafter, while the freedoms from fear and from want were distinct New Deal creations of Roosevelt. It was not surprising then that religious liberty was also the freedom that made the most appearances in many of his public speeches as well as his private correspondence at a time when the United States looked grimly across the Atlantic at the onset of another European war. Ironic as it might seem given the perilous waters of religious factionalism in the American domestic scene, where widespread and persistent anti-Catholicism and anti-Semitism still held sway, Roosevelt's turn to religion and religious liberty in the years leading up to the war grew out of a pragmatic recognition that it would speak to a large swath of the American population, most of whom remained insistent on isolationism.[17]

The key to American preparation for war, even as the majority clamored for neutrality, was the promotion of ideals of freedom and democracy, especially the ideal of religious liberty in the face of German fascism. This, Roosevelt, the consummate practitioner of American civil religion since Abraham Lincoln, did not find difficult to do. Even before he became preoccupied with foreign affairs, FDR had always made effective use of biblical symbols, religious language, and moral injunctions in his public addresses. In cultivating much-needed support for his New Deal program for instance, FDR successfully employed the ideas and imagery of a "Good Samaritan" and "a national covenant to drive out the moneychangers of the temple" as justifications for the creation of a welfare state.[18] In fact, some have argued that for all its secular appearance, the New Deal was essentially a Protestant project in spirit.[19] While Roosevelt was a deeply religious man and in fact a practicing Episcopalian, he had no patience for theological nuances. His was, in the words of his wife Eleanor, "a simple faith."[20] Thus, he could genuinely speak about religion and its importance, but he was not wedded to a particular conception of it. His speechwriter and friend, Samuel Rosenman, described him as a "new man in politics—one who did not seem to care or even know whether you were a Catholic, Protestant or Jew."[21] Indeed, an unprecedented number of Catholics and Jews were appointed to government positions during his years in office—and became a perennial target for his critics.[22] The two groups, by that time already crucial constituencies of the Democratic Party, had their own reasons to favor him. Among others, his New Deal program resonated with them as it sought to ameliorate the conditions of the poor and the weakest in the aftermath of the Great Depression. But more than out of mere political astuteness, Roosevelt himself also clung to the traditional republican idea in which religion was seen as an indispensable basis of morality, and without it a proper democracy would be impossible. In a remark to Postmaster General Jim Farley in 1933, he stated that a "proper attitude toward religion, and belief in God, will in the end be the salvation of peoples."[23]

As the president partook of a veritable American tradition of pluralism and the invocation of the sacred in public affairs, he also transformed it when he included non-Protestants in the process. In a letter to the head of the Federal Council of Churches (FCC), an umbrella organization of Protestant groups, over protests concerning the appointment of an American representative to the Vatican, he stated that when he was a small boy, the Protestant Episcopal prayer book contained a prayer "calling down divine wrath on Jews, Turks and other infidels. I think that most American Christians have advanced considerably in their religious thought in the past half century."[24] This was a rather significant change. Not more than half a century ago, President William McKinley offered the Christianization of the largely Catholic Philippine Islands as a principal justification for American humanitarian imperialism.

But the president was not only looking inward but also outward. This recognition and appreciation of the interconnectedness between domestic and foreign questions defined his foreign policy and sharply distinguished him from his ill-fated predecessor Woodrow Wilson.[25] He also emphasized the necessity of religion especially in the realm of foreign affairs. At the 1936 Inter-American Conference in Argentina, Roosevelt told his fellow heads of state that their common faith in democracy will not be complete "if we fail to affirm our faith in God." He pointed out that while freedom of religion was embedded in "the constitutions and in the practice of our nations," these words presuppose "a belief and trust in God."[26] He was not yet prepared, however, to make it an official policy to intervene in other countries on its behalf. At the height of anticlericalism and religious persecution in Mexico, even as he asserted the right of all people to enjoy religious freedom, he refused to intervene as a matter of maintenance of peaceful relations.[27] Adhering to the Good Neighbor policy, the Roosevelt administration cast aside congressional appeals and private pleas to defend religious freedom south of the Rio Grande.

Nevertheless, as Europe drifted toward war, Roosevelt became increasingly stumped. Various European leaders were desperately urging him to take the initiative for peace, while the majority of his fellow Americans remained adamantly opposed to any form of involvement in European affairs. His 1937 Quarantine Speech at Chicago, in which he proposed a rather mild policy of isolation against unspecified aggressor nations to stop the "epidemic of world lawlessness,"[28] had not been effective in arousing American sentiments. In fact, it was met with public hostility.[29] During the following year, the British and French capitulated to German demands in Munich.[30] If Roosevelt had any misgivings about the inevitability of war with Hitler, the Munich conference finally prompted him to act otherwise. But unable to confront Nazi Germany directly and militarily, he set about on a path to support the other Western democracies, educate the American people to his views, and simultaneously build up the country's military capabilities. At this juncture, the president turned to religious freedom protection as both a crucial justification and objective of American participation. Prior to the Japanese attack at Pearl Harbor, that participation would take the form of material and moral support to her allies.

In his 1939 State of the Union Address, Roosevelt characterized the brewing storms from abroad as challenges to the three institutions indispensable to Americans: religion, democracy, and international good faith. Roosevelt carefully painted a picture of the indivisibility of liberty and offered his most eloquent defense of religious freedom to date, warning that:

> where freedom of religion has been attacked, the attack has come from sources opposed to democracy. Where democracy has been overthrown, the spirit of free worship has disappeared. And where religion and democracy have vanished, good faith and reason in international affairs have given way to strident ambition and brute force. . . . There comes a time in the affairs of men when they must prepare to defend, not their homes alone but the tenets of faith and humanity on which their churches, their governments and their very civilization are founded. The defense of religion, of democracy and of good faith among nations is all the same fight. To save one, we must now make up our minds to save all.[31]

Religion, he explained, enabled this liberty by "teaching man his relationship to God, giv[ing] the individual a sense of his own dignity and teach[ing] him to respect himself by respecting his neighbors." Thus, it would be a building block for democracy and international good faith, crucial components of a functioning and, more important, a moral international order. Samuel Rosenman, the presidential speechwriter, recounted that FDR wanted to convey the falseness of a philosophy prevailing among some American industrialists that "we can do business with Hitler." To this, FDR countered that "we can do business with him all right but in the process we would lose everything that America stands for."[32]

As part of his turn to religion and its defense to marshal support both from home and abroad, FDR appointed Myron C. Taylor as his personal representative to the Vatican, in a Christmas Day message of the same year addressed to the pope.[33] It was a telling testament to the state of interfaith tensions in American society at that time that Roosevelt went to great lengths at home to portray the appointment as sui generis and that it did not mean the establishment of any form of diplomatic relations with the Vatican.[34] Though Taylor's job description was kept deliberately ambiguous, the president did explain that he wanted to "mobilize the moral forces of the world" and that establishing effective contact with Roman Catholics all over the world required some kind of relationship with the pope.[35] Nonetheless, there were vociferous protests from various Protestant churches, which assailed the appointment as a violation of the constitutionally mandated separation of church and state.[36] Roosevelt pressed on, however, and sought to allay those fears in a personal note to George A. Buttrick, president of the FCC, reiterating the unique and temporary character of the appointment and stating that the primary motive behind it was simply to assist endeavors of peace and to alleviate the suffering of peoples.[37]

Though it was decidedly controversial on the home front, Roosevelt's religion-related moves that year accomplished three goals. They suggested the intended portrayal of the defense of religion as something that resonated with all Americans without regard to religion and thus a way to build domestic consensus with regard to the nation's road to war. The Vatican appointment was Roosevelt's ultimately unsuccessful attempt to divide the Axis powers in enlisting Vatican help to keep Italy out of the conflagration. Last, and perhaps more important, it laid the early groundwork for the role of religion and religious freedom in his postwar vision. In the 1940 State of the Union Address, Roosevelt reminded his listeners to "look ahead and see the kind of lives our children would have to lead if a large part of the rest of the world were compelled to worship a god imposed by a military ruler, or were forbidden to worship God at all. . . ."[38] Tapping into the religious liberty concerns of all Americans, he cited a Nazi plan to "abolish all existing religions—Catholic, Protestant, Mohammedan, Buddhist, Hindu and Jewish alike and in the place of the churches of our civilization, there is to be set up an International Nazi Church staffed with orators of the Nazi regime,"[39] depicting everyone as likely victims of Nazi oppression in order to convince them of the Allied cause.

When Hitler invaded the Soviet Union, the question of whether U.S. Lend-Lease support, which was already being given to several countries fighting the Axis, should also be extended to Russia further highlighted domestic concerns about religious liberty.[40] Four years earlier, a previous pope—Pius XI—had issued the encyclical *Divini Redemptoris* in which he warned the church faithful about the intrinsic evils of atheistic communism and forbade those who wished to defend Christian civilization from any collaboration with it.[41] For many American Catholics, the Soviet Union was no better than Nazi Germany. It was thus preferable to see the two godless totalitarian states destroy each other.[42]

Roosevelt characteristically showed deep interest in making this course of action acceptable to Catholics in the United States or at least in preventing their strong opposition to it. The Myron Taylor appointment proved especially useful in this debacle insofar as FDR's domestic objectives were concerned. Roosevelt coursed through Taylor a message to Pope Pius XII in which he depicted Russia as less dangerous to the world than a victorious Nazi Germany and explained that, insofar as he was informed, "churches in Russia are open. I believe there is a real possibility that Russia may as a result of the present conflict recognize freedom of religion in Russia, although of course without recognition of any official intervention on the part of any church in education or political matters within Russia. I feel that if this can be accomplished it will put the possibility of the restoration of real religious liberty in Russia on a much better footing than religious freedom is in Germany today."[43] Pope Pius XII reluctantly acceded to FDR's requests to convey his support for the American aid policy to Russia and for the principles stated in the Atlantic Charter by sending the apostolic delegate in Washington a more lenient interpretation of the 1937 encyclical. Following the suggestion of Roosevelt and Taylor, the new interpretation held that aiding the Russian people was distinct from aiding its communistic system of government.[44] The linguistic sleight of hand worked. As one historian observed, the effect was noticeable shortly thereafter as members of the American Catholic hierarchy began advancing the same justification to their followers.[45]

The Lend-Lease controversy was an episode in the broader and persistent trajectory of Roosevelt to enlist the rhetoric of religious freedom as the country inched closer to war. At the beginning of 1941, with much of Europe having already fallen to the advancing Wermacht, he had enumerated his famous four freedoms as he proposed the Lend-Lease bill in his annual message to Congress.[46] These four freedoms, the president stressed, were intended to be secured throughout the world. While it may appear as the first definite articulation of a vision for human rights, as many later commentators elaborated,[47] Roosevelt was, in reality, describing his ideal international order. The concern for these freedoms was relevant to the extent that having them made for stable democracies. To this end, these four freedoms were what he deemed as necessary ingredients of such an order: secure democracies, both politically and economically. Without the four freedoms, he said, "democracy would be superseded by slavery. . . . We will accept only a world consecrated to freedom of speech and expression, freedom of every person to worship God in his own way. . . ."[48] Thus, religion and religious freedom were important components of these democracies. In a letter to Dr. Buttrick, the president expressed his intentions to reach out and mobilize all the churches, including the "Mohammedan Church" for "internationally decent moral relations."[49] Taken together, Lend-Lease and the four freedoms represented the material and moral aspects of the defense of democracy and the freedoms that could only be made possible and flourish under such a system.

For his American audience, the president had to offer more than just the military defeat of Nazi Germany. He had to lay out his long-term peace objectives, which certainly appealed more to them. Thus, the inclusion of the "freedom of every person to worship God in his own way—everywhere in the world" in the four freedoms, though a continuation of his earlier policies, served a useful purpose. It was not only a matter of rhetoric in terms of articulating an important war *and* peace aim; it also allowed him to connect with religious constituencies and organizations in support of the war effort. Inexplicably, it was omitted from the Atlantic Charter, a historic statement of Anglo-American wartime cooperation between Roosevelt and British prime minister Winston Churchill signed seven months after the Four Freedoms Speech.[50] It did reappear in the internationalization of the Atlantic Charter—the 1942 Declaration of the United Nations that was initially signed by twenty-six countries.[51] Rosenman opined that the omission was a result of inadvertent oversight in drafting but not condoned.[52] When press secretary Stephen Early cabled the president about the negative domestic reactions to this oversight, the president was recorded to have replied: "I have heard the commentator who said freedom of press and religion were given up. He is either senile or an ass. The same happy thought applies to press queries as to whether principles of civilization apply today or next week or a year hence. Tell the boys [of the press] I said so off the record."[53]

In a more diplomatic manner, Roosevelt subsequently reported to Congress that it was unnecessary to point out that the "declaration of principles includes of necessity the world need for freedom of religion. . . . No society of the world organized under announced principles could survive without these freedoms which are a part of the whole freedom for which we strive."[54] A reason for the opposition was that it became live ammunition at the hands of those critical of aid to the godless Soviet Union, in particular, and Roosevelt's policy of accommodation toward the Russians, in general. Back in 1933, Roosevelt had already encountered a similar religious opposition to the American recognition of the Soviet Union. Appealing to the Jewish roots of the Soviet foreign minister Maksim Litvinov, he was able to secure a guarantee that the religious freedom of American nationals would be protected in exchange for American recognition. This time, Roosevelt's concern extended to all believers in Russia. For the president, this was not entirely a matter of immediate political expediency. Shortly before the end of the war in 1945, he had sent his close associate and a leading Democratic politician, Edward J. Flynn, on a secret mission to the Soviet Union to inquire about the position of the Roman Catholic Church in Russia and the Balkans after the war. With a sense of foreboding, Roosevelt felt that there could be "no permanent peace unless the large Catholic populations in Poland, Lithuania and the Balkans were permitted to practice their faith freely."[55] The mission would be cut short by his death and the complete breakdown of U.S.-Russian relations shortly after.

In his effort to defend the aid policy, the president asked the Soviet ambassador Konstantin Oumansky to get some positive publicity into the United States regarding freedom of religion in Russia because it might have "a fine educational effect before the next [Lend-Lease] bill comes up in Congress."[56] On the domestic front, Roosevelt pointed out during a press conference that Article 124 of the Soviet Constitution guaranteed freedom of conscience and of religious worship, as well as freedom to propagandize against religion,[57] much to the dismay of his critics who pointed out the incredulous sophistry in this example. The president arguably knew full well the lack of such freedom in the Soviet Union, but beyond the immediate problem of aiding the Russians, he was more concerned about the bigger picture he was painting for his fellow Americans to help them sign on to the case for the country's likely involvement in the war: the contrast between Nazi totalitarianism and Anglo-American freedom. Thus, he wanted to place the Russians in the latter camp.[58] The Russians surprisingly complied with this request and promptly proclaimed that freedom of worship was allowed in the Soviet Union as long as it did not challenge the authority of the state.[59] Later, over the initial complaints of the Russians who thought the inclusion of freedom of religion in the 1942 declaration was unnecessarily provocative, Roosevelt understandably stood firm. Making a distinction between the phrase "religious freedom" and "freedom of religion," he managed to convince Litvinov, who had become Soviet ambassador to the United States at this time, that religious freedom also included the freedom to have no religion.[60]

The declaration, which began with "being convinced that complete victory over their enemies is essential to defend life, liberty, independence and religious freedom, and to preserve human rights and justice in their own lands as well as in other lands, and that they are now engaged in a common struggle against savage and brutal forces seeking to subjugate the world . . . ," was addressed to a broad international audience. Its message was repeated in the president's clarification that the Atlantic Charter was intended to apply to the whole world and implement the four freedoms in the whole world, not just those parts that border the Atlantic.[61] It was also present in his commemoration of the first anniversary of the Atlantic Charter.[62] Compared to the charter, the notion of human rights as a war aim was more central in the declaration. Its name was coined by Roosevelt, who was reported to have excitedly proposed it to Churchill while the latter was bathing during his stay in the White House.[63] Religious freedom was mentioned separately from human rights—no doubt an effort to rectify its omission from the Atlantic Charter. In all these iterations of the declaration, a defense of religious freedom was included. But the call was not addressed primarily to Americans anymore. A month before the declaration, Japanese military forces launched a surprise bombing attack at Pearl Harbor. The United States was now officially at war against the Axis.

Religious Liberty and the Ghost of Woodrow Wilson

American postwar planning began early.[64] An advisory committee within the State Department on postwar foreign policy first met in February 1942, armed with the only available presidential policies to date: the four freedoms, the Atlantic Charter, and the declaration by the United Nations. But Franklin Roosevelt, like Wilson before him, was, for the most part, his own secretary of state. While mindful of Wilson's mistakes—for example, he did not go outside the State Department for postwar planning, which is what Wilson did with The Inquiry—he shared with his predecessor an inclination to formulate policies on the most important matters on his own. The result was that State officials were often kept in the dark or even held conflicting positions when it came to presidential intentions—a problem that resulted in animosities among key State officials.[65]

Nevertheless, FDR instructed them to begin developing a blueprint for a postwar international organization guided by these declarations. According to Benjamin Welles, son and biographer of undersecretary for state and chief architect of the U.S. plans for the United Nations organization Sumner Welles, the president did not want details about frontiers or other problems. What he told Welles was "to prepare the necessary number of baskets and the necessary number of alternative solutions for each problem. When the time comes, all I have to do is reach into a basket and fish out solutions that are sound and from which I can make my own choice."[66] Although a number of prominent government officials and private individuals worked on various aspects of a postwar international organization, it was Welles who almost single-handedly crafted a draft UN charter by working from the model of the League of Nations Covenant.

The issue of human rights, however, was not yet on the table. Welles did consider the new international organization as the vehicle through which the four freedoms would be protected.[67] But while the draft UN charter contained a reference to human rights in its preamble,[68] there was an obvious need to spell out and translate that into more concrete and detailed provisions. Various State subcommittees considered the inclusion of a possible bill of human rights throughout the year, culminating in a draft international bill of rights by the end of it.[69] The provisions were a blend of traditional American negative constitutional liberties and New Deal–esque positive economic and social rights, including the right to have minimum standards of economic well-being. Article IV on religious freedom, which was among those not debated, did not use the language in the First Amendment but was formulated with a caveat against conflicting with public order or good morals, traditional language found in international documents such as treaties and in the League Covenant. The proposal was characteristically sensitive to American separation of church and state concerns. Article VIII, on the proposed right to public education, carried a caveat that students shall not be obliged to participate in religious instruction of a faith to which they or their parents do not adhere.[70]

Alongside these official efforts was an explosion of proposals and studies from U.S. private organizations on the problem of postwar peace and organization. A State subcommittee was mandated to serve as a liaison to these nongovernmental groups working on postwar issues.[71] The failure of Wilson to enlist domestic support for the League of Nations and the dire consequences of such failure were the clear motivating forces behind this new public and private partnership. Many of these private proposals, although primarily focused on the structural aspects of the international organization, also included several human rights charters. The American Law Institute (ALI), for example, after consultation with various groups and consideration of the views of different cultures, issued an influential "Essential Statement of Human Rights,"[72] which John Humphrey, a principal drafter of the UDHR, later recounted that he found especially useful in his own drafting process.[73] The ALI statement combined the traditional American negative freedoms, which included religious liberty, together with its New Deal additions. Religious groups such as the World Jewish Congress and the FCC likewise submitted their proposed bills of rights to the State Department. The Commission to Study the Bases for a Just and Durable Peace, a body created by FCC and headed by future secretary of state and preeminent cold warrior John Foster Dulles, came up with the "Six Pillars of Peace," which featured freedom of religion as part of its proposed international bill of rights.[74]

Riding the momentum created by Roosevelt's stirring declarations on rights and freedoms for the past two years, these emboldened groups projected the strong and deeply rooted American rights tradition as encapsulated in the Bill of Rights of the U.S. Constitution. Not only a response to the immediate atrocities committed during the European conflict, the tradition also addressed what they perceived as one of the underlying causes of the war—the failure of the minority protection regime (MPR). Jewish groups in particular felt that the safest recourse was not to single themselves out as a minority but to ensure that individual rights for all would be guaranteed. For U.S. government officials, the aim behind crafting the draft international bill of rights in 1942 (later renamed the Declaration of Human Rights because the term was more recognizable outside the United States and to avoid confusion with the American Bill of Rights) was precisely to forestall demands to have a new MPR after the war.[75] In enumerating a list of essential individual rights, it would be diffusing the political difficulties involved in crafting and implementing a workable and effective minority protection regime. The draft was appended as a binding annex to Welles's draft constitution of the envisioned postwar international organization. After much reworking, the constitution was approved by Roosevelt in February 1944. It did not contain a reference to human rights, only that, as part of the general purposes of the organization, it would "promote through cooperative effort the . . . social advancement of nations and peoples."[76]

The State Department debated the merits of such a bill of rights but in the end, it was considered an international intrusion into what was properly regarded as the domestic sphere. U.S. officials were concerned that it would make the protection of individual rights paramount to the safety of the state. It was not surprising then that the American negotiators decided against including the draft as part of the U.S. proposals by the time they went to Dumbarton Oaks.[77]

In the meantime, the United States signed the Moscow Joint Four-Nation Declaration in October 1943, which incorporated the principles of the 1942 declaration, established the necessity of the creation of a postwar international organization for the maintenance of international peace and security, and pronounced Allied policies with regard to Italy and Austria.[78] In the particular attempt to democratize Italy, similar to what would be prescribed for Japan in the Potsdam Declaration,[79] the freedoms of speech, religious worship, political belief, the press, and public meeting, among others, were promised to be restored to the Italian people.

At the initiative of the American delegation, an enumeration of these human rights provisions, including freedom of religious worship, was proposed during the first meeting of the Council of Foreign Ministers, held in London from September to October 1945. These provisions were included in the 1947 Paris Peace Treaties, which the victorious Allied Powers signed with countries affiliated with the Axis forces such as Italy, Romania, and Hungary. Under Section VI on Nationality and Civic Rights in Ceded Territories, the U.S. proposal of Article 13 (4) under "Part One—The Territorial Clauses" read: "The State to which the territory is transferred shall take all measures necessary to secure to all persons within the territory, without distinction as to race, sex, language or religion, the enjoyment of human rights and of the fundamental freedoms, including the freedom of expression, of press and publication, of religious worship, of political opinion and of public meeting."[80] This is repeated in Article 14 under "Part Two—The Political Clauses," which reads: "Italy shall take all measures necessary to secure to all persons under Italian jurisdiction, without distinction as to race, sex, language or religion, the enjoyment of human rights and of the fundamental freedoms, including the freedom of expression, of press and publication, of religious worship and of political opinion and of public meeting."[81] The provisions of the peace treaty with Italy would be the model for the rest of the Axis affiliates. According to James F. Byrnes, a former Supreme Court justice who resigned and was later appointed by President Truman as secretary of state to succeed Edward Stettinius Jr., the American delegation was at every stage of the negotiations concerned with the ideal of fundamental human rights and liberties. "Everything that we could possibly do to assure those rights and freedoms, we did."[82]

Italy and Romania protested the inclusion of these provisions because it seemed to them a pretext for outside intervention in their domestic affairs and inconsistent with the declared principle of equality among members of the UN. The concern was that it preestablished responsibilities that the other member-states of the UN had yet to undertake. In the course of discussing these individual freedoms and liberties, the American delegation once again had the opportunity to discuss whether to reinstitute the MPR in these former enemy states. Singling out the impracticality of such action, Samuel Reber, the political adviser of the U.S. delegation, deemed the nondiscrimination rule and the guarantee of individual freedoms as sufficient to protect members of minority groups.[83] And without recognizing the legal personality of the minority groups, it would be futile to maintain such a system. Recognition was probably not politically possible, if impracticable, as the concerns of State Department officials as early as 1942 showed.[84] At a time when the nation-state was being consolidated, both U.S. and British delegates categorically declared that these peace treaties should seek the assimilation rather than perpetuation of various kinds of minorities.[85]

In his report to the Senate on these treaties, Byrnes stated that these clauses constitute an international obligation and grant other states the right to see to it that they are maintained.[86] In his view, it also solved the traditional conundrum associated with international rights protection: enforcement. Through mutual agreement, the state itself undertakes to guarantee the protection of these rights. The four peace treaties concluded in Paris in addition to Italy, those of Bulgaria, Hungary, Finland, and Romania, also featured religious freedom and other human rights in similar individual rights language. In the process, the minority protection regime was forever abandoned and there was no chance that it could have been revived during the crafting of the UDHR.

During the first meeting of all three heads of state in Tehran in December 1943, the three powers—Roosevelt, Churchill, and Stalin—reiterated their dedication toward working for "the day when all peoples of the world may live free lives, untouched by tyranny, and according to their varying desires and their own consciences."[87] And they continued the offensive against the Axis and reaffirmed their commitment to the creation of a United Nations organization. These lofty-sounding concerns were not duly reflected, however, in what would become the Dumbarton Oaks Proposals, published on October 9, 1944, which were the result of informal, technical, and exploratory talks among the United States, Great Britain, the Soviet Union, and China concerning the establishment of an international organization.[88] Because of the considerable amount of time, skill, and expertise devoted to the preparation of the American proposal prior to the talks, it became the basis for discussion during the conversations.

The proposals dealt with three key issues, none of which related to human rights: the organizational structure of the UN, the decision-making procedures within it, and the availability of an international force to enforce its decisions. The resulting proposals were touted as being recommendations only, thus they were also necessarily incomplete. Because they were written by military and foreign affairs experts, the proposals were also as dry as bone. It was particularly criticized as lacking in humanity and warmth, though this was, according to the British delegate and historian Charles Webster, a matter of design.[89] The necessary language for an appeal to posterity would have to wait until the conference in San Francisco.

Despite the decision not to include the draft declaration of human rights in the American proposal, the U.S. government was determined to keep it on the agenda. Although it was solely an American initiative during the conversations to include the promotion of the observance of human rights as a purpose of the organization, it was kept deliberately general and vague.[90] Piqued by the mention of human rights in the draft, a Chinese delegate had asked if that meant the drawing of an international bill of rights, but the Americans replied that it would be left to the General Assembly. Even this was found unacceptable, however, by both the British and the Russians due to concerns about state sovereignty.[91] The British also felt that this was an underhanded American attempt to weaken British imperial power. Nonetheless, the members of the American group persisted, explaining that there was great interest throughout the United States in a possible international bill of rights.

To address the issue of noninterference in domestic affairs, lawyer Ben Cohen, a member of the American delegation and a personal representative of Roosevelt, formulated the following novel provision that attempted to solve this dilemma:

> The International Organization should refrain from intervention in the international affairs of any state, it being the responsibility of each state to see that conditions prevailing within its jurisdiction do not endanger international peace and security and to this end, to respect the human rights and fundamental freedoms of all its people and to govern in accordance with principles of humanity and justice.[92]

But Cadogan, the British representative, pointed out that the second part of the paragraph contradicted the first, and voiced his worry that it still sanctioned criticism of the internal administration of member states. The Russian ambassador Gromyko further added that this bore no relation to the task of an international security organization. The Americans themselves, led by Stettinius, Cohen, and Leo Pasvolsky who was then head of the State Policy Planning Staff, were also concerned about possible congressional reaction to a prospective international body that could investigate the problematic racial and immigration policies in the United States, but they were hesitant not to mention human rights at all. They had suggested three areas in which the term *human rights* could be mentioned: first, under the chapter involving the General Assembly; second, under Chapter I on the general purposes of the organization; or third, under Chapter IX on economic and social affairs. None of these, however, were appealing to both the British and the Soviets. Eventually, it was decided to drop the Cohen suggestion altogether, though with an American reservation for the right to mention human rights somewhere in the document. According to historian Elizabeth Borgwardt, it was only after Roosevelt expressed his personal interest in the matter that Gromyko sought instructions from Moscow for a concession.[93] When he finally obtained permission to accept a reference to human rights, the British followed suit. The result was the mention of human rights under Chapter IX of the proposals, under Social and Economic Rights: "With a view to the creation of conditions of stability and well-being, which are necessary for peaceful and friendly relations among nations, the Organization should facilitate solutions of international economic, social and other humanitarian problems and promote respect for human rights and fundamental freedoms."[94] It was the first mention of the term *human rights* in an international document. Stettinius recounted that this gratified the president because he felt that the inclusion of the human rights sentence was extremely vital for the success and acceptance of the plan.[95] Whether he was referring to a domestic or international acceptance of the plan was unclear.

The holding of a conference for the establishment of the United Nations was agreed to during the controversial Yalta Conference in February 1945, the second of three meetings among the leaders of the three powers.[96] Yalta's main purpose was to hasten the defeat of Nazi Germany and "to build the foundation for an international accord which would bring order and security after the chaos of the war."[97] It became notorious later for what amounted to American and British acquiescence to the Russian annexation of Poland and other Eastern European countries as de facto Soviet satellite states. Though the issue of religion was not discussed in detail during the conference, it was during this time that Roosevelt asked Vyacheslav Molotov, the Russian foreign minister, to allow Edward Flynn to travel to Moscow to investigate Soviet religious freedom policy. Cognizant of strong Vatican opposition to the Yalta agreement because of the deliberately ambiguous status of Poland, Roosevelt continued his earlier policy of mitigating domestic Catholic opposition in the United States by relating their concerns with that of the Vatican agenda. By sending Flynn to Moscow after the war to address concerns, such as allowing Catholic clergy in Eastern Europe to exercise their vocation, the president would simultaneously appeal to both American Catholics and the Vatican; deflect opposition to American cooperation with the Soviet Union; and, consequently, ensure the success of the establishment of the United Nations organization itself.

Perhaps it was also out of genuine concern for the fate of peoples in Eastern Europe, or even out of guilt. Roosevelt had responded to his chief of staff, who remarked that the terms of the Yalta agreement were so elastic that it could fit any Russian interpretation, that "it was the best he could do for Poland at this time."[98] Whatever the main motivation might be, it explains the special mention of religious freedom in his emotional, if circuitous, Report to Congress on the Crimea Conference. Elaborating on his postwar vision, Roosevelt described his envisioned world peace as beyond the work of a single person or government; it would be "a peace based on the sound and just principles of the Atlantic Charter—on the concept of the dignity of the human being and on the guarantees of tolerance and freedom of worship"[99]—the only instance of enumeration of human rights in the entire, almost 6,000-word speech. Shortly after Yalta, Stalin suspended the state policy of persecution of the Russian Orthodox Church and allowed the election of an Orthodox patriarch for the first time in more than twenty years.[100]

The perceived betrayals at Dumbarton Oaks and Yalta notwithstanding, many attempted to salvage whatever moral capital was left from these official declarations in order to establish an ideal charter at San Francisco. For all the pronouncements that the proposals were simply proposals, the American delegation stuck to them as the official blueprint for negotiation and discussions. This subtly imposed the limitations present at Dumbarton Oaks onto what could be accomplished at San Francisco. Only the human rights–related provisions would decidedly make the UN Charter, as approved, considerably significant from its Dumbarton Oaks predecessor.[101] The private organizations made their mark on this aspect. Mindful of the mistakes surrounding the failed Senate ratification of the League of Nations Covenant, the State Department had already launched and conducted a broad public educational campaign on behalf of the Dumbarton Oaks Proposals even before the date of the San Francisco conference was announced at Yalta.[102] This ensured long-running public support and involvement that was strategically designed to influence congressional decisions and thus ratification.

In addition to the bipartisan delegation of senators and congressional representatives to San Francisco, the State Department also took the unprecedented step of designating an advisory group made up of forty-two representatives of various nongovernmental organizations as official consultants to the U.S. delegation.[103] Initially staying on the sidelines, these private consultants eventually asserted their rights and demanded a bigger role during the talks. Their influence was felt in three important areas of the charter: education, human rights, and the formal recognition of the consultative role of nongovernmental organizations (NGOs) at the UN. None of these appeared in the Dumbarton Oaks Proposals. In an oft-cited account of a meeting on May 2, 1945, Virginia Gildersleeve, one of the U.S. delegates and the dean of Barnard College, had previously warned Clark Eichelberger, director of the American Association for the United Nations, about the omission of any mention of human rights in the draft charter being debated by the delegates, including the establishment of a commission on human rights. He quickly informed the other consultants and, together with a few others, drafted the proposed amendments and presented it to Stettinius, urging him to take a "position of leadership" on the issue of human rights.[104] The NGO memorandum proposed that human rights must be identified as a purpose of the charter; that all member-states should assume the obligation of guaranteeing human rights; and that a commission on human rights be established by name in the charter,[105] warning that it would be a "grievous shock" if the charter failed to provide some mechanism to guarantee and secure human rights.

Judge Joseph Proskauer of the American Jewish Committee then delivered an eloquent speech and implored the secretary of state that "the voice of America was speaking in this room . . . if you make a fight for these human rights proposals and win, there will be glory for all. If you make a fight for it and lose, we will back you up to the limit. If you fail to make a fight for it, you have lost the support of American opinion—and justly lost it. In the event, you will never get the Charter ratified."[106] Stettinius was reported to have remarked that he had no idea of the "intensity of feeling on this subject."[107] Later, after he announced that the U.S. delegation would incorporate the suggestions, he informed the consultants that they could justly claim credit for getting a consideration of human rights into the charter.[108]

Whether this incident could be credited as the catalyst for the inclusion of human rights is not as clear.[109] As previously shown, ideas regarding human rights have long been percolating inside the White House and the State Department prior to San Francisco, as clearly evidenced by the 1942 draft international bill of rights. While indeed the Dumbarton Oaks Proposals were criticized as lacking any "soul," State Department planners had taken these comments into account when they drafted a revised set of proposals concerning human rights a month before the infamous May 2 meeting.[110] These revised proposals were in sync with what the consultants eventually presented to Stettinius: a more substantial status for the protection of human rights in the charter and the establishment of a commission on human rights under the ECOSOC. The reason why the president instructed Stettinius to include a reference to human rights in the Dumbarton

Oaks Proposals was presumably the same reason why the State Department engaged in a massive public relations campaign surrounding the establishment of the new international organization. Roosevelt had learned from Wilson's mistakes.

The involvement of these private groups ensured American participation in a revived internationalist project, a remarkable feat given the tragic fate of the League of Nations just over two decades earlier.[111] Indeed, for many of them, there was no question about the necessity of U.S. membership in the United Nations. It was this international order or nothing.

But lost in the seemingly uphill battle for the inclusion of the ambiguous phrase "human rights"[112] was its precise definition. This was the ambiguity confronting the delegates in the Commission of Human Rights at Lake Success, New York, in June 1947, where they had assembled to draft an international bill of rights.[113] Three Latin American countries, Chile, Cuba, and Panama, had previously proposed their own versions of bills of rights to be incorporated in the UN Charter at San Francisco but to no avail. Now the members of the commission were asked to come up with a list of rights that would clarify what the charter was intended to promote and protect. At some point during the war, the four freedoms collapsed into a more vague "human rights and fundamental freedoms," at least insofar as the U.S. government was concerned. Contrary to its unique importance during wartime, religious liberty protection was transformed into making religion part of a general rule of nondiscrimination. Even in the articles concerning trusteeship and dependent territories—one of the most controversial subjects of discussion during the conference and one of the areas in which the divide between rhetoric and reality was most obvious[114]—the specific freedom of conscience provision for mandate territories under the League Covenant was replaced with the generic phrase "to encourage respect for human rights and for fundamental freedoms for all without distinction as to race, sex, language or religion. . . ."[115]

There are no clear explanations for this overall development. Perhaps it was partly due to the untimely demise of President Roosevelt, who was the one primarily responsible for human rights rhetoric and especially religious freedom protection during the war, just days before the San Francisco conference commenced. Or perhaps the Nazi atrocities in Europe, which started to come to light slowly after the Nuremberg trials, revealed the wide spectrum of essential rights and freedoms that needed protection beyond the four freedoms. Most likely, however, was that the Great Powers certainly cared less about the specific contents of the term *human rights* than about whether these—of any sort—could be used against them. The language of peace had given way to the language of security.

At Lake Success, the State Department began with a general policy of obtaining "a declaration which was a carbon copy of the American Declaration of Independence and Bill of Rights." That meant the liberal individualist variety. To achieve this, they counted on Eleanor Roosevelt to influence the work of the drafting committee as the planners from State wrote their own version.[116] It also meant that the U.S. government already had a concrete position insofar as the question of whether to have a nonbinding declaration or an enforceable covenant was concerned. Between these two poles, the U.S. government allowed the unpredictable forces of popular pressure, Cold War tensions, and the lobbying of other states to play themselves out. By 1946, it was far from evident that the framework of universal human rights would take the tripartite form of a single declaratory instrument and two enforceable covenants. Indeed, this proved to be one of the most contentious issues of discussion. The appointment of Eleanor Roosevelt as the U.S. representative was welcomed by many because of her background in the peace movement, and her world-class stature certainly lent much credibility to the commission, but by and large, she was there to follow the American position as laid out by the State Department.[117]

The commission started its work under the long shadow cast by the Cold War. Just a few months before, President Truman famously challenged the world to choose between two alternative ways of life: one characterized by the familiar individual guarantees of speech, religion, and freedom from political oppression, alongside free elections, or one featuring the suppression of these very personal freedoms.[118] The tension between the American and Soviet delegations was palpable throughout the work of the commission. It especially colored American insistence on the primacy of traditional political and civil liberties as opposed to social and economic rights, which, though part of the four freedoms had come to acquire an unpalatable communist flavor.[119]

Both of these positions influenced the resulting religious liberty guarantee. It was drafted by Frederick Nolde of the Joint Committee on Religious Liberty, a body set up by the Federal Council of Churches and the Foreign Missions Conference, who viewed religious freedom as primary among all other human rights.[120] Freedom of religion in the UDHR largely crystallized the two dominant currents of the time. The first was that freedom of religion coalesced solely around the individual compared to both the group and the individual protections present in the League Covenant. The UDHR starts from the premise that all human beings are endowed with dignity.[121] Reading the rest of the declaration in light of this premise, the intention to elevate the individual to primacy is evident. Despite the final wording of Article 18, in which the freedom to manifest such belief "alone or in community with others" was protected, the right itself regarded such collective protection as emanating from the primary desire to protect individual religious freedom.

Roosevelt herself believed in the original American position on minority rights protection, which is to say that she also deemed it dangerous and unnecessary. As originally formulated, the provision was as follows: "In States inhabited by a substantial number of persons of a race, language or religion, other than that of the majority of the population, persons belonging to such ethnic, linguistic or religious minorities shall have the right to establish and maintain their schools and cultural and religious institutions."[122] It morphed into a simpler but more vague version: "Minorities shall be entitled to preserve their culture, religion and language." But it was nonetheless voted down. Debating this draft minority protection provision introduced by the commission secretariat, Roosevelt, together with representatives from China, India, and the United Kingdom, dismissed concerns about a possible cultural genocide. The United Kingdom was particularly concerned that minority rights protection might be used to fuel anticolonial movements. Roosevelt, for her part, asserted that the "provision relating to minorities had no place in a declaration of human rights . . . minority questions did not exist in the American continent. United States experience with foreign groups residing within its borders had been happy; assimilation having been emphasized throughout."[123] This also stemmed from a belief that the existence of groups organized around racial, national, or religious categories impeded the consolidation of the nation-state. In a telling 1945 speech, she argued that the promise of the United States as the great melting pot of the world was being undermined by this very phenomenon.[124] Though she valued religious freedom, she upheld the American commitment to the principle of disestablishment, stating that government should be immune from any kind of church influence.[125]

None of this was surprising as American official thinking on this issue was clear as early as 1942. In view of the general rule of nondiscrimination, it also meant that there was to be no separate legal recognition of any form of communal diversity, whether by religion, language, or culture. The addition of the language of "in community with others" in Article 18 satisfied those, including Nolde, who were concerned about the corporate aspects of religious exercise, such as that of worship and teaching, without having to revive the minority protection regime.

A corollary to this individualist conception is the well-known discussion of whether such freedom included the right to change one's religion, a provision introduced by Charles Malik, the Christian Lebanese member of the UDHR drafting committee.[126] The right to change beliefs was a novel legal development.[127] Along with Nolde, Malik supported this provision with the plight of the missionaries in the Middle East in mind. It was the same concern that Jamil Baroody, the delegate from Saudi Arabia, stressed in his debate, oddly enough, with fellow Muslim representatives from India and Pakistan.[128] Baroody did not overtly base his objections on Islamic reasons but on the UDHR's general Western bias and characterized missionaries as forerunners of Western political intervention. Pakistani Zafrullah Khan, a Muslim from the marginalized Ahmadiyya sect, argued the concept of the missionary as intrinsic to Islamic teachings.[129] When the UDHR was put to a plenary vote in the General Assembly, Egypt and Syria set aside their earlier reservations and voted with the other Muslim states in its favor. The eight abstentions included the Soviet Union and Saudi Arabia, both of which viewed the UDHR as a Western imposition.

The other current was the international codification of rights. A mere twenty years earlier, Woodrow Wilson encountered extraordinary opposition to his proposal to include a universal guarantee of religious freedom in the League Covenant. In the years leading up to the war, even as sectarian tensions pervaded American society, Franklin Roosevelt turned it into a rallying cry for his countrymen and for the world, without opposition from others, save for the Russians who were already anti-religious on ideological grounds. As part of the original four freedoms, it was taken for granted and included without debate in the deluge of proposed bills of rights produced during the period, even occupying a privileged position in some of them. That it would be included in the UDHR as part of its itemization of the "human rights and fundamental freedoms" referred to in the UN Charter seemed a foregone conclusion. Mary Ann Glendon described the UDHR as the epitome of the "spirit of prolific constitution and treaty-making activity that followed WWII."[130]

Of course, one obvious explanation for the difference could be that the UDHR as a whole was merely declaratory and of no legal effect, while the

League Covenant was intended to bind the conduct of all its members. U.S. officials and Eleanor Roosevelt herself nonetheless took pains to emphasize its nonbinding character. Roosevelt clarified that the declaration was neither a treaty nor an international agreement—not law at all—but simply a statement of basic principles of human rights and freedoms.[131] It nonetheless had a ubiquitous presence in the international legal instruments that were concluded during the interim period between 1945 and 1948, such as the largely U.S.-drafted Paris Peace Treaties of 1947 and the UN-drafted General Assembly Resolution 181, which called for the partition of the British mandate of Palestine.[132]

While there were different schools of thought at that time regarding the precise juridical character of the UDHR—whether it was a purely moral instrument, whether it embodied some kind of legal character pursuant to its nature as a General Assembly issuance, or whether it was an annex to the UN Charter and thus possessed the same value as the charter—it was never simply the "paper declaration," as the Soviet delegate criticized it. Unlike the selective applications of religious freedom protection in the League Covenant, in principle, the same protection was now universal in scope and carried the moral authority of an international consensus behind it. Thus, despite its lack of legal enforcement, it was a monumental advance in international law. Universal freedom of religion was now an idea and ideal beyond dispute. Even with the sui generis character of the UDHR as a whole, the very codification of this litany of rights contained therein testified more to the slow acceptance of the erosion of the walls of state sovereignty on the part of the Great Powers, especially the United States, than a question on the intrinsic validity of these rights. Not unlike Woodrow Wilson's aspirations for the League Covenant, the UDHR, in the words of its initial drafter John Humphrey, would find ways to develop its own implementation.

Like the broader, if more ambiguous, category of human rights,[133] religious liberty protection eventually entered the American postwar anticommunist arsenal against the Soviet Union as Truman drew a Manichean line between the two competing ideologies with his eponymous doctrine. But steps toward that direction were hardly inevitable, as U.S. official reluctance toward the controversial case of Cardinal Aloysius Stepinac of Yugoslavia showed, happening as it were as the UDHR was being debated and discussed.[134] American Catholic groups and interested members of the House of Representatives sought the assistance of the State Department to intercede on behalf of Stepinac, who was arrested and convicted by the Tito communist government on charges of treason and war crimes. But it was only nine days after the trial ended that Acting Secretary of State Dean Acheson replied with a condemnation of the lack of due process surrounding the cardinal's trial and the violation of his religious freedom. In addition, the U.S. delegation refused domestic pleas to bring the matter to the attention of the General Assembly because delegation members were concerned that the same might be done to them on account of the racial problem in the United States.[135]

As the chilly winds of the Cold War began to blow over international relations and shape American foreign affairs, religious liberty protection, with an emphasis on *religious*, would occupy center stage for several years. The God-fearing democracy of FDR, bent on upholding international good faith against Nazi Germany, slowly turned into the Christian nation of Harry Truman, ready to export its ideals in the battle against Communism, with far-ranging consequences for the rest of the world.[136] In the meantime, the promises and aspirations of the UN Charter and the UDHR lay suspended, until such time that history would see fit to retrieve them.

* * *

Freedom of religion as a binding transnational legal norm would not be realized until 1950 and 1966 with its enactment, respectively, in the European Convention of Human Rights (Article 9) and the International Covenant on Civil and Political Rights (Article 18). Both instruments trace their genesis, however, to the authoritative moral foundations laid down by the UDHR and the human rights imperatives of the UN Charter. Few documents today could claim the same moral cachet as the UDHR. Nevertheless, the conventional narrative surrounding these instruments still considers U.S. foreign relations history and the history of international organizations such as the UN as separate histories. How the two are more interconnected than is commonly known is shown through the lens of the shaping of the international law on religious liberty. Though there was nothing particularly American about the idea of religious freedom, its privileged position in American society and history allowed Franklin Roosevelt to highlight it in the wartime effort to fight Hitler and Nazi Germany. It formed part and parcel of his stirring speeches and declarations, such as the Four Freedoms Speech and the Declaration by the United Nations, which many consider to be the precursor and catalyst for the explosion of human rights thinking in the immediate postwar period. That

FDR seemed to make sheer instrumental use of it at times, which became exceptionally clear in its role with regard to his fragile wartime alliance with Stalin, did not detract from its effectiveness or nobility, for that matter, as a war aim.

While it does not completely discount the possibility that Roosevelt, the pragmatic idealist, genuinely believed in its protection, religious freedom in his wartime pronouncements was also anything but a response to the perceived atrocities of the Axis forces. He was concerned about the security of states rather than individuals. This concern for security, in the form of a democratic type of government, has been accurately reflected in the historical circumstances surrounding the creation of the charter and the UDHR. Although the exact degree of hegemony of the United States by the end of the war could be debated, it exercised an overwhelming influence in the drafting processes of these foundational documents. Consequently, it was able to champion the codification of these freedoms, including religious liberty, without the corresponding legal obligation to protect them. From then on, religious liberty in these documents would be a key freedom for export from the world's arsenal of democracy.

Regardless of the intentions of its framers, however, the ideals and vision of a new world order in the charter and the UDHR have since been claimed by many from all over the world and adapted to their own circumstances. The very freedoms that FDR enumerated for the political and economic security of states would pave the way for the individual citizen to transcend them.

4

Spiritual Disarmament

> So we come to the second phase of our war against Japan—what might be called the spiritual disarmament of the people of that nation—to make them want peace instead of wanting war. This is in some respects a more difficult task than that of effecting physical disarmament. . . . To bring about the spiritual disarmament of the Japanese we intend to have removed all obstacles such as oppressive laws and practices which in the past have closed the door to truth and have stifled the free development of democracy in Japan.
>
> —*Press Statement of Secretary of State James F. Byrnes, September 1, 1945*

Harold Gould Henderson, a Columbia University professor and then a lieutenant colonel in the U.S. army, was lying down on the bed in his small Tokyo hotel room, while imagining himself to be Hirohito, the 124th Emperor of Japan.[1] Pen and paper in hand, he wondered what would be the most appropriate words to use in an imperial rescript if he were to strip himself of any semblance of divinity. The key sentence, he decided, would be as follows: "The ties that bind us with our people do not depend on outworn superstitions."[2] The resulting human emperor would remain a symbol of Japanese unity but devoid of any mystical properties. A few weeks later, Henderson's draft would be incorporated in the real Hirohito's Humanity Declaration. Centuries after the founding of Japan, the emperor-deity was now suddenly all too human.

It was November 1945, and the American military occupation of Japan was well underway. As an officer tasked with the elimination of Japanese ultranationalism and militarism, what Henderson himself termed as the reeducation of Japan, he was initially concerned with the effects of an existing Imperial Rescript on Education, first promulgated under Meiji rule in 1890. The Rescript on Education inculcated filial piety and loyalty to the emperor.[3] This emperor-centered philosophy served as the primary tool of national unification in the face of rapid societal changes brought about by the Westernization efforts of the Meiji government and facilitated the militarism that involved Japan in various aggressive wars of expansion in the early twentieth century. Considered one of the most significant and influential documents ever issued in Japan, it was worshipped along with the imperial portrait, and schoolchildren were required to know it by heart. As Henderson thought, the text of the Rescript itself contained nothing objectionable per se, but its place and function in daily school ceremonies prior to and up to the Second World War were such that it served to perpetuate the myth of imperial divinity, something that clearly ran against the principles and goals of the U.S. occupation.

What was to become of the emperor? When U.S. military forces landed in Tokyo in late August 1945, no other question vexed the Allied powers more than the status and future of the Japanese imperial throne. In fact, no transformation of such magnitude that Henderson was contemplating had been envisioned by the relevant departments focused on postwar planning. Planning for Japan began after Pearl Harbor. While the diplomatic and military branches of the U.S. government debated the question, for years even,[4] they did not reach a definitive answer until General Douglas MacArthur, then Supreme Commander of the Allied Powers (SCAP), categorically decided that, as a practical matter, the emperor was indispensable in governing Japan and conveyed such message clearly to Washington.[5] The emperor question implicated more than just the determination of Hirohito's war responsibility. It pointed to the very raison d'être of the U.S. occupation, that is, the establishment of a peacefully inclined and democratically responsible Japan. Whether changing Hirohito could indeed change an entire people remained foremost in American minds.

Throughout the wartime years, American war propagandists were careful to cultivate and project an image of the Japanese people as an innocent herd led astray by its sinister militarist leaders.[6] Under this view, the Japanese military leadership alone was responsible for the nation's disastrous plunge into war. Depending on whose views one considered, the emperor was either a part of this innocent herd or not, a question that engulfed the State Department for several years, nearly putting Hirohito on trial as a war criminal. Because of pragmatic concerns, the policy that eventually prevailed involved retaining the imperial throne and Hirohito himself in order to achieve the purposes of the U.S. occupation. Although the success of this approach could not have been foreseen at the outset, the gamble was nonetheless made largely because of the perception that the Japanese people revered the emperor as a matter of religious patriotism—a practice without any comparison in the Western tradition—and thus using the emperor as a conduit for Allied reforms would make for a less costly occupation.

The irony of this situation could not be any clearer. The same emperor that Japan's military caste utilized to accomplish their goal of putting the "eight corners of the world under one roof"[7] would be the same one that the Allied forces, particularly the U.S. government, would use to fulfill the objectives of the Potsdam Declaration in creating a peaceful and democratic Japan. The key to this revolutionary transformation was the introduction of religious freedom in the broad and narrow senses of the term. American officials labored very early to restore the people's civil liberties that were denied them under the previous regime, including the freedom to worship as they pleased, through the issuance of various SCAP directives.[8] The Civil Liberties Directive of October 1945 and the Shinto Directive of December 1945 were the most relevant. The Shinto Directive, in particular, dramatically altered the shape and landscape of Japan's indigenous religion and forever changed the interaction of religion and state in Japan.

If the problem was largely spiritual in substance—indeed, the problem was officially phrased as one of reeducation and reorientation—the solution must also be of like character.[9] Hence, it would not have been sufficient to give the Japanese people these civil liberties alone. The spiritual font of the previous regime must be destroyed. Whereas previously the emperor stood as a deity in whose name military leaders engaged in acts of aggression, he now stood as the unflinching secular symbol of Japanese national unity in the country's march toward democratization and fellowship in the community of nations. The initial plan bandied about among U.S. officials involved transforming the imperial arrangement into a British-style constitutional monarchy with which the Western world was more familiar. The specifics on how to effect such changes were still in murky waters when an even better moment of happenstance ended with Hirohito issuing an Imperial Rescript denying his divinity, mollifying his Western critics, and satisfying his supporters alike.

The terms of the Potsdam Declaration, under which Japan offered unconditional surrender, did not mention anything about constitutional change.[10] But U.S. officials in either Tokyo or Washington would not accept only superficial or no revisions at all to the existing Meiji constitution. In addition, if the United States wanted to preserve the changes it had made through SCAP directives, which would expire on the formal termination of the occupation, writing them into a fundamental law would be the surest guarantee of entrenching them for the future, long after American military boots would have left Japanese soil. The new constitution, in addition to shifting the source of authority from the emperor to the Japanese people, guaranteed religious freedom and various other rights and freedoms without the old qualification of "as may be limited by requirements of public necessity or order."[11] In doing so, it crystallized and institutionalized all the revolutionary gains and changes it made during the first few months of the occupation. That these changes would endure for the next half century despite its largely imposed origins remains one of the remarkable successes of U.S. foreign policy.[12]

While a prodigious amount of literature exists on the U.S. occupation of Japan, very few have considered the role of religious freedom in facilitating the goals of the U.S. government. Unlike race, education, and economics,[13] for example, interpretive accounts of the relationship between religion and the U.S. occupation of Japan have been narrowly focused on the efforts of MacArthur to propagate Christianity in Japan[14] or discussed simply as part of a more comprehensive account of the occupation, especially its role in the constitutional drafting process.[15] But religious freedom, through the legal instruments available to the United States in remaking Japan, also had a distinct place in the creation of a postwar Japanese democracy. This could be fully appreciated in the context of the motivations of its principal architects and against the background of what came before it.

Similar to the underpinnings of the largely American-sponsored, new international order inaugurated by the UN Charter, the United States promoted religious freedom not out of concern for any human right or flourishing of Japanese individuals but precisely, in the words of the Potsdam Declaration, to "strengthen the democratic tendencies among the Japanese people,"[16] one that is more closely aligned with American international security goals. The story that follows shows the transformative power of one ideal and how it created the necessary space during the early years of military occupation for occupier and occupied to negotiate and achieve their separate and, in the end, not necessarily conflicting goals.

The Emperor's New Clothes

The photograph, the "most famous visual image" of the American occupation of Japan, conveyed everything about the character and intent of the occupation.[17] It depicted MacArthur and Emperor Hirohito, standing side by side: the taller and older general in a casual, relaxed pose towering over the younger emperor who stood stiffly in a full morning dress. Prior to the Japanese surrender, such a photograph, much less its publication, would have been unthinkable. But aside from establishing the reality of occupation to the Japanese, it also sent a message of what the American government hoped to achieve. Hirohito was still emperor, at least for the time being, but he was human, not a living god.

As the singular symbol of Japan's national moral and spiritual edifice, the future of Hirohito and the imperial institution was foremost among the minds of U.S. officials as they debated his place in an occupied Japan:[18] Abolish the throne, keep it, or change it. The choices underwent as many permutations as there were interested bureaucrats within the U.S. foreign policy establishment. The inclination to view almost everything in Japan through the emperor, however narrow and bizarre, nonetheless made the situation more intelligible for American policymakers. To discuss the emperor meant discussing different aspects of Japanese culture and society that would be affected, and indeed targeted, by the impending occupation. Hirohito was ruler, military leader, and a god. His fate would significantly change Japan's politics and culture, its army, and its religion. Japan's road toward democracy would start with the emperor's new clothes.

American conceptions of religion and general misunderstanding of the Orient produced starkly negative views about the nature of the Japanese imperial throne and of Hirohito himself.[19] The idea of emperor worship—his English language titles included Son of Heaven—bordered on the blasphemous for many Westerners, especially Christians. Indeed, the origins myth of the emperor as a direct descendant of the sun goddess Amaterasu was already an object of ridicule in the American press even before the attack at Pearl Harbor and unsurprisingly intensified after it.[20] On May 21, 1945, with Japan in the throes of defeat, *Time* magazine featured Hirohito on its cover, with the title "The God-Emperor."[21] Written in a half-serious, rather mocking tone, the lead article characterized the emperor as the total embodiment of the Japanese enemy, and it described Shinto as "a spiritual totalitarianism more primeval and more potent than anything Nazism ever dreamed of."[22]

The Potsdam Declaration was silent on the issue of the imperial institution, a product of open-ended confusion rather than deliberate policy. In fact, Secretary of State James F. Byrnes erased the statement that the monarchy would be preserved—if Japan made peace—from the original draft of the document just before he left for the Potsdam conference upon the last-minute advice of his predecessor Cordell Hull.[23] Up to that point, despite the negative American public views of the emperor, official U.S. war policy avoided "military strikes against imperial sites or even the verbal denigration of Emperor Hirohito."[24] This sensitivity was shown out of pragmatic considerations. The Japanese were thought to hold a religious devotion to the emperor; thus, any such attacks might encourage more intense, even suicidal, retaliation. As Japan scholar John Dower argued, there was an increasing awareness that the emperor might prove useful in the consequent occupation.[25]

That usefulness clearly lay in the emperor's claim to spiritual authority. As the high priest of Shinto and crux of the national *kokutai* ideology, which propelled the militarist machine, American officials saw in him possibilities of order as well as chaos. Before the occupation formally began, there was no indication which way it was most likely to go. The uncertainty fueled the oft-cited rift between what came to be known as the Japan and China crowds within the State Department during presurrender planning.[26] The Japan crowd, so-called because most of its members spent some time in Japan (such as Joseph Grew, who served as a former U.S. ambassador to Japan during the prewar years), maintained that the imperial institution should be retained to advance the goals of the occupation. Grew described the Japanese people in a widely covered speech in 1943 "as a whole somewhat like sheep," and therefore Shintoism, insofar as it involved paying homage to the emperor, "could be an asset in reconstructing Japan as a peaceful nation."[27] Testifying before the Senate in 1944, Grew also likened the Japanese emperor to a queen bee in a hive and thus the figure who held the key to Japanese surrender,[28] a metaphor he later reiterated as an argument for retention.[29] As a practical matter, retaining the institution of the emperor meant fewer occupation personnel and the establishment of peace and order in Japan with the least possible delay. It was also pointed out that the laws of war prohibited a military occupant from making any decisive or substantial change to the political structure of an occupied country.[30]

The China crowd, on the other hand, counted among its members George Atcheson, later appointed political adviser to MacArthur in Tokyo; Dean Acheson; Stanley Hornbeck; and James Byrnes. War, their collective argument went, was the natural consequence of Japan's false ideology. Breaking the power of the emperor as an incarnate deity in the minds of the Japanese people was crucial in order to free them from subordination to authority. To achieve this, the emperor must be removed before democracy could take root in Japan;[31] otherwise, it would defeat American efforts to destroy the very system that made Japan an aggressor state in the first place. Echoing a question that would be repeated in a slightly different form within U.S. government circles more than half a century later, Hornbeck asked how Japan could possibly have a government that was based simultaneously on democratic principles as well as on the concept of a god-emperor and a God-given national destiny.[32]

Before the victor could use the emperor, however, the emperor had to be saved from the taint of war responsibility. Uncertain about the prospects of democratization, the United States nevertheless adopted the wedge policy toward Japan, separating the people from the military leadership first in order to obtain Japanese surrender, but later, subsequent to the bombing of Hiroshima and Nagasaki, to prepare for an efficient occupation. As Washington was debating which side the emperor was on,[33] Japanese court officials were busy driving their own wedge between the emperor and the military in order to save Hirohito and the institution.[34] In the meantime, other Allied countries such as China, the Soviet Union, the Philippines, and New Zealand were clamoring for the emperor's head. U.S. lawmakers criticized the Truman administration for what was turning out to be a velvet glove policy toward the emperor. Senator Richard Russell, a Democrat from Georgia, referred to the emperor as the "head and heart of Japanese imperialism" and called for his arrest as a war criminal.[35] Russell's focus was also on the spiritual effects of Hirohito's authority. Such a trial, the senator thundered, would show him to be an ordinary human being and strip him of the false divinity with which he had been cloaked.[36] Shortly after Russell's speech, the Senate issued a unanimous resolution calling for President Truman to have the emperor arrested.[37]

The ambiguity of the Potsdam Declaration offered no relief to those in favor of keeping the emperor as a tool of democratization because it referred only to the establishment of a peacefully inclined and responsible government "in accordance with the freely expressed will of the Japanese people."[38] Not even the formal surrender document signed by MacArthur and Japanese foreign minister Mamoru Shigemitsu, which explicitly mentioned the emperor but only to state that he was subject to the authority of SCAP,[39] helped. As late as mid-October 1945, when preparations for the establishment of the Tokyo war crimes tribunal were starting, the security of his person, never mind the throne and the national ideology that came with it, remained up in the air.[40]

Fortunately for Hirohito, SCAP was going to stand by him. In his *Reminiscences,* MacArthur stated that he already knew how he was going to implement occupation policies through the emperor and the existing machinery of the Japanese government on his appointment as SCAP.[41] His apparent overconfidence was no accident. Claiming to possess a unique insight into the Oriental mind, MacArthur felt and acted as if, in John Dower's words, there was only a fine line between supreme commander and supreme being.[42] Many factors contributed to the general becoming the very embodiment of the U.S. military occupation in Japan, among them, the distance from Washington and the larger-than-life personality of MacArthur himself.

Far removed from the bureaucratic tussles of Washington, MacArthur was acutely aware of the historical and spiritual dimensions of the ensuing occupation and reconstruction. Indeed, he saw Japan as a great experiment in the liberation of a people from totalitarianism. And he was not alone in this sentiment. When American Protestant church leaders sought permission from Washington to travel to postsurrender Japan, they obtained a letter of endorsement from President Truman, who not only endorsed their aim but also quoted MacArthur's statement that "the problem in [Japan] is theological and involves a spiritual recrudescence and improvement of human character." The president concluded that "your [the church leaders'] deputation should in large measure aid in solving this fundamental problem facing Japan."[43] For MacArthur, to save Hirohito and the throne was not a mere matter of expediency but an opportunity to undertake the spiritual regeneration of Japan. His famous cable, replete with apocalyptic rhetoric, to army chief of staff Dwight Eisenhower in January 1946, put the issue of trying the emperor for war crimes to rest once and for all.[44]

In MacArthur's mind, spiritual regeneration had two inseparable components: democracy, specifically the American model, and Christianity.[45] Reminiscent of William McKinley and the Philippines, he also styled himself as an emancipator of a people "stunted by ancient concepts of mythological teachings"[46] but who can nonetheless be uplifted by a demonstration of these twin ideals. For him, there was no contradiction between propagating Christianity in Japan and upholding the principle of freedom of religion.[47] Indeed, the latter could not be possible without the existence of Christian ideals. General anxiety toward the creeping onset of communism was probably as plausible an explanation as MacArthur's sincere belief in the democratizing power of Christianity.

Much to the chagrin of the rest of SCAP bureaucracy, the supreme commander lent his official support and sponsorship for American Christian missionary groups seeking to enter the country—the first nonmilitary group to do so—even though this clearly went against the freedom of religion guarantee found in many policy documents concerning surrender, such as the Potsdam Declaration and the Basic Initial Post-Surrender Directive. He even exhorted them to "fill the spiritual vacuum"[48] and send missionaries and a million Bibles to Japan.[49] SCAP staff members, particularly those in the Religions Division, often faced complaints from domestic Shinto and Buddhist groups regarding the occupation's aggressive support of the Christian cause. At one point, MacArthur even considered the emperor as a potential Christian convert.[50]

His peculiar personal goal of Christianizing Japan certainly influenced MacArthur's determination to keep Hirohito on the throne. But Hirohito himself also proved to be a cooperative partner in many respects. Because of the uncertainty hanging over his head, the emperor already entertained the idea of addressing the issue of imperial divinity in a rescript even before Henderson innocently suggested the matter to his court liaison, a British citizen named Reginald Blyth who was then teaching at the Peers' school. Thus, the suggestion was eagerly welcomed in the imperial household as soon as it was received. Prodded by Blyth to come up with a draft quickly (the head of Civil Information and Education [CIE], General Ken Dyke, was absent at that time), Henderson hurriedly drafted his own version of the rescript over lunch break. The draft rescript was floated to both MacArthur and the imperial court circle and underwent several translations under the shroud of complete secrecy before its approval by the Cabinet. The resulting imperial rescript, issued on New Year's Day 1946, retained the essence of Henderson's lunch break draft.[51] But perhaps as a faltering act of defiance, it also downplayed the humanity declaration, which was buried toward the end of the document. What the rescript highlighted instead was an affirmation of the Meiji Charter Oath in full, reportedly with MacArthur's wholehearted endorsement, in which it showed the unmistakable continuing fusion of monarchy and democracy.[52]

All those who read the Japanese language document in its entirety saw that there was no attempt on the part of the emperor to repudiate completely his Shinto-based origins myth. And yet the Western press nonetheless chose to focus on the Humanity Declaration. The *New York Times* hailed the rescript as a blow from which "the jungle religion Shinto" could scarcely recover.[53] *Time* magazine called it an "ideological *hara-kiri* for the anachronistic body of Shinto."[54] MacArthur likewise responded that "the Emperor's New Year's statement pleases me very much. By it he undertakes a leading part in the democratization of his people. He squarely takes his stand for the future along liberal lines. His action reflects the irresistible influence of a sound idea. A sound idea cannot be stopped."[55]

The rescript undoubtedly achieved its purpose. In this way, that sound idea, presumably democratization and the concomitant separation of religion and state, moved both Japan and the United States one step closer toward their respective goals: liberation for the occupied, and the accomplishment of the objectives of Potsdam for the occupier.

Separating Shinto and State

The importance of religious freedom as a means to achieve occupation goals was clear from its existence in all the major documents guiding SCAP.[56] Shinto was both a religious and political ideology, and it had to be dealt with accordingly. But because Shinto was also a religion, U.S. officials had earlier wondered how they could distinguish genuine religions from the nationalistic Shinto used by the previous regime.[57] An interdepartmental memo, prepared by two State Department officials in 1944, sought to differentiate sectarian Shinto from the state Shinto as practiced in nationalist shrines, and further recommended that these ancient temples be kept open and that Christian churches should be liberated by restoration of freedoms to organize and to worship.[58] Roman Catholic and Protestant missionaries in the country, they advised, could help determine the identity of these nationalist shrines. Both the Potsdam Declaration and the Basic Initial Post-Surrender Directive to SCAP, as far as religious freedom was concerned, drew from this document.

In Tokyo, connected with the transformation of the emperor was the consequent liberation of the Japanese people from subordination to the iron grip of what was perceived to be a corrupted version of Shinto. The SCAP cleaning of the so-called Japanese house to prepare it for democratization began with the removal of all previous restrictions through the Civil Liberties Directive of October 4, 1945, dubbed the Magna Carta of Japan. It ordered the government to remove all restrictions on political, civil, and religious liberties in furtherance of the Potsdam objective to "encourage the revival and strengthening of democratic tendencies" among the Japanese.[59]

On the religious liberty front, the directive abrogated and suspended the existing Religious Organizations Law and the notorious Peace Preservation Law, which was used to stifle dissent during the prewar years.[60] Those imprisoned for their religious beliefs or for denigrating state Shinto were likewise released. The directive immediately caused the existing Japanese government to resign en masse the following day. It was replaced with a more moderate group, led by Baron Kijuro Shidehara, who would be instrumental during the subsequent constitutional revision process.

Given the extant Japanese official position that Shinto shrines were not religious institutions and therefore worship in these shrines was not considered religious,[61] the directive did not immediately affect Shinto. This strange shape of things was not a recent creation of the militarist clique of the 1930s but ironically traces its origins to the heyday of the imperialist age of the nineteenth century. Under considerable Western pressure, the Meiji rulers introduced religious freedom, however qualified, in the 1889 constitution in order to win equal recognition from the Western powers and thus remove Japan from the ambit of its unequal treaties with "lesser nations." Mindful of the possible negative effects of the Meiji restoration (a period of great national transformation and modernization through adoption of Western technology and practices) on Japanese culture and society,[62] the ruling elite fashioned a national Shinto-based ideology centered on the emperor to minimize internal conflicts, increase social cohesion, and prevent a thorough Westernization of Japan.[63] The Imperial Rescript on Education, the effects of which Henderson was interested in curbing, was crucial in spreading this ideology. Shinto rituals were deliberately fused with imperial rites until eventually they became one and the same.

The resulting *kokutai* ideology, the closest English translation of which would be something akin to a family-state, regarded the emperor as an incarnate deity and drew from Shinto myths to portray him as one and indivisible with the land and the people. By separating state Shinto from church or sectarian Shinto and casting it as a civic and patriotic, rather than a religious, duty,[64] the Meiji government was able to oblige all Japanese, regardless of their religious beliefs, to participate in these national rituals. Starting from the Russo-Japanese War of 1905, the ruling elite would conscript these national rituals in the service of an expansionist ideology, indoctrinating schoolchildren, and glorifying the war dead. In the 1930s, babies were dedicated to the emperor, and houses were required to have an additional *kami*-shelf, a miniature altar ubiquitous in Japanese homes, for offerings to the nation's imperial and divine ancestors.[65] State Shinto also justified and undergirded the belief in Japanese ethnic and racial superiority. Daniel Holtom, an American Shinto scholar who wrote on the ideology of Shinto as early as 1922, argued that Shinto myths have been utilized and carefully manipulated to "surround a doctrine of political absolutism with the final sanctions of religious belief."[66]

Because the Civil Liberties Directive did not affect state Shinto, it was necessary to have another directive address the issue. Aside from MacArthur's personal interest in the religious aspects of the occupation, SCAP dealt with religions in Japan institutionally through the Religions Division of its CIE section. Its head, Lieutenant Commander William Bunce, was tasked to draft what would become known as the Shinto Directive, a task that took him seven weeks to finish and earned him the Legion of Merit as recognition. Bunce was guided by two main principles during the process. First, all references to state Shinto and to the divine origins of the emperor should be removed from the Meiji constitution and excised from all current and future legislation. Second, there should be no references in any official documents or pronouncements to the allegedly divine origins of the emperor, the Japanese people, and the nation as a source of inherent national superiority.[67]

The danger in the directive was that it walked a thin line between disestablishment and violation of the very principle of religious freedom that it purported to uphold. Even though shrine Shinto propagated ultranationalist and militarist ideology, it held itself out as a civil religion—a means to deepen national sentiment—and consequently used religious rites to achieve this, notwithstanding its official designation as a nonreligious cult.[68] The mix of the religious and the secular in what was in any case a complex ideology presented SCAP with a conundrum. Abolishing state Shinto was out of the question. Thus, the SCAP solution lay in the separation of Shinto from state, a two-pronged approach that required the withdrawal of state support and funding, on the one hand, and the transformation of the peculiar political system generated by the emperor-centered state Shinto ideology (which allowed the concentration of power with a few unaccountable individuals), on the other. The first could be addressed by directives mandating religious freedom; the second could be secured through a revision of the Japanese constitution.[69]

The separation of Shinto from state as embodied in the Shinto Directive involved a total severance of state support, endorsement, or participation in any Shinto ritual, reducing it to a voluntary religious organization.[70] It also eliminated the teaching of Shinto in schools.[71] Although it attempted to separate sectarian from state Shinto and sought only to circumscribe the effects of the latter, the directive and other related pronouncements nevertheless ended up removing Shinto in all its forms altogether from Japanese public life. It prohibited participation of public officials in state funerals and memorial services for the war dead.[72] It also removed any representations of Shinto in postage stamps,[73] currency,[74] and textbooks.[75] Visits to the shrines by any public educational institution or private schools receiving any amount of state funding were prohibited.[76] Confusion broke out especially with regard to the place of religion in schools. Several Japanese were of the view that it was impossible to teach ethics or any sort of morality without religion in schools, an erstwhile familiar episode during the nineteenth century in the United States. The Imperial Rescript on Education was withdrawn by the Ministry of Education, and the imperial portraits were removed from the schools. SCAP recognized the emotional value of the national shrines to the people, so one concession that SCAP did make was to allow the national shrines to continue, with the caveat that no public funds could support them.

Despite its name, the Shinto Directive did not cover Shinto only but all kinds of religion, including Christianity and Buddhism. It categorically stated that its purpose was "to separate religion from the state"; "to prevent misuse of religion for political ends"; and "to put all religions, faiths and creeds upon exactly the same basis, entitled to precisely the same opportunities and protection."[77] Bunce's acknowledgment that the U.S. Constitution was the primary inspiration for the directive was apparent in the use of the phrase "separation of church and state" in the first two drafts, notwithstanding the Christian connotations of the word *church*.[78] It was later changed to *religion* in the third draft. The extraordinary strictness with which the American drafters of the directive construed the degree of separation allowed in the Japanese context sharply contrasted with the fluid and contested nature of separation between religion and state on the American home front at that time.[79] This could be explained by the view that the introduction of separation, a natural corollary of religious freedom in the American mind, was a necessary means to facilitate the democratization of the country. Given Western beliefs, however mistaken, about Japanese society and culture, religion was deemed too dangerous to have any sort of role in the public sphere. The provisions of the directive were later enshrined in Articles 20 and 89 of the new Japanese constitution. More important, it would influence the judicial interpretation of these religion-related constitutional provisions long after the directive's binding force ceased on the signing of the San Francisco peace treaty in 1952.[80]

The Constitutional Moment

Notwithstanding a lack of clear directive from Washington, the matter of constitutional revision found support from the basic policy documents concerning the occupation. The confusion was nonetheless evident during a visit of the Far Eastern Advisory Commission, later renamed the Far Eastern Commission (FEC), to meet with SCAP officials in Tokyo in January 1946. The FEC was created by the Moscow Communique of December 1945 to enable joint Allied oversight and policymaking for the occupation of Japan, similar to the arrangement for postwar Germany.[81] During an oft-quoted exchange between Tomas Confesor, the Philippine representative to the FEC, and Charles Kades, a member of SCAP, Kades declared that constitutional amendments were "a long-range problem concerning fundamental changes in the Japanese constitutional structure which is within the province of your Commission."[82] A perplexed Confesor replied that he did not understand why constitutional revision was not part of the Government Section's (GS's) work.

The Potsdam Declaration had stated that its purposes, among others, were "to remove all obstacles to the revival and strengthening of democratic tendencies among the Japanese people" and to establish "freedom of speech, of religion and of thought, as well as respect for fundamental human rights."[83] And though it seemingly assigned these tasks to the Japanese government, it was well understood that SCAP could direct the Japanese government to effect such changes should they fail to accomplish them. Just how much direction SCAP could give, however, was unclear. MacArthur's overarching concern, rightfully so it seemed in retrospect, was that any resulting document should be considered by the Japanese as a Japanese product, or it would not last very long.[84] The moment American forces were withdrawn, he was certain the Japanese would get rid of such a constitution. But at the same time, only a revised constitution would ensure that the democratization goal of the occupation would be achieved. The dizzying tale of constitutional reform during the first year of the occupation followed this tension and confusion-filled script.

Shortly after the new Japanese prime minister Baron Kijuro Shidehara was appointed in October 1945, MacArthur conveyed to him the importance of constitutional revision and that the United States considered it a requirement for Japan's compliance with the Potsdam Declaration. In a separate conversation, he also suggested the same to Prince Fumimaro Konoe, a member of the previous cabinet who still maintained links with the Imperial House. This suggestion spurred a series of events that ended tragically with Konoe's suicide after he was included in the list of war criminals to be tried by the soon-to-be-established Tokyo war crimes tribunal.[85] As a consequence of its involvement in the Konoe affair, the State Department, in the person of George Atcheson, was completely cut off from discussions involving the Japanese constitution.[86] From then on, constitutional revision was contained in Tokyo and became a SCAP monopoly.

At that point, SCAP was content to let the Japanese government take the lead in effecting changes to the Meiji constitution. In his "Statement to the Japanese Government" dated October 11, MacArthur declared that "the traditional social order under which the Japanese people for centuries have been subjugated will be corrected. This will unquestionably involve a liberalization of the Constitution."[87] He had wanted the Japanese to initiate what could turn out to be a long drawn-out process of revision. The precise extent of liberalization would become the point of divergence, however, between American prodding and Japanese intent.

One of the means identified in MacArthur's statement to correct the previous order was the introduction of, among others, freedom of religion in order to free the people from all sorts of state intrusion, which had held them in virtual slavery. This prescription dovetailed with the earlier findings of Milo Rowell, the judicial affairs officer of Government Headquarters and a lawyer in civilian life, who was assigned to make a preliminary report on the text and operation of the Meiji constitution.[88] His findings highlighted its major defects, foremost among them the lack of effective rights of individual citizens and a government generally not responsible to the people at large.[89] His subsequent recommendations listed several individual rights that would appear familiar to anybody versed in U.S. constitutional law, including not only the right to freedom of religious worship but also rights against double taxation and ex post facto laws and the right to privacy.

Given these significant shortcomings of the Meiji constitution, it seemed inevitable that a thorough revision was needed. Unknown to SCAP, a debate on precisely this point was going on among the members of the Constitutional Problem Investigation Committee (known as the Matsumoto Committee), the body appointed by Prime Minister Shidehara to study the question of constitutional reform. The committee was headed by Joji Matsumoto, a Minister without Portfolio and a law professor at Tokyo Imperial University who was also a prominent commercial lawyer. Both Shidehara and Matsumoto were of the view that no revision at all was necessary and that the Meiji constitution was flexible enough to allow democratization through appropriate legislation.[90] The previous problems were not caused by the charter's inherent flaws but rather by the way it was applied. One committee member also considered it highly inappropriate to revise a constitution while under foreign occupation.[91] Matsumoto's own guiding principles for the duration of the committee's work were the exact opposite of Rowell's recommendations. For example, there was to be no change in the principle that the emperor shall exercise the rights of sovereignty, and the rights and freedom of the Japanese "subjects" would not be restricted except by laws enacted by the National Diet.[92] Despite the presence of liberal voices within the committee, Matsumoto's views ultimately prevailed.

Because there was no contact between SCAP and Matsumoto during the drafting process, the Americans were as surprised as everybody else when a Japanese newspaper scooped a draft of what the Matsumoto committee was working on and released it.[93] The press reaction to the Matsumoto draft was wholly negative because it was rather conservative and reactionary in character. For instance, the Matsumoto draft provides that the "Emperor is the monarch and exercises the rights of sovereignty according to provisions of the present constitution." For SCAP, it meant only one thing. The Japanese government was unwilling and incapable of making any proposals that would meet the requirements of the Potsdam Declaration. What made that particularly clear to Courtney Whitney, chief of the GHQ, and others was that dozens of liberal and progressive proposals had been submitted by various private organizations, such as the Japan Bar Association and the Constitutional Research Association.[94] Even Konoe's ill-fated draft contained progressive language.[95] Thus, it was not for lack of any liberal or democratic inclinations on the part of the Japanese but rather sheer stubbornness on the part of its government. SCAP felt it had no choice but to take the lead.

Coincidentally, Whitney had sent a memo to MacArthur, the same day the Matsumoto scoop was published, in which he assured that the supreme commander had unrestricted authority to effect constitutional change in Japan,[96] with two stipulations. The first was that any decision to remove the emperor should have the prior concurrence of the Joint Chiefs of Staff; the second indicated that this unrestricted authority persisted only for as long as the FEC had not yet commenced its policymaking duties,[97] a deadline that influenced the GS's handling of the matter. The memo did not trace its origins to Japanese actions but rather to the January visit of the FEC and Kades's exchange with Confesor. The following day, MacArthur directed Whitney and the Government Section to come up with a detailed outline of the required revisions subject only to three basic principles: the emperor shall be head of state and responsible to the Japanese people, war was to be forever renounced as an instrument of national policy, and the feudal system shall cease.[98] With those guidelines at hand, American lawyers and military personnel proceeded to work for eight historic days as a constitutional convention to draft a new Japanese constitution.[99]

Religious freedom was affected by three sections of the draft MacArthur constitution.[100] The first section was the role of the emperor,[101] the second was on the fundamental rights and liberties of all the inhabitants in Japan,[102] and the third dealt with withdrawal of public funding for any religious properties or from religious associations.[103] All three had been dealt with by the emperor's earlier Humanity Declaration as well as previous SCAP directives involving civil liberties and the separation of Shinto and state.

Under the Meiji constitution, the Japanese were guaranteed freedom of religion, not unlike their Western counterparts.[104] Because of this provision in the constitution, an essential component of what was considered to be a superior Christian civilization in the nineteenth century, the United States accepted Meiji Japan as an equal on the world stage. American officials and missionaries were able to find common ground with Japan, especially during its 1905 war against Russia. President Theodore Roosevelt in fact remarked that the Japanese at that time were a welcome addition to the community of nations "because they played the game of civilized mankind."[105] But this right was also highly qualified by the phrase "not prejudicial to peace and order and not antagonistic to their duties as subjects." In addition, Shinto shrines in reality were accorded privileged status, and public worship in them was enforced by state authorities. The shrines and their officials were organized and closely monitored by a government ministry. As previously noted, the explanation for this paradoxical situation was that Shinto shrines were not considered religious in the same way as Buddhist shrines or Christian churches. Hence, government support of them was not considered a violation of religious freedom.

That logic, however, had perpetrated the very abuses brought about by Japanese military aggression. Guiding the GS drafters was the intent to "purge Shinto from the state" and "to prevent Shinto from ever again becoming entrenched in the government and the educational system of the country."[106] According to one of the drafters, there was no conscious desire on the part of the GHQ drafters to secularize the state, nor was there any overarching theory regarding the separation of religion and state.[107] That statement was belied by the fact that, taken together, the religious freedom–related provisions of the MacArthur draft fully implemented the democratization goal of the occupation. Even the infamous renunciation of war clause, as provided in Article 9, could be considered related to the goal of separation of church and state because it removed an avenue for aggressive action that could be taken as a result of any nationalist or religious dogma. In a rather uncannily similar fashion to how the Meiji constitution functioned as the implementation of the Charter Oath of Emperor Meiji,[108] the draft constitution did the same in the pursuit of the objectives stated in the Potsdam Declaration.

But these goals did not always coincide with one another. Liberty did not always go hand in hand with democracy. Occupiers, however well intentioned, have had to engage in a balancing act between their own objectives and the interest of the people under their authority. In the realm of religious freedom, the U.S. occupation of Japan was no exception. To illustrate, the original formulation of Article 20 not only guaranteed freedom of religion but forbade all ecclesiastics from political activity of any kind. A debate ensued among the drafters regarding its wisdom and practicality.[109] On the one hand, the denial seemed to amount to violations of the freedoms of speech and of the press for such ecclesiastics, but on the other hand, given the recent history of Japan, the constitution should ensure that spiritual authority could no longer be abused for political ends. Colonel Pieter Roest, the proponent of this blanket prohibition, argued the need for such because Japan has been "a priest-ridden country for generations."[110]

The original article reflected the same anxiety when it not only forbade ecclesiastics from all sorts of political activity but also maintained that no religious body would be recognized if it should disrupt public order under the guise of religion. Alfred Hussey, another GS member, cautioned, however, that this could be used by the state to suppress new religious sects. If no religious figures could engage in political activity, the state should likewise not be given any opportunity to interfere with religion.[111]

In the Japanese government draft presented to the cabinet on March 4, 1946 (in reality, this was the SCAP draft preliminarily negotiated and translated with Shidehara and members of the Matsumoto Committee[112]), freedom of religion was guaranteed through a more succinct three-pronged approach: All people shall have freedom of religion and there was to be no compulsion in terms of worship; no religious entity shall take part in politics or receive privileges from the government, and the state was prohibited from any involvement in religious education or similar activities.[113] To drive home the importance of democratization and yet not limit the source of antidemocratic tendencies to religions, a separate article guaranteed freedom of thought and conscience for everybody.[114] Constitutionalizing the separationist thrust of the Shinto Directive, a prohibition was made on government grants and assistance to sectarian associations; the wording of the text was modeled after a similar provision in the 1935 Philippine Constitution, which held commonwealth status vis-à-vis the United States at the time.[115] This formulation was retained in the final version approved by both MacArthur and the emperor.

The constitution's article on the emperor was intended to be the linchpin of the new democratic order. This was evident from the original GS draft, which put the emperor and the people together in one heading,[116] which would have been unimaginable under the previous regime. Although the chapter concerned was later renamed, the strong emphasis on the symbolic authority of the emperor, now devoid of any mystical powers, and the transfer of sovereignty to the people at large was maintained and even amplified as changes were made throughout the drafts. Matsumoto later lamented this transformation as making the emperor nothing more than a glorified notary.[117]

All of MacArthur's points on the emperor were kept. Most important, the emperor was now part of the new Japanese constitutional order as a symbol of the state and the unity of the people. These points also closely tracked the requirements indicated in SWNCC (State-War-Navy Coordinating Committee) 228, entitled Reform of the Japanese Governmental System,[118] the major document expressing U.S. policy regarding the revision of the Meiji constitution. SWNCC 228 emphasized the creation of a government responsible to the people and the guarantee of fundamental individual liberties, and was in fact used as the control document during the SCAP drafting process. The inversion of the locus of sovereignty from the emperor to the Japanese people achieved several goals. Obliterating the myth that the emperor was "sacred and inviolable,"[119] the draft removed the possibility that leaders could use the imperial authority as a smokescreen for irresponsible acts.[120] More important, it made the people accountable for their government. The constitution was no longer a gift handed down from the emperor, as the previous one was,[121] but a transformative charter that the people could use to create their own future. In the view of the Americans, these were sufficient safeguards against a repeat of the militarism of the past.

By this time, the Matsumoto Committee was still in the dark that a parallel draft was in the works inside GHQ. The surprise, or rather, shock, on Matsumoto's face when he read the SCAP draft later handed unceremoniously to him by Whitney was described as similar to someone who had just swallowed boiling water.[122] It was a useful mirror with which to view the unstated but palpable asymmetry of power present in the room, a general state of affairs referred to subsequently in documents and conversations by Japanese officials as "the situation." Starting with the preamble, which began oddly with "We the Japanese people," nobody except Matsumoto, who had studied in the United Kingdom, could understand the SCAP draft. He was especially aghast at the idea of the emperor as a symbol, a term he thought more appropriate for literary criticism rather than a constitution.[123] A subsequent marathon session days later between the two sides in order to go over the Japanese translation of the SCAP draft involved a bitter confrontation between Charles Kades and Matsumoto, who was still adamant about preserving the core of the Meiji constitution, particularly the powers of the emperor, and ended with the latter leaving the building in a huff without returning.[124]

The new draft constitution that Emperor Hirohito approved for promulgation, in accordance with the revision procedure laid out in the Meiji constitution, did not veer far from the SCAP model draft of February 13, 1946, notwithstanding efforts to Japanize it.[125] Rightfully called the single most important accomplishment of the Occupation by MacArthur himself,[126] it revolutionized Japanese society. Contestation over its provisions, including those concerning religious freedom, continued long after the Occupation formally ended in 1952, but for the most part, these debates took place under the very democratic rubric inaugurated by the Constitution itself. The constitutional autocracy of the Meiji order had given way to a democratic constitutional monarchy. With that transformation, the American spiritual disarmament of Japan was complete.

***

The promotion of religious freedom in Japan by the U.S. military authorities did not end when the new postwar Japanese constitution came into effect on May 3, 1947. But the overarching American-style principles of religious freedom and separation of religion and state laid down throughout the occupation using various legal means established an entirely new framework for religion-state relations and profoundly shaped the role of religion in Japanese public life since. These principles, especially as they were entrenched in the new postwar constitution, were woven into the Religious Juridical Persons Law, School Education Law, Local Autonomy Law, and the Fundamental Law of Education, to name a few—laws that are still in force in Japan today.

Even before the occupation formally began, American policymakers already saw religious freedom as a crucial component for the democratization and demilitarization of Japan. This was evident from the ambiguity and indecision that pervaded the official discussions on the fate of the emperor. Americans' apprehension was influenced by what they saw as the dangerously pliable and ultimately destructive consequences of a state religion run amok. But they also saw in its malleability a powerful transformative idea for a wholesale societal change. An extraordinary confluence of events saw both occupier and occupied taking advantage of the fluid landscape of military occupation. Religious freedom was an important site of this confluence, even unintended cooperation, as the episode involving the emperor's Humanity Declaration showed.

The Americans were also determined not to have a repeat of Japan's militarist past; indeed, this was the ultimate goal of the U.S. occupation. Leaving it to chance was not an option. Democratization not only meant handing sovereignty back to the people but also freeing their minds from the stranglehold of what Americans deemed a misused religion in the first place. In the minds of many SCAP officials, the Japanese did not know what real freedom and democracy were like. Looking to the U.S. constitutional experience as a model, they proclaimed religious freedom for everyone and thoroughly separated religion from state through SCAP directives. More important, through the extraordinary constitutional moment in which American lawyers and military officers drafted a constitution for Japan, these were all enshrined as constitutional guarantees.

As constitutions go, these provisions are not self-interpreting. But they also function somewhat as baselines, providing Japanese people with essential trumps against government encroachments. That American conceptions of separation of church and state permeated its origins does not prevent its appropriate adaptation for Japanese life, as the Japanese in fact later did.[127] In 1977, the Japanese Supreme Court backtracked on the absolute separation envisioned by the SCAP drafters when it held that separation between church and state is not an absolute and that some involvement by the state in religion is virtually inevitable.

For its American drafters, it was enough that the constitution guaranteed these freedoms. What the Japanese people would do with it afterward was precisely the point of democratization.

5

Cold War, Hot Rights

> This ought to be the basis of our international relations. These ought to be the things of which we speak to the world; a concern for our fellow human beings, knowing that we are one family regardless of distance and descent or any other kind of barrier, concern for their right to freedom of religion, for their right to travel and be unified with their family.
>
> —*U.S. Representative Millicent Fenwick, May 4, 1976*

In the beautiful, granite Finlandia Hall located in the center of Helsinki, the capital of Finland, foreign ministers and heads of state from countries in Europe and North America gathered in resplendent fashion to witness the signing of the Helsinki Final Accords (HFA) on August 1, 1975.[1] A long bare wooden table lay before them with nothing but thirty-five pens, one for each leader to sign the historic document. The HFA, not unlike the Universal Declaration of Human Rights (UDHR), which was issued with similar fanfare almost three decades earlier, was not in any way legally binding. And yet it somehow possessed the same, if not greater, political and moral force carried by the UDHR. For the first time, the communist states, including the Soviet Union, that had abstained from the UDHR in 1948 now publicly accepted that respect for human rights was as important an international principle as respect for state sovereignty.

But in the first few months after its signing, many criticized the HFA. For those in the West, the main complaint was that the HFA legitimized the Soviet annexation of Eastern Europe, already a reality after World War II. Indeed, the Soviet government proudly reprinted the entire final text of the act in various newspapers, including the official state newspaper *Izvestia*. Understandably, the criticism was particularly vociferous inside the United States. Even before the signing, influential media outlets such as the *Wall Street Journal* and the *New York Times* had written editorials asking President Gerald Ford to forego the trip to Helsinki and not to sign the act.[2] Influential Democratic Party senator Henry "Scoop" Jackson charged that "there are times in international diplomacy when the president of the United States ought to stay home. By cooperating with Brezhnev at the Helsinki summit, and in fostering the illusion that substantive progress toward greater security in Europe has been made, President Ford is taking us backward, not forward, in the search for genuine peace."[3] Democratic presidential candidate Jimmy Carter likewise lamented the American ratification of a "Russian takeover of Eastern Europe."[4] To many observers at the time, the HFA represented the moral abyss to which the policy of détente, constructed painstakingly under the previous administration by President Richard Nixon and his enigmatic secretary of state Henry Kissinger, inevitably led.

Conventional accounts portray the accords as the height, if not the quintessential expression, of the much-maligned policy.[5] Seen in that light, it was indeed quite ironic to count Kissinger as one of the biggest skeptics of what the accords could accomplish. In his view, it was, at best, an exercise in satisfying public opinion,[6] and a necessary show of solidarity with Western European governments who were also members of NATO.[7] A devoted student of the realist tradition in international relations, Kissinger cared about geopolitical realities, not sentimentalities. "What is it that suddenly possesses the West to believe that it can affect the domestic structure of the Soviet Union through a treaty signed . . . of peripheral significance?" he characteristically mused.[8]

But it was also an extraordinary story of unintended consequences. Today, the HFA is better known as the accidental catalyst of a process ultimately ending with the dramatic collapse of the Soviet Union and the demise of communism as a viable political ideology.[9] Drawing on preexisting legal norms such as those contained in the Universal Declaration of Human Rights, the HFA provided an internationally agreed-upon framework around which different groups could mobilize and hold their various governments accountable. The accords were divided into three sections that were also known informally as baskets: the political and military aspects of security, including the ten guiding principles for the relations among the participating states; the economic and environmental aspects; and the human aspects of cooperation and security. Later, Principle VII of the Declaration on Principles Guiding Relations between Participating States in the first basket, which had taken longer than any other principle to negotiate, would stand out and become the rallying point for many human rights groups around the world. It stated: "The participating States will respect human rights and fundamental freedoms, including the freedom of thought, conscience, religion or belief, for all without distinction as to race, sex, language or religion."[10] Contrary to popular interpretations of the accords, there is no such thing as a "human rights" basket. What the third basket of the HFA contained were various matters involving human contacts covered by the broad umbrella phrase "Cooperation in Humanitarian and Other Fields," including family reunification,[11] marriage across states,[12] freedom of travel,[13] cultural and educational exchanges,[14] and freedom of information.[15] Given the emphasis on liberalization of contacts rather than the guarantee of particular political freedoms, it was, in one commentator's words, a Cold War approach to a Cold War problem.[16]

It was precisely this particular Cold War approach that had been denounced by many in the American domestic political scene. Long before the Helsinki effect was to dawn on everybody, including the Soviets themselves, U.S. lawmakers led by Scoop Jackson took charge of an anti-Soviet assault that reached its peak upon the signing of the Jackson-Vanik amendment (JVA) to the 1974 Trade Reform Act into law.[17] If the HFA was the height of détente, the JVA was its principal antithesis. It explicitly linked American cooperation with its communist superpower rival to ideological and moral axes. The JVA was intended to destroy détente, not prop it up. In the face of an escalating nuclear arms race between the two superpowers, critics of the JVA charged it as a reckless and irresponsible piece of legislation. But Jackson and his fellow congressional crusaders were unfazed. The pursuit of American ideals and national interest were not mutually exclusive, they claimed. By conditioning the grant of favorable trade status on the observance of human rights norms, particularly the freedom of emigration, the JVA crystallized the focus on human rights in the conduct of U.S. foreign relations and restored the place of ideals and morality swept aside by the erstwhile overall pragmatism of détente. Although the JVA did not feature religious language explicitly, its emphasis on increasing the emigration numbers of Soviet Jews had always involved a religious liberty component. In doing so, it opened the floodgates for the increased participation of religious actors in the foreign policy arena and reintroduced the protection of religious liberty garbed in the newfound language of human rights as a legitimate foreign policy goal.[18]

Despite their contradictory origins then, the JVA and the HFA complemented each other in their efforts to extend U.S. religious freedom protection for believers in the Soviet Union and Eastern Europe. More important, both resuscitated the rights and freedoms enshrined in the UDHR against the backdrop of the Cold War. This was completely new. While ideals and morality have long been part of the American foreign policy tradition, this marked the first time that appeals to international legal norms were made, long a bête noire of the conservative movement.

The JVA followed a long precedent of earnest congressional efforts to push for greater religious freedom in the Soviet Union, while the HFA and its mandated follow-up meetings were, in essence, forums within which the Soviet Union could be held to its treaty commitments, including the UDHR and the International Covenant on Civil and Political Rights (ICCPR), which it signed in 1966 and then ratified seven years later. The American genesis of these two seemingly disparate instruments bore witness to the deeper structural changes that occurred in and consequently transformed American domestic politics and society in the early 1970s.[19] Many became crucial antecedents to the explosion of human rights rhetoric under the administration of Jimmy Carter and the revival of 1950s godless Soviet Union rhetoric in the "evil empire" characterization of Ronald Reagan. The emergence of the silent majority, which would eventually become the religious right, and its active engagement in American politics, the institutionalization of human rights within the foreign policymaking apparatus of the U.S. government and the recovery of human rights language on the global stage were all legacies of these changes.

But above all else, at the turn of the new (if tumultuous in hindsight) decade, the resort to human rights law—religious freedom's new clothes—as a weapon against the communist enemy set the stage for the eventual piercing of the walls of state sovereignty, walls that would remain up but nonetheless permeable to this day.

From Godless to Oppressive

Whatever fragile connection there was between the United States and the Soviet Union that Franklin Roosevelt had shrewdly and carefully sustained before and during the war, it promptly broke down upon his untimely death.[20] Although his appeal to religious freedom protection as one of the war aims was meant to tap into the religious sensibilities of his domestic constituency, his emphasis on freedom sounded secular enough to encompass nonbelief and thus obtain Soviet acquiescence.[21] This delicate balancing act officially dissipated into thin air as soon as his successor, Harry Truman, in what amounted to a declaration of the Cold War, announced his eponymous containment doctrine in a March 1947 speech before a joint session of Congress.[22] As he announced U.S. military and economic support for Greece and Turkey, he also drew broad ideological battle lines between two "alternative ways of life." It was shortly followed by the reappointment of Myron Taylor as a personal envoy of the president to the Vatican, notwithstanding continuing controversy,[23] with an assertion to Pope Pius XII that the United States was "a Christian Nation."[24] Within the same context, he claimed that "freedom of conscience, ordained by the Fathers of our Constitution to all who live under the flag of the United States, has been a bulwark of national strength, a source of happiness, from the establishment of our Nation to this day."[25] From then on, religious freedom became *religious* freedom.

Far from being an entirely spontaneous and organic outgrowth, Truman and key members of his administration carefully orchestrated and nurtured a national moral and spiritual offensive against the Soviet Union using religion as their main weapon.[26] After all, religion was perhaps the primary anticommunist principle that could provide people with the necessary motivations and wherewithal to withstand its pressures. It also helped that, as the Cold War intensified, the Soviet Union fit squarely into American perceptions of the Manichean good versus evil, free versus enslaved narrative by its relentless public persecutions of religious believers and churches in its territories, including its Eastern European satellites. Consequently, Truman exhorted his fellow Americans to practice their religious faiths actively. Freedom of religion was not merely a negative right directed against the state but a positive duty on the part of every citizen in the form of active participation in religious life or community. Like Roosevelt before him, Truman sincerely believed that religion was an indispensable source of morality. Spiritual nourishment was therefore necessary to reinforce this unique American national strength. But he also knew that religion was the key in winning the ideological battle between the forces of freedom and democracy and that of tyranny and conformity.

The resulting domestic spiritual awakening led to an infusion of a religious "soul" in American foreign relations.[27] Tapping into the religious boom of the immediate postwar years,[28] President Dwight Eisenhower and his secretary of state John Foster Dulles consciously recast communism as a kind of faith—a dangerous religious creed—and thus set the stage for the framing of the Cold War as a modern-day holy war.[29] In the years following, anticommunism became a resolute bipartisan effort at the highest levels of government, especially in the official use of religion against the spiritual bankruptcy of communism. Though not particularly religious himself before becoming president, Eisenhower became a visible member of the National Presbyterian Church during his two terms in office. In addition, religiosity was equated with patriotism. In 1954, he signed into law Public Law 81, a bill passed without any floor debate, which adopted "In God We Trust" as the national motto,[30] the same year that the phrase "under God" was incorporated into the Pledge of Allegiance.[31] The Supreme Court appeared to join the effort when it upheld the constitutionality of a New York law that permitted students to leave school during school hours for purposes of religious instruction or practice.[32] In the most cited part of the decision, Justice William Douglas stated that "the Court's validation of the New York law rests in part on its statement that Americans are a religious people whose institutions presuppose a Supreme Being."[33] A congressional prayer room was also opened in 1955.

But American official perceptions of the Soviet Union did not always stay the same. By the time Richard Nixon took over the presidency in 1969, Washington no longer saw in the Soviet Union a godless tyranny headed by a malevolent dictator. Instead, it saw another superpower not unlike itself. While competition between the two persisted, both sides no longer employed apocalyptic or ideological rhetoric.[34] This chastened posture, at least from the American point of view, could be attributed to many factors, domestic and foreign alike. Foremost among them was that the disastrous nuclear brinkmanship that led to the Cuban missile crisis was no longer an available option. Another major factor for the eventual demise of the "spiritual-industrial complex" was the breakdown of consensus among American religious believers themselves. The more important question, however, is not why the shift occurred but what it produced: the rise of modern American conservatism.[35]

Nixon straddled both sides of the political fence during his administration. While he rode the conservative train on domestic issues, he implemented a new foreign policy, characterized by rapprochement, with regard to the Soviet Union.[36] *Détente,* a French term meaning "relaxation of tensions," referred to the normalization of relations between the United States and the Soviet Union during the middle period of the Cold War. It was a period marked by the signing of important bilateral treaties involving arms control and reduction and increased trade in the early 1970s as well as symbolic acts that included personal meetings between Nixon and his Soviet counterpart, Leonid Brezhnev.[37] Still reeling from the ferocious early Cold War battles against communism, conservatives, both religious and secular, criticized the new approach. Both were united in their anticommunism, but for different reasons. For religious conservatives who have always cast the conflict with the Soviet Union in theological terms,[38] détente was a blasphemous retreat from the offensives of the early Cold War. For the rest, it appeared to be tantamount to an acceptance of the legitimacy of communist ideology, a downright abhorrent idea.

Cold War Democrats such as Scoop Jackson saw détente as unduly emphasizing the common interests shared by the two superpowers and accepting coexistence with a fundamentally oppressive regime. A veteran legislator from Washington State, Jackson was a staunch anticommunist, a strong supporter of Israel and other threatened democracies, and a critic of arms limitations. He especially believed that the Cold War was a struggle with an end point—the breakup of the Soviet Union and the collapse of its totalitarian system.[39] Cooperation with the Soviet Union thus appeared to be a further surrender to the cynicism and despair engendered by the Vietnam fiasco.

Perhaps the fault could be attributed to the inability of Nixon and Kissinger to convey clearly their actual conceptions of what détente was and what it was intended to achieve. Détente was central to Nixon's foreign policy; he needed Soviet help to end the Vietnam War and to maintain leverage in the burgeoning U.S. relationship with China. By playing the two communist powers against each other, the United States would be able to dominate both. In addition, strategic weapons parity between the United States and the USSR certainly made measures oriented toward manageable coexistence imperative. With this end in mind, détente was a strategy, not an objective, a "structure of peace" as envisioned by Kissinger. In other words, superpower competition must correspond with the reality of coexistence.[40] The alternative was a third world war. In practice, this meant that a web of complex, interlocking relationships encompassing mainly issues of economics, arms control, and educational exchanges was deliberately spun in order to manage and contain Soviet power. Détente was the means through which the United States would control the Soviet Union by drawing it into a de facto acceptance of, and assimilation into, the existing world order.

The difficulty, however, was that, in the words of historian Robert Litwak, "while the network of ties was intended to influence Soviet thinking, it also had unanticipated effects on American opinion. The American public perceived the growing network of ties with the Soviet Union as implying shared values and interests to a greater extent than was justified or reflected in U.S. as well as Soviet policy."[41] Kissinger's realpolitik insistence on removing ideology in American relations with the Soviet Union exacerbated the problem. Testifying before the Senate Foreign Relations Committee in what was the first major foreign policy pronouncement of the Ford administration, he urged Congress to approve the 1972 U.S.-Soviet trade pact and not to tie such agreements to internal Soviet political developments such as human rights abuses.[42] He pointed out that, for as long as the Soviet Union engaged in responsible international behavior, its internal affairs should not be a subject of outside pressure. From Kissinger's point of view, "the temptation to combine détente with increasing pressure on the Soviet Union . . . would be disastrous. We would not accept it from Moscow; Moscow will not accept it from us. We will finally wind up again with the Cold War and fail to achieve either peace or any human goal."[43] For Kissinger, the preservation of human life and international order were moral values as worthy of, if not more, protection as were human rights.[44]

Notwithstanding the UDHR and the several human rights treaties that had subsequently been drafted and ratified, the idea that domestic human rights could be a legitimate matter of international concern was still considered radical at that time. This was true for the United States as well as the Soviet Union. From the very beginning of the Cold War, the deplorable state of race relations inside the United States had prevented it from taking a more active stance in promoting and realizing the hortatory ideals written in the foundational juridical texts it was largely responsible for bringing into being.[45] In tandem with the efforts to strengthen national godliness to counteract Soviet atheism, the U.S. government also saw the need to remove the problem of race as an obstacle to its general Cold War ideological offensives against the Soviet Union. It could not export freedom abroad given racial injustice formally enshrined in its laws at home. A sentence contained in the amicus brief of the U.S. government in the landmark case of *Brown v. Board of Education* was particularly telling: "It is in the context of the present world struggle between freedom and tyranny that the problem of racial discrimination must be viewed."[46] As the United States started to recover its moral standing after a series of seminal civil rights legislation was passed in the 1960s, it was likewise emboldened in the process to criticize repressive Soviet internal abuses.

This ran against détente, however. For its many opponents, especially those in Congress tired of deferring to the executive branch, the danger was that, in the Nixon administration's amoral pursuit of order in international affairs, the unfortunate victim would be American ideals. In light of Vietnam and Watergate, and freed from the constraints of domestic problems on race, the promotion of human rights thus offered a way to restrain executive power and to restore the rightful place of ideals and morality in official affairs. What they did in order to address that problem took two main forms. The first was a congressional revolt against American military and security aid to repressive though friendly foreign regimes, while the second aimed its sights at the dismal human rights record of the Soviet Union and strove to change it. And thus began the congressional human rights revolution.[47]

Congressional Crusaders and the American Human Rights Moment

Contrary to popular accounts, the American human rights moment did not begin with the presidency of Jimmy Carter, though the idea of human rights caught fire during his administration.[48] It was inaugurated instead in 1974 by a landmark congressional report entitled *Human Rights in the World Community: A Call for U.S. Leadership*,[49] which was issued by the House Subcommittee on International Organizations and Movements. The subcommittee was chaired by Donald Fraser, a Democrat from Minnesota. The report was the result of fifteen hearings held during the previous year that inquired into U.S. bilateral policy toward governments guilty of committing egregious human rights violations against their own citizens, including the governments of Bangladesh, Burundi, Brazil, Chile, and South Africa. It observed that the "human rights factor is not accorded the high priority it deserves in our country's foreign policy. Too often it becomes invisible in the vast foreign policy horizon of political, economic and military affairs."[50] It was one of the most searing critiques of détente yet. A direct result of the Fraser subcommittee hearings is Section 502B of the Foreign Assistance Act, initially a nonbinding resolution that eventually became part of the statute. It stated that "except in extraordinary circumstances . . . no security assistance may be provided to any country which engaged in a consistent pattern of gross violations of internationally recognized human rights."[51] A Bureau of Human Rights and Humanitarian Affairs within the State Department was also created in 1975 pursuant to the numerous recommendations of the Fraser Report.

But it was not the only important or lasting legacy of this renewed legislative assertiveness. Much of the surprising congressional revolt against the "imperial presidency" revolved around the role of missing American ideals in the conduct of U.S. foreign policy.[52] Many structural and societal factors made this development possible, among them the rise of ethnic lobbies and technological progress insofar as they facilitated easier dissemination of information. As a result, lawmakers generally became more attuned to popular pressures and public opinion. During a remarkable period of congressional effort to "restore its role and that of public law"[53] in the formulation of foreign policy, Congress ended U.S. involvement in Vietnam, passed the War Powers Resolution despite a presidential veto,[54] imposed an arms embargo against Turkey, and generally legislated foreign policy contrary to the aims of an unwilling executive. Underlying all these was not only an attempt to check an executive power run amuck but the reintroduction of forgotten ideals in the conduct of American foreign affairs. The promotion of human rights by Congress aimed at the oppressive nature of the Soviet regime thus became the defining feature of this impasse.

The Jackson-Vanik amendment (JVA) to the 1974 Trade Reform Act was easily the most significant of these early congressional efforts to insert morality back into American foreign relations. It also brought together an unusual coalition, one that would have far-reaching repercussions more than thirty years later. As Kissinger himself acknowledged, Scoop Jackson, the senator behind the amendment, was the indispensable link between the two groups critical of détente: the liberals preoccupied with human rights, and the conservatives who were anxious about any sort of negotiations with the Soviets.[55] They came together in a rare convergence, as Kissinger wrote, like an eclipse of the sun.

The amendment sought to deny any economic concessions such as credits or credit guarantees and the conclusion of any commercial agreements between the United States and any nonmarket economy that denies its citizens the right or opportunity to emigrate, or imposes a tax or fine that is not nominal to any citizen who wishes to exercise such freedom.[56] On paper, the JVA had nothing to do with the promotion of religious liberty and neither was it especially about Jews.[57] Jackson introduced his amendment to the comprehensive trade bill that followed as a result of the historic Moscow trade pact between President Nixon and Soviet premier Brezhnev in 1972, which involved the U.S. extension of most favored nation (MFN) status to imports from the Soviet Union and the provision of much-needed credits to the Soviets. In this amendment, Jackson managed to combine his unwavering support for Israel and his fervent antipathy toward the Soviet Union in one fell swoop. For the first time in American legislative history, the UDHR and, in particular, Article 13(2), was invoked, referring to a citizen's right to leave and return to one's own country, as the principal inspiration for the piece of legislation.[58] Its passage was never in question. More than three-quarters of the Senate and well over half the membership of the House of Representatives supported the measure. The JVA applied to all nonmarket economies, not just the Soviet Union, and sought to protect everyone regardless of race, religion, or national origin. In reality, however, Jackson finally found a tangible weapon with which to bludgeon the Soviet Union. And it had everything to do with religious liberty.

Official concern for religious believers in the Soviet Union was already widespread in both houses of Congress, and it dated back to the anticommunism crusade of the 1950s and 1960s and lasted well into Nixon's term. In 1964, the Senate issued Resolution 204 condemning religious persecution in the Soviet Union. Its author, Abraham Ribicoff, a Democrat from Connecticut, was initially concerned about the particular plight of Soviet Jewry. In his cosponsorship speech, Republican Jacob Javits listed the litany of historical events in which the U.S. government had intervened to aid Jews dating back to the period of the Ottoman Empire. At the insistence of Senator Bourke Hickenlooper, a fellow Republican from Iowa, the resolution was expanded to cover other oppressed religious minorities, in addition to Soviet Jews.

During the same year, Congress also condemned Soviet religious persecution in an amendment to the Foreign Assistance Act of 1964,[59] and added discrimination on the grounds of religion as another basis with which to deny American official aid to a foreign country. Subsequently, a joint resolution was issued expressing a similar "sense of Congress" that religious persecution in the Soviet Union and other Eastern European countries should be condemned, and that such governments "be urged to cease such persecution and to permit full and free exercise of religion. . . ."[60] The resolution was introduced by Ribicoff and cosponsored by Scoop Jackson, among others. The House of Representatives was just as busy as their upper house counterpart on this subject. Anti-religious activities in the Soviet Union and in Eastern Europe were the focus of several days of hearings by the Subcommittee on Europe of the House Committee on Foreign Affairs.[61]

In all these cases, the concern for religious freedom behind the Iron Curtain was not limited to a few senators nor was it simply out of pure humanitarianism. Hearings on the subject of "The Communist Exploitation of Religion" were convened by the subcommittee to investigate the administration of the Internal Security Act of the Senate Committee on the Judiciary,[62] while a similar theme was discussed in hearings before the House Committee on Un-American Activities.[63] Many of these congressional resolutions were akin to public statements, functioning as reflections of public concern as well as the conveyance of information to a wider audience intended to shape popular attitudes through the legislative mill.

But as far as actually effecting any sort of change on Soviet policies, these unsurprisingly fell on deaf ears. It did not help that the executive branch did not seem to share the legislative agenda in campaigning for a more humane treatment of Soviet citizens belonging to various religious communities. Prior to the historic 1972 Moscow summit, the House of Representatives issued a resolution, by a vote of 360 to 0, with 70 abstentions, urging the president to "1) call upon the Soviet government to permit the free expression of ideas and the exercise of religion by all its citizens; 2) utilize formal and informal contacts with Soviet officials in an effort to secure an end to discrimination against religious minorities; and 3) request the Soviet government that it permit its citizens the right to emigrate."[64] The Senate, for its part, issued the unopposed Brock-Jackson concurrent resolution, which demanded a governmental commitment against Soviet oppression of minorities and emigration restrictions. It reiterated the contents of the House resolution and particularly called on the State Department to raise in the General Assembly of the United Nations the issue of the Soviet Union's violations of the UDHR. In his sponsorship speech, Jackson explained that the Senate was "calling upon the President to use America's influence to help eliminate those restraints which hinder individuals from freely developing their abilities, personalities and cultural identities."[65] In focusing on freedom of emigration, Jackson clearly intended it as a means to facilitate the exercise of religious freedom, stating that "[i]t is a tragic crime for the Soviet or any other government to imprison its own citizens in a society where they can neither practice their religion nor make their way to countries where they might give full expression to their religious and cultural identity."[66]

As part of this broad congressional offensive on behalf of religious freedom in the Soviet Union, senators also sponsored resolutions and issued various statements urging, for example, that the broadcast of Voice of America be undertaken in the Yiddish language,[67] and further condemnation of government persecution of Soviet Jewry.[68] Despite these strongly worded protestations, there was no indication that Nixon even brought up the issue during his Moscow meeting with Brezhnev.[69]

Various congressional efforts also attempted to put some teeth into these pronouncements, including the Soviet Jews Relief bill of 1971, proposed by Edward Koch of New York, which sought to permit the immigration of 30,000 more Soviet Jews above existing limits into the United States. Another was a proposed amendment by Representative Thomas Rees of Los Angeles, California, to the 1969 Export Administration Act, which was due for renewal in 1972. The amendment would have authorized the president to prohibit commodity exports or the export of information to any nation that prohibited freedom of religion and emigration.[70] Both bills were defeated for various reasons. In Koch's case, Attorney General John Mitchell promised to ease immigration restrictions for Soviet Jews into the United States, while the Rees amendment failed to get any support in the House Banking Committee.[71] A reason for this failure was the very reluctance on the part of some politicians to link emigration to Soviet-American trade, which had undergone significant liberalization since the time Nixon assumed office. Nobody was eager to rock the boat of détente.

Nonetheless, the idea of linking economic concessions to the observance of human rights norms took hold. After the Soviet Union imposed a punitive "diploma tax" on all its would-be emigrants in August 1972, Jackson seized the opportunity he had been waiting for. While the Soviet constitution guaranteed freedom of emigration, like freedom of religion, it was routinely violated in practice. An exit tax imposed in 1972, ostensibly to recoup state financing of higher education, made emigration legally difficult if not impossible. Prohibitive fees ranged from USD$5,000 to USD$30,000 depending on one's educational credentials. Soviet Jews were particularly affected by this measure because many of them had advanced university degrees. In a statement to the Senate proposing his amendment to the East-West Trade Relations Act of 1971, Jackson outlined the contents of Section 10(a), which conditioned the extension of MFN status or participation in any U.S. government program that grants credits, credits guarantees, or investment guarantees on the observance of the freedom of emigration for its citizens.[72]

In its original formulation, the nascent JVA embodied language that portrayed the right to emigration as a means to facilitate other freedoms, particularly religious and cultural ones. Any attempt, for instance, by the president to grant MFN status, or the like, in accordance with the provisions of the trade law was to be accompanied by a report on, among other issues, prevailing legal and policy frameworks on emigration as well as existing restrictions applied to people wishing to emigrate, specifically their national and religious backgrounds.[73] Jackson framed the measure against a whole slew of human rights violations within the Eastern bloc, singling out the plight of Roman Catholic demonstrators in Lithuania demanding religious freedoms and the Jews in the Soviet Union seeking to emigrate to Israel, and eventually making the unavoidable analogy between the Soviet regime and the Third Reich.[74]

To the criticism that the JVA was undue interference on the internal affairs of another sovereign state, Jackson pointed out the obvious. The United States was actually *giving* money to the Soviet Union, which made it the business of the United States, "quite apart from the dedication to our own high principles,"[75] to be concerned with what was going on in the country. "By acceding to the International Convention on the Elimination of All Forms of Racial Discrimination in 1969, the Soviet Union acknowledged that emigration policy goes beyond the limits implied by the term *internal affairs*. . . . The Jackson Amendment far from being an intrusion into anyone's internal affairs is one small step along the road to an international community based on law."[76] As if to drive home the point of his message, he officially introduced his proposed amendment on the very same day that the Soviet trade minister arrived in Washington to sign the trade agreement.

Downplaying the potential consequences of the Jackson amendment down the road, the White House initially went into a quiet diplomacy mode with the Soviets in order to secure concessions regarding emigration. By this time, Jackson had persuaded and enlisted a broad swath of domestic Jewish groups to support his amendment, stating that "the time has to come to place our highest human values ahead of the trade dollar by firm and immediate action that the Russians can understand."[77] His chief aide, a young Richard Perle, took charge of cultivating and strengthening the grassroots support for the JVA within a divided American Jewish community. Initially, the quiet diplomacy seemed to work. Forty-four Soviet Jews were allowed to leave the country without paying the diploma tax in two days, and several more families followed thereafter. Soviet officials claimed that the tax was waived for the time being, though it would remain on the statute books. Aware of the leniency, Jackson pressed ahead nevertheless. Charging that the Soviet relaxation was a fraud, he countered, "Now I have heard it said that the Soviets are going to keep the ransom tax on the statute books but they won't apply it in practice. I say that we are going to put the Jackson amendment on the statute books but in the hope that it won't apply to the Soviet Union because they will be in compliance with its free emigration provision."[78]

Jackson and his aides moved deftly and swiftly, securing more than adequate support from both houses of Congress, including Abraham Ribicoff and Jacob Javits in the Senate, both well-known and respected Jewish voices, and Charles Vanik, the chair of the House Ways and Means Committee who brought along with him more than 200 cosponsors.[79] Vanik was also a logical choice. Ethnic groups formed a large part of his constituency,[80] and his own roots were from Czechoslovakia. As part of the trade pact, the president was to grant MFN status to the Soviet Union, which he then sought to get, together with the power to raise and lower tariffs in one comprehensive trade bill from Congress. On the same day that Nixon sent the bill to Congress, Jackson included his amendment as a rider.

Upon hearing of the amendment's reintroduction, Nixon flew into a rage.[81] The bill, which now featured the JVA, threatened the unraveling of the delicately woven web of détente. Because the JVA encouraged emigration without regard for race, nationality, and religion, it also attracted broad domestic support, apart from Jewish groups. The JVA not only united Jews with other ethnic groups but also enlisted them, under the all-encompassing banner of "human rights," alongside liberals and conservatives in a unique coalition. The administration's various attempts to shelve the amendment included inviting Jewish leaders to the White House in order to persuade them to abandon their support for the JVA. In a 1974 hearing before the Senate Foreign Relations Committee, Kissinger opposed the amendment, stating that the administration had been protesting the Soviet crackdown on its dissidents, but it would not serve the interests of either country to make a formal protest or to tie foreign policy to domestic changes.[82] In a private conversation with the president, Kissinger was heard to go so far as to say, "[T]he emigration of Jews from the Soviet Union is not an objective of American foreign policy. And if they put Jews into gas chambers in the Soviet Union, it is not an American concern. Maybe a humanitarian concern."[83] The brutality of the statement was an indication of how Kissinger prized international order above all, and the depths of frustration to which the JVA was driving him.

The face-off between the two Henrys—Kissinger and Jackson—revolved around the goals and purposes of détente. With Nixon in the sidelines because of Watergate, Kissinger took over the reins of mitigating the potential effects of the JVA on U.S.-Soviet relations. For some, the primary goal of Jackson, very much the cold warrior of old, was twofold: to fight for human rights and to deter the normalization of relations between the two superpowers.[84] For others, his objective was more domestically focused. Jackson threw his hat into the presidential race in 1972 and 1976. Whatever the main motivation was, the edifice of détente remained the target as far as it shielded the internal practices of the Soviet Union from American and, by extension, international scrutiny.

Conveniently for Jackson, the fight for religious and cultural freedoms of Soviet Jewry, whether in the form of freedom to practice them within the country or freedom to seek them elsewhere, provided a rallying cause that seamlessly merged the two. The Yom Kippur War between Israel, on the one hand, and Egypt and Syria, on the other, complicated matters, however. In what was one of Kissinger's last attempts to dissuade Jewish groups from supporting it, he told them that passing the JVA would represent an ungrateful affront to the Soviets at a time when their cooperation was badly needed in order to avert a full-scale war in the Middle East, but his efforts to link the two failed.[85] It also mattered enormously that the broad language of the JVA went beyond Jews and religious freedom, thus increasing its humanitarian appeal. Neither term appeared in the famous exchange of letters between Jackson and Kissinger in 1974 as they negotiated on an acceptable version,[86] the main feature of which was the grant of MFN status and extension of credits in exchange for 60,000 exit visas from the Soviet Union annually. As support for the amendment irrevocably coalesced, Senator George McGovern asked on the Senate floor, "[I]f we don't interfere in internal affairs, then what the hell were we doing in Vietnam?"[87] Robert Bauman, a Democrat from Maryland, summed up the moral imperatives involved: "Those who see this measure solely in economic terms ignore two centuries of American dedication to the cause of human freedom. We must not walk away from those who plead for our help."[88] On December 18 of the same year, the Soviet Union publicly denounced the JVA as "gross interference" in its internal affairs and as contrary to the agreed-upon principles of U.S.-Soviet relations.

It was a different but similarly reluctant president who signed the JVA into law as part of the 1974 Trade Reform Act on January 3, 1975, finally ending the two-year struggle. Within the same month, Congress also voted to restrict the extension of Export-Import Bank credits to the Soviet Union to a paltry sum of $300 million over the next five years.[89] An angry Kremlin revoked the trade pact a week after the bill's passage. The JVA would remain on the statute books until its repeal well after the end of the Cold War, a towering reminder of a newly awakened congressional human rights consciousness.[90]

But with respect to its goal of facilitating religious freedom and freedom of emigration in the Soviet Union, the JVA appeared to be a dismal failure. From 35,000 emigrants in 1973, the emigration numbers of Soviet Jews, many of them headed to Israel, went down drastically, to a little more than 13,000 in 1975.[91] Nevertheless, Soviet emigration continued for a variety of reasons, among them the desire of the Soviets to hold a European security conference to ratify the postwar division of Europe. Allowing limited emigration for family reunification purposes was part of the Soviet efforts to get the Western powers to come to the negotiating table and sign what would become known as the Helsinki agreement. As for getting the Soviet Union to recognize the rights and freedoms of its citizens, ironically enough, it would take an international accord intended to affirm détente to accomplish what Jackson had begun with his amendment in order to destroy it.

The Helsinki Effect

The official U.S. delegation, composed of career diplomats from the State Department, departed for Dipoli, a conference center in Finland, in 1972, armed with but one oral instruction of a general nature: "You know what you're supposed to do. Don't screw it up!"[92] Such was the degree of importance, or lack thereof, given by Kissinger and Nixon to an obscure, technocratic security conference that would become known as the Conference on Security and Cooperation in Europe (CSCE). The CSCE was originally a Soviet idea, dating back to the early 1950s, that called for a pan-European security pact and excluded the United States and Canada. But the conference did not convene until 1969, when the West took seriously the Soviet desire to conclude a multilateral agreement that would renounce the use of force, recognize existing European borders, and improve relations between the East and West. The United States knew full well that the real goal of the Soviets in holding this conference was to obtain a juridical recognition of what was, in any case, an accepted territorial status quo post–World War II and increase the legitimacy of the existing governments within the Eastern bloc.[93] Thus, there was a lack of enthusiasm amounting to general indifference for the conference at the highest policymaking circles. At best, the State Department saw it as an opportunity to lower current barriers on various freedoms, such as freedom of movement and cultural exchanges within Eastern Europe, with the view of reducing East-West tensions in Europe.[94] Kissinger eventually decided to participate in order to show American support for the European members of NATO as well as to prevent any agreements that could endanger U.S. interests.[95] Given considerable Soviet interest in the matter, it was thought that this conference could be the carrot used to buy Soviet support on more substantial questions, such as the Middle East crisis and international arms control. Consequently, the United States was content to let its Western European allies take the lead in the early stages of the CSCE.

The consequences of the CSCE, which would culminate in the signing of the HFA, could not have been foreseen by its participants, not even by State Department officials who, by and large, held a divergent view from that of Kissinger. Notwithstanding the obvious implications of Kissinger's skepticism toward the ongoing negotiations, he proved to be the decisive factor in getting the Kremlin to acquiesce on the human contacts provisions of basket three.[96] But as he did so, true to character, he did not forget to remind the Europeans that the Soviet Union had been in existence for fifty years and it would certainly not change because Western newspapers were now going to be sold in Moscow.[97]

The HFA embodied two religious freedom commitments to which signatories were to be held accountable. The first was Principle VII, which pertains to the right to hold beliefs and to worship freely, alone or in concert with others. This principle was included as part of basket one (or the security basket), not in the famous basket three. Under its general heading, section (1) prescribes that human rights and fundamental freedoms shall be respected by the participating States for all without distinction as to, inter alia, religion, while section (3) states that "the participating States will recognize and respect the freedom of the individual to profess and practice, alone or in community with others, religion or belief acting in accordance with the dictates of his own conscience."[98] The other provision that dealt with religious freedom is found in basket three, which emphasized the movement or communication of peoples for purposes of the exercise of their religious beliefs.[99] Principle VII would ultimately serve as the basis for the Western demand, by governments and—unexpectedly—a powerful transnational network of human rights activists alike,[100] that communist governments comply with their Helsinki commitments and would raise questions accordingly for such ends. It is true that all ten principles in the HFA were intended to be of equal importance.[101] But the powerful paradox that was at the heart of the HFA was that this simply meant that the HFA contained the prized Soviet guarantee of noninterference, and it also nevertheless contained an obligation for all its signatory states to respect human rights in their territories. In this way, the concept of linkage at the heart of détente became transformed from that of economics for peace to human rights for peace. In the early years of implementing the HFA, religious persecution would be one of the most highlighted human rights violations.

All this was lost on the outside world as soon as the HFA was signed. Because of how Kissinger and the administration downplayed the significance of the CSCE in public and in private, the HFA was vilified by many in the United States. That President Ford was going to Helsinki in order to sign a document nobody had heard of was enough to raise suspicions regarding another American favor to the Soviets. Ford compounded the confusion by declaring in his infamous television debate with Jimmy Carter that "there is no Soviet domination of Eastern Europe."[102] As far as everybody else was concerned, the only accomplishment of the HFA was that it sold out Eastern Europe to the Soviet Union, the ultimate sin committed in the name of furthering détente.

Given the combination of apathy, underappreciation, and confusion on the part of the executive on the matter of the HFA, a few members of Congress took responsibility for injecting life into the text of the HFA. Two months after its signing, Millicent Fenwick, a New Jersey Republican, joined a special congressional fact-finding delegation to Moscow, where she interviewed several Soviet dissidents, including the famous dissident and physicist Yuri Orlov.[103] Orlov suggested to Fenwick that the West should use the HFA to pressure the Kremlin in honoring its human rights obligations. This eventually led her, along with Clifford Case, a Senator and her fellow legislator from New Jersey, to introduce a bill that proposed to create an official government commission to monitor Helsinki compliance of various signatory states.[104] Many of the groups and associations that testified before Congress in support of the commission's creation advocated for religious freedom of their coreligionists in Eastern Europe. The proposed commission, which would become the U.S. Helsinki Commission, was a sui generis institution because it fused executive and legislative elements of government together. It included representatives from all executive departments responsible for implementing the HFA: State, Defense, and Commerce, together with members of the Senate and the House of Representatives. Its primary task was to monitor and make recommendations. The House endorsed the bill in May 1976, and the Senate followed suit shortly thereafter. Scoop Jackson was among its cosponsors, notwithstanding his earlier criticisms of Ford and the signing of the HFA. The bill was signed into law a month later. The administration considered the legislation similar to the JVA: as an unwarranted intrusion into the executive constitutional prerogative in the realm of foreign affairs.[105]

In the inaugural meeting of the commission, Fenwick captured the new idea that the congressional crusade appeared to be cultivating, an idea that would not reach its high point until the Carter presidency, though with much unacknowledged prodding from members of the Helsinki Commission. "It is fair to explore the question of how those diverse national groups within the Soviet Union do coexist and how militant communism and religious conviction can survive side by side . . . we recognize that the subjects of our two hearings were commonly called internal affairs: now they are a matter of international agreement and that is a substantive change."[106]

The HFA finally legitimized the idea that human rights were a matter of international concern, a fact seemingly amplified by Brezhnev's personal signature on the document, but it did not change the emphasis on religious liberty protection by Congress. There are two main reasons for the continued emphasis. One is the traditional communist antipathy toward religion. Thus, it remained a focal battleground between the two conflicting ideologies. It certainly helped that violations of this freedom were visible and could easily be measured. In one of the House hearings held by the Fraser subcommittee, a "sense of Congress" concurrent resolution was passed, expressing concern about the deprivation of religious liberty in the Soviet Union. The content was similar to previous congressional resolutions on the matter, but this time, it deployed the moral and political leverage of the Soviet signature on the HFA. Urging the release of Georgi Vins, an imprisoned Baptist preacher, and appealing to allow other persecuted Christians and religious believers to worship God freely, the resolution noted that the "Soviet policy contravenes the spirit, if not the letter of the Helsinki agreement and by doing so raises serious doubts as to the commitment of the Soviet Union to that agreement."[107] In fact, during the first four formative years of the U.S. Helsinki Commission, four out of sixteen hearings were devoted to the subject of protection of religious and minority rights in the Soviet Union and in Eastern Europe.[108] In these hearings, dozens of witnesses testified to the deplorable state of religious freedom in the Soviet Union. A 1975 amendment to then existing Soviet law on religion, passed on the eve of the signing of Helsinki, had restricted religious liberties even further. Religious congregations were required to be registered with the Council on Religious Affairs; proselytization was completely prohibited; and no form of religious education was allowed, including private parental instruction.[109]

Another reason is that it has always been a traditional American freedom, and therefore violations of religious freedom have always had a special historical resonance with the public. Because of Vietnam and Watergate, there was also a timely and pressing need to bring back morality and idealism in U.S. foreign relations. The election of Carter provided the necessary spark to do just that, but it was the congressional crusaders who had persuaded him that human rights should be a core part of his new policy. As sanctioned by the HFA, the advocacy of religious freedom as a human right was given a new impetus and a new package. In her statement before the Helsinki Commission bill was put to a final House vote, Fenwick singled out freedom of religion and freedom of emigration as the two biggest concerns for the would-be commission and declared that these two freedoms are essentially "what this bill is all about."[110] A related factor was that religious freedom concerns readily mobilized many diverse ethnic and religious groups within the American population. Similar to the JVA, it obtained support not only from Jews but also from Christians concerned with the plight of their coreligionists in the Soviet Union. The proliferation of ethnic lobbies that similarly concerned themselves with the troubles of their Eastern European brethren ensured that there was constant pressure on American legislators to hold the Soviet Union to its HFA commitments within the available legal and political forums.[111] As the commission interviewed a gamut of witnesses, ranging from Soviet Jews to Ukrainian Greek Catholics and Estonian Lutherans, it established itself as something akin to a global "religious freedom" police, providing a rough template for the creation of the U.S. Commission on International Religious Freedom more than twenty years later.

The HFA facilitated this process of global shaming in two ways. The first was through the official instrumentality of the U.S. Helsinki Commission. Prompted by the human rights–focused policy of Jimmy Carter, the commission issued reports on the state of human rights in the Soviet Union and its Eastern European satellites. The other was that it spurred the formation of private nongovernmental organizations in order to monitor Soviet compliance.[112] Helsinki Watch, the precursor of present-day Human Rights Watch, was among the most prominent of these groups. What made both modalities particularly effective was that the HFA itself provided for periodic review meetings in which to present these findings. According to one Helsinki scholar, a follow-up meeting mandated in the HFA, where implementation of the accords was reviewed, lent the accords a semi-juridical and politically binding character.[113] That it was unclear whether the HFA possessed any legal significance or whether it rested on an explicitly juridical basis seemed a less important question than its political implications.[114] Because its human rights provisions drew their strength from the UDHR, it could be argued that it possessed legal effects, even if they were somewhat limited.

In any case, the U.S. government took full advantage of this unique forum. Carter had appointed Arthur Goldberg, a former secretary of labor and U.S. Supreme Court justice, as the head of the American delegation to Belgrade, the first scheduled follow-up meeting after the HFA signing. The delegation included all members of the U.S. Helsinki Commission, representatives and senators, which lent it a prestige not present with the delegation of other states. In fact, early U.S. Helsinki Commission hearings had been geared toward acquiring information in order to present it at Belgrade. Goldberg took an unusually high-profile approach at the meeting. He publicly criticized communist human rights abuses, hence initiating a crucial ingredient of the U.S. strategy in its dealings with the Soviet Union that would persist until the end of the Cold War.[115] Goldberg, a "highly political Jew and truly sensitive to Soviet behavior toward its Jewish citizens,"[116] aggressively focused on the implementation review, naming offending countries and singling out oppressive practices, much to the distress of the other delegates and especially the Soviets. Belgrade would set the template for the rest of the CSCE meetings.

Notwithstanding the HFA taking on a life of its own and with a human rights–minded president, Congress never let up on its crusade for human rights, including religious freedom, in the Soviet Union. On the eve of the Belgrade meeting, for instance, the House of Representatives issued a concurrent resolution expressing indignation at what was termed as "religious genocide" committed by Soviet authorities against Ukrainian churches.[117] More important, through the institution of the U.S. Helsinki Commission, the HFA permanently entrenched the link between détente and human rights, which was the central feature of the JVA only a few years earlier. Natan Sharansky, another famous Soviet dissident who spent more than a decade in a Soviet gulag for practicing his religion and an ardent supporter of the JVA, insisted that it was Henry Jackson who was instrumental in bringing about the extraordinary consequences of the HFA's human rights provisions.[118] And he was right. Jackson and his fellow congressional crusaders understood very early that the United States could not deal with the Soviet Union while ignoring the issue of human rights. For the most part, Kissinger's stark realism in foreign relations did not resonate with an American public clamoring for the return of moralism and idealism in government affairs.

By the time the Helsinki effect was finally felt by everybody, the vocabulary of linkage and the discourse of human rights set in motion by the JVA through the efforts of the fierce opponents of détente became readily available to those who sought to harness its potential in the new and last phase of the Cold War. Up to his untimely death in 1981, Jackson continued to maintain the pressure on Soviet violations of religious freedom, this time armed with information provided by the transnational network spawned by the HFA. The JVA, he clarified, was not just about Jews. "Too many people think that Jackson-Vanik applies only to Soviet Jewry. It does not, and never has."[119]

* * *

The opposing currents of détente and unilateralism in U.S. foreign relations accidentally coalesced into a legal and political safety net for religious believers and advocates of human rights worldwide. By enacting the Jackson-Vanik amendment into law and vigorously implementing the human rights provisions of the HFA, the U.S. government found itself yet again at the forefront of transnational religious freedom protection, now couched in the language of human rights. Given the traditional fate of human rights treaties in Congress and the general lack of popularity of various forms of internationalism,[120] it seemed a surprising result. But the transformation of religious freedom as a human right was also necessarily part and parcel of a broader battle over the shape and form that American foreign policy would take in the midst of the Cold War against the United States' superpower rival. Domestic factors in the U.S. political and cultural milieu played themselves out on the field of foreign policy precisely over this issue. Conservatives opposed détente, worried as they were that this policy was changing the country into one without any resemblance to its history and traditions. Détente, with its emphasis on a centralized decision-making apparatus, also marginalized Congress, much to its discontent. The advocacy and promotion of religious freedom in the Soviet Union and its satellites responded directly to the difficulties posed by both the ideological underpinnings and practical implications of this policy. In so doing, American efforts created and shaped the early content of international human rights law. The 1970s ended with human rights conditions in states regarded as legitimate matters of international concern, and the provisions of the UDHR and the ICCPR as operationalized by the HFA were now weapons against an ideological enemy.

From a domestic point of view, it meant that these conditions have become key factors in U.S. diplomacy. The institutional apparatus developed during this period still exists today, and it includes the U.S. Helsinki Commission, and the Bureau of Democracy, Human Rights, and Labor in the State Department. Their primary mechanisms, country-monitoring reports and economic sanctions against violators, likewise date their origins to the congressional revolution of this period. But the most important development was the unforeseen consequences of both the JVA and the HFA. Inside the United States, the JVA and HFA catalyzed religious and ethnic groups into greater political involvement. Outside the United States, the HFA empowered dissenters all over Eastern Europe and the Soviet Union, throwing the lid off a simmering cauldron of human rights activism. Almost three decades after the UDHR, the international protection of individual human rights, including religious freedom, finally emerged as a reality.

6

Age of Exceptionalism

> When this bill passes, in small villages in southern Sudan, people with their little crystal radio sets, people in villages in China with their crystal sets when they hear that the U.S. Congress, the people's House, the House of Representatives has voted for this legislation, it will send a message to the people who are being persecuted around the world that this Congress and this country stands with them.
>
> —*Representative Frank R. Wolf, May 11, 1998*

L. Paul Bremer III, the head American civilian administrator in Iraq, was in a pickle. The leading Shiite cleric in Iraq, the Grand Ayatollah Ali al-Sistani, had just issued a *fatwa,* the Islamic legal equivalent of an opinion in American law, in which he stated, "[T]hose forces have no authority to appoint the members of the constitution preparation assembly . . . there must be a general election so that every Iraqi citizen—who is eligible to vote—can choose someone to represent him in a foundational constitution preparation assembly."[1] Prompted by a concern that the Americans would write the Iraqi constitution similar to what Douglas MacArthur did in postwar Japan,[2] Sistani exhorted all Iraqis to ensure that elections be undertaken for this purpose in order to safeguard Iraqi national interest and identity.

But to hold elections in June 2003 or at any time shortly thereafter, a mere month after Bremer flew into Iraq as the new head of the Office for Reconstruction and Humanitarian Assistance (ORHA), which has since been transformed into the Coalition Provisional Authority (CPA), seemed flat out impossible. After the decisive capture of Baghdad, things had turned sour quickly for U.S. forces. Order and security were nonexistent. Despite a heavy American military presence, looting was widespread, and bombs were still exploding.[3] He also had another reason to be apprehensive about Sistani's *fatwa*. To heed the cleric's *fatwa* was to undermine the cherished American ideal of separation of religion and state. On both principled and pragmatic grounds, it had negative connotations for the CPA. It would appear to give religious leaders the upper hand, which the occupation officials never wanted to give them in the first place. In addition, conceding to the inflexible Sistani demand at this time ensured that only the major Islamist groups or Baathist extremists would be organized and in a position to prevail in any elections conducted in the short term. The idea of an Iraqi theocracy not unlike that of its Iranian neighbor, sprouting from the ashes of the secular Saddam Hussein regime, was not something CPA officials could stomach.

Bremer was not the only American official anxious about the unpredictable role of Islam in the rebuilding of Iraq. Days before President George W. Bush would declare the end of major military combat operations in a much-maligned speech, the U.S. Commission on International Religious Freedom (USCIRF), an independent federal bipartisan government entity created through enabling legislation in 1998 to review circumstances of religious freedom violations internationally,[4] sent a letter to President Bush asking the "Administration to remain firm in its commitment to ensure freedom, including religious freedom for all Iraqis. The Administration should also promote in all its reconstruction programs the idea of a future Iraqi political system that practices religious tolerance and respects the universal human rights of all Iraqis."[5] It was not the first time that the USCIRF voiced its concerns about the state of religious freedom in Iraq, having designated it a country of particular concern (CPC) since the commission started issuing country reports in 1998.[6] But it was the first time that the USCIRF, indeed, the U.S. government in its entirety, was presented with a concrete opportunity to realize these goals as they engaged in yet another nation-building effort. As the Iraqis were in the process of drafting their own permanent constitution in 2005, President Bush proudly responded to a reporter's question that "we're watching an amazing event unfold: that is, the writing of a constitution which guarantees minority rights, women's rights, freedom to worship in a part of the world . . . in a country that only knew dictatorship. And so you're seeing people express their opinions and talking about a political process."[7] Singling out these particular features of the new Iraqi constitution was an especially telling sign of what was foremost in the minds of the highest policymakers when they found themselves confronted with the daunting task of reconstruction and nation building after the fall of Baghdad just two years earlier.

What explains the contemporary American concern about the uses and implications of religious liberty in international politics? At the end of the Cold War, the secularization thesis, which posited the demise of religion as a source of authority in direct correlation with the advance of modernity and scientific progress,[8] underwent the first of many of its own funerals in the years to follow. Religion did not cower before the forces of modernity but did the exact opposite. Scholars now confidently speak of the twenty-first century as "God's Century,"[9] an era characterized by the resurgence of religion in the public sphere. While two crucial events that mark this period have had a profound impact on U.S. foreign relations, namely, the Iranian Islamic revolution of 1979 and the tragic terrorist attacks in the United States on September 11, 2001, the origins of its contemporary religious freedom policy, as embodied in the 1998 International Religious Freedom Act (IRFA), were not in any way connected to their common denominator—Islamic extremism.

Instead, looking at the post–Cold War world, the United States, at the peak of its unipolar moment,[10] sought to justify its leadership by invoking the language of human rights and by promoting the spread of democracy in other parts of the globe. Religious liberty in this period was no longer a weapon against a rival superpower but an argument for justification for its own power. What was similar was that the cause of religious freedom did not rank high in the White House agenda. True, both Nixon and Kissinger were particularly averse to the use of morality and ideology as a matter of principle when it came to international diplomacy. But the 1970s was also a time when religion became a flashpoint for partisan mobilization in the broader culture wars.[11] The consequences of those early years of the culture wars were at the center of American cleric and public intellectual Richard John Neuhaus's classic jeremiad *The Naked Public Square,* which exposed the contradiction that the values of the American people, overwhelmingly grounded in religious belief, had been systematically excluded from consideration at the highest policymaking levels. This phenomenon identified by Neuhaus led to, among others, the misleading perception that U.S. foreign policy had been secularist.

After the Cold War, as human rights became an ascendant secular lingua franca, privatization of religion persisted. In her memoir, former U.S. secretary of state Madeleine Albright candidly admitted that U.S. foreign policy under her watch deliberately ignored religion.[12] Not even the August 1998 al-Qaeda bombing of the U.S. embassies in Kenya and Tanzania could make the Clinton administration change its stance.[13] It thereupon fell on a resolute group in Congress to promote the same cause it had championed since the 1970s,[14] which culminated in the enactment of the IRFA in October 1998. The IRFA recovered religious freedom from a plethora of human rights and restored it to a prominent position among other rights in U.S. foreign relations, much to the chagrin of its critics.[15] For the representatives and senators who have been the strongest supporters of the IRFA, the Cold War was largely won with the use of human rights against the Soviet Union, and chief among those human rights was the right to religious freedom. Now alone at the helm of a world freed of the perverse balance of the Cold War but grappling with the religious, cultural, and ethnic fault lines revealed by its demise, American lawmakers and intellectuals alike generally saw U.S. leadership as a stabilizing force and moral beacon for the rest of the world. Similar to the struggle around the Jackson-Vanik amendment (JVA) from the Nixon years, executive and legislative branches in the post–Cold War world battled anew for the place of religious liberty in U.S. foreign policy.

It took only a few years for the executive to see eye to eye with Congress on this issue as the American realist worldview was suddenly shattered by the arrival of Islamic nonstate terrorism on that fateful Tuesday in September 2001. The promotion of religious freedom and the protection of minority rights for the inhabitants of Iraq were not the animating forces behind Operation Iraqi Freedom, but faced with the daunting task of nation building, they became a prime objective of the U.S. government soon after the removal of the Iraqi dictator Saddam Hussein.[16] In the 2004 Transitional Administrative Law (TAL) written under the watchful gaze of the CPA, this objective was formally realized through a novel constitutional experiment: the blending of principles of Islam and democracy, with an explicit guarantee of freedom for all individuals to their own religious belief and practice.[17] The subject of intense focus from the White House, Congress, and various domestic religious and secular human rights groups, the process that led to the compromise outcome in the TAL set the groundwork for the subsequent explosion of literature on the compatibility of the demands of religion, Islam in particular, with the requirements of democracy.[18]

The writing of religious freedom guarantees into the 2004 Iraqi TAL presented a new window through which to view the institutionalized role of religious freedom in U.S. foreign policy in action, as established by the IRFA. Scholars in the fields of law, religion, and international politics have generally studied and analyzed the Iraqi TAL and the IRFA separately. But the circumstances surrounding the Iraqi TAL could only be fully understood by looking at the origins of the IRFA. At the same time, the possibilities presented by the IRFA can only be appreciated in what has been done through the Iraqi TAL. Each promoted religious freedom as part of U.S. foreign policy in order to justify American power. In both cases, religious freedom as an individual human right was institutionalized and entrenched. In IRFA, the promotion of religious freedom was statutorily incorporated in U.S. foreign policy, while the Iraqi TAL constitutionalized religious freedom. Ideological and security considerations underpinned the two latest efforts of the U.S. government to incorporate religious freedom guarantees in these laws. Only when we view the two stories as part of a single continuum do we realize the myriad ways in which religious freedom as a legal idea appealed to lofty and long-held American ideals as well as to its worldly and ever-changing national interests.

Remembering the Persecuted, Again

Political scientist Allen Hertzke, one of only two scholars who has written a history of the IRFA,[19] has credited the unlikely and remarkable alliance between Christian and Jewish activists in producing the statute. In his account, the initial Christian evangelical mobilization behind the legislation would not have been sufficient had it not included other religious groups such as the American Catholic, Jewish, Buddhist, and Baha'i communities. In fact, it was largely the zealous efforts of Michael Horowitz, a former Reagan administration official and a fellow at the Hudson Institute, that contributed to the formation of this unique interfaith coalition that ensured the passage of the IRFA. Painting evangelical Christians as the Jews of the twenty-first century, Horowitz lent credibility to the cause using his self-identification as a Jew and frequent analogies between the lessons of the Holocaust and the contemporary scourge of Christian persecution around the world.[20] To evangelical Christian leaders who were reluctant to lobby for the plight of their persecuted co-religionists abroad, he said, "I'm a Jew. I'm interested in this. Why aren't you?"[21] Horowitz, together with Nina Shea, a conservative Roman Catholic activist affiliated with the nongovernmental organization (NGO) Puebla Institute, which was later absorbed by the group Freedom House, became the formidable force behind the initial push for what would eventually become the IRFA.[22]

That account, however, is incomplete. Although it is true that religious civil society was responsible for the fast tracking and taking advantage of the critical mass of support that had built up around the various pieces of legislation that became the IRFA, longstanding congressional interest on the matter of religious freedom was independently built up since the fall of the Berlin Wall. Many of these representatives and senators were veterans of the anticommunist crusade from the Nixon to the Reagan years. Chris Smith of New Jersey and Frank Wolf of Virginia, for example, both well-known proponents of global religious freedom, were among the first American officials, as members of the U.S. Helsinki Commission, to visit the infamous Perm 35 Soviet gulag in 1989.[23] After the collapse of the Soviet Union, their attention turned to Muslim countries and still-existing communist regimes.[24] China, in particular, was a primary target. Because of the dismal state of Chinese human rights, especially after the 1989 Tiananmen Square massacre, both Congress and American civil society groups began to scrutinize U.S. policies with China closely, with a particular focus, once again, on using a familiar tool of economic leverage: the granting of most favored nation (MFN) status.

The term *MFN* is actually a misnomer. As Senator Dianne Feinstein of California was wont to point out in a hearing focused on the consequences of granting MFN status to China in 1996,[25] it simply meant normal trade relations, not preferential treatment. But for that part of Congress at odds with the executive on the direction of its China policy, MFN status held symbolic power. It was a card that would be played repeatedly by several representatives until the grant of permanent normalization of trade relations (PNTR) status to China in 2000.[26] As early as 1994, well before the momentum for the IRFA would surface in Capitol Hill, two congressional hearings were already focused on the linkage between U.S. economic policy and the repression of religious freedom in China. Several witnesses, among them Nina Shea, appeared and gave oral and documentary evidence on the brutal state repression of all religious activity in China before the committee. During those hearings, Tom Lantos, another Democrat from California and a longtime human rights advocate, urged his fellow legislators to send a signal to Chinese leaders that religious persecution was not acceptable under any circumstances and therefore not to renew MFN status for China.[27] As a regular witness in hearings on matters of religious persecution in China and Vietnam, including a 1996 Senate hearing on the consequences of MFN renewal in China, Shea likewise implored legislators to do the same.[28] Notably, religious freedom was the only human rights issue presented at the hearing.

Executive reluctance on the issue of religious freedom, and human rights in general, however, was quite clear. Despite an unprecedented earlier executive order that explicitly conditioned further MFN renewal on, among others, "taking steps to begin adhering to the Universal Declaration of Human Rights,"[29] and "releasing and providing an acceptable accounting for Chinese citizens imprisoned or detained for the non-violent expression of their political and religious beliefs,[30] President Clinton did a complete turnaround on the issue and announced the extension of MFN treatment for China the following year. This change was notwithstanding China's failure to improve its human rights record. Crucially, the extension was made together with the decision to delink MFN from human rights issues.[31] The president has extended MFN every year since.

Horowitz, Shea, and human rights groups focused on religious freedom issues entered the picture right when Congress was in the middle of the MFN debacle. Their religious freedom campaign was not limited to China—Sudan and most Muslim-majority countries were very much on their radar, although given China's outsized importance to American interests, it was easier to capture the attention of not only the legislators but also the public. Months before Clinton's turnaround on MFN status for China in 1994, legislators were on the offensive, using various forms of media to remind Beijing of the requirements of a U.S. extension. More often than not, these reminders pertained to the state of religious repression in the country. Horowitz's conversion to the religious freedom cause stemmed from his own frustrations in failing to secure U.S. asylum for his domestic help on grounds of religious persecution against Christians in Ethiopia.[32] This led him to connect with existing NGOs such as Shea's Puebla Institute. His newfound conviction then morphed into a zealous campaign to press the U.S. government to take on the issue of religious persecution abroad more seriously. It was, in one observer's words, a rare example of an "individual initiative taking Washington by storm."[33]

Despite the setback concerning China, the movement toward passing the IRFA began to galvanize. In January 1996, the National Association of Evangelicals (NAE) issued an influential statement of conscience.[34] Principally drafted by Horowitz, it included an extensive call to action addressed to various arms of the U.S. government, which included, among others, a call for the appointment of "a knowledgeable, experienced and compassionate Special Advisor to the President for Religious Liberty charged with preparing a report indicating needed changes in policies dealing with religious persecution and recommending remedial action."[35] This and many of the other recommendations would be incorporated in the final version of the IRFA. The statement triggered several congressional hearings on the subject of religious freedom, with a hearing separately focused on Christians, Jews, and Iranian Baha'is together with a general inquiry into the problem of religious persecution in the Middle East.[36] For Muslims, only Bosnians and the ethnic Uighurs in China appeared on the persecuted list. Militant Islam, alongside communism, became the bogeyman of both public and private religious freedom advocates. Indeed, if the literature cited by different legislators during the hearings was any indication, the campaign was clearly and foremost an effort to save persecuted Christians abroad against the scourge of communism and radical Islam. Most popular were Nina Shea's "In the Lion's Den" and Paul Marshall's *Their Blood Cries Out*.[37] Both were the go-to authorities for the main sound bite of the Horowitz-and-Shea-led campaign that "more Christians have died for their faith in the 20th century than in all other previous centuries combined,"[38] a claim critics derided as simplistic hype.

The campaign's increasing momentum both inside and outside Congress was not lost on the State Department. It was prompted to create an Advisory Committee on Religious Freedom Abroad in November 1996, the principal task of which was to advise the secretary of state on the enhancement, protection, and promotion of religious freedom abroad.[39] In addition, upon congressional request, it also released a report on all existing U.S. policies and actions concerning global religious freedom. Not surprisingly, the report was focused on the plight of Christians, as the title of the report itself indicates.[40] These policies ranged from purely executive branch actions (such as raising the religious freedom issue directly with fellow heads of state,[41] streamlining asylum conditions,[42] foreign assistance provision,[43] and the creation of the advisory committee itself[44]) to actions undertaken as part of its multilateral diplomacy (such as U.S. diplomatic activities on behalf of religious freedom in the UN Human Rights Commission and the General Assembly). The report's annex also listed religious freedom–related actions by the U.S. government in specific countries.

To private groups and several representatives devoted to the issue, however, these measures, because of their ad hoc and temporary nature, seemed inadequate. The executive was "always subordinating human rights to some other consideration. Whenever there is an array of issues on the table, human rights gets thrown to the back of the bus."[45] Clearly, the Chinese MFN debacle was still fresh in congressional memory. But in the same way that the Chinese MFN episode persisted as a reminder of the perennially low priority status given to human rights by the White House, the Jackson-Vanik amendment stood as a source of inspiration for public and private advocates alike. It provided a template for a successful results-oriented human rights mobilization. On the one hand, it showed the need for a religion-neutral language.[46] Jackson-Vanik, though intended primarily to aid Soviet Jewry, employed the universal language of free emigration and religious freedom. On the other hand, it also justified the utility of focusing on a specific cause or constituency. More important, it was proof that legislation made a difference.

The solution therefore was to draft a statute. Pursuant to the motivations of its early proponents, it was expressly intended to address the problem of religious persecution abroad[47] and not necessarily to cultivate a broader climate conducive for religious freedom. A number of consequences necessarily follow from this distinction, one of which was the shape of an effective enforcement regime that would implement the legislation. Thomas Farr, for example, argues that this was the main difference between the Wolf-Specter bill and the contending Nickles-Lieberman bill, which would eventually become the basis of the IRFA as enacted.[48]

The initial bill proposed by Wolf and cosponsored by Republican Senator Arlen Specter, aptly titled the Freedom from Religious Persecution Act (also known as the Wolf-Specter bill), was the legislative embodiment of the call to action of the NAE 1996 Statement of Conscience. It was instantly met by strong opposition from a variety of sectors—the White House, the State Department, the business community, and several members of Congress. The proposed legislation had two key features: First, it created an office of religious persecution monitoring inside the White House, thus by implication putting it outside the State Department,[49] and second, it introduced a variety of mechanisms to prod foreign governments into action regarding the state of religious persecution in their respective countries, chiefly through the employment of sanctions and termination of nonhumanitarian aid.[50] It also sought to adjust existing criteria used by immigration authorities in order to grant expedited asylum for those seeking it on the ground of religious persecution.[51] The goal, as Horowitz explained, was to expose the otherwise marginalized issue of religious persecution abroad in the highest policymaking circles and, in the process, exact accountability from its violators using the different tools available to the U.S. government.[52]

But what were considered the key features of the bill were the very sources of opposition to it. John Shattuck, the lead human rights official of the Clinton administration in his capacity as assistant secretary of the Bureau of Democracy, Human Rights and Labor in the State Department, voiced his concern during the hearings on the Wolf-Specter bill that it "takes a one-size-fits-all approach to religious persecution." He described it as a blunt instrument that "provide[s] no flexibility—sanctions would be automatic"[53] and that "by creating the position of Director, the bill would duplicate existing State Department functions."[54] Shattuck's concerns predictably revolved around the preservation of that wide latitude for maneuver deemed essential for the effective conduct of foreign relations. The bill, for instance, authorizes the director of the Office of Religious Persecution Monitoring to make a determination whether a particular country is engaged in religious persecution, which would then trigger the automatic imposition of sanctions. The president, under particular circumstances and after following certain procedures, could waive the imposition of sanctions,[55] but only the director would have the power to terminate them,[56] a rather disproportionate concentration of authority in one person. The idea of automatic sanctions also elicited a frank remark from President Clinton himself when he stated that it would put pressure on officials to "fudge an evaluation of the facts of what is going on"[57] in order to maintain the necessary flexibility for diplomatic conduct.

But for Wolf, Horowitz, and other supporters of the bill, a blunt instrument was precisely what was needed in order to achieve the purpose of reducing and eliminating religious persecution abroad. It would serve as a stern warning to foreign governments that the U.S. government is serious about ending global religious persecution and at the same time also hammer home the message to its domestic skeptics that it was a serious problem that needed addressing. To illustrate, the decision to place the Office of Religious Persecution Monitoring outside the State Department was not only a deliberate move to show their distrust of the department, a skepticism that would produce the USCIRF, but was also designed to ensure that the issue of religious freedom would remain visible to the highest officials in the executive branch.

In addition to the institutional difficulties presented by the proposed bill, Shattuck also challenged the notion that religious freedom was exceptional in the wide panoply of human rights. Even as he emphasized that addressing religious persecution was a foreign policy priority, he also warned that the bill created a de facto hierarchy of human rights that would compromise the government's ability to protect all other basic civil and political rights abroad.[58] Proponents of a global religious freedom bill, regardless of their views on Wolf-Specter, denied the charge and characterized the effort as simply restoring the issue to a visible place in the national agenda. This charge would stick even with the final version of the IRFA.

Certain that the Wolf-Specter bill would never pass in the Senate, a separate group of legislative staffers had begun crafting an alternative bill.[59] Don Nickles, a Republican from Oklahoma, picked up the main sponsorship duties, along with Joseph Lieberman, a Democrat from Connecticut, for what would be known as the Nickles-Lieberman bill. Led by John Hanford, then an aide to Senator Richard Lugar, the drafters of the Nickles-Lieberman bill worked largely in secret, much to the consternation of Horowitz and the supporters of Wolf-Specter. When the alternative bill made its debut in a March 1998 hearing of the Senate Foreign Relations Committee, it found a more receptive audience. The Nickles-Lieberman bill corrected what were deemed to be the objectionable features of Wolf-Specter by building on existing mechanisms. For instance, it used the definition of religious persecution under Article 18 of the UDHR and Article 18 of the ICCPR,[60] and returned the proposed Office of International Religious Freedom (OIRF) to the State Department.[61] For the sake of flexibility, it expanded the number of measures available to the president to address reports of such violations by providing a menu of sixteen calibrated actions, ranging from a private demarche to a cutoff of economic relations.[62] It also established the USCIRF as a federal independent body tasked with the consideration of the report issued by the OIRF and to make separate recommendations to the president.[63] This was salvaged from an aborted proposal of a Senate task force in an earlier effort to revise the Wolf-Specter bill. As Horowitz shifted his position on the Nickles-Lieberman bill from one of opposition to vigorous support,[64] he also ensured the inclusion of the USCIRF, patterned after the U.S. Civil Rights Commission, to institutionalize what was essentially a deep-seated distrust of the State Department. In other words, the USCIRF would function as a check against the OIRF. President Clinton, no doubt influenced by the upcoming midterm election and burdened with an ongoing scandal, signed the bill into law with several reservations three weeks after the Senate vote.[65]

The seemingly lopsided final vote in favor of the IRFA—it passed 98 to 0 in the Senate and 375 to 41 in the House—obscured a tortuous path marked with acrimonious debates before its passage. But these debates focused by and large on the appropriate methods by which the right to religious freedom should be promoted or secured abroad. Part of the reason why the IRFA enjoyed such wide congressional support was that everyone involved, including influential members of religious civil society who had earlier expressed support for Wolf-Specter, such as the Southern Baptist Convention, the Episcopal Church, and the American Jewish Committee, held the view that a law—any law, in fact—using U.S. influence as the government monitored and responded to violations of this particular human right was necessary.[66] The campaign for global religious freedom was propelled by momentum occurring simultaneously inside and outside Capitol Hill. Hence, assertions that the statute was mainly a product of the lobbying efforts of the Christian right are plain wrong.[67] What was lost in the discussions, however, was the first-order question of whether the United States indeed had an obligation to promote religious freedom abroad, whether by itself or as part of a pantheon of basic rights and freedoms.

Congress justified the official concern to reduce or eradicate religious persecution abroad on American exceptionalist terms. This belief was shared by all those who supported the bill. In the same hearing when the Wolf-Specter bill was first announced, for instance, Senator Sam Brownback stated that, "as Americans, I believe that we have a unique obligation to speak out against religious persecution. . . . We must not fail to defend a principle that our Founding Fathers viewed as fundamental to our democracy. . . . To fail to protect those who suffer persecution would be to repudiate our convictions before the world."[68] He was not the only one who sought to characterize the nascent IRFA as an American moral responsibility. As early as 1993, Tom Lantos had argued that the United States, as "a country that has made the championing of religious freedom a defining trait of its national character," cannot turn "a blind eye to the denial of this most basic human right."[69] Indeed, during a consultation over the implications of the newly enacted IRFA, Hanford candidly admitted that, "while many nations may not like it, America has long maintained as part of its agenda to meddle in other nations' affairs, in order to assert its influence where justice and basic human rights are denied."[70] That official concern found fruition in the IRFA as it established a permanent foreign policy apparatus that would strategically leverage American influence on behalf of religious freedom around the world.

In the inaugural report of the Office of International Religious Freedom in 1999,[71] a voluminous 1,000-page document on the state of religious freedom in 194 countries as mandated by the new statute, the U.S. policy of promotion of religious freedom was explained in its accompanying executive summary as follows:

> It happens when an American diplomat, sometimes at the risk of safety, presses authorities to know where the priest has been taken and why. It happens when the US speaks out in the UN Commission on Human Rights or other multilateral institutions on behalf of prisoners of conscience. It happens when a U.S. Ambassador, after discussing with a senior official his country's important strategic relationship with the U.S., raises that "one more thing"—access to the imprisoned mufti or information on the missionary who has disappeared. It happens when senior U.S. officials responsible for balancing and pursuing all of America's vital national interests make it clear that a single persecuted human being, perhaps obscure and insignificant in the grand affairs of state, matters to the world's most powerful nation.[72]

This dramatic formulation emphasized the flexing of American muscle in order to encourage a culture in which freedom to believe could flourish rather than simply punishing its violators, whether or not these violations were state-sponsored. Two criticisms nonetheless stuck to the statute even in its drastically revised version.[73] Coming from domestic critics, the first was that the IRFA created an irrational hierarchy of human rights in U.S. foreign relations that made the act "vulnerable to politicization and the abuse of the human rights agenda."[74] Another described the unilateral approach as a failure of international cooperation and only served to weaken existing multilateral regimes. Outside the United States, the IRFA was characterized as an exercise of American imperial overreach.[75]

Despite the lofty inspiration of Jackson-Vanik, the human rights edifice that the IRFA invoked bore little resemblance to its Cold War predecessor. The fragmentation of human rights in the post–Cold War years gave the idea a distinct home in its many guises: as a philosophy, a discourse, a social movement, and a legal regime.[76] Two decades before, human rights provided the individual a language of global morality where salvation, for the most part, lay beyond the state. After the collapse of the Berlin wall, the same language of global morality would be enforced both inside and outside sovereign states through a proliferation of international committees, transnational courts, and domestic human rights institutions such as the very regime that the passage of the IRFA had inaugurated. The momentum of the 1970s might have sowed the seeds for such a transformation, but it was only upon the thawing of Cold War tensions that its present-day polycentric incarnation could fully materialize.

The result was that contemporary human rights norms adoption and enforcement in the international order occur in multiple directions. Viewed in this way, unilateralism is not always problematic, especially if such an approach is employed in order to enforce recognized international human rights norms.[77] To the contrary, a unilateral approach, whether by imposition of sanctions or other means and if used properly, might aid the internalization of these norms by forcing political attention to it. Another question was whether enacting the IRFA indeed created a hierarchy of human rights and, if so, ascertaining what that entails. Supporters of the statute have consistently claimed that what it does is simply "mainstream" religious liberty as a foreign policy concern given its relatively neglected prior status.[78] Doing so does not marginalize related freedoms but instead cultivates them, especially those freedoms necessary to facilitate freedom of belief such as the rights to free speech and expression and public assembly. Opponents deplored singling out religious freedom instead of promoting human rights as a whole because, among others, "human rights is premised on fundamental principles of human dignity, liberty and equality" and therefore should not be subject to the usual trade-offs in weighing policy considerations.[79] Putting an undue priority on religious freedom might therefore relegate the task of promoting other equally important civil rights and liberties on a lower plane.

But this characterization of human rights mistakenly treats it as a set of trump cards, the function of which is to bring political disputes to closure and conclusion.[80] As a set of legal, moral, and political claims that limit the exercise of state sovereignty, human rights are a product of historical and contingent political processes.[81] They should therefore be seen instead as offering a vocabulary and a set of institutional arrangements for further dialogue and contestation. Human rights are also not a monolith nor are they a single indivisible set of rights.[82] Rather they are a set of fragmented and possibly conflicting ones.[83] When rights conflict, balancing becomes inevitable.[84] That the U.S. government singled out the right to religious freedom as a policy choice does not necessarily mean that other similar rights are less important. It is worth noting that the creation of various other ambassadors-at-large positions to focus on specific issues such as war crimes, counterterrorism, AIDS, women's issues, and global trafficking of persons did not invite the same magnitude of criticism that one focusing on religious freedom did.[85]

In the wake of the tragic events of September 11, 2001, President George W. Bush and his national security team recalibrated American foreign policy at the dawn of the global war on terror and embodied it in the National Security Strategy (NSS) of 2002. The NSS traces its intellectual history to the world of the same group of cold warriors that once occupied the Senate office of Scoop Jackson during the period of détente with the Soviet Union. It elevated the strategies of preemption and unilateralism in the pursuit of a free international order, one that is guaranteed by American military and economic power. Continuing a century-old American tradition, freedom of worship once again occupied a prominent place in that strategy. Consequently, one of its declared means to achieve that goal was "to take special efforts to promote freedom of religion and conscience and defend it from encroachment of repressive governments."[86]

And in Iraq, that was exactly what the U.S. government did.

Human Rights and the Road to the Iraqi TAL

The road from September 11 to the invasion of Baghdad was short.[87] Starting from what turned out to be nonexistent weapons of mass destruction (WMDs), one justification after another disappeared until the only one that remained was the restoration of democracy and promotion of human rights in Iraq.[88] That these rights were certainly nonexistent throughout the three decades of iron-fisted rule by Saddam Hussein made it a rather compelling argument for the rebuilding of Iraq. But the Bush administration also had a particular vision of what a post-Saddam Iraq would look like—a model Arab secular democracy that protected individual rights and guaranteed religious freedom and gender equality—one that could fit into President Bush's "forward strategy of freedom in the greater Middle East."[89] This vision failed, however, to take into account the role of religion, Islam in this case, in setting the bounds of acceptable constitutional politics. In the end, the American plan for a secular and democratic Iraq grudgingly gave way to the emergence of an Islamic democracy that nonetheless guaranteed minority religious freedoms and women's rights.

The constitutional experiment in Iraq was not the first of its kind. In January 2004, the Afghan constitution, likewise written in the aftermath of an American military operation against the erstwhile ruling Taliban government, enshrined a constitutional synthesis between Islam and democracy. The constitution declared Afghanistan an Islamic republic, establishing Islam as a state religion and including a nonrepugnancy clause stating that no law can be contrary to Islam.[90] At the same time, it also guaranteed its citizens several fundamental rights and liberties, including religious freedom for those belonging to other faiths.[91] Nonetheless, the broader picture enveloping the two situations could not be any different. Many accounts critical of the American twenty-first-century foray into the Middle East trace countless difficulties in the transition process to the "original sin" of occupation.[92] Operation Iraqi Freedom was a controversial war that did not attract broad international support, including that of the United Nations. As a result, the United States found itself practically alone with the extraordinarily comprehensive authority of an occupying power as soon as its forces reached Baghdad, an authority later recognized though not endorsed by UN Security Council Resolution 1483.[93]

The window of opportunity in which the possibilities of remaking Iraq seemed to abound, notwithstanding the occupation's frantic early days under the ORHA, lasted only a short while. Indecision on the ground in Iraq and infighting in Washington dogged the process. Aside from the general guideline of setting Iraq on a path to democratic self-government, no agreement within the U.S. government was reached on how to achieve such goal. In fact, no post-conflict plan, save for a quick transfer of power to a group of Iraqi exiles, existed. As Bremer recalled, he was instructed by President Bush to "[g]et over there and give us your recommendation."[94] Cobbled together hastily, the initial CPA postwar reconstruction plan was nevertheless ambitious. It involved extensive nation building, a process that would necessarily involve a delayed transfer of sovereignty to Iraqi hands,[95] whether by direct elections or otherwise. One reason motivating the officials in Washington was that the only way to get a nontheocratic system was to go slowly. At the time, the only organized and well-funded political organization was the Islamist group called the Supreme Council of Islamic Revolution in Iraq (SCIRI), which was rumored to be funded and influenced by the Iranian government.

Alongside the obvious practical difficulties of holding an election, Bremer shared the view that the United States should proceed slowly. He thought it imperative to establish first what he termed the shock absorbers of society, which would mediate the power of the state and help protect individual rights.[96] When asked by Senator Lincoln Chaffee at a Senate Foreign Relations Committee hearing if there was an American plan for a scenario in which the Iraqis elected an "Iranian-style theocracy," he even briefly entertained the hopeful notion that "fewer than 33 percent of the people in Iraq even want an established religion."[97] Bremer was careful to note, however, that the CPA believed it was important for the constitution to be written by Iraqis.[98]

The CPA placed great emphasis on the writing of a new constitution from the outset. A constitution was seen as a vital prerequisite before any transfer of power could be made to any Iraqi body, so that it could concretely define the boundaries of Iraqi political life.[99] It would establish the structure of the new government; enshrine the basic principles of democracy, including individual rights; and ensure national unity. Rory Stewart, a British diplomat who was assigned as a deputy governor of two of Iraq's provinces, recounted how Bremer fervently believed that the TAL would become an important part of the new Iraq, a proud part of the nation's identity, just as the U.S. Constitution had become central to U.S. identity.[100]

In Bremer's seven-point plan, which appeared in the *Washington Post* in September 2003, a new constitution was indeed the focal point of American efforts to restore Iraqi sovereignty.[101] The CPA plan included the creation of the Iraqi Governing Council (IGC), a twenty-five-member group representing different sectors of Iraqi society and intended to put an Iraqi face to the occupation.[102] The IGC, in turn, would convene a preparatory committee that would propose a system for writing the constitution. In the meantime, the IGC would be given an increased number of day-to-day responsibilities together with appointed local deputies to oversee several government ministries. After the constitution was written, it would be circulated and debated by the Iraqi people and endorsed accordingly in a referendum. Only after elections had been held and concluded would the CPA be dissolved and the reins of government handed to the elected Iraqis. Bremer did not include a specific timetable, but it was, at the very least, a two-year plan.

The plan did not sit well with Washington. Bremer did not consult anybody before it was published and, worse, it also implied an extended U.S. presence that could very well last beyond the November 2004 U.S. presidential elections, a deadline important to President Bush. But U.S. officials halfway across the world were not the only ones unhappy about the CPA plan. Iraqis obviously were not happy either. Although the CPA had initially managed to ignore Sistani's June 2003 *fatwa*—at one point, high-ranking CPA officials thought they could get Sistani to change his mind or worse, to have another ayatollah issue a contradictory *fatwa*[103]—they could not do so any longer by November. The inordinate delay in the consideration of the Sistani *fatwa* was perhaps the best indication of a lack of appreciation, much less proper understanding, on the part of the CPA of the importance of Islam's role; Sistani's commitment to the preservation of that role in Iraqi society and government; and, for that matter, the role of Sistani himself. The *fatwa* called for a constitution drafted by elected representatives, an entirely reasonable demand based on democratic principles that the United States had purported to be standing for in Iraq. Even the preparatory committee felt constrained. And the *fatwa* was all but law as far as the Shi'i bloc in the IGC was concerned, even though they themselves favored a quick handover of power.

Despite his earlier concerns about heeding the *fatwa*, Bremer had no choice but to face the reality of the Iraqi situation and change course.[104] To make matters more complicated, both the State and Defense departments changed their views about going slowly in Iraq. Both had started pressuring the CPA with their own ideas and proposals for an early transfer of sovereignty.[105] And while everyone was looking for the quickest route to end the occupation, the level of violence throughout the country was increasing. The Americans did not help themselves by their inability to provide local security and basic services. Faced with a dwindling set of options and time running out fast, Bremer buckled under pressure and discarded his seven-point plan. His team came up with an alternative plan to have the IGC itself write an interim constitution by March 2004. A transitional assembly would be chosen via provincial and local caucuses by the end of May. The United Nations, previously sidelined by the U.S. government, was asked to help oversee the transition process, no doubt an attempt to shore up its legitimacy. The interim constitution would go into effect after the CPA handed over sovereignty to an interim government formed from the members of the transitional assembly on June 2004. National elections would be held the following year for the convention tasked to draft the permanent constitution. After obtaining the requisite approval from Washington for the revised plan, the CPA and the IGC stipulated these terms, among others, in the November 15 Agreement, which set out the important points and principles of the new and accelerated road map toward Iraqi sovereignty.[106]

The Transitional Administrative Law was the fundamental law envisioned in the agreement and was so-called only to avoid going against Sistani's *fatwa,* though it was an interim constitution in all but name. It was intended to enshrine the principles that would provide guidance during the transitional period, including a bill of rights that would guarantee equality and basic freedoms for all Iraqis.[107] It was also widely understood that the TAL would serve as a model for a future permanent constitution, so various factions in the IGC fought tooth and nail to have their respective interests protected and guaranteed in the document. At that point, nobody was certain if there was going to be a permanent constitution.

Islam was not the most contentious issue in the drafting process. That accolade easily belonged to federalism. But as far as those outside Iraq were concerned and considering that the promotion of human rights was a raison d'être of the U.S. occupation, religion was a rather important issue. It certainly was for the CPA. When he was contemplating the demand of the Sistani *fatwa,* Bremer privately worried what the CPA would do if Sistani became more emboldened and asked that Shari'a law be applied throughout Iraq.[108] In December 2003, the IGC, under the rotating presidency of Abdul al-Aziz al-Hakim of the main Shi'i Islamist group, SCIRI, had passed GC Resolution 137, which sought to apply Islamic law to all matters of family law in Iraq according to the individual's specific religious affiliation within Islam. The resolution declared invalid all previous laws, decisions, and directions regarding family law that was contrary to Islamic law. Essentially, it was a revocation of the 1959 Family Code, which provided a unified system of rules applicable to all Muslim Iraqis regardless of their personal beliefs.[109] Iraq's Shi'i clerics had been chafing against the code since its enactment because of the eclectic way the statute was put together, mixing strands from different Islamic jurisprudential schools and then requiring all Iraqi Muslims to adhere to it. But the code also guaranteed more rights for women; when Resolution 137 sought a return to the precode situation, most mistakenly concluded that this would be an imposition of shari'a law, with all its negative connotations. The SCIRI ploy generated controversy both inside and outside Iraq, and Bremer publicly refused to sign the resolution, which was necessary to give it legal effect.[110]

Given this preview, U.S. officials in both Washington and Baghdad were predictably anxious about the shape and form that Islam would take in the TAL, for two reasons. First, Iraq was to serve as an experiment in democracy and human rights, and thus become a beacon of hope in the Middle

East. But a more geopolitically relevant reason was that the Shi'i majority in Iraq could prove to be vulnerable to Iranian influence, a not implausible probability. Remarkably enough, curbing the role of Islam in the incipient Iraqi constitutional order became a point of convergence for interest groups as diverse as secular international human rights organizations and the Christian right in the United States, the same groups that were at loggerheads during the drafting of the IRFA.

Legal scholar Noah Feldman pointed out the irony for those belonging to the Christian right to be pushing for a secular Iraqi constitution, given its own domestic predilections about the U.S. Constitution not being a secular document, and finding such an arrangement not incompatible with notions of democracy.[111] They were also the constituency with direct access to the powers in Washington: Congress and President Bush himself. In a September 2003 Senate Foreign Relations Committee hearing for the release of Iraq reconstruction funds, a conspicuous concern among the senators present, including well-known evangelical and later Roman Catholic convert Sam Brownback of Kansas, was whether the CPA had a plan in place should the Iraqis elect an Iranian-like, anti-American theocratic regime.[112] Brownback and Frank Wolf subsequently sought to condition the release of these funds on the guarantee that a religious freedom provision be included in a not-yet-drafted Iraqi constitution, stating that there is a "need to have that separation of mosque and state."[113] President Bush, an avowed born-again Christian evangelical, also conveyed to Bremer and the IGC members the importance of including a religious liberty provision in the TAL.[114] "I'd like to be sure that if I came to Iraq as a Christian, I would be free to practice my religion," said the president, directing his remarks to al-Hakim, the Islamist in the delegation. Al-Hakim seemed taken aback by the statement. He emphatically stated that the rights of all religious groups in Iraq were respected. Speaking in a television interview, Bush later assured his domestic audience, though perhaps also himself, that the Iraqis would not establish an extremist Islamic regime because that was what the IGC members who visited the White House promised him.[115]

Meanwhile, in Iraq, Bremer declared that the TAL "won't be an Islamic constitution" and warned that he would exercise his veto power on any attempts to make Islam "the" sole source of legislation.[116] The fact that U.S. officials even seriously considered omitting any mention of Islam in the TAL, much less prohibiting its establishment as a state religion, seemingly betrayed earlier American declarations that Iraqis would write their own constitution. While the drafting process could not be accurately described as an imposition reminiscent of MacArthur's example in Japan, the CPA did not simply facilitate its writing either.[117] The asymmetry of power in the room was not lost on the members of IGC. But the reality was that no such constitution would be deemed legitimate in Iraq. All previous Iraqi constitutions included a declaration of Islam as the state religion, and almost all Arab constitutions contain the same provision. As Feldman noted, even the secular communists in the IGC did not offer any objection to the designation of Islam as the official state religion.[118]

With that option off the table, the question turned on how best to protect members of minority religions and guarantee equal rights for women even with an established religion. While Islam was established as a state religion in previous Iraqi constitutions, it was not made a source of law in the same manner as Article 2 of the Egyptian constitution. The debate boiled down to whether Islam should be *a* or *the* source of legislation.[119] The non-Islamist members of the IGC naturally resisted the latter. After much wrangling, the Shi'i Islamists agreed to the "a source of legislation" formulation, that is, one source among many. In exchange, they brought a demand for a noncontradiction clause that prohibited laws contradicting Islam or its principles to be included.[120] This set off another round of discussions with Adnan al-Pachachi, one of the IGC's liberal members and the chair of the TAL drafting committee, finally breaking the impasse with a proposal to amend the noncontradiction clause to include not only Islam but also principles of democracy and the enumerated fundamental rights.[121] Thus, the final wording of Article 7(A) read: "Islam is the official religion of the State and is to be considered a source of legislation. No law that contradicts the universally agreed tenets of Islam, the principles of democracy, or the rights cited in Chapter Two of this Law may be enacted during the transitional period. This Law respects the Islamic identity of the majority of the Iraqi people and guarantees the full religious rights of all individuals to freedom of religious belief and practice."[122] Chapter Two, Article 13 guaranteed that "[e]ach Iraqi has the right to freedom of thought, conscience and religious belief and practice. Coercion in such matters shall be prohibited."

One should not conclude from this discussion that such freedoms would have been absent if not for the American insistence on them. Indeed, if the subject of Iraqi opposition meetings abroad for the ten years or so prior to 2003 was to be any indication, individual and minority rights were a regular fixture of an Iraqi-envisioned post-Saddam Iraq. For instance, as part of the controversial Future of Iraq project, a report called *Transition to Democracy in Iraq* included protections for freedom of religion, conscience, and thought (implying an individual right) as well as the protection of religious communities.[123] Various parts of the U.S. government, however, had their own ideas about what these rights and protections should mean—from using secular Turkey as a model, likewise encouraged by secularized Iraqi opposition leaders, down to the conception of religious freedom as involving an individual right to change one's religion, a controversial issue in Islamic scholarship and in Muslim countries. Under traditional Islamic law, a Muslim could not change his or her religion. Although there are also Islamic sources that prohibit compulsion in religion, apostasy remains a crime punishable by death in some Muslim countries. Given the historical association of Christian proselytizing in the Middle East with the all-too-recent memory of Western colonialism, the origins of this reticent interpretation is perhaps more complicated than what could strictly be attributed to religious doctrine.

Still, as far as the U.S. government was concerned, only a secular Iraq would be able to counter the Islamist threat. To be sure, the human rights records of other officially Islamic states such as Saudi Arabia and Pakistan were not sources of encouragement. But if the goal was to introduce democracy in Iraq, such democracy, to be accepted, would inevitably come in an Islamic package, whatever form that might take. Given the picture of Islam already pervasive in the U.S. government even before the September 11 attacks—which led to the passage of the IRFA—and especially after it, an Islamic democracy was a dangerous oxymoron.

These concerns were apparent in several U.S. official interventions made on behalf of religious freedom during the drafting of the TAL. One such intervention, by four U.S. senators who were all associated with global religious freedom causes, was sent in a letter to national security adviser Condoleezza Rice detailing their concerns regarding the circulating TAL drafts.[124] The letter singled out the document's wording that Islam was to be a source of legislation without recognizing other possibly countervailing sources such as "principles of democracy, pluralism, rule of law and individual human rights."[125] Islam, as such, they asserted, was vague and could easily be interpreted as anathema to human rights. But by the term *human rights,* they meant only its liberal individual variety. The senators conveyed their main concern that the "religious freedoms enumerated in the draft are expressed mostly in terms of group rights rather than the rights of individuals" and offered an alternative text to protect such rights. The letter gave the example of an individual Muslim woman who would not be able to "opt out of Islamic dress codes, or discriminatory inheritances and forced marriages" without an explicit individual right to religious freedom.[126]

In his analysis of a later TAL draft, Middle East Studies scholar Nathan Brown attributed the change in the wording of Article 13 to mean individual religious freedom—a departure from the regional conception of religious freedom as a communal right—to the abovementioned letter.[127] The senators were not the only ones, however, airing such concern. The USCIRF also sent a letter, this time addressed directly to Bremer, requesting that the TAL be amended to include an "explicit guarantee that everyone has the right to freedom of thought, conscience and religion" and an "explicit commitment to protect the fundamental rights and freedoms of individuals."[128] The USCIRF request focused on the importance of rights that would facilitate free expression and public debate without which Iraqis could be subjected to accusations of blasphemy, apostasy, or offending Islam.

Apart from President Bush's personal intervention on behalf of religious liberty, there was no clear evidence that the CPA, as the entity directly overseeing the writing of the TAL, brought the message of these letters into the drafting room. But it did not have to. The major themes of the 2002 National Security Strategy—hegemony, preemption, the conflation of power and principle, and the promotion of democracy and human rights as antidotes to the scourge of terrorism—were not new products of the post–September 11 world. They were the main intellectual strands that arose from the glaring fissures left by the collapse of the Soviet Union. Much academic writing after the end of the Cold War, the most famous of which were Samuel Huntington's *Clash of Civilizations* and Francis Fukuyama's *End of History*, attempted to map out what lay ahead, only to be proven both wrong and right down the road. This unparalleled vista from which the United States could look at the rest of the world fueled groups as disparate as veteran, if nostalgic, cold warriors in the U.S. Congress agitating on behalf of religious freedom for Chinese citizens and prompted influential conservatives to establish think tanks such as the Project for the New American Century (PNAC). Many would find themselves in official positions in the administration of George W. Bush arguing for U.S. global military dominance.[129]

These conservatives were realists, not starry-eyed human rights activists. Even Richard Perle, a member and contributor to PNAC, an influential figure in the Bush administration as member of the Defense Policy Board, and Scoop Jackson's aide during the Jackson-Vanik episode in the 1970s, saw the JVA not only for its human rights consequences but primarily for what it represented: an American offensive against the Soviet Union.[130] But in Iraq, their interests coincided. A democratic Iraq and guaranteed rights and freedoms for individual Iraqis reflected varied American notions of what it means to be a leader of a fractured world order. That both the Iraq Liberation Act and the International Religious Freedom Act were passed by the same Congress in 1998 testified to this convergence. The attacks of September 11 finally gave clarity of purpose to post–Cold War U.S. foreign policy.

It seems less an important question then to ask if the IRFA would have made any difference during the TAL drafting episode. They were both products of the post–Cold War milieu. Questions such as whether Islam and democracy could be made compatible were only possible in this environment. In any case, Bremer shared all these concerns himself and made sure that the TAL respected individual rights of all Iraqis, especially non-Muslims and women,[131] thus completing the circle on what amounted to an incredible American effort to marginalize official Islam in Iraq. Taken together, these efforts show a significant convergence of official thinking on religious freedom as a means to serve national security interests. Shortly afterward, the State Department removed Iraq's designation as a country of particular concern (the language of the IRFA) for 2004, which covered the U.S. overthrow of the Saddam Hussein regime.

For a constitutional provision that most legal and political commentators agree is largely symbolic,[132] the position of Islam in the Iraqi TAL generated a disproportionate amount of effort and attention, not only from the Iraqis themselves but especially from the U.S. officials anxious to leave with the goal of a democratic Iraq accomplished. But judging from the way U.S. officials closely followed and drew the outer limits within which religious identities could be expressed in a constitutional document, it is hardly an exaggeration to say that the accomplishment of an Islamic democracy in Iraq was far from symbolic. Perhaps more for the Americans rather than the Iraqis, it was a realization that democracy and the protection of individual rights need not and could not come in one shape and size.

By enacting the IRFA into law and ensuring that adequate religious freedom guarantees were written into the Iraqi TAL, the U.S. government brought together its old and new ways of promoting international religious freedom. The IRFA is the culmination of a long American tradition of advocating for religious freedom through and by law, but it also represented a new form of enforcing international human rights norms, that is, by unilateral effort, and one that would be subsequently emulated by several other Western governments. The old way had involved participation in standard setting, by imposition if need be, which dates to the emergence of the United States as a global power in 1898, while the new way, inaugurated by the statute creating the U.S. Helsinki Commission in the 1970s, involves continuous participation in the interpretation and implementation of those standards, and an entire foreign policy apparatus to back that endeavor. More important, this new mode involves Congress and, through it, the broader American public, which built on the institutional foundations created by a unique Cold War backdrop. Now freed from its Cold War context and constraint, however, religious freedom as one human right among many has become an enduring argument for American power. The origins and outcomes of the IRFA and the TAL were both justified and vindicated by that very goal.

What does this mean for the future of global religious freedom? And to what extent will that be further determined and shaped by the fortunes of American power? If there is anything that the contingent story of American understandings of religious freedom has indicated to us thus far, it is that the possibilities for its transformation remain open-ended, as are its consequences.

Conclusion

The spread of religious liberty in the international legal order accompanied the rise of American power. In its various guises, religious liberty responded to a felt need; it corresponded with prevailing ideologies and continues to provide an enduring ideal in the conduct of U.S. foreign relations. To say that this is purely instrumental is to fail to comprehend the powerful grip of religious freedom in the American national imagination, even though it is contested now more than ever before.[1] For a nation that wrestled and continues to render intelligible the question of what it means to be a great power and everything that such status entails, the export of this American ideal served both U.S. material and moral interests, though certainly not always in equal terms. What the history suggests is that it served as a point of confluence between the pursuit of naked national interest, on the one hand, and the aspirations of political morality, on the other, and how one can indubitably form part of the other. That was evident in U.S. efforts to include religious freedom as part of the Philippine, Japanese, and Iraqi constitutions during various periods of military occupation. Attempts by Woodrow Wilson, Franklin Roosevelt, Scoop Jackson, and the drafters of the International Religious Freedom Act to promote religious freedom outside the milieu of military occupation and establish it as the norm through international treaties and domestic legislation only illustrate the malleability and utility of religious freedom. Religious freedom is a rallying cry for the American people as well as for the rest of the world.

As the United States laid down the building blocks of international religious freedom, its promotion abroad was undertaken for different purposes. From the vantage point of American power, it proved essential in its civilizing mission in the Philippines as well as in Woodrow Wilson's effort to construct a new world order, as epitomized by the Covenant of the League of Nations. The achievement of the necessary political liberty became inextricably tied to the existence of a protestant, individualist notion of religious liberty, one that was considered to be impossible within the context of religions such as Catholicism and Islam.[2] When a similar global conflagration confronted Franklin Roosevelt, he recognized that religious liberty would play a central role in enlisting domestic support against Nazi totalitarianism, representing as it did a world antithetical to the Nazi vision. Never mind that his fragile wartime alliance also included another type of totalitarianism, that is, the Soviet kind. That would have to wait until another kind of war. What Roosevelt did realize from Wilson's mistakes was the need to ensure that his moral vision would survive the war, hence the American emphasis on including admittedly diluted human rights provisions in the foundational documents of the postwar order and consequently ensuring American participation in it. Religious freedom in these documents was not guaranteed, however, out of any primary concern for individual welfare beyond the confines of the nation-state but was based on a prior belief that democratic orders that guarantee this liberty and many other liberties for its inhabitants would create a stable international system. The American aims in the drafting of the postwar constitution of Japan were evidence of this belief.

The rediscovery of human rights and the subsequent couching of religious freedom in that language during the tumultuous decade of the 1970s became a useful weapon in the hands of the U.S. government against the Soviet communist scourge. There was never any official consensus on the role morality should play on the precarious chessboard of international Cold War diplomacy, but out of that tussle between the executive and legislative branches, a space emerged where citizens' movements could go beyond the narrow strategies devised by seasoned diplomats. It would unintentionally start a spiral of activism that would end with the fall of the Berlin Wall.[3] In its aftermath, veterans of this period reclaimed religious freedom as a human right and continued to promote its protection worldwide in the form of the International Religious Freedom Act. Bereft of a superpower rival, the promotion of religious freedom as a human right now served and continues to serve enduring American power. Post–U.S. invasion Iraq would provide yet another opportunity for the U.S. government to insist on religious freedom and separation of church and state in the interim constitution, which, though written by Iraqis, was finished under the close supervision of the Coalition Provisional Authority (CPA). That Islam remained the established state religion despite American wishes to the contrary only illustrated the limits, not the ambitions, of American power.

Illuminating as it is to note that the path taken was marked with contingencies, what difference does it make that we understand religious freedom this way today? And more important, does it matter that it is law? The first and foremost answer is that ideas matter. It matters what kinds of narratives we subscribe to, as do the symbols and ideals with which we rally the people—ourselves. As political scientist Harold D. Lasswell stated in 1941, "[S]ymbols that release the energy of millions must be connected with a unified view of the world, a comprehensive ideology that stands out against every rival."[4] Religious freedom forms part of that ever-changing, tractable, and yet comprehensive prism with which U.S. officials view the world inasmuch as it provided a means to achieve their purposes.

But different kinds of prisms offer varying possibilities as well as constraints. For one, it might be easier to state that modern-day assertions of human rights are no more than a contemporary incarnation of civilizing missions of the past.[5] In a very wishful address before a joint session of the Philippine Congress in October 2003, President George W. Bush equated the American accomplishments in the Philippines with what awaited the American presence in Iraq.[6]

Nothing could have been more mistaken. The methods might be similar and the participants might be familiar, but the liberalism of empire is not the same as the empire of liberalism, no matter how hard we might want to make them so.[7] Civilizing missions cannot occur, as they did in the past, in an era marked by the universal language of rights and self-determination, and in a world composed not only of states but also of individuals and other nonstate groups. We care about democratic states and even more so about the freedoms and welfare of individual persons.[8] Today, everyone can use human rights language in a way that was not possible before. That alone should be a source of hope and empowerment.

But this is also a critical history. Speaking of religious freedom, using the ubiquitous language of human rights makes it susceptible to the same critiques leveled at this enterprise, particularly its claims to universality and neutrality. What the foregoing account shows is that religious freedom is no less protean, no less a political project, than other human rights. Contrary to conventional wisdom, the promotion of religious freedom abroad goes beyond the protection of religious believers in those countries.[9] It has also been sustained by a set of normative premises that did not and still does not see itself as only one form of culture among many. Losing sight of this liberal conceit paves the slippery slope to the reduction of freedom to mere rights and the unfortunate impoverishment of the broader political sphere in receiving societies.[10] That we appeal to religious freedom today as a matter of international law and not simply as good policy or good morals makes this need for sensitivity all the more urgent. Law is a distinct normative space where claims are allowed or excluded, where sanctions and denials of liberty are meted. The U.S. army officers writing the draft of the Japanese constitution had something of the nature of law in mind when they initially debated whether to allow political liberties such as freedom of speech for ecclesiastics. And Eleanor Roosevelt's position that minority protections had no place in a declaration of human rights surely had profound consequences on the current practice of religious liberty.

We are no closer to that world free from religious strife than it was to Woodrow Wilson a hundred years ago. Modern international religious freedom law might have begun as a handmaiden of empire, but its future as a universal human right is not yet written in stone. The point is not to despair. The many challenges that lie ahead of us do not allow such recourse. This book is not only meant to expose the biases and assumptions in the current international law on religious freedom as a result of decisions made in the past by a global power; but also to argue that the slow realization of religious freedom in a society is and should be a profoundly political act, one that is built on continuing deliberation, contestation, and mutual recognition. These are a few lessons we would do well to heed today.

NOTES

BIBLIOGRAPHY

ACKNOWLEDGMENTS

INDEX

Notes

Introduction

1. William Sorsby to the Secretary of State, Sept 12, 1906, in U.S. Department of State, Foreign Relations of the United States 1906, 106–107 (hereafter FRUS).
2. Mr. Hay to Mr. Bridgman, Sept 1, 1899, in FRUS 1899, 112–113. Hay was concerned with the general state of religious liberty in South American republics. A telegram of a similar nature also went out to the U.S. legations in Peru and Ecuador at around the same time.
3. Mr. Hay to Mr. Cooper, Oct 30, 1900, in FRUS 1900, 224 (China); Mr. Seward to Mr. McMath, Dec 9, 1863, in FRUS 1864, 410–434. See generally Cyrus Adler and Aaron M. Margalith, *With Firmness in the Right: American Diplomatic Action Affecting Jews, 1840–1945* (New York: The American Jewish Committee, 1946 [Ottoman Empire]); Mr. Hay to Mr. Wilson, July 17, 1902, in FRUS 1902, 905–915. Hay appealed to the provisions of the 1878 Treaty of Berlin even though the United States was not party to it, invoking its principles as natural moral principles (Romania).
4. Secretary of State to American Ambassador, Termination of Treaty of 1832 between Russia and the United States, Dec 15, 1911, in FRUS 1911, 695–699.
5. For example, Noah Feldman, *Divided by God: America's Church-State Problem—and What We Should Do About It* (New York: Farrar, Straus and Giroux, 2005); Steven D. Smith, *The Rise and Decline of American Religious Freedom* (Cambridge, MA: Harvard University Press, 2014).
6. Mitt Romney, "Faith in America," speech delivered Dec 6, 2007, at the George Bush Presidential Library, College Station, Texas. Full text is found at www.npr.org/templates/story/story.php?storyId=16969460.
7. For the debate about whether this is desirable, see Thomas Farr, "International Religious Freedom and Moral Responsibility," in Gerard V. Bradley, ed., *Challenges to Religious Liberty in the Twenty-First Century* (2012); Chris Seiple and

Dennis Hoover, "Religious Freedom and Global Security," in Allen Hertzke, ed., *The Future of Religious Freedom: Global Challenges* (New York: Oxford University Press, 2013), 315–327. But see Elizabeth Shakman Hurd, "The Global Securitization of Religion, The Immanent Frame," March 23, 2010, http://blogs.ssrc.org/tif/2010/03/23/global-securitization/.

8. Eric Hobsbawm, *On Empire: America, War and Global Supremacy* (New York: Pantheon Books, 2008), viii.
9. For the lone exception, see John Noonan, *The Lustre of Our Country: The American Experience of Religious Freedom* (Berkeley: University of California Press, 1998), 263–356. However, this account suffers somewhat from a triumphalist tone and ignores the historical and imperial contexts of religious freedom as a matter of American export.
10. I use the term *international law on religious freedom* expansively, including not only international documents on religious freedom such as the UN Declaration on Human Rights or the League of Nations Covenant but also provisions in national constitutions and regional conventions that form the building blocks of the international regime. For an example of such use of the term, see Anat Scolnicov, *The Right to Religious Freedom in International Law: Between Group Rights and Individual Rights* (London: Routledge, 2011). The only existing account of religious freedom in international law is in Malcolm Evans, *Religious Liberty and International Law in Europe* (New York: Cambridge University Press, 1997). A more philosophical-historical investigation is found in Peter Danchin, "The Emergence and Structure of Religious Freedom in International Law Reconsidered," *Journal of Law and Religion* 23, no. 2 (2007): 455–534.
11. Because they did not always see religious liberty in the same way, government and missionaries often entered into a fragile entente so that each side could accomplish its goal. See Elizabeth Foster, *Faith in Empire: Religion, Politics and Colonial Rule in French Senegal,* 1880–1940 (Stanford, CA: Stanford University Press, 2013); Heather Sharkey, *American Evangelicals in Egypt: Missionary Encounters in an Age of Empire* (Princeton, NJ: Princeton University Press, 2008); Andrew Porter, *Religion versus Empire? British Protestant Missionaries and Overseas Expansion, 1700–1914* (Manchester: Manchester University Press 2004); Davide Rodogno, *Against Massacre: Humanitarian Interventions in the Ottoman Empire, 1815–1914* (Princeton, NJ: Princeton University Press, 2012).
12. Saba Mahmood and Peter C. Danchin, eds., "Politics of Religious Freedom: Contested Genealogies," Special Issue, *The South Atlantic Quarterly* 113, no. 1 (2014); see also Saba Mahmood, "Religious Freedom, the Minority Question and Geopolitics in the Middle East," *Comparative Studies in Society and History* 54, no. 2 (2012): 418–446.

13. See Samuel Moyn, *The Last Utopia: Human Rights in History* (Cambridge, MA: Belknap Press of Harvard University Press, 2010).
14. See, for example, W. Cole Durham Jr., Matthew K. Richards, and Donlu D. Thayer, "The Status of and Threats to International Law on Freedom of Religion of Belief," in Hertzke, *The Future of Religious Freedom*, 31–32.
15. Canada Office of Religious Freedom, available at www.international.gc.ca /religious_freedom-liberte_de_religion/; Commission of the Bishops' Conferences of the European Community, A Compilation Report on Religious Freedom at the European Parliament and the European External Action Service, Jan 2010–Sept 2012 (compiling EU Parliament resolutions and recommendations on religious freedom insofar as EU External Relations is concerned), available at www.comece.org/site/en/activities/policyareas /fundamentalrights/religiousfreedom/article/5321.html?SWS=8ddf1b9e9f9a 9240ae1a07ac6b8fcbf9; Pasquale Annicchino, "Recent Developments Concerning the Promotion of Freedom of Religion or Belief in Italian Foreign Policy," *Review of Faith and International Affairs* 11, no. 3 (2013): 61–68.
16. Nehal Bhuta, "Two Concepts of Religious Freedom in the European Court of Human Rights," *South Atlantic Quarterly* 113, no. 1, pp. 10–36 (2014); Samuel Moyn, "From Communist to Muslim: European Human Rights, the Cold War and Religious Liberty," *South Atlantic Quarterly*, 113, no. 1, pp. 63–86 (2014).
17. See Moyn, *The Last Utopia*.
18. See, for example, Mark Mazower, *No Enchanted Palace: The End of Empire and the Ideological Origins of the United Nations* (Princeton: Princeton University Press, 2009). On the imperial contexts of the spread of religious freedom, see Mahmood, "Religious Freedom."
19. See Chapter 4 of this book for an illustration.
20. Paul A. Kramer, "Power and Connection: Imperial Histories of the United States in the World," *American Historical Review* 116, no. 5 (2011): 1348–1391, 1349.
21. A pioneering introduction for this "new international history" approach is found in Thomas Bender, ed., *Rethinking American History in a Global Age* (Berkeley: University of California Press, 2002). Examples exist in abundance today. See, for example, David Armitage, *The Declaration of Independence: A Global History* (Cambridge, MA: Harvard University Press, 2007); Erez Manela, *The Wilsonian Moment: Self-Determination and the International Origins of Anticolonial Nationalism* (New York: Oxford University Press, 2007); Sarah Snyder, *Human Rights Activism and the End of the Cold War* (New York: Cambridge University Press, 2011). In legal scholarship, some examples are David Golove and Daniel Hulsebosch, "A Civilized Nation: The Early American Constitution, the Law of Nations, and the Pursuit of International Recognition," *New York University Law Review* 85, no. 4 (2010): 932–1066; Mary

Dudziak, *Cold War Civil Rights: Race and the Image of American Democracy* (Princeton, NJ: Princeton University Press, 2000). Many of these are about the import, the international reception, and transnational cross-fertilization of norms and ideas, not the export of them, which this book focuses on.

22. A magisterial treatment is Andrew Preston, *Sword of the Spirit, Shield of Faith: Religion in American War and Diplomacy* (New York: Knopf, 2012); see also Daniel Walker Howe, *What Hath God Wrought: The Transformation of America, 1815–1848* (New York: Oxford University Press, 2007); Michael Oren, *Power, Faith, and Fantasy: America in the Middle East, 1776 to the Present* (New York: W. W. Norton & Co., 2007).
23. For the claim that American foreign relations is largely shaped by American culture, see Walter Hixson, *The Myth of American Diplomacy: National Identity and American Foreign Policy* (New Haven, CT: Yale University Press, 2008); Preston, *Sword of the Spirit;* David Zietsma, "Building the Kingdom of God: Religious Discourse, National Identity and the Good Neighbor Policy, 1930–1938," *Rhetoric & Public Affairs* 11 (2008), 179–214.
24. The term is originally by Oliver Wendell Holmes., Jr., who described law "as in a magic mirror we see reflected not only our own lives but the lives of all men that have been! When I think on this magic theme, my eyes dazzle." Mark DeWolfe Howe, ed., *The Occasional Speeches of Justice Oliver Wendell Holmes* (Cambridge, MA: Harvard University Press, 1962), 20–21.
25. Preston, *Sword of the Spirit,* 8.
26. Philip Hamburger, *Separation of Church and State* (Cambridge, MA: Harvard University Press, 2002). See also Sehat, *Myth of American Religious Freedom;* Feldman, *Divided by God.*
27. For a focus on Mormons, see Sarah Barringer Gordon, *The Mormon Question: Polygamy and Constitutional Conflict in Nineteenth-Century America* (Chapel Hill, NC: University of North Carolina Press, 2002); for Catholics and Jews, see John Higham, *Strangers in the Land: Patterns of American Nativism* (New Brunswick, NJ: Rutgers University Press, 1955); for the Indians, see Francis Prucha, *The Great Father: The United States Government and the American Indians* (Lincoln: University of Nebraska Press, 1984).
28. For an elaboration of long-term history oriented toward this goal, see David Armitage and Jo Guldi, "The Return of the *Longue Durée:* An Anglo-American Perspective," *Annales, Histoire, Sciences Sociales* 69 (2014).
29. The irony produced by the settlement at Westphalia in 1648 was that, even though religious freedom for European princes became the basis of state sovereignty, the same principle of religious freedom would operate to challenge the very walls that state sovereignty had erected. See Daniel Philpott, "Religious Freedom and the Undoing of the Westphalian State," *Michigan Journal of International Law* 25, no. 4 (2004): 981.

30. On a genealogy of the concept of national security, see Andrew Preston, "Monsters Everywhere: A Genealogy of National Security," Stuart Bernath Lecture, *Diplomatic History* 38, no. 3 (2014), 477–500. Religious liberty became part of a new national security worldview during World War II.
31. See, for example, Kristine Kalanges, *Religious Liberty in Western and Islamic Law: Toward a World Legal Tradition* (New York: Oxford University Press, 2012).
32. Pew Research Project on Religion and Public Life, "Religious Hostilities Reach Six-Year High," January 12, 2014, available at http://www.pewforum.org/files/2014/01/RestrictionsV-full-report.pdf (last accessed July 31, 2014).
33. U.S. Department of State, *2013 International Religious Freedom Report,* available at http://www.state.gov/j/drl/rls/irf/religiousfreedom/index.htm#wrapper (accessed July 31, 2014).
34. See Elizabeth Shakman Hurd, "What's Wrong with Promoting Religious Freedom?," *Foreign Policy Magazine,* June 12, 2013, available at http://mideastafrica.foreignpolicy.com/posts/2013/06/12/whats_wrong_with_promoting_religious_freedom.

1. White Man's Burden

Epigraph: Speech before the Home Market Club, Boston, Massachusetts, February 16, 1899, in Speeches and Address of William F. McKinley (1900), 193.

1. For a brief background on the causes of the war, see "The War of 1898, the New Empire and the Dawn of the American Century, 1893–1901," in George C. Herring, ed., *From Colony to Superpower: U.S. Foreign Relations since 1776* (New York: Oxford University Press, 2011), 299–336.
2. Letter of Oscar F. Williams, U.S. consul in Manila to Secretary of State William R. Day, May 4, 1898, in *Reports of Rear Admiral George Dewey* (Washington, DC: U.S. Government Printing Office, 1900), 27–28.
3. For a history of expansionism as part of American nation building, see Aziz Rana, *The Two Faces of American Freedom* (Cambridge, MA: Harvard University Press, 2010); Walter Nugent, *Habits of Empire: A History of American Expansion* (New York: Alfred A. Knopf, 2008). To illustrate how and why the episode of 1898 was a break from previous expansions, see Bartholomew Sparrow, *The* Insular *Cases and the Emergence of American Empire* (Lawrence: University Press of Kansas, 2006). See also the first half of Gary Lawson and Guy Seidman, *The Constitution of Empire: Territorial Expansion and American Legal History* (New Haven, CT: Yale University Press, 2004).
4. The amendment stated, "[T]he United States hereby disclaims any disposition of intention to exercise sovereignty, jurisdiction or control over said island except for pacification thereof, and asserts its determination when

that is accomplished to leave the government and control of the island to its people." The United States occupied Cuba in all but name, however, under the military governorship of Leonard Wood until 1902. See H. Res. 233, April 18, 1898, Cong. Rec. 4041.

5. McKinley's designs on the Philippines varied from wanting to keep only the capital city of Manila as a suitable naval outpost in Asia to keeping Luzon, the largest among the islands in the Philippines, and later, because of geopolitical calculations of keeping the British and Germans at bay, to annexing all of the islands. See Frank Ninkovich, *The United States and Imperialism* (Malden, MA: Blackwell Publishers, 2001), 36. For a detailed account of the peace negotiations, see H. Wayne Morgan, ed., *Making Peace with Spain: The Diary of Whitelaw Reid* (Austin: University of Texas Press, 1965).
6. Ironically, the entire poem was read into the Congressional Record as part of a speech by anti-imperialist Senator Ben Tillman of South Carolina. See also William Jennings Bryan, ed., *Republic or Empire: The Philippine Question* (Chicago, IL: W. B. Conkey Co., 1900), 122.
7. Ninkovich, *The United States and Imperialism,* 17. Ninkovich's account focuses on the combined role of ideology and balance of power politics in the American decision to annex the Spanish insular possessions.
8. For an overview of the anti-imperialist views, see Robert Beisner, *Twelve against Empire* (New York: McGraw-Hill, 1968); E. Berkeley Tompkins, *Anti-Imperialism in the United States: The Great Debate, 1890–1920* (Philadelphia: University of Pennsylvania Press, 1970). For a focus on racial and religious arguments, see Susan K. Harris, *God's Arbiters: Americans in the Philippines* (New York: Oxford University Press, 2011).
9. The wide gamut of ideologies that were dominant and mutually reinforcing during this period ranged from Social Darwinism, Progressivism, and Protestant Christianity to racism and notions of national greatness, not unlike Manifest Destiny of the antebellum period. For a sense of how these ideas were translated into practice, see Richard Hoftstader, *Social Darwinism in American Thought* (New York: G. Braziller, 1959), chapter 9; Reginald Horsman, *Race and Manifest Destiny* (Cambridge, MA: Harvard University Press, 1981); Edward J. Blum, *Reforging the White Republic: Race, Religion, and American Nationalism, 1865–1898* (Baton Rouge: Louisiana State University Press, 2005); Paul Kramer, "Empires, Exceptions, and Anglo-Saxons: Race and Rule between the British and United States Empires, 1880–1910." *The Journal of American History* 88, no. 4 (2002): 1315–1353. See also Kristin Hoganson, *Fighting for American Manhood: How Gender Politics Provoked the Spanish-American and Philippine-American Wars* (New Haven, CT: Yale University Press, 1998).
10. For the two best and well-known accounts providing a largely economic interpretation for the plunge to war and expansion, see Walter LaFeber, *New Em-*

pire: An Interpretation of American Expansion, 1860–1898 (Ithaca, NY: Cornell University Press, 1963); William Appleman Williams, *The Roots of the Modern American Empire* (New York: Random House, 1969).

11. See Thomas J. McCormick, *China Market: America's Quest for Informal Empire, 1893–1901* (Chicago, IL: Quadrangle Books, 1967); LaFeber, *New Empire;* Thomas G. Paterson and Stephen G. Rabe, eds., *Imperial Surge: The United States Abroad, the 1890s–Early 1900s* (Lexington, MA: D.C. Heath, 1992).
12. For an illustration of how this exceptional empire was created, see Anna Leah Castañeda, "Creating Exceptional Empire: American Liberal Constitutionalism and the Philippine Constitutional Order, 1900–1916" (unpublished SJD dissertation, Harvard Law School, 2009), which argues that, without the structural checks and balances offered by the U.S. Constitution, including the principle of federalism, the colonial government cultivated and allowed unchecked exercises of power by executive officials in Manila, thus unleashing the latent despotisms within liberal legality.
13. Elihu Root summed up the ruling in the *Insular* cases with his remark that "the Constitution follows the flag, but it does not quite catch up with it." For an overview of the debates leading to the *Insular* cases, see James Edward Kerr, *The* Insular *Cases: The Role of the Judiciary in American Expansionism* (Port Washington, NY: Kennikat Press, 1982); Sparrow, *The* Insular *Cases.* The legal arguments that later appeared in the Supreme Court opinions were already prefigured in the pages of the special edition of the *Harvard Law Review* in 1898. See Christopher Langdell, "The Status of Our New Territories," *Harvard Law Review* 12, no. 6 (1899): 365–392; James Thayer, "Our New Possessions," *Harvard Law Review* 12 (1898): 464; Carman Randolph, "Constitutional Aspects of Annexation," *Harvard Law Review* 12, no. 5 (1898): 291–315.
14. See, for example, Christina Duffy Burnett and Burke Marshall, eds., *Foreign in a Domestic Sense: Puerto Rico, American Expansion and the Constitution* (Durham, NC: Duke University Press, 2001); Yves Dezalay and Bryant G. Garth, *Asian Legal Revivals: Lawyers in the Shadow of Empire* (Chicago, IL: The University of Chicago Press, 2010); Hilary M. Carey, *God's Empire: Religion and Colonialism in the British World, C. 1801–1908* (Cambridge: Cambridge University Press, 2011).
15. Philip C. Jessup, *Elihu Root* (New York: Dodd, Mead & Company, 1938), 354.
16. The American author Mark Twain, who was vice president of the Anti-Imperialist League from 1901 to its demise in 1921, wrote in his famous essay, *To the Person Sitting in Darkness,* that the United States was becoming more like "Europe." The dominant narrative in the early historiography of U.S. foreign relations is that the episode of 1898 was a "great aberration." See Samuel Flagg Bemis, *A Diplomatic History of the United States* (New York: Holt, Rinehart and Winston, 1965); Robert Osgood, *Ideals and Self-Interest in America's*

Foreign Relations (Chicago, IL: University of Chicago Press, 1953), stating that the United States acquired empire in a fit of absent-mindedness. For the view that the U.S. empire was not really exceptional, see Julian Go, *Patterns of Empire: The British and American Empires, 1688 to the Present* (New York: Cambridge University Press, 2011); see also Niall Ferguson, *Colossus* (New York: Penguin Press, 2004); Charles Maier, *Among Empires* (Cambridge, MA: Harvard University Press, 2006).

17. For a more detailed treatment of the Philippine-American war, see Stuart Creighton Miller, *Benevolent Assimilation: The American Conquest of the Philippines* (New Haven, CT: Yale University Press, 1982); David J. Silbey, *A War of Frontier and Empire: The Philippine-American War, 1899–1902* (New York: Hill and Wang, 2007).
18. A concise overview of this period is in "Cuba, the Philippines and the First Crusade," in Preston, *Sword of the Spirit* (New York: Knopf, 2012), 207–232.
19. See Robert T. Handy, *Undermined Establishment: Church-State Relations in America 1880–1920* (Princeton, NJ: Princeton University Press, 1991).
20. For a variety of American Protestant missionaries' views of Roman Catholicism, see Kenton J. Clymer, *Protestant Missionaries in the Philippines 1898–1916* (Urbana: University of Illinois Press, 1986), 93–113.
21. See Ian Tyrrell, *Reforming the World: The Creation of America's Moral Empire* (Princeton, NJ: Princeton University Press, 2010). Protestant groups opposed licensing and sale of opium, prostitution, and alcohol in the Philippines.
22. See generally Warren Zimmerman, *First Great Triumph: How Five Americans Made Their Country a World Power* (New York: Farrar, Straus and Giroux, 2002); Alfred Mahan Thayer, *The Harvest Within: Thoughts on the Life of The Christian* (Boston, MA: Little, Brown & Co., 1909).
23. Josiah Strong, *Expansion under New World Conditions* (New York: The Baker and Taylor Company, 1900).
24. Ibid., at 302.
25. Josiah Strong, *Our Country: Its Possible Future and Its Present Crisis* (New York: The Baker and Taylor Company, 1891).
26. Article III, Treaty of Peace between the United States and Spain, Dec 10, 1898. Last accessed on Nov 7, 2012, from http://avalon.law.yale.edu/19th_Century/sp1898.asp (hereafter Treaty of Paris).
27. "Future Work in the Philippines," *New York Times*, February 7, 1899, 6.
28. General James Rusling, "An Interview with President William McKinley," in *The Christian Advocate*, LXXVII, January 22, 1903. The interview took place on Nov 21, 1899, but was published four years later.
29. "Elihu Root," *New York Times*, July 30, 1899.
30. Jessup, *Elihu Root*, 215.

31. David Healy, *U.S. Expansionism: The Imperialist Urge in the 1890s* (Madison: University of Wisconsin Press, 1970), 153–157. Root would later become one of the main proponents of a legalist challenge to the Wilsonian moralist paradigm of international relations focusing on arbitration, judicial enforcement, and sanctions. See Stephen Wertheim, "The League That Wasn't: American Designs for a Legalist-Sanctionist League of Nations and the Intellectual Origins of International Organization, 1914–1920," *Diplomatic History* 35, no. 5 (2011): 797–836.
32. Jessup, *Elihu Root*, 345.
33. Annual Report of the War Department (1899), 32 (hereafter ARWD).
34. Jessup, *Elihu Root*, 346.
35. Elihu Root, *Military and Colonial Policy of the United States: Speeches & Addresses* (Cambridge, MA: Harvard University Press, 1916), 502.
36. Root Conversation with Philip Jessup, Sept 20, 1930, Box 1, Philip C. Jessup Papers, Library of Congress.
37. For an account of the evolution of Schurman's views before, during, and after his appointment, see Kenneth Hendrickson, Jr., "Reluctant Expansionist: Jacob Gould Schurman and the Philippine Question," *Pacific Historical Review* 36, no. 4 (1967): 405–421. The commission had two military members, General Elwell Otis and Admiral George Dewey, and two other civilians, Dean Worcester and Charles Denby.
38. Report of the Philippine Commission to the President (1900) (hereafter RPC 1900).
39. Article X, Treaty of Paris.
40. Papal bull *Inter caetera*, May 4, 1493 (granting Spain rights to all lands discovered or to be discovered . . . in exchange for a feudal obligation to convert the inhabitants to the Christian faith). See Bardo Fassbender et al., *The Oxford Handbook of the History of International Law*, 580 (Oxford: Oxford University Press, 2012).
41. Donald Parker, "Church and State in the Philippines, 1896–1906," *Philippine Social Science Review* 10, no. 4 (November 1938): 354–371.
42. Lewis L. Gould, "McKinley, Ida Saxton," American National Biography Online, February 2000. Retrieved from http://www.anb.org.ezp-prod1.hul.harvard.edu/articles/20/20-01377.html.
43. For example, Theodore Roosevelt wrote to a friend: "I emphatically feel as I have always told you that the chance for bettering the Catholic inhabitants of the tropic islands lies in bringing them up to the highest standard of American Catholicism. The worst thing that could happen both for them and for the Catholic church would be for the church to champion the inequities that have undoubtedly been committed not only by lay but by clerical leaders in the Philippines and elsewhere." TR to Maria Storer, Oyster Bay, New York, May 18,

1900, in *The Letters of Theodore Roosevelt*, vol. 2 (Cambridge, MA: Harvard University Press, 1951), 1298–1299.

44. Issues of nonsectarian education and the secular composition of the colonial government in Manila were constant matters of controversy. These concerns were important enough that all the members of the Taft Commission found the time to refute charges that they did not issue any ruling stating that they will not attend religious services while in Manila or ask the same from their subordinates. ("[I]t is as absolutely a matter of individual choice and discretion as it is in the United States. The officers and employees of the government include a very large number of Catholics and many Protestants of various denominations. The separation of church and state is absolute, complete and individual liberty on religious matters is the rule and the law.") Taft to Root, Sept 10, 1902, RG 350.3, Bureau of Insular Affairs, #1158, NARA.
45. RPC 1900, 85. The conclusion was based on an analysis of the local constitution drawn up by the Filipino revolutionaries who were fighting the Americans.
46. McKinley's Instructions to the Second Philippine Commission (hereafter McKinley's Instructions), April 7, 1900, Letterbook Container 173, Elihu Root Papers (hereafter Root Papers), Library of Congress, Manuscript Division.
47. Spooner Amendment to the Army Appropriations Bill of 1901, U.S. Statutes at Large, XXXI, 895. "[A]ll military, civil and judicial powers necessary to govern the Philippine Islands . . . shall until otherwise provided by Congress be vested in such person and persons and shall be exercised in such manner as the President of the United States shall direct, for the establishment of civil government and for maintaining and protecting the inhabitants of said islands in the free enjoyment of their liberty, property and religion." The same act included the Platt amendment for Cuba.
48. July 1, 1902, chapter 1369, 32 Stat. 691.
49. Bureau of Insular Affairs, *What Has Been Done in the Philippines: A Record of Practical Accomplishments* (Washington, DC: U.S. Government Printing Office, 1904).
50. Root to Seth Low, August 28, 1900, Box 228, Root Papers.
51. Root to Sen. John Morgan, May 8, 1902, Box 228, Root Papers.
52. Of course, race was the other major factor explaining the inferiority of the Filipino. For accounts of the American colonial project through the lens of race, the best treatment is Paul Kramer, *Blood of Government: Race, Empire, the United States and the Philippines* (Chapel Hill: University of North Carolina Press, 2006). See also Matthew Frye Jacobson, *Barbarian Virtues* (New York: Hill and Wang, 2000), 221–260.
53. ARWD 1901, 200. "[I]t remains the guide and rule of action of the insular government and all the steps taken in the government of the Philippines since that time have been in conformity to its provisions."

54. The Vatican initially attempted to prevent war between the United States and Spain through the efforts of Archbishop Placide Chappelle of New Orleans.
55. For a comprehensive view of TR's relationship with the American Catholic Church, see Frederick Zwierlein, *Theodore Roosevelt and Catholics, 1882–1919* (St. Louis, MO: V. T. Suren; for sale by Art Print Shop, Rochester, NY, 1956). See also Oscar Alfonso, *Theodore Roosevelt and the Philippines 1897–1909* (New York: Oriole Editions, 1974), 142–173.
56. The text is reprinted in Cameron Forbes, *The Philippine Islands,* vol. 2 (Boston, MA: Houghton Mifflin Co., 1928), 438. For a background of this proclamation, see Go, *Patterns of Empire,* 90.
57. See Creighton Miller, *Soldier as Diplomat* (New Haven, CT: Yale University Press, 1982).
58. The commanding officer of the U.S. Army, General Elwell Otis imposed a strict censorship on all cables going overseas so that Americans in the States knew about the outbreak of the war but not the ensuing guerrilla war, at least not immediately.
59. Democratic Party Platform of 1900. Retrieved from http://www.presidency.ucsb.edu/ws/index.php?pid=29587.
60. Republican Party Platform of 1900. Retrieved from http://www.presidency.ucsb.edu/ws/index.php?pid=29630.
61. For example, consider Article VIII, Treaty of Paris. "And it is hereby declared that the relinquishment or cession, as the case may be, to which the preceding paragraph refers, can not in any respect impair the property or rights which by law belong to the peaceful possession of property of all kinds, of provinces, municipalities, public or private establishments, ecclesiastical or civic bodies, or any other associations having legal capacity to acquire and possess property in the aforesaid territories renounced or ceded, or of private individuals, of whatsoever nationality such individuals may be."
62. See, for example, RPC 1901, vol. I, 25, 26.
63. Ibid. In fact, the two foundational novels of the Philippines, *Noli Me Tangere* (translated with an introduction by Harold Augenbraum, New York: Penguin, 2006) and *El Filibusterismo* (1891) written by the martyred hero Jose Rizal and for which he was executed by the Spanish authorities, were novels about abuses of clerical authority. Rizal's execution ignited the Philippine revolution in 1897, long before Americans entered the country.
64. For a detailed account of the friar lands issue, see Rene Escalante, *The American Friar Lands Policy* (Manila: De La Salle University Press, 2002), which focuses on the issue's implications for contemporary agrarian reform in the Philippines; John T. Farrell, "Background of the 1902 Taft Mission to Rome I," *The Catholic Historical Review* 36, no. 1 (1950): 1–32; Charles H. Cunningham,

"Origin of the Friar Lands Question in the Philippines," *The American Political Science Review* 10, no. 3 (1916): 465–480.

65. See RPC 1900, vol. II, 421.
66. Before the Philippine-American war officially broke out, General Otis had urged Emilio Aguinaldo, the Filipino leader, to release Spanish priests held by them, but Aguinaldo refused to do so because he had wanted to use them as bargaining chips with the Vatican to recognize the Filipino clergy. See *War Department, Correspondence Relating to the War with Spain, April 15, 1898, to July 30, 1902, vol. II*, 1121.
67. Taft to Root, Dec 14, 1900, Manila, Box 164, Root Papers. "Native priests are those who have held out longest in favor of the insurgents and against the Americans and I deem this action of great importance."
68. Frank Reuter, *Catholic Influence on American Colonial Policies, 1898–1904* (Austin: University of Texas Press, 1967), 70–80.
69. See Roosevelt to Root, July 16, 1902, Box 162, Root Papers, asking Root to get General Luke Wright in Manila to get a statement from American Catholics in the Philippines that the desire to expel the friars is the desire of Filipino lay Catholics themselves and a measure of prime importance for the tranquility of the islands.
70. James LeRoy, *Americans in the Philippines* (New York: AMS Press, 1970), 295, citing General Orders, Military Governor of the Philippines 1899, Order no. 68, Dec 18, 1899; ARWD 1900, 101.
71. ARWD 1900, vol. 1, 68. "10. As under the Constitution of the United States, complete religious freedom is guaranteed, and no minister of religion can be interfered with or molested in following his calling in a peaceful or lawful manner, and there must be complete separation of church and state."
72. RPC 1901 (Taft Commission Report), 29. "[C]hief ground of deep feeling cherished against the friars by the Filipino people . . . is to be found in the fact that to the Filipino the government in these islands under Spain was the government of the friars."
73. See McKinley's Instructions: "That the provision of the Treaty of Paris, pledging the United States to the protection of all rights of property in the islands, and as well the principle of our own Government which prohibits the taking of private property without due process of law, shall not be violated; that the welfare of the people of the islands, which should be a paramount consideration, shall be attained consistently with this rule of property right; that if it becomes necessary for the public interest of the people of the islands to dispose of claims to property which the commission finds to be not lawfully acquired and held disposition shall be made thereof by due legal procedure, in which there shall be full opportunity for fair and impartial hearing and judgment; that if the same public interests require the extinguishment of property rights lawfully

acquired and held due compensation shall be made out of the public treasury therefor; that no form of religion and no minister of religion shall be forced upon any community or upon any citizen of the islands; that upon the other hand no minister of religion shall be interfered with or molested in following his calling, and that the separation between state and church shall be real, entire, and absolute."

74. *Hearings on Lands Held for Ecclesiastical or Religious Uses in the Philippine Islands,* etc., 56th Cong., 2nd session (1901) (hereafter Friar Lands Hearings).
75. *Affairs in the Philippine Islands,* Hearings before the Committee of the Senate on the Philippines, April 10, 1902, 178.
76. Frank Reuter, *Catholic Influence,* 99.
77. David Alvarez, "Purely a Business Matter: The Taft Mission to the Vatican," *Diplomatic History* 16, no. 3 (1992): 357–370, which focuses on the diplomatic aspects of the negotiations for the United States and the Vatican rather than the implications of the negotiations for the U.S. pacification efforts in the Philippines.
78. Taft would be the chief troubleshooter throughout the Roosevelt presidency. As secretary of war beginning in 1903, Taft dealt with Japan in the aftermath of the Russo-Japanese War, negotiated the end of a local revolt in Cuba in 1906, and handled controversies relating to the construction of the Panama Canal.
79. Reuter, *Catholic Influence,* 139; Farrell, "Background of the Taft Mission," 12–13.
80. White House Memorandum for Governor Taft, April 24, 1902, Special Correspondence Root to Taft, Box 164, Root Papers. For an analysis of the mission from a legal perspective, see Simeon E. Baldwin, "Mission of Gov. Taft to the Vatican," *Yale Law Journal* 12 (1902):1–15.
81. But see Alvarez, "Purely a Business Matter," 366–370, for the point that the primary goal of the American mission was the withdrawal of the friars, and that the Vatican conceded to the point of the acquisition of the friar lands only because they already decided on their own to reorganize the Philippine church.
82. Henry Pringle, *The Life and Times of William Howard Taft,* vol. I (New York: Farrar & Rinehart, 1939), 232.
83. Jessup, *Elihu Root,* 355.
84. Sections 63 and 64, Philippine Organic Act, July 1, 1902, chapter 1369, 32 Stat. 691.
85. Sept 17, 1902. An English translation is printed in *American Catholic Quarterly Review* 28 (1903): 372–379.
86. William Pendergast, *The Catholic Voter in American Politics: The Passing of the Democratic Monolith* (Washington, DC: Georgetown University Press, 1999), 88.

87. Reuter, *Catholic Influence,* 147, citing Taft to Roosevelt, Manila, Sept 13, 1902. ("I do not state it too strongly when I say that the visit to Rome has done us a great deal of good in this country"); Escalante, *The American Friar Lands Policy,* 105; Preston, *Sword of the Spirit,* 219.
88. Escalante, *The American Friar Lands Policy,* 206.
89. Frank Reuter, "William Howard Taft and the Separation of Church and State in the Philippines," *Journal of Church and State,* 24, no. 1 (1982): 113.
90. *Friar Lands Hearings,* 174 (on the Faribault plan in the Philippines); Alfonso, *Theodore Roosevelt,* 166–170 (addressing charges of proselytizing in Philippine schools).
91. Interview with Gregorio Aglipai, Nov 21, 1902, Box 164, Root Papers. "The government occupied an entirely impartial and neutral position, defending worshippers of religion in their right to free worship and punishing only those who violated the rights of others or trespassed upon the law in some other way. . . . Father Aglipai at the close assured the Governor that all his influence and all that of his brethren would be exercised in favor of peace and loyalty to the United States."
92. Taft himself referred to this as policy of attraction in his annual report to the president as secretary of war. See William Taft, *Special Report of William H. Taft, Secretary of War, to the President, on the Philippines* (Washington, DC: U.S. Government Printing Office, 1908). This policy has been criticized by historians because it perpetuated an elite aristocracy. See, for example, Kramer, *Blood of Government,* 13.
93. Philippine independence was finally granted on July 4, 1945, but as early as 1916, eventual independence was promised in the form of the Jones Act, though no particular date was indicated.
94. For a classic overview of the history of the Moros, see Cesar Adib Majul, *Muslims in the Philippines* (Quezon City: Published for the Asian Center by the University of the Philippines Press, 1973).
95. An English translation of the Spanish copy of the 1878 treaty is in Najeeb M. Saleeby, *The History of Sulu* (Manila: Bureau of Printing, 1908), 229–231. Saleeby served in various capacities during U.S. military rule in Mindanao from 1901 to 1913. For a background of the events leading to the treaty, see Adib Majul, *Muslims,* 291–300.
96. Oscar Straus to John Hay, Constantinople, Sept 23, 1899, FRUS 1899, 770.
97. Ibid.
98. Peter Gowing, *Mandate in Moroland* (Quezon City: Philippine Center for Advanced Studies, University of the Philippines, 1977), 32.
99. Agreement between General John C. Bates, U.S. Army, and the Sultan of Sulu, August 20, 1899, Senate Document No. 136, 56th Cong. 1st sess., February 1, 1900, 1114–1116; reprinted in Appendix B, Gowing, *Mandate in Moroland,*

348 (hereafter Bates-Kiram Treaty). This actually involves less than what the 1878 treaty covered, and the sultan did not initially want to sign it but he was persuaded otherwise by his ruling council. One of the controversies surrounding the treaty was that there were significant translation discrepancies and that the Moro copy (in the Tausug language) did not mention the word *sovereignty.* See James R. Arnold, *The Moro War: How America Battled a Muslim Insurgency in the Philippine Jungle, 1902–1913* (New York: Bloomsbury Press, 2011), 9. The Bates Treaty technically only covered the Sultanate of Sulu.

100. Bates-Kiram Treaty, Art. I. "The sovereignty of the United States over the whole archipelago of Jolo and its dependencies is declared and acknowledged."
101. Bates-Kiram Treaty, Art. II. "The United States flag will be used in the archipelago of Jolo and its dependencies on land and sea."
102. Bates-Kiram Treaty, Art. III. "The rights and dignities of His Highness the Sultan and his *datos* shall be fully respected, the Moros shall not be interfered with on account of their religion, all their religious customs shall be respected, and no one shall be prosecuted on account of his religion."
103. Donna J. Amoroso, "Inheriting the Moro Problem: Muslim Authority and Colonial Rule in British Malaya and the Philippines," in Julian Go and Anne Foster, eds., *The American Colonial State in the Philippines: Global Perspectives* (Durham, NC: Duke University Press, 2009), 118–143. American colonial officials generally showed a favorable view toward British methods. A massive catalog comparing various colonial powers and their methods of governance was published in 1903 by Oscar Austin, an official with the U.S. Department of Treasury. See Oscar P. Austin, *Colonial Administration, 1800–1900: Methods of Government and Development Adopted by the Principal Colonizing Nations in Their Control of Tropical and Other Colonies and Dependencies* (Washington, DC: U.S. Government Printing Office, 1903).
104. Bates-Kiram Treaty, Art. X. "Any slave in the archipelago of Jolo shall have the right to purchase freedom by paying to the master the usual market value."
105. Michael Salman, *The Embarrassment of Slavery* (Berkeley: University of California Press, 2001), 37, quoting *The Anti-Imperialist,* Sept 1899. Salman's work situates U.S. colonial policy, including its Moro policy, within the discourse of slavery and emancipation.
106. See Sarah Barringer Gordon, *The Mormon Question: Polygamy and Constitutional Conflict in Nineteenth-Century America* (Chapel Hill: University of North Carolina Press, 2002), 55–84.
107. Salman, *The Embarrassment of Slavery,* 38.
108. Ibid., 39.
109. There are explicit Qur'anic verses on slavery. See, for example, Q5:89, "He (Allah) will call you to account . . . for the food of your families; or clothe them;

or give a slave his freedom"; Q90:12–13, "And what will explain to thee the path that is steep? It is the freeing of a captive from the bondage of slavery, debt and other afflictions"; Q24:33, "If any of your slaves ask for deed in writing (to enable them to earn their freedom for a certain sum, give them such a deed)."

110. See generally James Warren, *The Sulu Zone, 1768–1898: The Dynamics of External Trade, Slavery and Ethnicity in the Transformation of a Southeast Asian Maritime State* (Singapore: NUS Press, 2003).
111. 30 U.S. 1 (1831).
112. Root, *Military and Colonial Policy,* 321.
113. McKinley's Instructions: "In dealing with the uncivilized tribes of the islands the commission should adopt the same course followed by Congress in permitting the tribes of our North American Indians to maintain their tribal organization and government, and under which many of those tribes are now living in peace and contentment, surrounded by a civilization to which they are unable or unwilling to conform. Such tribal governments should, however, be subjected to wise and firm regulation; and, without undue or petty interference, constant and active effort should be exercised to prevent barbarous practices and introduce civilized customs."
114. See ARWD (1902), 560–561.
115. Root to James Henry Pierson Esq., February 12, 1900, Box 228, Root Papers.
116. Austin, *Colonial Administration,* 1329.
117. General George Davis's Report on Moro Affairs, in ARWD (1902), vol. 3, 270.
118. Statement of William Taft before the House Committee on Insular Affairs, March 4, 1902, 189; Root, *Military and Colonial Policy,* 283; ARWD (1900), vol. 3, 270.
119. An Act Providing for the Organization and Government of the Moro Province, Philippine Commission Act No. 787, June 1, 1903, RG 350, #5975–10, NARA.
120. Kramer, *Blood of Government,* 218.
121. A domestic reason was that Roosevelt wanted to get Wood out of the country because he was up for promotion as major-general and it would mean a bitter public fight in the Senate. TR did not want the senators to use Wood's appointment as a means to criticize U.S. policies in Cuba. See Jack McCallum, *Leonard Wood: Rough Rider, Surgeon, Architect of American Imperialism* (New York: New York University Press, 2006), 217. Sure enough, the confirmation hearings proved brutal for Wood. For his previous promotion to brigadier-general, he had jumped over 530 officers. Senators attacked his lack of military experience and insinuated that Roosevelt was playing favorites when he promoted Wood, a fellow Rough Rider. Wood's lingering bitterness over the episode would have repercussions for the Moros. During his three-year stint as governor of the Moro Province, he oversaw and participated in a total of sixty-seven military

operations, including the infamous Massacre at Bud Dajo, killing more than 800 Moros, which presumably remedied the gap in his military résumé. See Jack C. Lane, *Armed Progressive: General Leonard Wood* (San Rafael, CA: Presidio Press, 1978), 180. For an account of the massacre, see Arnold, *Moro War,* 139–168. Another reason was that TR wanted to lure Taft back to Washington as secretary of war. Taft had already turned down offers of a Supreme Court seat by TR to do more work as governor-general in the Philippines. See Wayne Thompson, "Governors of the Moro Province" (unpublished PhD dissertation, University of California–San Diego, 1975).

122. Kramer, *Blood of Government,* 218. For a comprehensive treatment of American views of the Moros, see Karine Walther, "A Door into the Mohammedan World: Islam and U.S. Foreign Policy, 1821–1913" (unpublished PhD dissertation 2008, Columbia University).

123. "An Act Creating a Bureau of Non-Christian Tribes," Philippine Commission Act no. 253, October 2, 1901, in RG 350, #3833, NARA.

124. *Letters of Theodore Roosevelt Accepting the Republican Nomination for President of the United States* (Oyster Bay, NY: Theodore Roosevelt, 1904), 29. "[T]o abandon control over the Moros would amount to releasing these Moros to prey upon the Christian Filipinos."

125. *Annual Report of the Governor of the Province of Moro* (Washington, DC: U.S. Government Printing Office, 1903), vol. 3, 302 (hereafter RGMP). "[I]f it is contemplated to change the customs and habits of these people and bring them to an intelligent understanding and appreciation of our methods of government, it will be necessary to eradicate about all the customs that have heretofore governed their habits of life. They are an essentially different people from us in thought, word and action and their religion will be a serious bar to any efforts towards Christian civilization. So long as Mohammedanism prevails, Anglo-Saxon civilization will make slow headway."

126. Arnold, *The Moro War,* 76.

127. Wood to Taft, Oct 7, 1903, Box 33, Leonard Wood Papers, Manuscript Division, Library of Congress (hereafter Wood Papers). For example, Wood had his Moro Legislative Council replace the Moro religious courts with Western-style courts.

128. ARWD 1904, vol. xii, part II, 585. "[T]he Jesuits in the Moro province had helped a great deal in subduing the natives. The good effects of the missions established by the Jesuits at many places in the interior of this Island are everywhere apparent and the work which this society has done has implanted in many remote parts of the island not only the principles of the Christian religion but the principles of law and order and respect for authority."

129. Wood to Taft, Dec 16, 1903, Wood Papers (memo recommending the abrogation of the Bates-Kiram Treaty).

130. Ibid.
131. Ibid. Wood cited eight reasons in total to abrogate the treaty, among them, Moro disregard of the stipulation against slavery.
132. Letters of Theodore Roosevelt, 29. "To abandon the Moro country would be as if we withdrew the army and the civil agents . . . at a time when the Sioux and the Apache were still the terror of our settlers. It is a criminal absurdity. . . ."
133. Wood to J. St. Loe Strachey, Jan 6, 1904, Box 33, Wood Papers. "[O]ur policy is to develop individualism among these people and little by little, teach them to stand up on their own feet independent of petty chieftains. In order to do this the chief or headman has to be given some position of more or less authority under the Government, but he ceases to have any divine rights."
134. Arnold, *The Moro War,* 96.
135. John P. Finley, "The Commercial Awakening of the Moro and Pagan," *The North American Review* 197, no. 688 (1913): 325–334. Finley served as military governor of Zamboanga beginning in 1903; see RGMP 1904, 17.
136. RGMP 1905, 9–10; RGMP 1904, 16–17.
137. RGMP 1904, 17.
138. RGMP 1904, 16.
139. Act No. 8 of the Legislative Council of the Moro Council, Sept 24, 1903, in RGMP 1904, 36–37. See also Gowing, *Mandate in Moroland,* 132–133; RGMP 1905, 11.
140. Wood to Taft, October 7, 1903, Wood Papers.
141. See Arnold, *The Moro War,* for a more complete treatment of how the U.S. army battled the Moro insurgency. See also Gowing, *Mandate in Moroland.*
142. Appendix C, Sultan Jamal ul-Kiram II to Governor-General Luke E. Wright, April 1904, in Gowing, *Mandate in Moroland,* 350–351.
143. The term is taken from the classic book by Sidney Mead, *The Lively Experiment: The Shaping of Christianity in America* (New York: Harper & Row, 1963).

2. Removing the Fertile Sources of War

1. John Milton Cooper, *Breaking the Heart of the World* (Cambridge: Cambridge University Press, 2001), 118.
2. Address to the French Chamber of Deputies, Paris, February 3, 1919, in August Heckscher ed., *The Politics of Woodrow Wilson: Selections from His Speeches and Writings* (New York: Books for Libraries Press, 1970), 343.
3. For the rare account that takes a somewhat sympathetic view of the events and achievements of the Paris Peace Conference, see Margaret MacMillan, *Paris 1919: Six Months That Changed the World* (New York: Random House, 2002).
4. The Congress of Berlin was a meeting of the European powers and the Ottoman Empire in the wake of the Russo-Turkish war in 1877–1878. The

resulting treaty conditioned the recognition of Serbia, Montenegro, Romania, and Bulgaria as states on protections of religious minorities within its territories. For the full text of the Treaty of Berlin, see R. B. Mowat, *Select Treaties and Documents to Illustrate the Development of the Modern European States System, 1815–1916* (Oxford: Clarendon Press, 1916), 79–83.

5. Article 22: "Other peoples, especially those of Central Africa, are at such a stage that the Mandatory must be responsible for the administration of the territory under conditions which will guarantee freedom of conscience and religion, subject only to the maintenance of public order and morals, the prohibition of abuses such as the slave trade, the arms traffic, and the liquor traffic, and the prevention of the establishment of fortifications or military and naval bases and of military training of the natives for other than police purposes and the defence of territory, and will also secure equal opportunities for the trade and commerce of other Members of the League."
6. Annex No. 28, Article 50: "Under the control of the Governing Commission the inhabitants will retain their local assemblies, their religious liberties, their schools and their language."
7. Article 86: "The Czecho-Slovak State accepts and agrees to embody in a Treaty with the Principal Allied and Associated Powers such provisions as may be deemed necessary by the said Powers to protect the interests of inhabitants of that State who differ from the majority of the population in race, language, or religion."
8. Article 93: "Poland accepts and agrees to embody in a Treaty with the Principal Allied and Associated Powers such provisions as may be deemed necessary by the said Powers to protect the interests of inhabitants of Poland who differ from the majority of the population in race, language, or religion."
9. Fourteen Points Speech, January 8, 1918. Retrieved from http://avalon.law.yale.edu/20th_Century/wilson14.asp.
10. Supplementary Agreement VII: "Recognizing religious persecution and intolerance as fertile sources of war, the Powers signatory hereto agree and the League of Nations shall exact from all new States and all States seeking admission to it the promise that they will make no law prohibiting or interfering with the free exercise of religion and that they will in no way discriminate, either in law, or in fact, against those who practice any particular creed, religion, or belief whose practices are not inconsistent with public order or public morals." See Wilson's Third Draft (Second Paris Draft), January 20, 1919, in David Hunter Miller, *The Drafting of the Covenant*, vol. 2 (New York: GP Putnam's Sons, 1928), 105.
11. John Milton Cooper, *Woodrow Wilson: A Biography* (New York: Alfred A. Knopf, 2009), 491.
12. Joseph P. Tumulty, *Woodrow Wilson as I Know Him* (Garden City, NY: Doubleday, Page & Co., 1921), 235.

13. See Erez Manela, *The Wilsonian Moment* (Oxford: Oxford University Press, 2007) (a detailed account of the international response to the Fourteen Points).
14. Woodrow Wilson, Second Inaugural Address, in Halford Ryan, ed., *The Inaugural Addresses of Twentieth-Century American Presidents* (Westport, CT: Praeger, 1993). For an application of these principles, see Lloyd Ambrosius, *Wilsonian Statecraft: Theory and Practice of Liberal Internationalism during World War I* (Wilmington, DE: SR Books, 1991).
15. Woodrow Wilson's War Message to Congress, April 2, 1917, 65th Cong. 1st Sess., Senate Doc. No. 5, No. 7264 (Washington, DC: U.S. Government Printing Office, 1917), 3–8.
16. MacMillan, *Paris 1919*, 9.
17. Leslie Bethell, ed., *Cambridge History of Latin America* (Cambridge: Cambridge University Press, 1984), 107.
18. Woodrow Wilson, "Peace without Victory" address to the U.S. Senate, January 22, 1917.
19. Ibid.
20. Macmillan, *Paris 1919*, 9; Address of President Woodrow Wilson, Columbus, Ohio, Sept 4, 1919.
21. See Trygve Throntveit, "The Fable of the Fourteen Points," *Diplomatic History* 35, no.3 (June 2011).
22. John Milton Cooper and Woodrow Wilson International Center for Scholars, *Reconsidering Woodrow Wilson: Progressivism, Internationalism, War, and Peace* (Washington, DC: Woodrow Wilson Center Press, and Baltimore, MD: Johns Hopkins University Press, 2008), 239.
23. Allen Lynch, "Woodrow Wilson and the Principle of National Self-Determination: A Reconsideration," *Review of International Studies* 28, no. 2 (April 2002): 419–436, 424.
24. Woodrow Wilson, "The Study of Administration," *Political Science Quarterly* 2, no. 2 (1887): 197–222.
25. Mark Benbow, *Leading Them to the Promised Land: Woodrow Wilson, Covenant Theology, and the Mexican Revolution, 1913–1915* (Kent, OH: Kent State University Press, 2010), 10.
26. For the line of scholarship that considers Woodrow Wilson and religion, see John Mulder, *Woodrow Wilson: The Years of Preparation* (Princeton, NJ: Princeton University Press, 1978); Arthur S. Link, *The Higher Realism of Woodrow Wilson, and Other Essays* (Nashville, TN: Vanderbilt University Press, 1971); Benbow, *Leading Them to the Promised Land;* Malcolm Magee, *What the World Should Be: Woodrow Wilson and the Crafting of a Faith-Based Foreign Policy* (Waco, TX: Baylor University Press, 2008); Ambrosius, *Wilsonian Statecraft,* 132; Milan Babik, "George D. Herron and the Eschatological Foundations of Woodrow Wilson's Foreign Policy 1917–1919," *Diplomatic History* 35 no. 5 (2011): 837–857.

27. Cary T. Grayson, *Woodrow Wilson: An Intimate Memoir* (New York: Holt, Rinehart, and Winston, 1960), 106.
28. For a detailed exploration of the legalist paradigm in U.S. foreign relations, see Benjamin Coates, "Transatlantic Advocates: American International Law and U.S. Foreign Relations, 1898–1919" (unpublished PhD dissertation, Columbia University, 2010). To see the sharp contrast between the legalists and Wilson's vision, see Stephen Wertheim, "The League of Nations: A Retreat from International Law?," *Journal of Global History* 7, no. 2 (2012): 210–232. This divide would plague Wilson's domestic push for the treaty's acceptance. See Thomas Knock, *To End All Wars: Woodrow Wilson and the Quest for a New World Order* (New York: Oxford University Press, 1992).
29. Woodrow Wilson, "The Lawyer and the Community," Address at the 1910 Annual Meeting of the American Bar Association, cited in Kazimierz Grzybowski, "Woodrow Wilson on Law, State, and Society," *George Washington Law Review* 30 (1962): 812.
30. Milton Cooper, *Woodrow Wilson,* 474.
31. Papers of Woodrow Wilson (hereafter PWW) 54: 4.
32. Moria Paz, "Non-Territorial Ethnic Network and the Making of Human Rights Law: The Case of Alliance Israelite Universelle," *Interdisciplinary Journal of Human Rights Law* 4 (2010), 1–105.
33. Letter from John Hay to the American Minister at Bucharest, William Sorsby to the Secretary of State, Sept 12, 1906, in U.S. Department of State, Foreign Relations of the United States 1906, 106–107 (hereafter FRUS), July 17, 1902, 910–915.
34. Ibid.
35. John Milton Cooper, "A Friend in Power?: Woodrow Wilson and Armenia," in Jay Winter, ed., *America and the Armenian Genocide of 1915* (New York: Cambridge University Press, 2003), 103–112.
36. Point Twelve of the Fourteen Points Speech. Retrieved from http://avalon.law.yale.edu/20th_century/wilson14.asp.
37. Wilson address at Salt Lake City, Utah, Sept 23, 1919, in PWW 62:458.
38. Diary of Lord Cecil, February 3, 1919, PWW 54:460.
39. Fourth to sixth meeting of the Commission on the League of Nations, February 8, 1919, 10:30 a.m., PWW 55:6.
40. Miller, *Drafting of the Covenant,* vol. 1, 196.
41. Ibid., 269. Wilson himself would also bury the racial equality clause for good by suddenly requiring a unanimous vote when Makino proposed that a reference to equality of nations be included in the preamble of the covenant because it would raise substantial objections in the United States. See Miller, *Drafting of the Covenant,* vol. 2, 391–392. As a consequence, however, this gave Japan leverage on its claims over the Shandong territory in China, and Wilson did allow Japan to take possession of it.

42. Miller, *Drafting of the Covenant,* vol. 1, 183.
43. Thomas Burkman, *Japan and the League of Nations: Empire and World Order, 1914–1938* (Honolulu: University of Hawaii Press, 2008), 82.
44. Minutes of the 15th meeting of April 11, 1919, of the League of Nations Commission, PWW 57: 261.
45. 1 Deering's Gen. Laws, Act 261 (1913). For a general overview of the Japanese question in U.S. domestic politics during the time of the Peace Conference, see Kristofer Allerfeldt, "Wilsonian Pragmatism? Woodrow Wilson, Japanese Immigration, and the Paris Peace Conference," *Diplomacy and Statecraft* 15, no. 3 (2004), 545–572; Noriko Kawamura, "Wilsonian Idealism and Japanese Claims at the Paris Peace Conference," *Pacific Historical Review* 66, no. 4 (1997), 503–526.
46. PWW, 56:188–189.
47. Wilson had already gone head to head with California governor Hiram W. Johnson on this issue in 1913. See Naoko Shimazu, *Japan, Race, and Equality: The Racial Equality Proposal of 1919* (London: Routledge, 1998), chapter 3.
48. See Gary Gerstle, "Race and Nation in the Thought and Politics of Woodrow Wilson," in John Milton Cooper, ed., *Reconsidering Woodrow Wilson: Progressivism, Internationalism, War, and Peace* (Baltimore, MD: Johns Hopkins University Press, 2008), 93–124.
49. Miller, *Drafting of the Covenant,* vol. 1, 141.
50. Malcolm Evans, *Religious Liberty and International Law in Europe* (Cambridge: Cambridge University Press, 1997), 98.
51. President Wilson Address to Joint Session of Congress, February 11, 1918.
52. Address of President Wilson on Presenting the Draft of the Covenant of the League of Nations to the Third Plenary Session of Peace Conference, Paris, France, February 14, 1919.
53. PWW 54:308; Cooper, *Woodrow Wilson,* 471. For the quarrel between Wilson and Hughes of Australia, see Seth Tillman, *Anglo-American Relations at the Paris Peace Conference of 1919* (Princeton, NJ: Princeton University Press, 1961), 91–93.
54. Edward House, "The Versailles Peace in Retrospect," in Edward M. House and Charles Seymour, ed., *What Really Happened in Paris* (New York: Charles Scribner's Sons, 1921). The mandate system has often been derided as a mere twentieth-century version of European imperialism. For a more nuanced story of the relationship between the mandate system and the creation of non-European sovereignty, see Antony Anghie, "Colonialism and the Birth of International Institutions: Sovereignty, Economy and the Mandate System of the League of Nations," *New York University Journal of International Law and Politics* 343 (2002): 513. For the view that mandates were not colonies, see Michael D. Callahan, *A Sacred Trust: The League of Nations and Africa, 1929–1946* (Brighton: Sussex Academic Press, 2004). See also Susan Pedersen, "The

Meaning of the Mandates System: An Argument," *Geschichte und Gesellschaft* 32, part 4 (Oct–Dec 2006), pp. 560–582 (viewing the mandates as a mechanism to generate publicity and norms rather than a system of governance).

55. Michael Oren, *Power, Faith, and Fantasy: America and the Middle East* (New York: W. W. Norton & Co., 2007), 377.
56. Woodrow Wilson, Campaign speech, Jersey City, New Jersey, May 25, 1912.
57. Manela, *The Wilsonian Moment,* 28.
58. Wilson endorsed, in the election platform he wrote, the then-pending Jones Bill of 1914 and reiterated "our endorsement of the purpose of ultimate independence for the Philippine Islands, expressed in the preamble of the measure." See Democratic Party Platform of 1916. But see Paul Kramer, *Blood of Government* (Chapel Hill: University of North Carolina Press, 2006), pp. 360–363, for the contrary claim that Wilson blocked attempts to confer independence to the Philippines and that the Jones Act actually sacrificed Philippine political independence to U.S. moral independence.
59. Wilson report to the Third Plenary Session of the Peace Conference, February 14, 1919, Foreign office, Quai d'Orsay, PWW 55:176.
60. Compare the Second Paris Draft/American Draft and the draft covenant presented to the Plenary Session.
61. Text of the Mandate Agreement between the Council of the League of Nations and the British Empire over Togo, Appendix C, in Callahan, *A Sacred Trust,* pp. 202–204.
62. Oscar Janowsky, *Jews and Minority Rights (1898–1919)* (New York: Columbia University Press, 1933), 341.
63. Paul Mantoux et al., eds., *The Deliberations of the Council of Four (March 24–June 28, 1919)* (Princeton, NJ: Princeton University Press, 1992), 439 (hereafter Council of Four).
64. Letter from William Howard Taft to Woodrow Wilson (via Joseph Tumulty), May 5, 1919, PPW 58:461.
65. Interview of Manley O. Hudson, in Charles Seymour and Edward House, eds., *What Really Happened in Paris: The Story of the Peace Conference* (New York: Charles Scribner's Sons, 1921), 473.
66. There is consensus among historians that Jewish groups exerted the most influence on the American and British peace delegations, especially the U.S. delegation. At one point, the British foreign officer E. H. Carr noted, "Everyone is working in the dark and no one knows how far the Americans who are having strong Jewish influences brought to bear on them may press the question of Jewish rights." Fn. 56, Carole Fink, "The Minorities Question at the Paris Peace Conference: The Polish Minority Treaty, June 28, 1919," in Manfred F. Boemke, ed., *The Treaty of Versailles: A Reassessment after 75 Years* (Cambridge: Cambridge University Press, 1998), quoting E. H. Carr, April 24, 1919, 608, 61/129/4/1, GB, FO, PRO. But see generally C. A. Macartney, *National States*

and National Minorities (New York: Russell & Russell, 1968), pp. 280–286, for the criticism that, because of this influence, the MPT provisions relied too heavily on liberal, civil libertarian ideals, drawing largely from the Western European experience, which did not suit the conditions in Eastern Europe with its history of competing national cultures.

67. The Alliance Israelite Universelle has been engaged in this work since the Congress of Berlin. See Paz, "Non-Territorial Ethnic Network," 7–13. For more discussion on the conflicts between Eastern European and Anglo-American Jews on the issue of Jewish nationalism, see Carole Fink, *Defending the Rights of Others* (Cambridge, New York: Cambridge University Press, 2004).
68. Letter from Stephen Samuel Wise to Woodrow Wilson, March 2, 1919, PWW 55:368.
69. Letter from Woodrow Wilson addressed to Joseph P. Tumulty, responding to the letter of Louis Marshall and Julian Mack, which warned him of the danger of imminent pogroms against Jews in all Eastern European countries but especially those in Poland and Romania. They urged Wilson to take action to prevent the expected massacres and suggested that the recognition of new nations such as Poland should depend on the safeguarding of Jewish and other minority rights. Nov 13, 1918, PWW 53:67.
70. Article 3: "Polish Treaty. Poland admits and declares to be Polish nationals ipso facto and without requirement of any formality German, Austrian, Hungarian or Russian nationals habitually resident at the date of the coming into force of the present Treaty in territory which is or may be recognized as forming part of Poland, but subject to any provisions in the Treaty of Peace with Germany or Austria respectively relating to persons who became resident in such territory after a specified date." This still left a lot of ambiguity with regard to people who were forced to flee before the war. As a result, millions of stateless Polish Jews remained unprotected by the MPR. See Fink, *Defending the Rights of Others,* 258.
71. Memo from Manley Hudson to Woodrow Wilson, June 1919, Papers of Manley Hudson, Box 35, Folder 11.
72. Council of Four, May 17, 1919, 91.
73. Council of Four, June 17, 1919, 481–482. The example used was that of Brazil or Greece checking Poland.
74. For an elaboration of how this category implicated conflicting visions of the new international order and how it was subsequently interpreted and adjudicated in cases during the interwar period, see Nathaniel Berman, "'But the Alternative Is Despair': European Nationalism and the Modernist Renewal of International Law," *Harvard Law Review* 106 (1993): 1792–1903.
75. Fink, *Defending the Rights of Others,* 128.
76. Council of Four, June 23, 1919, 526.

77. FRUS, vol. 1, 17–20.
78. Jewish nationalists lobbied the British and argued that Yiddish is indispensable for the intellectual and cultural life of the Jewish masses. Lewis Namier described to Headlam-Morley that "the Polish language and Polish culture is strange to us and hostile. It is permeated by the spirit of Roman Catholicism and by the most rampant, aggressive, intolerant anti-Semitism. To make the Jew feed on it is the same as to make men eat straw or wood." See Fink, *Defending the Rights of Others,* 253.
79. The full text is in Council of Four, vol. 2, 487.
80. Fink, *Defending the Rights of Others,* 264.
81. Address of President Woodrow Wilson at the Metropolitan Opera House, New York City, Sept 27, 1918.
82. Kazimierz Grzybowski, "Woodrow Wilson on Law, State, and Society," *George Washington Law Review* 30 (1962): 808, 829. ("Law is growth and the result of growth. It is the growth of society recorded in institutions and practices.")

3. A God-Fearing Democracy

1. Memo from Stettinius to Cordell Hull, Sept 9, 1944, William Sorsby to the Secretary of State, Sept 12, 1906, in U.S. Department of State, Foreign Relations of the United States 1906, 106–107 (hereafter FRUS), 1944, 789. See generally Edward R. Stettinius, Thomas Campbell, and George C. Herring, eds., *The Diaries of Edward Stettinius Jr.* (New York: New Viewpoints, 1975), 132, 143.
2. FRUS 1944; Washington Conversations on International Organization, Dumbarton Oaks (Washington, DC: Government Printing Office, 1945) 789.
3. Mark Mazower, "The Strange Triumph of Human Rights," *Historical Journal* 47 no. 2 (2004), 392. "[R]ights talk came more naturally to Americans, with their constitution, than it did to the British. . . ."
4. Chapter IX. Section A. 1. "With a view to the creation of conditions of stability and well-being which are necessary for peaceful and friendly relations among nations, the Organization should facilitate solutions of international economic, social and other humanitarian problems and promote respect for human rights and fundamental freedoms. Responsibility for the discharge of this function should be vested in the General Assembly and, under the authority of the General Assembly, in an Economic and Social Council." Washington Conversations on International Peace and Security Organization, Oct 7, 1944. *The United Nations: Dumbarton Oaks Proposals for a General International Organization,* Department of State Publication 2297, Conference Series 66 (Washington, DC: U.S. Government Printing Office, 1945).
5. The term *human rights* appears in the Preamble, and in Articles 1(3), 13(1)(b), 55, 62(2), 68, and 76.

6. Article 1 (3). "To achieve international co-operation in solving international problems of an economic, social, cultural, or humanitarian character, and in promoting and encouraging respect for human rights and for fundamental freedoms for all without distinction as to race, sex, language, or religion. . . ." Charter of the United Nations, Oct 24, 1945.
7. Preamble, Charter of the United Nations, Oct 24, 1945. It must be noted, however, that it was Jan Smuts, the South African premier and champion of the British Empire, who wrote the initial draft of the preamble. See Mark Mazower, *No Enchanted Palace: End of Empire and the Ideological Origins of the United Nations* (Princeton, NJ: Princeton University Press, 2009), 28–64.
8. The Four Freedoms appeared in its entirety in the Preamble of the General Assembly Resolution adopting the UDHR. See Universal Declaration of Human Rights, GA Res. 217A (III), UN Doc. A/810 (1948): "Whereas disregard and contempt for human rights have resulted in barbarous acts which have outraged the conscience of mankind and the advent of a world in which human beings shall enjoy freedom of speech and belief and freedom from fear and want."
9. See Elizabeth Borgwardt, *A New Deal for the World: America's Vision for Human Rights* (Cambridge, MA: Belknap Press of Harvard University Press, 2005).
10. Andrew Preston illustrates the full historical context of FDR's thinking on religion and religious freedom in *Sword of the Spirit* (New York: Knopf, 2012). This chapter makes a further connection between FDR and the foundational documents of the postwar order.
11. Richard Primus, *The American Language of Rights* (Cambridge: Cambridge University Press, 1999), 178.
12. Mazower makes a similar argument. See Mazower, "The Strange Triumph."
13. George C. Marshall, Address to United Nations General Assembly, Paris, France, Nov 1948.
14. Nehemiah Robinson, *The Universal Declaration of Human Rights: Its Origin, Significance, Application, and Interpretation* (New York: Institute of Jewish Affairs, World Jewish Congress, 1958), 42.
15. John Foster Dulles, *War or Peace* (New York: Macmillan Company, 1950), 204.
16. For an analogous argument, see Mazower, *No Enchanted Palace,* which focuses on the imperial origins of the UN as evidenced by the role and ideas of key British figures Jan Smuts and Alfred Zimmern. See also Tony Evans, *U.S. Hegemony and the Project of Universal Human Rights* (Houndmills, UK: Macmillan Press, 1996); Moyn, *The Last Utopia* (Cambridge, MA: Belknap Press of Harvard University Press, 2010), 44–83.
17. See Steven Casey, *Cautious Crusade: Franklin D. Roosevelt, American Public Opinion, and the War against Nazi Germany* (New York: Oxford University Press, 2001), which argues that most Americans remained isolationists even

after the Japanese attack at Pearl Harbor; Preston, *Sword of the Spirit,* 333–364.

18. For Roosevelt and religion, see Ronald Isetti, "The Moneychangers of the Temple: FDR, American Civil Religion and the New Deal," *Presidential Studies Quarterly* 26, no. 3 (1996): 678–693; Merlin Gustafson and Jerry Rosenberg, "The Faith of Franklin Roosevelt," *Presidential Studies Quarterly* 19, no. 3 (July 1, 1989): 559–566.
19. Michael A. Janson, "A Christian Century: Liberal Protestantism, the New Deal and the Origins of Postwar American Politics" (unpublished PhD dissertation, University of Pennsylvania, 2007).
20. Gustafson and Rosenberg, "The Faith of Franklin Roosevelt," 561. See also Frances Perkins, *The Roosevelt I Knew* (New York: Viking Press, 1946), 141; Preston, *Sword of the Spirit,* 315–326.
21. Samuel Rosenman, *Working with Roosevelt* (New York: Harper & Bros, 1952), 24. FDR also supported New York governor Al Smith in the 1929 presidential election, but Smith lost because of his Catholic religion.
22. Jews became so closely associated with the FDR administration that his anti-Semite critics branded his program as the "Jew Deal." In addition, Roosevelt had to fend off criticisms from Protestants when he decided to send Myron Taylor as a personal representative to the Vatican. On Roosevelt and Jews, see Thomas Philip Wolf et al., *Franklin D. Roosevelt and Congress: The New Deal and Its Aftermath* (Armonk, NY: M. E. Sharpe, 2001); Henry Feingold, *Bearing Witness: How America and Its Jews Responded to the Holocaust* (Syracuse, NY: Syracuse University Press, 1995). On Catholics, see George Q. Flynn, *Roosevelt and Romanism: Catholics and American Diplomacy, 1937–1945* (Westport, CT: Greenwood Press, 1976); John Conway, "Myron C. Taylor's Mission to the Vatican, 1940–1950," *Church History* 44, no. 1 (1975): 85–99. *Religion: Protestants v. Pope,* Time Magazine, April 15, 1940.
23. James Farley, *Jim Farley's Story: The Roosevelt Years* (New York: Whittlesey House, 1948), 36.
24. Letter to George Buttrick, March 14, 1940, cited in Kurt Klingbeil, "F.D.R. and American Religious Leaders: A Study of President Franklin D. Roosevelt and His Relationship to Selected American Religious Leaders" (unpublished PhD dissertation, New York University, 1972), 143.
25. For a magisterial treatment of Roosevelt in the realm of foreign affairs, see Robert Dallek, *Franklin D. Roosevelt and American Foreign Policy, 1932–1945* (New York: Oxford University Press, 1995). Much of the isolationist sentiment during the 1930s was a direct result of the costly American intervention during World War I.
26. Speech to the Inter-American Conference for the Maintenance of Peace, Dec 1, 1936, Franklin D. Roosevelt and Foreign Affairs, Series 1, vol. 3, 521 (hereinafter FDRFA).

27. Letter to Mr. Martin Carmody, Supreme Knight, Knights of Columbus, Nov 13, 1935, in Papers and Public Addresses of Franklin Delano Roosevelt, 450–452. FDR also did not want to contravene his own Good Neighbor policy and he deemed it would only divide American Catholics and Protestants even further. In any case, U.S. Catholics were not united on the issue. See E. David Cronon, "American Catholics and Mexican Anticlericalism, 1933–1936," *Mississippi Valley Historical Review* 45, no. 2 (1958): 201–230; David Zietsma, "Building the Kingdom of God: Religious Discourse, National Identity and the Good Neighbor Policy, 1930–1938," *Rhetoric & Public Affairs* 11, no. 2 (2008): 179–214.
28. PPAFDR 1937, 406–411. See Dorothy Borg, "Notes on Roosevelt's Quarantine Speech," *Political Science Quarterly* 72 (Sept 1957): 405–433, for a description of the drafting process.
29. Ruth B. Russell, *A History of the United Nations Charter: The Role of the United States, 1940–1945* (Washington, DC: Brookings Institution, 1958), 13. See also Dallek, *FDR*, 151–152.
30. For a detailed treatment of the 1938 Munich Conference, see David Faber, *Munich, 1938: Appeasement and World War II* (New York: Simon & Schuster, 2009).
31. State of the Union Address, January 4, 1939, in PPAFDR, 1–11.
32. Rosenman, *Working with Roosevelt*, 182.
33. Letter to Pope Pius XII, December 23, 1939, in PPAFDR, 608–609.
34. Some form of consular relations existed between the United States and the Papal States as early as 1797, but no official relations would be established until 1984. An 1867 statute passed by Congress withdrew appropriations for the support of an American legation in Rome. See Act of February 28, 1867, chapter 99, 14 Stat. 412, 413 (1867), merely codifying what was already a non-existent relationship.
35. George Q. Flynn, "Franklin Roosevelt and the Vatican: The Myron Taylor Appointment," *Catholic Historical Review* 58, no. 2 (1972): 172.
36. Anson Phelps Stokes and Leo Pfeffer, *Church and State in the United States* (New York: Harper & Row, 1964), 110. Jewish leaders also denounced the appointment as a serious breach in the separation of church and state. See Allen Hertzke, *Representing God in Washington* (Knoxville: University of Tennessee Press, 1988), 37–38. One significant offshoot of the Protestant opposition to this appointment was the creation of the Protestants and Other Americans United for the Separation of Church and State (POAU), which was especially instrumental in litigating many pivotal domestic church–state cases in the 1950s and 1960s. See Sarah Barringer Gordon, *Spirit of the Law* (Cambridge, MA: Belknap Press of Harvard University Press, 2010), 56–95.
37. Letter on the Status of Myron Taylor to Rev. George A. Buttrick, March 14, 1940, in PPAFDR, 101–102.

38. 1940 Annual Message to Congress, January 3, 1940, in PPAFDR, 1.
39. Rosenman, *Working with Roosevelt,* 195.
40. For a detailed account of the origins and details of the Lend-Lease program, see William L. Langer and S. Everett Gleason, *The Undeclared War, 1940–1941* (New York: Published for the Council on Foreign Relations by Harper, 1953), chapters 8 and 9. For a particular look at Russia, see Raymond Dawson, *The Decision to Aid Russia, 1941: Foreign Policy and Domestic Politics* (Chapel Hill: University of North Carolina Press, 1959).
41. Pius XI, Divini Redemptoris (Divine Redeemer), March 19, 1937. Retrieved from http://www.vatican.va/holy_Father/pius_xi/encyclicals/documents/hf_p-xi_enc_19031937_divini-redemptoris_en.html.
42. But this attitude was not limited to American Catholics alone. See Les K. Adler and Thomas G. Paterson, "Red Fascism: The Merger of Nazi Germany and Soviet Russia in the American Image of Totalitarianism, 1930s–1950s," *American Historical Review* 75, no. 4 (1970): 1046–1064.
43. Letter from FDR to Pius XII, Sept 3, 1941, in *Wartime Correspondence between President Roosevelt and Pope Pius XII: With an Introduction & Explanatory Notes by Myron C. Taylor* (New York: MacMillan, 1947), 61–62.
44. Ibid., at 57.
45. See Langer and Gleason, *The Undeclared War,* 794.
46. Annual Message to Congress, January 6, 1941, in PPAFDR, 663. FDR already hinted at these four freedoms several times during the previous year. See also Jan Herman Burgers, "The Road to San Francisco," *Human Rights Quarterly* 14 (1992): 470, for the argument that H. G. Wells's previously published "Rights of Man" influenced FDR.
47. This view is by now almost sacrosanct. See, for example, M. Glenn Johnson, "The Contributions of Eleanor and Franklin Roosevelt to the Development of International Protection for Human Rights," *Human Rights Quarterly* 9, no. 1 (February 1, 1987): 19–27.
48. Address at Annual Dinner of White House Correspondents' Association, March 15, 1941, in PPAFDR, 66.
49. Letter to Buttrick, March 14, 1940, cited in Klingbeil, "A Study of President Roosevelt," 143.
50. For a general treatment of the Atlantic Charter, see Borgwardt, *A New Deal for the World.*
51. Declaration by the United Nations, January 1, 1942, in FRUS, 1942, 1:25–26. The total number of signatories is 46.
52. See James MacGregor Burns, *Roosevelt: Soldier of Freedom* (New York: Harcourt Brace Jovanovich 1970), which states that FDR felt remorse that freedom of religion was left out of the Atlantic Charter, 183. See also Rosenman, *Working with Roosevelt,* 316; Borgwardt, *A New Deal for the World.*

53. Johnson, "The Contributions," 22, citing Steve Early to FDR, Safe File, President's Secretary's Files, FDR papers.
54. Report to Congress, August 21, 1941, PPAFDR, 1941, 334.
55. Edward Flynn, *You're the Boss* (New York: Viking Press, 1947), 185.
56. Franklin Delano Roosevelt and Susan Butler, *My Dear Mr. Stalin: The Complete Correspondence of Franklin D. Roosevelt and Joseph V. Stalin* (New Haven, CT: Yale University Press, 2005), 43. American recognition of the Soviet Union in 1933 was already a prelude. Roosevelt told Litvinov that he expects "the nationals of the United States within the territory of the Union of Soviet Socialist Republics will be allowed to conduct without annoyance or molestation of any kind of religious services and rites of a ceremonial nature, including baptismal, confirmation, communion, marriage and burial rites." *New York Times,* Nov 18, 1933, 3; See also Dallek, *FDR,* 78–81; Donald G. Bishop, *The Roosevelt-Litvinov Agreements* (Syracuse, NY: Syracuse University Press, 1965), 61–86.
57. Roosevelt and Butler, *My Dear Mr. Stalin,* 24; Art. 124, 1936, Constitution of the USSR.
58. See Dallek, *FDR,* 298.
59. Letter from U.S. Ambassador to the Soviet Union Steinhardt to Cordell Hull, Oct 6, 1941, FRUS 1941, 1:1002. They warned, however, that the "Soviet government will give lip service and make a few gestures to meet the President's wishes but is not yet prepared to give freedom of religion in the sense that we understand it."
60. See Rosenman, *Working with Roosevelt,* 316. Rosenman recounted how Roosevelt told the story with great satisfaction.
61. Fireside Chat on the Progress of the War, February 23, 1942, PPAFDR, 115.
62. Franklin Roosevelt, message of August 14, 1942, cited in Paul Gordon Lauren, *The Evolution of International Human Rights: Visions Seen* (Philadelphia: University of Pennsylvania Press, 1998), 149. Churchill could not be persuaded to sign this statement because of the concern that the message endorsed the demise of the British imperial order. See James Hubbard, *The United States and the End of British Colonial Rule in Africa, 1941–1968* (Jefferson, NC: McFarland, 2011), 11.
63. Townsend Hoopes and Douglas Brinkley, *FDR and the Creation of the U.N.* (New Haven, CT: Yale University Press, 1997), 110.
64. U.S. postwar planning actually started even *before* its entry into the war because of the assumption that the European wars would end quickly with a negotiated peace between Britain and Germany, but FDR only gave formal approval for real postwar preparation in 1942. See A. W. Brian Simpson, *Human Rights and the End of Empire* (Oxford: Oxford University Press, 2004), 175. For an account of early planning, see Department of State and Harley A. Notter, *Postwar Foreign Policy Preparation 1939–1945* (Washington, DC: U.S. Government Printing Office, 1949), 7–61.

65. The rift between Secretary of State Cordell Hull and Undersecretary Sumner Welles is one legendary example. For a more detailed account of these disagreements, see Stephen C. Schlesinger, *Act of Creation: The Founding of the United Nations* (New York: Basic Books, 2003), 33–51.
66. Benjamin Welles, *Sumner Welles: FDR's Global Strategist: A Biography* (New York: St. Martin's Press, 1997), 328.
67. Sumner Welles, *The World of the Four Freedoms* (New York: Columbia University Press, 1943).
68. "The United Nations . . . having subscribed to a common program of human rights." Preamble, Draft Constitution of International organization, Appendix 13, July 14, 1943, in Notter, *Postwar Foreign Policy Preparation,* 472.
69. See Notter, *Postwar Foreign Policy Preparation,* Appendix A, 483–485. The final draft was formulated by the Legal Subcommittee composed of Adolf Berle, Hamilton Fish Armstrong, James Shotwell, and Benjamin Cohen.
70. Draft International Bill of Rights, in Notter, *Postwar Foreign Policy Preparation,* Appendix 14, 484.
71. See Lauren, *The Evolution of International Human Rights,* 167–173.
72. See William Draper Lewis, "The Statement of Essential Human Rights by Representatives of the Principal Cultures of the World," *Proceedings of the American Philosophical Society* 89, no. 3 (Oct 11, 1945), 489–494.
73. John Humphrey, *Human Rights and the United Nations: A Great Adventure* (Dobbs Ferry, NY: Transnational Publishers, 1984), 32.
74. Federal Council of the Churches of Christ in America, *A Righteous Faith for a Just and Durable Peace* (New York: Commission to Study the Bases of a Just and Durable Peace, 1942), 101, 103.
75. Russell, *A History of the UN Charter,* 323.
76. Russell, *A History of the UN Charter,* 328. Text of draft constitution, Notter, *Postwar Foreign Policy Preparation,* Appendix 12, 470–471.
77. Kirsten Sellars, *The Rise and Rise of Human Rights* (Stroud, Gloucestershire: Sutton, 2002), xii.
78. Moscow Joint Four-Nation Declaration, Oct 1943. Retrieved from http://avalon.law.yale.edu/wwii/moscow.asp.
79. Potsdam Declaration, July 26, 1945. For a closer look at the relationship between religion and democracy in the American military occupation of Japan, see Chapter 4 of this book.
80. Department of State, *Paris Peace Conference, 1946: Selected Documents* (Washington, DC: U.S. Government Printing Office, 1947), 85.
81. Ibid., at 86.
82. Testimony of James F. Byrnes, on Treaties of Peace with Italy, Rumania, Bulgaria, and Hungry: *Hearings before the Committee on Foreign Relations,* United States Senate, 80th Congress, 1st Session (1947).

83. Memo to Secretary Byrnes from Samuel Reber, Political Adviser, U.S. delegation, August 19, 1946, FRUS, 838. "[I]t is our contention that the human rights clause in these treaties provides protection for all minorities from the point of view of guaranteeing fundamental freedoms and non-discrimination. . . . If proposals are accepted on behalf of any one group they will inevitably lead to the presentation of demands by other special groups and to an unending discussion of whose particular needs are greater."
84. Stephen D. Kertesz, "Human Rights in the Peace Treaties," *Law and Contemporary Problems* 14, no. 4 (1949): 627–646.
85. Joseph B. Schechtman, "Decline of the International Protection of Minority Rights," *Western Political Quarterly*, 4, no. 1 (March 1, 1951): 1–11.
86. James F. Byrnes, *Report by the Secretary of State on the Paris Peace Conference* (Washington, DC: U.S. Government Printing Office, 1946).
87. Declaration of the Three Powers, Dec 1, 1943, Tehran, Iran. Retrieved from http://www.yale.edu/lawweb/avalon/wwii/tehran.htm.
88. For a general account of what transpired at Dumbarton Oaks, see generally Robert C. Hilderbrand, *Dumbarton Oaks: The Origins of the United Nations and the Search for Postwar Security* (Chapel Hill: University of North Carolina Press, 2001); Roger Normand and Sarah Zaidi, *Human Rights at the United Nations: The Political History of Universal Justice* (Bloomington: Indiana University Press, 2008); Townsend Hoopes and Douglas Brinkley, *FDR and the Creation of the U.N.* (New Haven, CT: Yale University Press, 1997), 133–158.
89. Russell, *A History of the UN Charter*, 420, citing Charles Webster, "The Making of the UN Charter," *History* 32, no. 15 (March 1947), 26.
90. The British did propose, however, that a purpose of the organization should be to guard humanity's freedom by creating institutions for removing social wrongs, while China suggested that the organization be based specifically on the principle of the equality of races as well as of states. Russell, *A History of the UN Charter*, 423; Lauren, *The Evolution of International Human Rights*, 162.
91. Russell, *A History of the UN Charter*, 423.
92. FRUS, 1944, 789. See Russell, *A History of the UN Charter*, 423.
93. Borgwardt, *A New Deal for the World*, 167.
94. Russell, *A History of the UN Charter*, 424.
95. Edward Stettinius Jr., *Diaries*, entry for Sept 27, 1944, FRUS, 1944, 1:842.
96. The controversy surrounding the conference involved the de facto annexation of Poland by the Soviet Union and perceived American acquiescence, although Senator Arthur Vandenberg himself recognized that Roosevelt would not enter a war against the Soviet Union on behalf of Poland. Many consider the conference to be the key event in the emergence of the Cold War between the two countries. For a general treatment of the Yalta conference, see, for example, Edward Stettinius Jr., *Roosevelt and the Russians* (Garden City,

NY: Doubleday & Co., 1949); Serhii Plokhy, *Yalta: The Price of Peace* (New York: Penguin, 2010).

97. Russell, *A History of the UN Charter,* 546. Roosevelt Report on the Crimea Conference, *New York Times,* March 1, 1945; PPAFDR, 579.
98. Russell, *A History of the UN Charter,* 525. See also Normand, *Human Rights at the UN,* 315–316.
99. Roosevelt Report to Congress on the Crimea Conference, March 1, 1945, in PPAFDR, 579. The Yalta Conference is sometimes called the Crimea Conference.
100. Plokhy, *Yalta,* 374. Stalin moved away from this accommodationist policy at the onset of the Cold War.
101. Borgwardt, *A New Deal for the World* 184. For a side-by-side comparison, see *UNCIO: Selected Documents,* appendix 2, Table of Correspondence between the Charter and the Dumbarton Oaks Proposals, 989–991. See also Edward Stettinius Jr., "Human Rights in the United Nations Charter," *Annals of the American Academy of Political and Social Science* 243 (January 1, 1946), 1–3.
102. For a detailed treatment of American private participation in the making of the UN Charter, see, for example, Dorothy B. Robins, *Experiment in Democracy: The Story of U.S. Citizen Organizations in Forging the Charter of the United Nations* (Glendale, NY: Parkside Press, 1971); Clark Eichelberger, *Organizing for Peace: A Personal History of the Founding of the United Nations* (New York: Harper & Row, 1977).
103. The complete list of the consultants and private organizations represented at San Francisco is in *Charter of the United Nations: Report to the President on the Results of the San Francisco Conference* (Washington, DC: U.S. Government Printing Office, 1945), Appendix D, 262–266.
104. William Korey, *NGOs and the Universal Declaration of Human Rights: A Curious Grapevine* (New York: Palgrave, 2001), 36.
105. Korey, *NGOs,* 36.
106. Ibid., at 37.
107. Ibid., at 37; See also Schlesinger, *Act of Creation,* 124.
108. Schlesinger, *Act of Creation,* 124. See also Stettinius, *Diaries.* Korey also attributes more importance to the lobbying role of U.S. NGOs than the efforts of "small" nations in the drafting process of the charter.
109. Sellars, *The Rise and Rise of Human Rights,* 1–3, which declares that this interpretation is plain wrong and not supported by the verbatim transcripts; Borgwardt, *A New Deal for the World,* 190, which states that the NGO meeting lasted only half an hour and its transcript suggests no such emotional tone, and that Stettinius was already committed to the human rights–related provisions in the first place. The private organizations nonetheless made an original contribution in securing the formal role of NGOs within the UN system.

110. Sellars, *The Rise and Rise of Human Rights,* 4, citing NARA, RG 59, Records of the U.S. Delegation to the UN Conference of International Organization, 1944–1945, Box 208: Promotion of Respect for Human Rights and Fundamental Freedoms, July 4, 1945.
111. But see Robert Divine, *Second Chance: The Triumph of Internationalism in America during WWII* (New York: Atheneum Press, 1967), which argues that the longstanding efforts of private groups during the interwar period helped ensure American acceptance of the UN.
112. Louie Henkin noted that the first use of the term *human rights* in an international document was made at Dumbarton Oaks but that the records show nobody thought much about it. Louis Henkin, "Human Rights from Dumbarton Oaks," in Ernest R. May and Angeliki E. Laiou, eds., *The Dumbarton Oaks Conversations and the United Nations 1944–1994* (Washington, DC: Dumbarton Oaks Research Library and Collection; Distributed by Harvard University Press, 1998), 97–104.
113. This chapter will not retell the story of the drafting process. For comprehensive treatments of the drafting of the UDHR, see, for example, Johannes Morsink, *The Universal Declaration of Human Rights: Origins, Drafting, and Intent* (Philadelphia: University of Pennsylvania Press, 1999); Mary Ann Glendon, *A World Made New: Eleanor Roosevelt and the Universal Declaration of Human Rights* (New York: Random House, 2001); Simpson, *Human Rights,* 323–461; Humphrey, *Human Rights and the United Nations,* 1–63; Robinson, *Experiment in Democracy*; Normand, *Human Rights at the UN,* 177–196. See also Susan Waltz, "Reclaiming and Rebuilding the History of the Universal Declaration of Human Rights," *Third World Quarterly* 23, no. 3 (2002): 437–448, which argues that the role of small states in drafting the UDHR has been overlooked.
114. For example, Roosevelt wanted a separate category of trust territories for certain Pacific islands that were crucial to U.S. military interests. Unlike the League mandate system, the UN trusteeship system did not have independence as its goal. See Lauren, *The Evolution of International Human Rights,* 187.
115. UN Charter, Chapter XII, Art. 76 (c). Compare with Article 22 of the League Covenant.
116. Stephen Andrew James, *Universal Human Rights: Origins and Development* (New York: LFB Scholarly Pub LLC, 2007), 166, quoting James P. Hendrick, a lawyer with the State Department who was the principal adviser to Eleanor Roosevelt throughout the drafting process. See also Joseph P. Lash, *Eleanor: The Years Alone* (New York: Norton, 1972), 62.
117. Simpson, *Human Rights,* 357–359; Glendon, *A World Made New,* 82. But see Lash, *Years Alone,* 62. "Policy was formulated by an interdepartmental committee. But in effect, Mrs. Roosevelt set the policy. She was a presidential ap-

pointee, a woman of world stature and the State Department was eager to do what she wanted."

118. Truman address to Congress, March 5, 1947.
119. Glendon, *A World Made New,* 115–116; Normand, *Political History* (Bloomington: Indiana University Press, 2008), 190–191.
120. Theo Van Boven, "The Role of Non-Governmental Organizations in International Human Rights Standard-Setting: A Prerequisite of Democracy," *California Western International law Journal* 20 (1989): 212; Preston, *Sword of the Spirit,* 406. For a closer look at the role of the international ecumenical movement and Nolde specifically, see John Nurser, *For All Peoples and All Nations: The Ecumenical Church and Human Rights* (Washington, DC: Georgetown University Press, 2005).
121. Article 1, UDHR. "All human beings are born free and equal in dignity and rights. They are endowed with reason and conscience and should act towards one another in a spirit of brotherhood."
122. Simpson, *Human Rights,* 441.
123. Ibid., at 442, which describes it as a "perverse position." Rene Cassin, one of the prominent drafters of the UDHR, also saw minority rights as incompatible with human rights. For an interpretation of the politics involved, see Linde Lindkvist, "The Politics of Article 18: Religious Liberty in the Universal Declaration of Human Rights," *Humanity: An Interdisciplinary Journal for Human Rights* 4, no. 3 (2013): 429–447. Lindkvist argues that Roosevelt's position was not a reaction against the interwar experiment on minority protection but a defense of the American assimilationist project. However, the State Department position was a reaction to 1919. In any case, Roosevelt largely followed State Department guidelines, although it is also true that Roosevelt personally disliked the idea of minority protections.
124. "From the Melting Pot: An American Race," July 14, 1945, in Allida Black, ed., *The Eleanor Roosevelt Papers: The Human Rights Years 1945–1948* (vol. 2) (Charlottesville, VA: University of Virginia Press, 2010). See also Lindkvist, "Shrines and Souls: The Reinvention of Religious Liberty and the Genesis of the Universal Declaration of Human Rights" (PhD dissertation, Lund University, 2014).
125. ER was highly critical of the American Catholic Church, and her view on religious schools dovetailed with the Supreme Court in its landmark decision in *Everson v. Board of Education* in 1947. A more detailed treatment of Roosevelt's views is in Lindkvist, "Shrines and Souls."
126. Glendon, *A World Made New,* 69. For a deeper background on Malik's worldviews and how they influenced the UDHR, see Linde Lindkvist, "Shrines and Souls."
127. This is one of the main claims in Lindkvist, "Shrines and Souls."

128. See John Kelsay, "Saudi Arabia, Pakistan and the Universal Declaration of Human Rights," in David Little et al., eds., *Human Rights and the Conflict of Cultures: Western and Islamic Perspectives on Religious Liberty* (Columbia, SC: University of South Carolina Press, 1988), 48.
129. UN Doc A/C.3/SR.128 (1948), 405; UN Doc. A/C.3/247/Rev.1 (1948).
130. Glendon, *A World Made New,* 174.
131. A/C.3/SR 93, p. 12—Department of State Bulletin, Dec 19, 1948, 751.
132. General Assembly Resolution 181 Part I (B)(10)(d), Nov 29, 1947 ("Guaranteeing to all persons equal and non-discriminatory rights in civil, political, economic and religious matters and the enjoyment of human rights and fundamental freedoms, including freedom of religion. . . .")
133. See Moyn, *Last Utopia,* 71–83.
134. For an extended account of the Stepinac affair, see Charles Gallagher, "The United States and the Vatican in Yugoslavia, 1945–1950," in Dianne Kirby, ed., *Religion and the Cold War* (New York: Palgrave, 2003).
135. The most famous example of this conundrum occurred when Eleanor Roosevelt refused the pleas of W. E. B. DuBois to bring the National Association for the Advancement of Colored People's (NAACP's) quest for UN intervention on the issue of racial segregation in the United States before the General Assembly. See Carol Anderson, *Eyes off the Prize* (New York: Cambridge University Press, 2003), 102. The U.S. government responded with a report entitled *To Secure These Rights* by the Presidential Committee on Civil Rights, which framed the racial issue as a matter of civil rights not a minority one. See U.S. President's Committee on Civil Rights, *To Secure These Rights: The Report of the President's Committee on Civil Rights* (Washington, DC: U.S. Government Printing Office, 1947).
136. *Letter from Harry Truman to Pius XII,* August 6, 1947. Retrieved from http://www.presidency.ucsb.edu/ws/?pid=12746. "Your Holiness, this is a Christian Nation. More than a half century ago that declaration was written into the decrees of the highest court in this land. . . . Freedom of conscience, ordained by the Fathers of our Constitution to all who live under the flag of the United States, has been a bulwark of national strength, a source of happiness, from establishment of our Nation to this day."

4. Spiritual Disarmament

1. For the full story behind the New Year's Day Rescript, which included the Declaration of Humanity, see John Dower, *Embracing Defeat* (New York: W. W. Norton & Company, 2000), 308–318; William Woodard, *Allied Occupation of Japan 1945–1952 and Japanese Religions* (Leiden: Brill, 1972), 250–268.

2. The Reminiscences of Harold G. Henderson, June 1, 1961, 59, in the Columbia Center for Oral History Collection (hereafter CCOHC).
3. For the text of the 1890 Rescript, see Edward R. Beauchamp and James M. Vardaman, eds., *Japanese Education since 1945: A Documentary Study* (Armonk, NY: M. E. Sharpe, 1994), 37–38.
4. The question came up as early as the months immediately following Pearl Harbor, but the first policy paper on the status of the emperor came out on May 25, 1943. A long debate ensued between the so-called Japan crowd and the China crowd within the State Department during the subsequent years. See Robert E. Ward, "Presurrender Planning, Treatment of Emperor and Constitutional Changes," in Robert Ward and Sakamoto Yoshikazu et al., eds., *Democratizing Japan* (Honolulu: University of Hawaii Press, 1987), pp. 1–41. See also Hugh Borton, "Preparation for the Occupation of Japan," *The Journal of Asian Studies* 25, no. 2 (1966): 203–212; Marlene J. Mayo, "American Wartime Planning for Occupied Japan," in Robert Wolfe, ed., *Americans as Proconsuls: United States Military Government in Germany and Japan, 1944–1952* (Carbondale: Southern Illinois University Press, 1984), 3–50.
5. MacArthur's telegram to the U.S. Joint Chiefs of Staff Dwight Eisenhower on January 25, 1946, FRUS, vol. 8, 395–397 (1971). For a contrary view, see Hal Brands, "Who Saved the Emperor?," *Pacific Historical Review* 75, no. 2 (May 1, 2006): 271–305, which argued that, contrary to the consensus historiography, MacArthur simply reinforced and executed preexisting Washington policy on Hirohito.
6. See, for example, U.S. Office of War Information, *Enemy Japan* (Washington, DC: U.S. Government Printing Office, 1945).
7. *Hakko ichiu* in Japanese literally means "universal brotherhood." It was based on an imperial decree of Emperor Jimmu, the first emperor of Japan, and was actively propagated in order to justify Japanese expansionism. *Eight directions* was a Chinese expression meaning "the entire world," while the term *under one roof* meant "the world is one family." The term was used in the Imperial Rescript of September 27, 1940, where Japan announced its Tripartite Pact with Germany and Italy. See Herbert Bix, *Hirohito and the Making of Modern Japan* (New York: HarperCollins, 2001), 383.
8. SCAPIN 93, Removal of Restrictions on Political, Civil and Religious Liberties, October 4, 1945 (Civil Liberties Directive); SCAPIN 448, Abolition of Governmental Sponsorship, Support, Perpetuation, Control and Dissemination of State Shinto, December 15, 1945 (Shinto Directive). The full text of each is in *The Political Reorientation of Japan,* 463 and 467, respectively.
9. Edwin Reischauer, *The United States and Japan* (Cambridge, MA: Harvard University Press, 1965), 251; Rudolf V. A. Janssens, *"What Future for Japan?": U.S. Wartime Planning for the Postwar Era, 1942–1945* (Amsterdam:

Rodopi, 1995), 134, quoting Erle Dickover ("I would like to educate the Japanese out of their present glorification of military might and into an appreciation of humanity and fair dealing"). For a great account of how American perceptions of Japan changed after World War II, see Naoko Shibusawa, *America's Geisha Ally* (Cambridge, MA: Harvard University Press, 2009).

10. Proclamation Defining Terms for Japanese Surrender, Potsdam, Germany, July 26, 1945 (hereafter Potsdam Declaration), Clause 12: "The occupying forces of the Allies shall be withdrawn from Japan as soon as these objectives have been accomplished and there has been established in accordance with the freely expressed will of the Japanese people a peacefully inclined and responsible government."
11. See Chapter II, Rights and Duties of Subjects, 1889 Meiji Constitution. Retrieved from http://www.ndl.go.jp/constitution/e/etc/c02.html.
12. Ray Moore and Donald L. Robinson, *Partners for Democracy: Crafting the New Japanese State under MacArthur* (New York: Oxford University Press, 2004); Theodore Cohen and Herbert Passin, *Remaking Japan: The American Occupation as New Deal* (New York: Free Press, 1987).
13. The best treatment of this topic is John Dower, *War without Mercy: Race and Power in the Pacific War* (New York: Pantheon Books, 1986) (race); Toshio Nishi, *Unconditional Democracy: Education and Politics in Occupied Japan, 1945–1952* (Stanford, CA: Hoover Institution Press, 2004) (education); Cohen and Passin, *Remaking Japan* (economics).
14. Ray Moore, *Soldier of God: MacArthur's Attempt to Christianize Japan* (Portland, ME: MerwinAsia, 2011); Lawrence S. Wittner, "MacArthur and the Missionaries: God and Man in Occupied Japan," *Pacific Historical Review* 40, no. 1 (February 1, 1971): 77–98; Okazaki Masafumi, "Chrysanthemum and Christianity: Education and Religion in Occupied Japan, 1945–1952," *Pacific Historical Review* 79, no. 3 (2010): 393–417; Jai-keun Choi, "MacArthur's Religious Policy in Occupied Japan," *Theological Forum* 40 (2005): 135–154.
15. See pertinent portions of John Dower, *Embracing Defeat: Japan in the Wake of World War II* (New York: W. W. Norton & Company, 2000); Moore, *Partners for Democracy;* Dale Hellegers, *We, the Japanese People* (Stanford, CA: Stanford University Press, 2002); Eiji Takemae et al., *Inside GHQ* (New York: Continuum, 2002), 371–381.
16. Potsdam Declaration, Clause 10. The only book that discusses religion and the Allied occupation is Woodard, *Allied Occupation.* In this account, he categorically states that "the reason religious freedom was established by SCAP directive was because it was regarded as a sine qua non of a democratic society," 9.
17. See Dower, *Embracing Defeat,* 292. Dower narrates colorfully the background behind the publication of this photo and how, "in a single stroke, it established

both MacArthur's authority and the fact that he would stand by the emperor," 292–294.

18. A sampling of the major themes in these debates as they played out in different agencies of the U.S. government is in Janssens, *What Future,* 119–251. See also Mayo, "American Wartime Planning," 3–51.
19. See, for example, Robert Ballou, *Shinto, the Unconquered Enemy* (New York: Viking Press, 1945); Ruth Benedict, *The Chrysanthemum and the Sword: Patterns of Japanese Culture* (Boston, MA: Houghton Mifflin Co., 1946).
20. See, for example, Ernest O. Hauser, "Son of Heaven: Japan's Last Liberal, the God-Emperor Hirohito Is Prisoner of His Own Power," *Life Magazine,* June 10, 1940; Andrew Roth, *Dilemma in Japan* (Boston, MA: Little, Brown and Company, 1945); Willard Price, *Japan and the Son of Heaven* (New York: Duell, Sloan and Pearce, 1945); Ballou, *Shinto, the Unconquered Enemy.*
21. "The God-Emperor," *Time* magazine, May 21, 1945, 33–36. The cover photo itself was a provocation. When *Time* magazine put Hirohito on its cover in 1932, it was requested by the Japanese government that copies of the issue lie face upward on all tables and no object be placed upon Hirohito's likeness.
22. Ibid.
23. James F. Byrnes, *Speaking Frankly* (New York: Harper, 1947), 206. See also Letter from Cordell Hull to Secretary Byrnes, July 16, 1945, FRUS 1960, vol. 2, 1267.
24. Dower, *Embracing Defeat,* 281; Janssens, *What Future,* 130.
25. Dower, *Embracing Defeat,* 281.
26. Accounts of this rift are in Kiyoko Takeda, *The Dual-Image of the Japanese Emperor* (New York: New York University Press, 1988), 8–15; Howard Schonberger, *Aftermath of War: Americans and the Remaking of Japan, 1945–1952* (Kent, OH: Kent State University Press, 1989); Roth, *Dilemma in Japan;* Byrnes stated that he was aware of the differences in the State Department at the time he went to Potsdam. Byrnes, *Speaking Frankly,* 204.
27. Address by Joseph Grew, Annual Banquet celebrating the 90th Anniversary of the Illinois Education Association, Chicago, December 29, 1943, in Joseph C. Grew, *Ten Years in Japan* (New York: Simon and Schuster, 1944). Grew was heavily criticized for his sympathetic views toward Japan and the emperor.
28. Masanori Nakamura, *The Japanese Monarchy: Ambassador Joseph Grew and the Making of the "Symbol Emperor System," 1931–1991* (Armonk, NY: M. E. Sharpe, 1992), 66.
29. Dean Acheson charged Grew as "The Prince of Appeasers" for his views on retention, but he admitted later that he was glad to have been proven wrong. See Dean Acheson, *Present at the Creation* (New York: W. W. Norton, 1969), 112.
30. See Article 43, 1907 Hague IV Convention Respecting Laws and Customs of War on Land, October 18, 1907, 36 Stat. 2277, 1 Bevans 631, which states that

"the authority of the legitimate power having in fact passed into the hands of the occupant, the latter shall take all the measures in his power to restore and ensure as far as possible, public order and safety, while respecting, unless absolutely prevented, the laws in force in the country." Retrieved from http://avalon.law.yale.edu/19th_Century/hague02.asp.

31. Janssens, *What Future,* 233.
32. Mayo, "American Wartime Planning," 22. This was a rather prescient question that would resurrect itself in the post–Cold War and post-9/11 worlds in the context of the debates on the compatibility between Islam and democracy.
33. See Hal Brands, "The Emperor's New Clothes: American Views of Hirohito after WWII," *Historian* 68, no. 1 (2006): 1–28.
34. Bix, *Hirohito,* 557–559; Dower, *Embracing Defeat,* 277–301. Both Bix and Dower give excellent illuminations of Hirohito's wartime role.
35. U.S. Senate, Congressional Record, 91st Cong. 2nd sess., Sept. 18, 1945, 8671–80.
36. Ibid., at 8679: "He is the symbol of state and church used by the war lords in generating Japanese fanaticism. He is the god-Emperor in the direction of whose imperial palace millions of Japanese faced and prostrated themselves in the dust in abject apology for their failure to kill enough Americans to win the war. . . . If we were to leave this arch criminal upon his throne . . . we will forever perpetuate the fiction of his godliness and the myth that he is the Son of Heaven."
37. S. J. Res. 94, referred to Committee on Military Affairs, Ibid. at 8680.
38. Potsdam Declaration Clause 10.
39. Instrument of Surrender, September 2, 1945, in *Political Reorientation,* 419–420.
40. On November 29, 1945, the Joint Chiefs of Staff instructed MacArthur to gather information and evidence relating to the emperor's possible war guilt. Ward and Yoshikazu, *Democratizing Japan,* 15.
41. Douglas MacArthur, *Reminiscences* (New York: McGraw-Hill, 1964), 262. JCS 1380 was a directive for MacArthur stating this course of action. What made MacArthur different, however, was that he decided unilaterally to retain Hirohito. See Hellegers, *We, the Japanese People,* 223–233. *Time,* SCAP success, and Hirohito's own cooperation made the emperor issue less controversial down the road. See Brands, *American Views.*
42. Dower, *Embracing Defeat,* 361. See also Moore, *Soldier of God,* 55–57. For a comprehensive picture of MacArthur's idiosyncratic, enigmatic, if narcissistic personality, see William Manchester, *American Caesar* (Boston, MA: Little, Brown, 1978).
43. Truman letter to Luman J. Schafer, October 8, 1945, in Dennis Merrill, ed., *Documentary History of the Truman Presidency: Creating a Pluralistic*

Democracy in Japan (Bethesda, MD: University Publications of America, 1996), 17.

44. General of the Army Douglas MacArthur to the Chief of Staff, United States Army, Eisenhower, January 25, 1946, FRUS 1971, vol. 8, 395–397.
45. Woodard, *Allied Occupation,* 359; Moore, *Soldier of God,* 54.
46. Douglas MacArthur, Address on Second Anniversary of Surrender, Sept 2, 1947, in *Political Reorientation,* 775.
47. Woodard, *Allied Occupation,* 358; Moore, *Soldier of God,* 58.
48. Moore, *Soldier of God,* 58. In a letter to the president of the Southern Baptist Convention, December 13, 1946, he wrote, "Due to the vacuum which events have left in the spiritual phase of Japanese life, there now exists an opportunity without counterpart since the birth of Christ for the spread of Christianity among the peoples of the Far East." Woodard, *Allied Occupation,* 355.
49. MacArthur, *Reminiscences,* 311; Woodard, *Allied Occupation,* 359.
50. Moore, *Soldier of God,* 49; Woodard, *Allied Occupation,* 270–275.
51. Woodard, *Allied Occupation,* 317–319.
52. Dower, *Embracing Defeat,* 308–314.
53. *New York Times,* January 2, 1946, at 15.
54. *Time,* January 16, 1946.
55. General MacArthur's Comment on the Imperial Rescript of January 1, 1946, in *Political Reorientation,* 746.
56. Potsdam Declaration, Clause 10; U.S. Initial Post-Surrender Policy for Japan, Part III (3), Encouragement of Desire for Individual Liberties and Democratic Processes. August 29, 1945: "Freedom of religious worship shall be proclaimed promptly on occupation. At the same time, it should be made plain to the Japanese that ultranationalistic and militaristic organizations and movements will not be permitted to hide behind the cloak of religion." Joint Chiefs of Staff, Basic Initial Post-Surrender Directive to SCAP, JCS 1380/15, November 3, 1945, (9)(e): "Freedom of religious worship shall be proclaimed promptly by the Japanese Government. To the extent that the security of your military occupation and the attainment of its objectives are not prejudiced . . . you will insure freedom of opinion, speech, press and assembly."
57. Memorandum on Freedom of Worship, March 15, 1944, Inter-Divisional Area Committee on the Far East, FRUS vol. 5 (1965), 1207–1208.
58. Ibid.
59. Civil Liberties Directive, in *Political Reorientation,* 463–465.
60. Woodard, *Allied Occupation,* 51.
61. There is no particular law designating Shinto as a nonreligion. However, a number of ordinances provided legal basis, the most important of which was Imperial Ordinance No. 163, April 26, 1900, which placed shrines and everything concerning them under a Shrine Bureau in the Home Ministry and

"all affairs pertaining to religion" under a Bureau of Religions in the same ministry. The latter was shortly transferred to the Ministry of Education, where it stayed until 1945. See Ken Dyke, "Shinto: A Study Prepared by General Headquarters SCAP CI&E Section," December 3, 1945, *Contemporary Religions in Japan* 7, no. 4 (1966): 348–350.

62. For a general treatment of the Meiji Restoration, see William Beasley, *The Meiji Restoration* (Stanford, CA: Stanford University Press, 1972); Marius B. Jansen, "The Meiji Restoration," in Marius B. Jansen, ed., *The Cambridge History of Japan* vol. 5, The Nineteenth Century (New York: Cambridge University Press, 1989).
63. See Helen Hardacre, *Shinto and the State, 1868–1988* (Princeton, NJ: Princeton University Press, 1989), 21–39.
64. For a great general overview of state Shinto and its relation to other religions during the prewar years, see generally Hardacre, *Shinto and the State.*
65. David M. O'Brien with Yasuo Ōgoshi, *To Dream of Dreams: Religious Freedom and Constitutional Politics in Postwar Japan* (Honolulu: University of Hawaii Press, 1996), 46.
66. Daniel C. Holtom, *The Political Philosophy of Modern Shinto* (Tokyo: Asiatic Society of Japan, 1922), 236. This was his doctoral dissertation at the University of Chicago. Holtom was offered a position with SCAP, but he declined for health reasons. He continued advising occupation officials in an informal capacity, and his book *The National Faith of Japan* (1938) was required reading for all occupation officials. As an illustration of Holtom's assertion, see for example, O'Brien with Ohkoshi, *To Dream of Dreams,* 46: "In 1940, when the Religious Organizations Law was presented to the Diet, Prime Minister Kiichiro Hiranuma claimed that, 'In our country the way of the kami is the absolute way. Teachings which differ from this and conflict with it are not allowed to exist.'"
67. Woodard, *Allied Occupation,* 63.
68. For an illustration of how this was effected, see Hardacre, *Shinto and the State,* 100–113.
69. Dyke, *Shinto: A Study Prepared,* 336.
70. See the text of the Shinto Directive in *Political Reorientation,* 467–468.
71. Shinto Directive: "(f) All public educational institutions whose primary function is either the investigation and dissemination of Shinto or the training of a Shinto priesthood will be abolished and their physical properties diverted to other uses. Their present functions, duties, and administrative obligations will not be assumed by any other governmental or tax-supported agency; (g) Private educational institutions for the investigation and dissemination of Shinto and for the training of priesthood for Shinto will be permitted and will operate with the same privileges and be subject to the same controls and restrictions as any other private educational institution having no affiliation with the government; in no case, however, will they receive support from public funds, and in no case will they propagate and disseminate militaristic and ultra-nationalistic

ideology; (h) The dissemination of Shinto doctrines in any form and by any means in any educational institution supported wholly or in part by public funds is prohibited and will cease immediately.

1) All teachers' manuals and text-books now in use in any educational institution supported wholly or in part by public funds will be censored, and all Shinto doctrine will be deleted. No teachers' manual or text-book which is published in the future for use in such institutions will contain any Shinto doctrine.

2) No visits to Shinto shrines and no rites, practices, or ceremonies associated with Shinto will be conducted or sponsored by any educational institution supported wholly or in part by public funds."

72. Shinto Directive: "(m) No official of the national, prefectural, or local government, acting in his public capacity, will visit any shrine to report his assumption of office, to report on conditions of government, or to participate as a representative of government in any ceremony or observance."
73. SCAPIN 947, Prohibition of Certain Subjects in Designs of Japanese Postage Stamps and Currency, May 13, 1946, in Woodard, *Allied Occupation,* Appendix B, 6, 299.
74. Ibid.
75. Shinto Directive: "(h) (1) All teachers' manuals and text-books now in use in any educational institution supported wholly or in part by public funds will be censored, and all Shinto doctrine will be deleted. No teachers' manual or text-book which is published in the future for use in such institutions will contain any Shinto doctrine."
76. Shinto Directive: "(h) (2) No visits to Shinto shrines and no rites, practices, or ceremonies associated with Shinto will be conducted or sponsored by any educational institution supported wholly or in part by public funds."
77. Shinto Directive (2): "(a) The purpose of this directive is to separate religion from the state to prevent misuse of religion for political ends, and to put all religions, faiths, and creeds upon exactly the same legal basis, entitled to precisely the same opportunities and protection. It forbids affiliation with the government and the propagation and dissemination of militaristic and ultranationalistic ideology not only to Shinto but to the followers of all religions, faiths, sects, creeds, or philosophies."
78. Takemae, *Inside GHQ,* 377. The difficulty was in finding the appropriate Japanese term because Japan and the West had different understandings of the word *religion.*
79. Although the phrase "separation of church and state" had its origins in the American Founding period, it does not appear anywhere in the text of the U.S. Constitution, and its definite contours were not delineated until February 10, 1947, in the U.S. Supreme Court decision of *Everson v. Board of Education,*

wherein the majority opinion held that the Establishment Clause is incorporated against the states, and that separation was defined as no state can support or aid one religion or all religions. See 330 U.S. 1 (1947). The phrase was considered at that time a veneer for anti-Catholic sentiment in the United States. See generally Philip Hamburger, *Separation of Church and State* (Cambridge, MA: Harvard University Press, 2002).

80. O'Brien with Ōgoshi, *To Dream of Dreams*, 53–61.
81. Agreement of Foreign Ministers at Moscow on Establishing a Far Eastern Commission and Allied Council for Japan, December 27, 1945, in *Political Reorientation*, 421–422. The FEC was a constant source of frustration for MacArthur.
82. Moore, *Partners for Democracy*, 89.
83. Potsdam Declaration, Clause 10.
84. Memorandum by the Secretary General of the FEAC, January 30, 1946, in FRUS, vol 8, 123.
85. The Konoe affair is eloquently recounted in Hellegers, *We, the Japanese People*, 438–460. See also Theodore McNelly, *Origins of Japan's Democratic Constitution* (Lanham, MD: University Press of America, 2000); Moore, *Partners for Democracy*, 64–80.
86. Indeed, the only time that the State Department knew about the draft constitution was when the Japanese government draft was released by the Cabinet on March 4, 1946. State officials immediately recognized the SCAP imprint on the draft.
87. *Political Reorientation*, vol. 2, Appendix II, 741.
88. See Milo Rowell, Report of Preliminary Studies and Recommendations of Japanese Constitution, December 6, 1945. Retrieved from http://www.ndl.go.jp/constitution/e/shiryo/03/046shoshi.html (hereafter Rowell Report). See also Ray Moore and Donald Robinson, eds., *The Japanese Constitution: A Documentary History of Its Framing and Adoption* (Princeton, NJ: Princeton University Press, 1998) (CD-ROM) (hereafter Moore and Robinson, *Documentary History*).
89. See Rowell Report. This is also found in Hellegers, *We, the Japanese People*, 499–502.
90. Hellegers, *We, the Japanese People*, 468–469; Dower, *Embracing Defeat*, 353; Moore, *Partners for Democracy*, 76–77; Takemae, *Inside GHQ*, 273.
91. This was the view of Tatsukichi Minobe, an eminent professor of constitutional law at Tokyo Imperial University. See Dower, *Embracing Defeat*, 355.
92. For Matsumoto's Four Points, see Moore, *Partners for Democracy*, 75; Hellegers, *We, the Japanese People*, 472.
93. The Mainichi draft was not even as conservative as what the committee was planning to submit on February 8. See The Tentative Plan of the Constitution

Problem Investigation Committee, Mainichi Shimbun, February 1, 1946, in *Political Reorientation,* 611.

94. Eiji Takemae, *The Allied Occupation of Japan* (New York: Continuum International Publishing Group, 2003), 273–274; Dower, *Embracing Defeat,* 356–357.
95. Moore, *Partners for Democracy,* 72.
96. Memorandum from Courtney Whitney to the Supreme Commander on Constitutional Reform, February 1, 1946, in *Political Reorientation,* 622–623.
97. Ibid., at 623.
98. MacArthur's Three Points, February 4, 1946. Retrieved from http://www.ndl.go.jp/constitution/e/shiryo/03/072shoshi.html; Hellegers, *We, the Japanese People,* 519.
99. Ruth Ellerman was the designated note taker during the drafting process, and her notes are considered the minutes of the GHQ constitutional convention. Both Moore and Robinson's *Documentary History* and Hellegers's *We, the Japanese People* include her notes for each constitutional provision.
100. The following provisions are from the original SCAP draft. For a side-by-side comparison of the SCAP draft and the Japanese government draft of March 2, 1946, which was the result of a marathon translation session, see Hellegers, *We, the Japanese People,* Appendix J, 673–709.
101. Chapter I, The Emperor. Article 1: "The Emperor shall be the symbol of the State and of the Unity of the People, deriving his position from the sovereign will of the People and from no other source."
102. Chapter III. Rights and Duties of the People. Article 9: "The people of Japan are entitled to the enjoyment without interference of all fundamental human rights"; Article 10: "The fundamental human rights by this Constitution guaranteed to the people of Japan result from the age-old struggle of man to be free. They have survived the exacting test for durability in the crucible of time and experience and are conferred upon this and future generations in sacred trust, to be held for all time inviolate"; Article 18: "Freedom of thought and conscience shall be held inviolable"; Article 19: "Freedom of religion is guaranteed to all. No religious organization shall receive special privileges from the State nor exercise political authority. No person shall be compelled to take part in any religious acts, celebration, rites or practices. The State and its organs shall refrain from religious education or any other religious activity."
103. Chapter VII, Finance. Article 83: "No public money or property shall be appropriated for the use, benefit or support of any system of religion or religious institution or association or for any charitable, educational or benevolent purposes not under the control of the State."
104. 1889 Meiji Constitution, Article 28: "Japanese subjects shall, within limits not prejudicial to peace and order, and not antagonistic to their duties as subjects, enjoy freedom of religious belief."

105. Joseph Henning, *Outposts of Civilization: Race, Religion, and the Formative Years of American-Japanese Relations* (New York: New York University Press, 2000), 145.
106. Woodard, *Allied Occupation,* 78.
107. Ibid., citing a letter dated August 28, 1967, from Frank Rizzo, one of the GS drafters and in charge of the finance provisions of the Constitution.
108. The full text of the Charter Oath of the Meiji Restoration is quoted in its entirety in the Imperial Rescript of January 1, 1946; see *Political Reorientation,* 470.
109. Hellegers, *We, the Japanese People,* 601, footnote 58, citing Ellerman's minutes.
110. Civil Rights: First Discussion of Draft, February 8, 1946, Meeting of the Steering Committee with Committee on Civil Rights, in Moore and Robinson, *Documentary History,* citing Takayanagi Kenzo, Ohtomo Ichiro, and Tanaka Hideo, eds., Nihonkoku kenpo seiti nokte, 2 vols. (1972). The first draft of the article read as follows: "Article 13. Freedom of Religion is guaranteed to all. No religious organization shall receive privileges from the State or its national or local authorities, nor any ecclesiastical functionaries abuse their spiritual authority for political purposes. No person shall be compelled or pressed to take part in any religious acts, celebrations, rites or practices. No religious body will be recognized as such if under the disguise of religion, it should stir up and practice antagonism in others or should weaken instead of strengthen public order or morality. The State and its organs shall refrain from religious education or any other religious activity."
111. Hellegers, *We, the Japanese People,* 601, footnote 58, citing Ellerman's minutes.
112. For the Japanese process from translation of SCAP draft to promulgation by the Japanese Cabinet, see Dower, *Embracing Defeat,* 374–404; Hellegers, *We, the Japanese People,* 534–544.
113. *Political Reorientation,* 625.
114. Ibid.
115. Section 23(3) of the 1935 Philippine Constitution: "No public money, or property shall ever be appropriated, applied, or used, directly or indirectly, for the use, benefit, or support of any sect, church, denomination, sectarian institution or system of religion, for the use, benefit, or support of any priest, preacher, ministers, or other religious teacher or dignitary as such except when such priest, preacher, minister, or dignitary is assigned to the armed forces or to any penal institution, orphanage or leprosarium." See Woodard, *Allied Occupation,* 78; Hardacre, *Shinto and the State,* 138.
116. "Chapter II, The Emperor and the People," SCAP First Draft, in Moore and Robinson, *Documentary History.*
117. Hellegers, *We, the Japanese People,* 529.

118. SWNCC 228, Reform of Japanese governmental system, FRUS 1971, vol. 8, 99–103. Technically it was just a guiding document for MacArthur because his directives can only come from the Joint Chiefs of Staff, and SWNCC was an interdepartmental document.
119. Article III, Meiji constitution. In the commentary of Ito Hirobumi, the principal author of the Meiji constitution, on this article, he wrote: "The Sacred Throne was established at the time when the heavens and the earth became separated. The Emperor is Heaven-descended, divine and sacred; He is preeminent above all his subjects. He must be reverenced and is inviolable." Ito Hirobumi, *Commentaries on the Constitution of the Empire of Japan* (Westport, CT: Greenwood Press, 1978), 6.
120. Explanatory Notes, February 13, 1946, in Moore and Robinson, *Documentary History.*
121. Whitney made this clear in an exchange with Matsumoto regarding the procedure with which to introduce the new constitution: "Our concept of a Constitution is that it comes up from the people, not down to the people. . . . In effect, the Emperor suggests to the people that they shall adopt the principles embodied in the Constitution. Then General MacArthur will proclaim to the world—this is the Constitution now accepted by the Japanese people." See Matsumoto and Shigeru meet with SCAP, GS Transcript, February 22, 1946, in Moore and Robinson, *Documentary History.*
122. See, for example, Dower, *Embracing Defeat,* 391–394; Hellegers, *We, the Japanese People,* 534–536; Moore, *Partners for Democracy,* 109.
123. Hellegers, *We, the Japanese People,* 528.
124. Matsumoto's testimony during the March 4 and 5 drafting sessions, in Moore and Robinson, *Documentary History*; Matsumoto quarreled with Kades over the Japanese translation of the powers of the emperor, and he claimed Kades was attempting to alter not only the constitution but the Japanese language as well. Richard B. Finn, *Winners in Peace: MacArthur, Yoshida, and Postwar Japan* (Berkeley: University of California Press, 1992), 100.
125. See Kyoko Inoue, *MacArthur's Japanese Constitution: A Linguistic and Cultural Study* (Chicago, IL: University of Chicago Press, 1991), which argues that the Japanese constitution was a product of Japanese effort as well as American imposition through the translation process and that tradition survives in the Japanese language text. It took the National Diet several months to debate the government draft before Hirohito approved it on November 3, 1946.
126. MacArthur, *Reminscences,* 671.
127. In an important case decided by the Japanese Supreme Court in 1977 regarding a Shinto grounds purification ceremony at public expense (*jichinsai*), the court held that separation between church and state is not an absolute and what is proscribed are ceremonies that carry a religious meaning and whose effect is to

support, encourage, or promote religion or to interfere with it. See Hardacre, *Shinto and the State,* 149–50.

5. Cold War, Hot Rights

1. All NATO and Warsaw Pact countries, the United States, and Canada, participated in the CSCE discussions. Only Albania opted out of the talks. The negotiations lasted for three years and involved almost 400 diplomats.
2. "Jerry, Don't Go," *Wall Street Journal,* July 23, 1975, at 14. "European Security and Real Détente," *New York Times,* July 21, 1975, at 14. For a closer look at the sources of U.S. domestic opposition to the HFA, see Sarah B. Snyder, "'Jerry Don't Go': Domestic Opposition to the 1975 Helsinki Final Act," *Journal of American Studies* 44, no. 1 (2010): 67–81.
3. Senate, Congressional Record, 94th Cong., 1st sess., July 22, 1975, 2410.
4. Edmund S. Muskie and Kenneth Rush et al., eds., *The President, the Congress and Foreign Policy* (Lanham, MD: University Press of America, 1986), 290.
5. *Détente* was a taboo word in the Nixon administration. It does not appear in the official foreign policy statements of the administration for the years 1970 to 1973. See generally Richard M. Nixon, U.S. Foreign Policy for the 1970s: A Strategy for Peace, A Report to the Congress, February 18, 1970; Nixon, U.S. Foreign Policy for the 1970s: Building for Peace, A Report to the Congress, February 25, 1971; Nixon, U.S. Foreign Policy for the 1970s: The Emerging Structure of Peace, A Report to the Congress, February 9, 1972; Nixon, U.S. Foreign Policy for the 1970s: Shaping a Durable Peace, A Report to the Congress, May 3, 1973. To date, only the Nixon administration has issued separate presidential reports on foreign policy.
6. Sarah B. Snyder, *Human Rights Activism and the End of the Cold War* (New York: Cambridge University Press, 2011), 22.
7. Michael Morgan, "The U.S. and the Making of the Helsinki Final Accords," in Fredrik Logevall and Andrew Preston, eds., *Nixon in the World: American Foreign Relations, 1969–1977* (New York: Oxford University Press, 2008), 169; Snyder, *Human Rights Activism,* 67–82.
8. Snyder, *Human Rights Activism,* 32; Oliver Bange and Gottfried Niedhart, *Helsinki 1975 and the Transformation of Europe* (New York: Berghahn Books, 2008), 71.
9. For the pioneering work on this topic, see Daniel C. Thomas, *The Helsinki Effect: International Norms, Human Rights, and the Demise of Communism* (Princeton, NJ: Princeton University Press, 2001); see also Snyder, *Human Rights Activism.*
10. Part (1)(a)(VII), Conference on Security and Cooperation in Europe, Final Act, Helsinki, Finland, August 1, 1975 (hereafter HFA). It was, in the terms of

one diplomat, "a solidly-worded Western achievement." For one of the classic insider accounts of the CSCE negotiations, see John Maresca, *To Helsinki: The Conference on Security and Cooperation in Europe, 1973–1975* (Durham, NC: Duke University Press, 1985), 108.

11. Part (3)(1)(b), HFA.
12. Part (3)(1)(c), HFA.
13. Part (3)(1)(d), HFA.
14. Part (3)(3) and Part (3)(4), HFA.
15. Part (3)(3) and Part (3)(4), HFA.
16. T. Jeremy Gunn, "The OSCE and the Rights of Religion or Belief," in Peter G. Danchin and Elizabeth A. Cole, eds., *Protecting the Human Rights of Religious Minorities in Eastern Europe* (New York: Columbia University Press, 2002), 231. Still, this was a big achievement. In the document "Basic Principles of Relations between the US and the USSR," signed on May 29, 1972, by Nixon and Brezhnev, human rights appeared nowhere in the text.
17. Section 401, Title IV of the Trade Act of 1974, P.L. 93–618, January 3, 1975. The literature surrounding the amendment is voluminous, but no one has analyzed it from the perspective of Congress and religious freedom. Nobody has made the claim that JVA was meant to espouse religious freedom. For works focusing on the role of the American Jewish lobby in the passage of the JVA, see William W. Orbach, *The American Movement to Aid Soviet Jews* (Amherst: University of Massachusetts Press, 1979), 117–154; Murray Freedman and Albert D. Chernin, eds., *A Second Exodus: The American Movement to Free Soviet Jews* (Hanover, NH: University Press of New England for Brandeis University Press, 1999). See also Gal Beckerman, *When They Come for Us, We'll Be Gone: The Epic Struggle to Save Soviet Jewry* (New York: Houghton Mifflin Harcourt, 2010), 273–310. For a look at the domestic executive-legislative interaction in the passage of this amendment, the best in-depth treatment is Paula W. Stern, *Water's Edge: Domestic Politics and the Making of American Foreign Policy* (Westport, CT: Greenwood Press, 1979). For a look at the point of view of Scoop Jackson and the relationship between the JVA and his opposition to détente, see Robert Gordon Kaufman, *Henry M. Jackson: A Life in Politics* (Seattle, WA: University of Washington Press, 2010), 261–300.
18. For the argument that the JVA and its freedom to emigrate provision contributed to the recognition of international human rights, see Jordan Chandler Hirsch, "The Gateway: The Soviet Jewry Movement, the Right to Leave and the Rise of Human Rights on the International Stage" (senior thesis, Columbia University, 2010). The thesis does not discuss religious freedom.
19. Barbara Keys, *Reclaiming American Virtue: The Human Rights Revolution of the 1970s* (Cambridge, MA: Harvard University Press, 2014), which argues that the American turn to human rights was a result of the national trauma

inflicted by the Vietnam War; Daniel Sargent, "Oasis in the Desert: America's Human Rights Rediscovery," in Jan Eckel and Samuel Moyn, eds., *The Breakthrough: Human Rights in the 1970s* (Philadelphia PA: University of Pennsylvania Press, 2014), 125–145. For a general picture of the epochal changes in American society in the 1970s, see pertinent portions of Daniel Rodgers, *Age of Fracture* (Cambridge, MA: Belknap Press of Harvard University Press, 2011). For a rendering of these changes on a worldwide stage, see generally Niall Ferguson, Erez Manela, et al., eds., *The Shock of the Global: The 1970s in Perspective* (Cambridge, MA: Harvard University Press, 2010); Thomas Borstelmann, *The 1970s* (Princeton, NJ: Princeton University Press, 2012).

20. See Frank Costigliola, *Roosevelt's Lost Alliances* (Princeton, NJ: Princeton University Press, 2012), which argues the postwar world depended on and was shaped by the personalities of FDR, Churchill, and Stalin.
21. See Chapter 3 of this book.
22. Harry S. Truman, Address Recommending Aid to Greece and Turkey, March 12, 1947. Retrieved from http://avalon.law.yale.edu/20th_Century/trudoc.asp.
23. The recognition of a Judeo-Christian tradition notwithstanding, the vitriol between Protestants and the Roman Catholic Church proved greater than any effort by Truman to put up a united national effort against communism. His attempt to appoint General Mark Clark, an Episcopalian and a war hero, to replace Myron Taylor upon the latter's retirement as the representative to the Vatican failed when Clark withdrew under intense criticism from various Protestant groups. See F. William O'Brien, "General Clark's Nomination as Ambassador to the Vatican: American Reaction," *The Catholic Historical Review* 44, no. 4 (January 1, 1959): 421–439; Samuel Eager Jr., "Constitutionality of the Proposed Appointment of an Ambassador to the Vatican," *Albany Law Review* 16 (1952): 208; Mark Edwards, "God Has Chosen Us: Remembering Christian Realism, Rescuing Christendom and the Contest of Responsibilities during the Cold War," *Diplomatic History* 33, no. 1 (2009): 67–94.
24. *Correspondence between President Truman and Pope Pius XII* (New York: n.p., 1953), 17.
25. Ibid.
26. See Jonathan Herzog, *The Spiritual-Industrial Complex: America's Religious Battle against Communism in the Early Cold War* (New York: Oxford University Press, 2011), which argues that the religious revival of the 1940s and 1950s was largely manufactured by commercial and governmental interests that weakened mainstream religion). This phenomenon was not limited to the United States. For the European experience, see Samuel Moyn, "From Communist to Muslim: European Human Rights, the Cold War, and Religious Liberty" *South Atlantic Quarterly* 113, no. 1 (Winter 2014): 63–86.

27. For the role of religion in U.S. foreign policy during the early Cold War, the relatively short canon includes William Inboden, *Religion and American Foreign Policy, 1945–1960: The Soul of Containment* (New York: Cambridge University Press, 2010); Andrew Preston, *Sword of the Spirit, Shield of Faith* (New York: Knopf, 2012): 411–495; Seth Jacobs, *America's Miracle Man in Vietnam* (Durham, NC: Duke University Press, 2005). See also Rachel Bronson, *Thicker Than Oil* (New York: Oxford University Press, 2006) (on how religion was mobilized to bolster the U.S.-Saudi relationship); T. Jeremy Gunn, *Spiritual Weapons: The Cold War and the Forging of an American National Religion* (Westport, CT: Praeger, 2009). For a treatment of how the early Cold War shaped the American domestic landscape, see generally Jason W. Stevens, *God-Fearing and Free* (Cambridge, MA: Harvard University Press, 2011); Angela M. Lahr, *Millennial Dreams and Apocalyptic Nightmares* (New York: Oxford University Press, 2007); Dianne Kirby, ed., *Religion and the Cold War* (New York: Palgrave, 2003), 211–231; Herzog, *The Spiritual-Industrial Complex.*
28. Seth Jacobs, "Our System Demands the Supreme Being: The U.S. Religious Revival and the Diem Experiment 1954–55," *Diplomatic History* 25, no. 4 (2001): 589–624.
29. It must be noted that Senator Joseph McCarthy's infamous domestic anticommunist crusade was not based on religious grounds, but the progenitors of today's Christian Right, Carl McIntire and Billy James Hargis, readily endorsed and lent their support to the senator. See Daniel K. Williams, *God's Own Party* (New York: Oxford University Press, 2010), 39–41; Herzog, *The Spiritual-Industrial Complex,* 88; Gunn, *Spiritual Weapons.*
30. 36 U.S.C. 186 (1954).
31. P.L. 83–396, 68 Stat. 249, H.J. Res. 243, enacted June 14, 1954. For the Cold War origins of the pledge, see Lee Canipe, "Under God and Anti-Communist: How the Pledge of Allegiance Got Religion in Cold War America," *Journal of Church and State* 45, no. 2 (2003): 305; Richard J. Ellis, *To the Flag: The Unlikely History of the Pledge of Allegiance* (Lawrence: University of Kansas Press, 2007).
32. *Zorach v. Clauson,* 343 U.S. 306 (1952). Compare this with the earlier case of *McCollum v. Board of Education,* 333 U.S. 203 (1948), in which the Court struck down an Illinois program setting aside class time for religious instruction.
33. *Zorach v. Clauson,* 3.
34. Compare, for example, the State of the Union addresses of Truman and Eisenhower with that of Kennedy, Johnson, and Nixon.
35. There are many reasons for the shift, aside from the demise of the spiritual-industrial complex. The literature on the great cultural shift in the 1960s is voluminous. For the rise of conservatism in the 1960s and 1970s and its

eventual entry into politics, see Maurice Isserman and Michael Kazin, *America Divided: The Civil War of the 1960s* (New York: Oxford University Press, 2008); Jonathan Schoenwald, *A Time for Choosing: The Rise of Modern American Conservatism* (New York: Oxford University Press, 2001); Matthew Moen, *The Christian Right and Congress* (Tuscaloosa: University of Alabama Press, 1989); William Martin, *With God on Our Side* (New York: Broadway Books, 1996); Williams, *God's Own Party.* See also Herzog, *The Spiritual-Industrial Complex,* 191–211.

36. For a general overview of U.S. foreign policy during the Nixon years, see Logevall and Preston, eds., *Nixon in the World.* Efforts toward détente already started during the Johnson administration, but they proceeded in fits and starts. It was only during the Nixon presidency that all essential ingredients came together for the policy to be implemented.
37. Soviet and American understandings of détente differed, which contributed to the early demise of this policy. The principal work on détente is Raymond Garthoff, *Détente and Confrontation* (Washington, DC: Brookings Institution, 1985). See also Robert Litwak, *Détente and the Nixon Doctrine* (New York: Cambridge University Press, 1984). Détente was also a core issue for Western Europe, but its aims and motives are different from that of the United States and thus are outside the scope of this chapter.
38. See Lahr, *Millenial Dreams,* which shows how evangelicals drew upon their premillenarian dispensationalist beliefs in finding common cause with mainstream Americans in the battle against communism.
39. Kaufman, *Scoop Jackson,* 250. See also Dorothy Fosdick, *Staying the Course: Henry M. Jackson and National Security* (Seattle: University of Washington Press, 1987), 114.
40. See Jeremi Suri, "Détente and Human Rights: American and West European Perspectives on International Change," *Cold War History* 8, no. 4 (2008): 527–545: "Human rights were not alternatives to the Cold War. They were in fact products of the Cold War. . . . Détente in both its West European and American formulations did not seek to end the Cold War but to make it easier to live with." But this only applies to the human rights included in the HFA, not the human rights envisioned by an assertive U.S. Congress with, for example, the JVA.
41. Litwak, *Détente and the Nixon Doctrine,* 91–92. For elaboration on domestic confusion about détente, see Julian Zelizer, "Détente and Domestic Politics," *Diplomatic History* 33 (2009): 653–670.
42. Hearings before the Senate Committee on Foreign Relations, Détente, 93rd Cong., 2nd sess., Sept 19, 1974, 247.
43. Statement by Henry Kissinger, "Détente with the Soviet Union: The Reality of Competition and the Imperative of Cooperation," Sept 19, 1974, *State Department Bulletin,* vol. 71, Oct 14, 1974, 518.

44. See Jeremi Suri, *Henry Kissinger and the American Century* (Cambridge, MA: Harvard University Press, 2007), for a sympathetic portrayal of Kissinger. Suri argues that his invocation of force and diplomacy was laden with moral purpose. But see Kissinger's surprising statement in 1976 when he spoke before the annual meeting of the Organization of American States (OAS) in Santiago, Chile, saying that "human rights are the very essence of a meaningful life." See "A Harsh Warning on Human Rights," *Time,* June 21, 1976.
45. See Keys, *Reclaiming American Virtue.* For example, despite her participation in the committee that drafted the UDHR, Eleanor Roosevelt refused to introduce a petition by W. E. B. DuBois critical of racial practices in the United States in the UN Commission on Human Rights, which she chaired, because it would provide the Soviet Union with Cold War ammunition against the United States. See Chapter 3 in this book. The path-breaking work exploring the Cold War origins of the U.S. civil rights revolution is Mary Dudziak, *Cold War Civil Rights: Race and the Image of American Democracy* (Princeton, NJ: Princeton University Press, 2000). Supporters of the Bricker amendment in the 1950s, which sought to restrict the scope and implementation of treaties entered into by the United States, were also motivated by fears that the federal government would use the treaties, particularly the Genocide Convention, to target the system of racial segregation in the American South.
46. Amicus brief for the United States, 6, *Brown v. Board of Education,* 347 U.S. 483 (1954).
47. The literature on this topic is too numerous to list. See Edmund S. Muskie et al., eds., *The President, the Congress, and Foreign Policy* (Lanham, MD: University Press of America, 1986); David Forsythe, *Human Rights and U.S. Foreign Policy: Congress Reconsidered* (Gainesville: University of Florida Press, 1988): 2, "It has been said that the Constitution invites a struggle between the political branches for control of foreign policy. After largely deferring to the executive branch for two decades, Congress accepted the invitation." It is not that Congress was largely passive before the Nixon years, but its impact was not as profound and enduring. For congressional activism prior to the Nixon years, see Robert David, *Congress and the Cold War* (New York: Cambridge University Press, 2006). For the argument that this revolution resulted in a permanent transformation of how U.S. foreign affairs are conducted and not necessarily in a positive way, the classic work is Thomas Franck and Edward Weisband, *Foreign Policy by Congress* (New York: Oxford University Press, 1979). To follow the trajectory of congressional human rights activism through human rights conditions on security assistance, see Barbara Keys, "Congress, Kissinger and the Origins of Human Rights Diplomacy," *Diplomatic History,* 34 (2010): 823–851.
48. This argument is elaborated on more fully in Moyn, *Last Utopia;* Michael C. Morgan, "The Seventies and the Rebirth of Human Rights," in Ferguson, Manela, et al., eds., *The Shock of the Global,* 237–250.

49. U.S. House of Representatives, *Report of the Committee on Foreign Affairs. Subcommittee on International Organizations and Movements,* March 27, 1974 (hereafter Fraser Report).
50. Ibid., at 9.
51. Sec. 502B (a)(1), Foreign Assistance Act of 1961 as amended, P.L. 87–195: "The United States shall, in accordance with its international obligations as set forth in the Charter of the United Nations and in keeping with the constitutional heritage and traditions of the United States, promote and encourage increased respect for human rights and fundamental freedoms throughout the world without distinction as to race, sex, language or religion. Accordingly, a principal goal of the foreign policy of the United States shall be to promote the increased observance of internationally recognized human rights by all countries." Sec. 502B (a)(2): "Except under circumstances specified in this section, no security assistance may be provided to any country the government of which engages in a consistent pattern of gross violations of inter-nationally recognized human rights."
52. Keys, *Reclaiming American Virtue.* For the origins of the term, see Arthur C. Schlesinger, *The Imperial Presidency* (Boston, MA: Houghton Mifflin, 1973).
53. Richard Campany, *The United States and Turkey: The Arms Embargo Period* (New York: Praeger, 1986), 78.
54. 50 U.S.C. 1541–1548 (1973). The resolution requires the president to notify Congress within 48 hours of committing armed forces to military action and forbids armed forces from remaining for more than sixty days without congressional authorization or a declaration of war. It was passed by two-thirds of Congress, thus overriding a presidential veto. It has been ignored by every president since. For a general overview of an assertive Congress in the realm of U.S. foreign policy during the Cold War, see Johnson, *Congress and the Cold War.*
55. Henry Kissinger, *Years of Upheaval* (Boston, MA: Little, Brown, 1982), 983.
56. Trade Act of 1974, § 402, P.L. No. 93–618, 88 Stat. 2056, current version at 19 U.S.C. 2432 (1988). Repealed December 14, 2012, see P.L. No. 208, Stat. 1496 ("Russia and Moldova Jackson-Vanik Repeal and Sergei Magnitsky Rule of Law Accountability Act of 2012").
57. See Exchange of Letters between Henry Jackson and Henry Kissinger, October 18, 1974, in Henry Kissinger, *Years of Renewal* (New York Simon & Schuster, 1999), 1088. See also Joseph Albright, The "Pact of Two Henrys," *New York Times,* January 5, 1975.
58. William Korey, *NGOs and the Universal Declaration of Human Rights: "A Curious Grapevine"* (New York: St. Martin's Press, 2001), 190.
59. P.L. 88–634, Foreign Assistance Act of 1961, as amended, October 7, 1964: "Sec. 501. It is the sense of Congress that the U.S. deeply believes in the freedom of religion for all people and is opposed to infringement of this freedom any-

where in the world. The Congress condemns the persecution of any persons because of their religion. It is the further the sense of Congress that all persons should be permitted the free exercise of religion and the pursuit of their culture."

60. S. Con. Res. 17, 89th Congress 1st Sess., March 17, 1965.
61. *Anti-Religious Activities in the Soviet Union and in Eastern Europe,* Hearings before the Subcommittee on Europe, Committee on Foreign Affairs, House of Representatives, 1st sess., 89th Congress, May 10–12, 1965.
62. *The Communist Exploitation of Religion,* Hearing before the Subcommittee to investigate the administration of the Internal Security Act and Other Internal Security Laws, Committee on the Judiciary, U.S. Senate, 2nd sess., 89th Cong., May 6, 1966.
63. *The New Communist Propaganda Line on Religion,* Hearing before the Committee on Un-American Activities, House of Representatives, 1st session, 90th Congress, August 10, 1967.
64. House of Representatives, Congressional Record, 92nd Congress, 2nd sess., 1972 CXVIII, no. 59, HB3057.
65. S. Con. Res. 33, 117 Congressional Record—Senate, July 12, 1971.
66. Ibid.
67. S. Res. 145, Congressional Record, July 7, 1971, 23695–23696: "Whereas the broadcasting by the Voice of America in the Yiddish language would bring to the Soviet Union's Jewish citizens knowledge of the worldwide sympathy for their plight and of the worldwide support for their being allowed religious and cultural freedom as well as freedom to emigrate."
68. S. Res. 209, Congressional Record, December 6, 1971, 44801–802.
69. Stern, *Water's Edge,* 15.
70. House H.R. 14806, A Bill to Amend the Export Administration Act of 1969 in order to Promote Freedom of Emigration, 92nd Congress, 2nd sess., Mr. Rees, Committee on Banking and Currency, CXVIII, pt. 13, p. 15862.
71. Stern, *Water's Edge.*
72. Senate, Congressional Record, 92nd Cong., 2nd sess., 1972, 32428–29.
73. Ibid.
74. Ibid.
75. Ibid.
76. Quoted in Orbach, *The American Movement,* 127.
77. Stern, *Water's Edge,* 32. In fact, Jackson mobilized a divided American Jewish community around this issue. See also Alan Weisman, *Prince of Darkness, Richard Perle: The Kingdom, the Power and the End of Empire in America* (New York: Union Square Press, 2007), 41. Beckerman, *When They Come for Us,* 290–296 (Nixon told Jewish leaders that it's a mistake to trust senators more than him and that they will save more Jews his way).

78. Stern, *Water's Edge,* 68–69. See also Beckerman, *When They Come for Us,* 290–291.
79. William Korey, "The Story of the Jackson Amendment, 1973–1975," *Midstream: A Jewish Review* 21, no. 3 (March 1975): 11.
80. The ethnic revival of the 1960s and 1970s is considered to be a major factor in the resurgence of human rights in U.S. foreign policy. Ethnic and religious issues in Eastern Europe were constant sources of concern for both Soviet leaders as well as their fellow kinsmen in the United States. See Nathan Glazer and Daniel Patrick Moynihan, *Beyond the Melting Pot* (Cambridge, MA: MIT Press, 1970), which argues that ethnic groups function largely as interest groups. See also Michael Novak, *The Rise of the Unmeltable Ethnics* (New York: Macmillan, 1972).
81. Kaufman, *Scoop Jackson,* 72. In fact, it is evidence of incredible neglect by the White House that the MFN provisions were included in the comprehensive trade bill, thus enabling Jackson to hold it hostage.
82. Testimony of Henry A. Kissinger, Senate Foreign Relations Committee, *Hearings on Nomination of Henry Kissinger as Secretary of State,* 93rd Congress, 1st sess., Sept 7, 10, 11, and 14, 1973, 42.
83. Tape Number 866, Oval Office, Nixon White House Tapes, March 1973, http://www.nixonlibrary.gov/forresearchers/find/tapes/finding_aids/march1973.php. (Nixon replied in the affirmative, saying, "I know, we can't blow up the world over it.")
84. Stern, *Water's Edge,* 21.
85. Painting the JVA as a Jewish issue, Kissinger tried to leverage his origins as a Jewish refugee from Nazi Germany with the American Jewish leaders. In both strategies, he emphasized the benefits of quiet diplomacy in order to prevent anti-Semitism in Russia as a result of the JVA. An angry Jackson rejected the connection between Israeli survival and Soviet Jewish emigration, telling Jewish leaders that Kissinger was a liar. See Stern, *Water's Edge,* 99; Noam Kochavi, "Insights Abandoned, Flexibility Lost: Kissinger, Soviet Jewish Emigration, and the Demise of Détente," *Diplomatic History* 29 (2005): 503–530; Orbach, *The American Movement,* 36. It also helped that Andrei Sakharov, a prominent Soviet dissident who won the 1975 Nobel Peace Prize, expressed his support for the JVA. See Andrei Sakharov, Open Letter to the Congress of the United States, Sept 14, 1973, in Walter Laquer and Barry M. Rubin, eds., *Human Rights Reader* (Philadelphia, PA: Temple University Press, 1979), 280. Sakharov implored that the JVA would not imperil détente and its abandonment would betray Jews and non-Jews alike who were fighting for freedom in the Soviet Union. For insights on Israeli views during the debates around JVA, see Noam Kochavi, "Idealpolitik in Disguise: Israel, Jewish Emigration from the Soviet Union and the Nixon

Administration, 1969–1974," *The International History Review* 29, no. 3 (2007): 550–572.

86. Exchange of Letters between Henry Jackson and Henry Kissinger, October 18, 1974, in Kissinger, *Years of Renewal,* 1088.
87. William Korey, "The Struggle over Jackson-Mills-Vanik," *The American Jewish Yearbook 1974–1975* (Philadelphia: American Jewish Committee and the Jewish Publication Society of America, 1976), 226.
88. Cited in Orbach, *The American Movement,* 128.
89. A further amendment was inserted into the trade bill by Senator Adlai Stevenson of Illinois weeks before the final version was approved on December 20, 1974. It provided that the $300 million credit ceiling could only be waived by the president with congressional approval. Both Jackson and the White House did not expect this move. See Korey, *The Promises We Keep* (New York: St. Martin's Press, 1993): 199.
90. Under the JVA, MFN status was extended to both Romania and Poland in 1977.
91. Orbach, *The American Movement,* 159.
92. William Korey, *Human Rights and the Helsinki Accords: Focus on U.S. Foreign Policy* (New York Foreign Policy Association, 1983), 24. See also Guy E. Coriden Jr., Interview, November 18, 1992, The Foreign Affairs Oral History Collection of the Association for Diplomatic Studies and Training, Library of Congress. Retrieved from http://memory.loc.gov/ammem/collections/diplomacy. "[N]obody really cared about it. We really felt that we were out there alone. We didn't have much instruction from Washington."
93. World War II, unlike World War I, ended without a formal peace pact, so the status of territories occupied by the Soviet Union as a result of the Yalta conference has always been on shaky legal grounds. In addition, Soviet reputation took a hit after its crushing of the 1968 Prague Spring and subsequent invasion of Czechoslovakia. See Michael C. Morgan, "The U.S. and the Making of the Helsinki Final Act," in Logevall and Preston, eds., *Nixon in the World,* 167.
94. The conflict between the White House and the Department of State when it came to the CSCE was resolved when Kissinger became secretary of state in 1973. On the origins of the Helsinki Final Act, see Morgan, "The U.S. and the Making of the Helsinki Final Act," 164–179. See also Snyder, *Human Rights Activism,* 15–37.
95. He considered the U.S. role in the CSCE as largely "damage control." Kissinger was correct as one of the Soviet objectives was to reduce American influence in Europe. See Korey, *The Promises We Keep,* xxii. Angela Romano, "Détente, Entente or Linkage? The Helsinki Conference on Security and Cooperation in Europe in U.S. Relations with the Soviet Union," *Diplomatic History* 33 (2009): 703–722.

96. Maresca, *To Helsinki,* 158; Snyder, *Human Rights Activism,* 51. See also Jussi Hanhimäki, "'They Can Write It in Swahili': Kissinger, the Soviets, and the Helsinki Accords, 1973–1975," *Journal of Transatlantic Studies* 1, no. 1 (2003): 37–58, which argues that Kissinger, while reluctant, deserves credit for bringing the CSCE to conclusion and that he helped produce significant concessions from the Soviet side.
97. Thomas, *The Helsinki Effect,* 78.
98. HFA, Part 1, Principle VII (3).
99. HFA, Part 3, Section (d). "The participating states . . . confirm that religious faiths, institutions, and organizations, practicing within the constitutional framework of the participating states, and their representatives can, in the field of their activities, have contacts and meetings among themselves and exchange information." The Vatican proposed this provision.
100. For a superb account of the transnational networks spawned by the HFA, see Snyder, *Human Rights Activism.* See also Christian Peterson, *Globalizing Human Rights: Private Citizens, the Soviet Union, and the West* (New York: Routledge, 2012), 14–29.
101. HFA, Principle X (4): "All principles set forth above are of primary significance and accordingly, they will be equally and unreservedly applied, each of them being interpreted taking into account the others."
102. The fact that the Soviets considered the HFA as an incredible coup against the West was also a big factor.
103. Orlov would later establish the private counterpart of the U.S. Helsinki Commission, the Moscow Helsinki Watch Group. See generally Paul Goldberg, *The Final Act* (New York: Morrow, 1988), for the story of the Moscow Watch Group.
104. Fenwick introduced H.R. 9466 to establish the U.S. Helsinki Commission on Sept 9, 1975, while Case introduced S. 2679 on November 17, 1975. See Hearings before the Subcommittee on International Political and Military Affairs, Committee on International Relations, House of Representatives, 94th Cong. (on H.R. 9466 establishing a Commission on Security and Cooperation in Europe), November 18, 1975, and S2679, May 4, 1976.
105. Act of June 3, 1976, P.L. No. 94–304, 90 Stat. 661 (codified as amended at 22 U.S.C. 3001–3009). Until Jimmy Carter assumed the presidency in January 1977, the Ford administration refused to cooperate with the Helsinki Commission, first by putting off the appointments of its executive members and later by instructing them to participate only as observers. See Korey, *The Promises We Keep,* 21–43. Many ethnic organizations of Eastern European origin lobbied for the passage of the bill, realizing that Congress could pressure the State Department into ensuring the adequate implementation of the HFA. See Madeleine Albright and Albert Friendly, "Helsinki and Human Rights," in

Edmund S. Muskie et al., eds., *The President, the Congress, and Foreign Policy* (Lanham, MD: University Press of America, 1986), 294–295.

106. *Implementation of the Helsinki Accords: Religious Liberty and Minority Rights in the Soviet Union,* Meeting of the U.S. Helsinki Commission, April 27, 1977, 1. Dante B. Fascell, a Democrat from Florida and the first chair of the U.S. Helsinki Commission, gave Carter the talking points about human rights, and Carter eventually highlighted these points in his inauguration speech.
107. House of Representatives, H.R. 726, 94th Cong., 2nd sess., June 24, 1976.
108. U.S. Congress, Implementation of the Helsinki Accords, hearings held Feb 23, 1977 to Dec 28, 1981 (hereafter HFA Implementation). The other subjects were as follows: human contacts and family reunification, information flow and cultural exchanges in Eastern Europe, Moscow Helsinki Watch reports on repression, right to citizenship in the Soviet Union, Soviet law and the Helsinki monitors, repercussions of the trials of the Helsinki monitors in the USSR, U.S. compliance on human rights, U.S. visa policies, Aleksandr Ginzburg on human rights situation in the USSR, Eastern European compliance with human rights provisions of Helsinki, and the crisis in Poland and its effects on the Helsinki process.
109. See Sabrina Petra Ramet, *Religious Policy in the Soviet Union* (Cambridge: Cambridge University Press, 1993), 23–30.
110. Hearings, House of Representatives, Committee on International Relations, Subcommittee on International Political and Military Affairs, to Establish a Commission on Security and Cooperation in Europe, May 4, 1976, 6–9.
111. See generally HFA Implementation.
112. Snyder, *Human Rights Activism;* Thomas, *The Helsinki Effect.* Both Snyder and Thomas make this argument.
113. Korey, *The Promises We Keep,* 61.
114. Alexandre Kiss and Mary Dominick, "The International Legal Significance of the Human Rights Provisions of the Helsinki Final Act," *Vanderbilt Journal of Transnational Law* 13 (1980): 293; Eric Manton, "The OSCE Human Dimension Process and the Process of Customary International Law Formation," *2005 OSCE Yearbook* (2007), 195–214. The USSR regarded it as virtually having a binding character at the beginning. At Helsinki, Brezhnev declared his assumption that all countries will implement the undertakings reached, and that the USSR will act precisely in this manner. The state newspaper *Izvestia* declared that the Helsinki principles should be made a law of international life that is not to be breached by anyone. See Korey, *Human Rights and the Helsinki Accords,* 19.
115. Snyder, *Human Rights Activism,* 110. Goldberg relied on the research of various private monitoring groups. See Korey, *The Promises We Keep,* xxv; Arthur

Goldberg, "Human Rights and the Belgrade Meeting," *Hastings Law Journal* 30 (1978): 249–253.

116. Ibid.
117. HFA Implementation, April 28, 1977, 96–101; H.R. 165, 95th Cong., 1st Sess., 154.
118. Kaufman, *Scoop Jackson,* 294.
119. Preston, *Sword of the Spirit,* 573, quoting Helsinki Watch press release, December 7, 1979.
120. The Bricker amendment is a collective name for a series of proposed constitutional amendments that sought to impose restrictions on the ratifications of treaties and executive agreements. It was named after its sponsor, Senator John Bricker of Ohio. See Frank Holman, *The Story of the "Bricker" Amendment* (New York: Committee for Constitutional Government, 1954); Natalie Kaufman and David Whiteman, "Opposition to Human Rights Treaties in the United States Senate: The Legacy of the Bricker Amendment," *Human Rights Quarterly* 10 no. 3 (August 1, 1988): 309–338; Louis Henkin, "U.S. Ratification of Human Rights Conventions: The Ghost of Senator Bricker," *American Journal of International Law* 89, no. 2 (April 1, 1995): 341–350.

6. Age of Exceptionalism

Epigraph: Congressional Record, 105th Cong. 2nd sess., May 11, 1998, 8648.

1. The reply by Grand Ayatollah Sayyid Ali Al-Hussaini Al-Sistani in response to an inquiry made by a group of Iraqi people regarding the preparation of the next Iraqi constitution, June 26, 2003, cited in Noah Feldman, "The Democratic Fatwa: Islam and Democracy in the Realm of Constitutional Politics," *Oklahoma Law Review* 58, no. 1 (2005): 6.
2. L. Paul Bremer, with Malcolm McConnell, *My Year in Iraq: The Struggle to Build a Future of Hope* (New York: Simon & Schuster, 2006), 94. See also Bob Woodward, *State of Denial* (New York: Simon & Schuster, 2007), 263. Bremer wrote in his memoirs that he explicitly told Ahmed Chalabi that the CPA had no intention of writing the Iraqi constitution. The CPA plan did involve, however, a constitutional drafting body whose Iraqi members were to be chosen by the CPA. See Feldman, "The Democratic Fatwa," 5. See also Jennifer Lee, "American Will Advise Iraqis on Writing New Constitution," *New York Times,* May 11, 2003 (on the appointment of Noah Feldman as senior constitutional adviser).
3. Descriptions of the early period of occupation are vividly captured in Larry Diamond, *Squandered Victory: The American Occupation and the Bungled Effort to Bring Democracy to Iraq* (New York: Times Books, 2005); Rajiv Chandrasekaran, *Imperial Life in the Emerald City: Inside Iraq's Green Zone* (New

York: Knopf, 2006); George Packer, *The Assassins' Gate: America in Iraq* (New York: Farrar, Giroux, Straus, 2005). See also James Dobbins et al., *Occupying Iraq: A History of the Coalition Provisional Authority* (Santa Monica, CA: RAND Corporation, 2009), 43.

4. Title II, Secs. 201–202, International Religious Freedom Act of 1998, Public Law 105–292, as amended by Public Law 106–55, Public Law 106–113, Public Law 107–228, Public Law 108–332, and Public Law 108–458.
5. Letter from USCIRF chair Felice D. Gaer to President George W. Bush, *Iraq: Religion and Reconstruction,* April 28, 2003: "Now that Saddam Hussein has been ousted, the U.S. Commission on International Religious Freedom believes strongly it is essential to ensure that the Iraqi people can exercise their religious freedom in full accordance with international human rights standards and the human rights treaties to which Iraq is a party. The United States can help make this become a reality." Retrieved January 25, 2013, from http://www.uscirf.gov/index.php?option=com_content&view=article&id=256.
6. Iraq has been designated a CPC in the language of the International Religious Freedom Act (IRFA) since the commission's inception in 1998. See State Department reports on religious freedom at http://www.state.gov/j/drl/rls/irf/.
7. George W. Bush, Remarks to the Travel Pool, Donnelly, Idaho, August 23, 2005, in *Public Papers of the Presidents of the United States: George W. Bush, Book II* (Washington, DC: U.S. Government Printing Office, 2005), 1342–1345.
8. The origin of the secularization thesis is in Max Weber, *Science as a Vocation* (Boston, MA: Unwin Hyman, 1989). For a contemporary critique and reexamination, see José Casanova, *Public Religions in the Modern World* (Chicago, IL: University of Chicago Press, 1994); Pippa Norris and Ronald Inglehart, *Sacred and Secular: Religion and Politics Worldwide* (New York: Cambridge University Press, 2004).
9. Monica Duffy Toft, Daniel Philpott, and Timothy Shah, *God's Century: Resurgent Religion and Global Politics* (New York: W. W. Norton & Company, 2011).
10. The term first appeared in an article in the magazine *Foreign Affairs.* See Charles Krauthammer, "The Unipolar Moment," *Foreign Affairs* 70, no. 1, America and the World (January 1, 1990): 23–33. The period immediately following the fall of the Berlin wall spawned a huge literature pondering the role of the United States in this new and unprecedented era. The most prominent of these is Francis Fukuyama, "The End of History?," *The National Interest,* 16 (1989): 3–18.
11. See Daniel T. Rodgers, *Age of Fracture* (Cambridge, MA: Harvard University Press, 2011); Richard John Neuhaus, *The Naked Public Square: Religion and Democracy in America* (Grand Rapids, MI: W. B. Eerdmans Pub. Co., 1984).

12. Madeleine Albright, *The Mighty and the Almighty* (New York: HarperCollins, 2006), 9. The Center for Strategic and International Studies issued a pioneering report called *Religion: The Missing Dimension of Statecraft,* in which participants interrogated the saliency of religion in U.S. diplomacy in early 1994.
13. Albright, *The Mighty and the Almighty,* 9.
14. See Chapter 5 of this book.
15. The creation of a hierarchy of rights and the perception that religious freedom was being singled out were and remain the biggest criticism against the act. See Peter Danchin, "U.S. Unilateralism and the International Protection of Religious Freedom: The Multilateral Alternative," *The Columbia Journal of Transnational Law* 41 (2002): 33–136, 102–104.
16. The arguments proffered by the Bush administration for the invasion of Iraq have changed numerous times, beginning with the removal of what turned out to be nonexistent weapons of mass destruction (WMDs) and ending with the spread of democracy and freedom in the Middle East. This topic remains controversial because it is still widely perceived that the invasion was particularly insisted on by private commercial interests, especially those involving oil. For a look at the difference between pre- and postinvasion arguments, see U.S. Senate Select Committee on Intelligence, *Report on Whether Public Statements Regarding Iraq by U.S. Government Officials Were Substantiated by Intelligence,* June 5, 2008 (Washington, DC: U.S. Government Printing Office, 2008). The majority concluded that the statements were not supported.
17. Article 7(A), Law of Administration for the State of Iraq for the Transitional Period (TAL), March 8, 2004. A revised version is reproduced in the 2005 permanent Iraqi constitution. "Article 2: First: Islam is the official religion of the State and it is a fundamental source of legislation:

    A. No law that contradicts the established provisions of Islam may be established.
    B. No law that contradicts the principles of democracy may be established.
    C. No law that contradicts the rights and basic freedoms stipulated in this constitution may be established.

    Second: This Constitution guarantees the Islamic identity of the majority of the Iraqi people and guarantees the full religious rights of all individuals to freedom of religious belief and practice such as Christians, Yazedis, and Mandi Sabeans."
18. Post-9/11 academic writing in various fields exploded with scholarship on the compatibility of Islam and democracy. For a small sampling, see John Esposito, *Unholy War: Terror in the Name of Islam* (New York: Oxford University Press, 2002); Noah Feldman, *After Jihad: America and the Struggle for Islamic Democracy* (New York: Farrar, Straus, and Giroux, 2003); Khaled abou

El-Fadl, *Islam and the Challenge of Democracy* (Princeton, NJ: Princeton University Press, 2004); Fatima Mernissi, *Islam and the Fear of the Modern World,* 2nd ed. (New York: Basic Books, 2002).

19. For all the attention that the statute has generated, only two books are devoted to this legislation. See Allen Hertzke, *Freeing God's Children* (Lanham, MD: Rowman & Littlefield, 2006), which argues that the IRFA came about as a result of an unlikely alliance among different religious groups; and Thomas Farr, *World of Faith and Freedom* (New York: Oxford University Press, 2008), which is an insider account of the early years of the Office of International Religious Freedom in the State Department. Much of the literature on the IRFA is found in law journals, and an overwhelming amount of the literature focuses on the statute as normatively undesirable law and policy.
20. Hertzke, *Freeing God's Children,* 149.
21. Ibid. See also Jeffrey Goldberg, "Washington Discovers Christian Persecution," *New York Times Magazine,* Dec 21, 1997.
22. That partnership was not without any hiccups. Shea reportedly detested Horowitz's self-aggrandizing efforts. See Goldberg, "Washington Discovers Christian Persecution."
23. R. C. Longworth, "Congressmen Visit Soviet Prison," *Chicago Tribune,* Aug 11, 1989; A. M. Rosenthal, "The Zones of Freedom," *New York Times,* Aug 25, 1989; "Congressmen Claim Gulags Still Exist," Associated Press, Aug 10, 1989.
24. See generally Religious Persecution, Hearings before the Subcommittee on International Security, International Organizations and Human Rights, Committee on Foreign Affairs, House of Representatives, Oct 28, 1993 and March 9, 1994 (hereafter 1994 Hearings). Compare with Goldberg, "Washington Discovers Christian Persecution," which claims that, before Horowitz and Shea entered the picture, the issue was not on the congressional agenda.
25. Consequences of MFN Renewal for China, Hearing before the Senate Foreign Relations Committee, 104th Cong. 2nd sess., June 6, 1996, 10.
26. Annual MFN debates involving China since 1989 have always been contentious. For a primer on China and MFN, see James R. Lilley, *Beyond MFN: Trade with China and American Interests* (Washington, DC: American Enterprise Institute, 1994).
27. 1994 Hearings, 30.
28. 1994 Hearings, 27: "The Puebla Institute urges the US Congress to use the leverage which it has to the maximum at this point with Vietnam before trade is reinstated, and as China nervously awaits our decision on MFN, to see these religious prisoners are freed and also that the policy itself is changed." See also Testimony of Nina Shea before Senate Foreign Relations Committee, 104th Congress, 2nd sess., June 6, 1996, 49–57.

29. Executive Order 12850—Conditions for Renewal of Most-Favored-Nation Status for the People's Republic of China in 1994, May 28, 1993. Retrieved from http://www.presidency.ucsb.edu/ws/index.php?pid=61546#axzz1yGsyu2A9.
30. Ibid.
31. For a terrific insider account of the struggle over MFN and human rights in China during the Clinton administration, see John Shattuck, *Freedom on Fire: Human Rights Wars and America's Response* (Cambridge, MA: Harvard University Press, 2009), 221–282.
32. Hertzke, *Freeing God's Children,* 157–160.
33. Christine McCormick, Comment, "Exporting the First Amendment," *Journal of International Legal Studies* 4 (1998): 283, 285.
34. Nina Shea, "In the Lion's Den: A Shocking Account of Persecution and Martyrdom of Christians Today and How We Should Respond" (1997), Appendix A, "Statement of Conscience," 95–102. Retrieved July 31, 2012, from http://www.pcahistory.org/pca/3-476.pdf.
35. See Shea, "Statement of Conscience."
36. The subcommittee on International Operations and Human Rights of the Committee on International Relations of the House of Representatives, 104th Cong., 2nd sess., conducted several hearings on *Worldwide Persecution of Jews,* February 27, 1996; *Persecution of Christians Worldwide,* February 15, 1996; and *Victims of Religious Persecution Around the World,* June 16, 1998, while the Subcommittee on Near Eastern and South Asian Affairs of the Senate Foreign Relations Committee held hearings on *Religious Persecution in the Middle East: Faces of the Persecuted,* May 1 and June 10, 1997; Subcommittee on African Affairs, "Religious Persecution in Sudan," September 25, 1997. See also H.R. Con. Res. 515, 104th Cong., S. Con. Res. 71, 104th Cong. (1996); H.R. Con. Res. 102, 104th Cong. (1996), for congressional resolutions on the issue of religious persecution abroad.
37. Paul Marshall and Lela Gilbert, *Their Blood Cries Out* (Dallas, TX: Word Publishing, 1997).
38. Shea, "In the Lion's Den," 1. See also Elizabeth Castelli, "Praying for the Persecuted Church: U.S. Christian Activism in the Global Arena," *Journal of Human Rights* (2005): 334, which characterizes the movement's framing of the issue as a "product to be sold, a media story to be mobilized, powerfully echoing the mythic framing of Americanness."
39. U.S. Department of State, *Final Report of the Advisory Committee on Religious Freedom to the Secretary of State and the President,* May 17, 1999 (Washington, DC: Department. of State, 1999).
40. "U.S. Policies in Support of Religious Freedom: Focus on Christians, Report Consistent with the Omnibus Consolidated Appropriations Act, Fiscal Year 1997, House Report 3610," released by the Bureau of Democracy, Human Rights and Labor Affairs, July 22, 1997.

41. Ibid.
42. Ibid.
43. Ibid.
44. Ibid.
45. Statement of Chris Smith, Hearings on Wolf-Specter, Administration witnesses, 105th Cong., 1st sess., September 9, 1997, 17.
46. Joseph Rees, the chief counsel for the Human Rights Subcommittee, had insisted that the language be universal, noting that "Jackson-Vanik was not just about Jews. Thus the new law can't just be about Christians." Cited in Hertzke, *Freeing God's Children,* 190.
47. Chris Smith, markup before the Subcommittee on International Operations and Human Rights of the Committee on International Relations, House of Representatives, 105 Cong., 1st sess., September 18, 1997, 3: "This bill is designed to help people whose situation is particularly compelling and who are suffering a terrible, horrific plight because of their belief system."
48. See Farr, *World of Faith and Freedom,* 113–124. See also T. Jeremy Gunn, "The United States and the Promotion of Freedom of Religion and Belief," in Tore Lindholm, W. Cole Durham Jr., and Bahia G. Thazib-Lie et al., eds., *Facilitating Freedom of Religion or Belief: A Deskbook* (Leiden: Martinus Nijhoff, 2004).
49. Wolf-Specter bill, Section 5.
50. See Wolf-Specter bill, Section 7, for a list of sanctions.
51. Wolf-Specter bill, Section 9.
52. Hertzke, *Freeing God's Children,* 192.
53. Testimony of Hon. John Shattuck, Assistant Secretary of State for Democracy, Human Rights and Labor, before the House International Relations Committee, Sept 9, 1997, 36.
54. Wolf-Specter bill, Section 5(e).
55. Wolf-Specter bill, Section 8(a): "Subject to subsection (b), the President may waive the imposition of any sanction against a country under section 7 for periods of not more than 12 months each, if the President for each waiver (1) determines (a) the national security interests of the United States justify such a waiver; or (b) that such a waiver will substantially promote the purposes of this Act as set forth in section 2, and (2) provides to the Committees on Foreign Relations, Finance, the Judiciary and Appropriations of the Senate and to the Committees on International Relations, the Judiciary, and Appropriations of the House of Representatives, a written notification of the President's intention to waive any such sanction."
56. Wolf-Specter bill, Section 11.
57. Elaine Sciolino, "Clinton Argues for Flexibility over Sanctions," *New York Times,* April 28, 1998.
58. National Security Advisor Sandy Berger, "Wrong Approach to Religious Freedom," *Washington Post,* May 14, 1998, at A23; Secretary Madeleine Albright

reportedly confronted Horowitz in a Washington, DC, restaurant and told him that the legislation would create a mess in U.S. foreign policy by sanctioning so many countries. Hertzke, *Freeing God's Children,* 203.

59. For a detailed account of the Nickles-Lieberman bill, see Hertzke, *Freeing God's Children,* 208–236. The personal recollections of these staffers are in Rosalind Hackett, Mark Silk, and Dennis Hoover et al., eds., *Religious Persecution as a U.S. Policy Issue: Proceedings of a Consultation Held at Trinity College, Hartford, September 26–27, 1999* (Center for the Study of Religion in Public Life, Trinity College, 2000), 7–17.
60. Nickles-Lieberman bill, Section 2(3).
61. Nickles-Lieberman bill, Section 101.
62. Nickles-Lieberman bill, S. 1868, 105th Cong. 2d sess., Sec. 405.
63. Nickles-Lieberman bill, Section 202(a).
64. Farr, *World of Faith and Freedom,* 118–119.
65. William J. Clinton, "Statement on Signing the International Religious Freedom Act of 1998," October 27, 1998. Online by Gerhard Peters and John T. Woolley, *The American Presidency Project.* Retrieved from http://www.presidency.ucsb.edu/ws/?pid=55155. Presidential signing statements are pronouncements issued by the president contemporaneously to the signing of a bill into law and include the president's interpretation of particular statutory language and constitutional objections. The subject has generated a voluminous literature in legal scholarship, particularly on whether it is contrary to the principle of rule of law and separation of powers.
66. This is evident from the range of groups that supported the statute, such as the U.S. Catholic Bishops Conference, the Family Research Council, the Union of Orthodox Hebrew Congregation, the Religious Action Center for a Reformed Judaism, and the Lutheran Church. Hertzke, *Freeing God's Children,* 197–199, 234–236.
67. See, for example, Peter Danchin, "U.S. Unilateralism and the International Protection of Religious Freedom: The Multilateral Alternative," *Columbia Journal of Transnational Law* 41 (2002), 48–49; McCormick, Comment, "Exporting the First Amendment," 285–286. It is more accurate to state, however, that the initiative came from groups associated with the Christian right but that it became an interfaith coalition quickly.
68. *Hearings on Religious Persecution in the Middle East,* May 1, 1997, U.S. Senate Subcommittee on Near Eastern and South Asian Affairs, Foreign Relations Committee, 105th Cong. 1st sess., 3. Senator Joseph Lieberman also defended the measure, saying, "[F]or Americans particularly, silence or disinterest on matters of religious freedom are not acceptable options. We in this great country bear a special obligation in this regard historically because our nation after all was founded by men and women seeking refuge from oppression for their religious faith." See U.S. Senate, Committee on

Foreign Relations, Hearings on Nickles-Lieberman bill, 105th Cong. 2nd sess. May 12, 1998.

69. 1994 Hearings, October 28, 1993, 1.
70. Rosalind J. Hackett, Mark Silk, and Dennis Hoover et al., eds., *Religious Persecution as a U.S. Policy Issue: Proceedings of a Consultation Held at Trinity College, Hartford, September 26–27, 1999* (Hartford, CT: Center for the Study of Religion in Public Life, Trinity College, 2000): 8. Hanford was appointed Ambassador at Large for International Religious Freedom in 2002.
71. Department of State, *Annual Report: International Religious Freedom* (Washington, DC: U.S. Government Printing Office, 1999).
72. Ibid.
73. The most comprehensive critique of the statute is in Danchin, "U.S. Unilateralism," 33. Legal scholarship critical of the statute has made similar arguments. For a rejoinder to Danchin's piece, see T. Jeremy Gun, "American Exceptionalism and Globalist Double Standards: A More Balanced Alternative," *Columbia Journal of Transnational Law* 41 (2002): 137.
74. Danchin, "U.S. Unilateralism," 41.
75. See, for example, "Egypt: Religious Freedom Delegation Gets Cold Shoulder," *Christianity Today*, May 21, 2001; Laura Cozad, "The United States' Imposition of Religious Freedom: The IRFA and India," *India Review* 4, no. 1 (2005): 59–83.
76. Philip Alston, "Does the Past Matter? On the Origins of Human Rights," *Harvard Law Review* 126 (2013): 2043–2081.
77. On this point, see Sarah Cleveland, "Norm Internalization and U.S. Economic Sanctions," *Yale Journal of International Law* 26 (2001): 1. This is an application of Harold Koh's transnational legal process theory. See Harold Hongju Koh, "Why Do Nations Obey International Law?" (book review), *Yale Law Journal* 106, no. 8 (June 1, 1997): 2599.
78. Hearings before House Committee on International Relations, Oct 6, 1999, 4 (on the first annual report on international religious freedom).
79. Danchin, "U.S. Unilateralism," 105.
80. Michael Ignatieff and Amy Gutmann, *Human Rights as Politics and Idolatry* (Princeton, NJ: Princeton University Press, 2001), 21.
81. This study is one such attempt to demonstrate the historicity and contingency of human rights, particularly that of religious freedom. See generally Samuel Moyn, *Last Utopia* (Cambridge, MA: Belknap Press of Harvard University Press, 2010); Lynn Hunt, *Inventing Human Rights* (New York: W. W. Norton, 2007).
82. Jack Donnelly, *Universal Human Rights in Theory and Practice* (Ithaca, NY: Cornell University Press, 2003), which defines an indivisible core list of human rights. *Indivisibility* connotes the equal importance of all rights.

83. See, for example, Donna J. Sullivan, "Gender Equality and Religious Freedom: Toward a Framework for Conflict Resolution," *New York University Journal of International Law and Politics* 24 (1991): 795.
84. A general treatment of the critique of rights is in Duncan Kennedy, *Critique of Adjudication* (Cambridge, MA: Harvard University Press, 1998), 315–338. For a list of criticisms against international human rights, see David Kennedy, "The International Human Rights Movement: Part of the Problem?," *Harvard Human Rights Journal* 15 (2002): 99.
85. For example, the Ambassador at Large for Global Women's Issues heads the Office on Global Women's Issues within the U.S. Department of State. It was created on August 10, 2012, by Executive Order 13623, Preventing and Responding to Violence Against Women and Girls Globally. Retrieved from http://www.gpo.gov/fdsys/pkg/FR-2012-08-16/pdf/2012-20259.pdf.
86. *National Security Strategy of the United States of America* (2002), 4. For a concise analysis of the paradigm shift necessitated by the NSS, see John Lewis Gaddis, "A Grand Strategy of Transformation," *Foreign Policy,* no. 133, (December 2002): 50–57.
87. Discussions of Iraq, regime change, and Saddam Hussein all appeared shortly after 9/11, as recounted in the memoirs of White House officials. See George W. Bush, *Decision Points* (New York: Crown Publishers, 2010), 228–229; Donald Rumsfeld, *Known and Unknown* (New York: Sentinel, 2011), 420–424; Douglas G. Feith, *War and Decision: Inside the Pentagon at the Dawn of the War on Terrorism* (New York: HarperCollins, 2008), 181–212. See also Packer, *The Assassins' Gate,* 40–46. The military started looking at plans to remove Saddam Hussein from power in November 2001, although the Iraq Liberation Act of 1998, Public Law 105–338, already made it U.S. policy to encourage regime change in Iraq prior to 2001. For a general account of the disastrous plunge to war, see Michael Gordon and Bernard Trainor, *Cobra II: The Inside Story of the Invasion and Occupation of Iraq* (New York: Pantheon Books, 2006).
88. Interview with Defense Deputy Secretary Paul Wolfowitz, *Vanity Fair,* May 9, 2003. Retrieved July 31, 2012, from http://www.defense.gov/transcripts/transcript.aspx?transcriptid=2594.
89. Turkey was often cited as a model of a secular Muslim-majority state. See Remarks of President George W. Bush on the twentieth anniversary of the National Endowment for Democracy, November 6, 2003. Retrieved July 31, 2012, from http://www.ned.org/george-w-bush/remarks-by-president-george-w-bush-at-the-20th-anniversary.
90. Chapter One, Articles 1–3, 2004 Constitution of the Islamic Republic of Afghanistan. The constitution was initially drafted by a constitutional drafting commission appointed by Hamid Karzai and ratified through consensus by a

500-delegate constitutional Loya Jirga ("grand council" in the Pashto language) on January 4, 2004. For an account of constitution making in post-Taliban Afghanistan, see J. Alexander Thier, "The Making of a Constitution in Afghanistan," *New York Law School Law Review* 51 (2006): 558.

91. Chapter One, Article 2; Chapter Two, 2004 Afghan Constitution.
92. Andrew Arato, "Post-Sovereign Constitution-Making and Its Pathology in Iraq," *New York Law School Law Review* 51 (2006): 536.
93. UN Security Council, Security Council resolution 1483 (2003), on the situation between Iraq and Kuwait, May 22, 2003, S/Res/1483 (2003). Retrieved July 27, 2012, from http://www.unhcr.org/refworld/docid/3f45dbe70.html. Although the United Kingdom was a major ally of the United States in Operation Iraqi Freedom, everybody knew it was largely an American operation. Rory Stewart, a British diplomat, for example, calls Bremer "our chief administrator" in Iraq. Rory Stewart, *The Prince of the Marshes* (New York: Houghton Mifflin Harcourt, 2007), 59.
94. Paul Bremer, Interview with PBS *Frontline*, "The Lost Year in Iraq," June 26 and August 18, 2006. All first-person accounts on the occupation offer conflicting versions of whether the United States intended to stay long after combat operations ceased, but this seems more a reflection on the general uncertainty about the nature of the U.S. role. A good overview of the government infighting involved is in Woodward, *State of Denial.*
95. Chandrasekaran, *Imperial Life at the Emerald City*, 162–165.
96. Bremer, *My Year in Iraq*, 12, 19. These practical issues included the absence of electoral laws, institutions, and defined geographies essential for a credible election. See also Bremer, Interview, "The Lost Year in Iraq."
97. Testimony of L. Paul Bremer III, Senate Foreign Relations Committee, Sept 24, 2003, 34.
98. Ibid.
99. Bremer, *My Year in Iraq*, 79.
100. Stewart, *The Prince of the Marshes*, 339.
101. L. Paul Bremer, "Iraq's Path to Sovereignty," *Washington Post*, Sept 8, 2003. The op-ed created a ruckus in Washington because Bremer did not consult anyone before it was published. Robert Blackwill told Bremer that handing sovereignty over to the Iraqis by the middle of 2004, that is, before the presidential elections, was important to President Bush. Chandrasekaran, *Imperial Life in the Emerald City*, 223. See also Feith, *War and Decision*, 453–454. Colin Powell reportedly saw it first in the *Washington Post.* Woodward, *State of Denial*, 248–249.
102. The twenty-five-member IGC was composed of representatives from different sectors of Iraqi society, but its nature as a governing body had always been up in the air. For example, while it managed to get powers for itself, these were not

on key matters such as control over financial resources or military and security matters. More often than not, it recommended, rather than decided. Constant tension governed the relationship between the IGC and the CPA. See David Philips, *Losing Iraq: Inside the Postwar Reconstruction Fiasco* (New York: Westview Press, 2006), 171; Ali Allawi, *The Occupation of Iraq* (New Haven, CT: Yale University Press, 2008), 166–167, 190; Noah Feldman, *What We Owe Iraq* (Princeton, NJ: Princeton University Press, 2003), 110–111.

103. Chandrasekaran, *Imperial Life in the Emerald City*, 91.

104. Sistani never met with U.S. officials, although he and Bremer communicated through intermediaries. See Bremer, *My Year in Iraq*, 166–167, 271–273, 301–304. For a brief analysis of the significance of the Sistani *fatwa*, see Feldman, "The Democratic Fatwa."

105. See James Dobbins et al., *Occupying Iraq* (Santa Monica, CA: RAND, 2009), 272–273; Arato, "Post-Sovereign Constitution-Making," 109–110; Bremer, *My Year in Iraq*, 217–218.

106. For the text of the November 15 Agreement, see John Ehrenberg, ed., *The Iraq Papers* (New York: Oxford University Press, 2010), 195–197. For a critical view of the November 15 Agreement, see Arato, "Post-Sovereign Constitution-Making," chapter 3: "Sistani versus Bremer," 99–134; Larry Diamond, "Lessons from Iraq," *Journal of Democracy* 16, no. 1 (2005). Note that Sistani also objected to the caucuses provision in the agreement and demanded that the transitional assembly be elected as well. UN intervention seemed to have assuaged his fears, however, and had him acquiesce to an appointed interim government, which would take office for a brief period. Philips, *Losing Iraq*, 181–183.

107. For first-person accounts of the drafting process behind the TAL, see Bremer, *My Year in Iraq*, 286–308; Feisal al-Istrabadi, "Reviving Constitutionalism in Iraq: Key Provisions of the Transitional Administrative Law," *New York Law School Law Review* 50 (2005): 269; Diamond, *Squandered Victory*, 140–78. See also Noah Feldman and Roman Martinez, "Constitutional Politics and Text in the New Iraq: An Experiment in Islamic Democracy," *Fordham Law Review* 75 (2006): 883, which examines the role of Islam and Islamic politics in the making of the TAL and the 2005 permanent constitution. Both Feldman and Martinez served in different capacities in the ORHA and CPA respectively.

108. Bremer, *My Year in Iraq*, 242.

109. For the history surrounding IGC Resolution 137 and the 1959 Family Code, see generally Kirsten Stilt, "Islamic Law and the Making and Remaking of the Iraqi Legal System," *George Washington International Law Review* 36 (2004): 695.

110. Dexter Filkins, "Iraqi Leaders Miss Deadline for an Interim Constitution," *New York Times*, Feb 29, 2004; "Bremer Will Reject Islam as Source of Law," *Associated Press*, Feb 16, 2004. See also Bremer, *My Year in Iraq*, 292; Philips, *Losing Iraq*, 186.

111. Noah Feldman, "Imposed Constitutionalism," *Connecticut Law Review* 37 (2004): 876.
112. *Iraq: Next Steps—What Will an Iraq 5-Year Plan Look Like?*, Hearings before the Senate Foreign Relations Committee, 108th Cong. 1st sess., Sept 24, 2003, 34. Paul Bremer was the only witness for this hearing. Sam Brownback converted to Roman Catholicism in 2002.
113. Senator Sam Brownback (Republican from Kansas) and Representative Frank Wolf (Republican from Virginia), Oct 23, 2003. Retrieved from http://wwrn.org/articles/6572/ (attempting to condition release of funds for Iraq reconstruction on guarantee of religious freedom in the yet-to-be drafted constitution).
114. Feldman, "Imposed Constitutionalism," 877; Bremer, *My Year in Iraq*, 283.
115. *Meet the Press* interview with Tim Russert, February 7, 2004. The president stated, "[T]he reason I can say that is because I'm aware of this basic law they're writing. They're not going to develop that because right here in the Oval Office, I sat down with Misters Pachachi and Chalabi and al-Hakim, people from different parts of the country that have made the firm commitment that they want a constitution eventually written that recognizes minority rights and freedom of religion." Transcript retrieved July 31, 2012, from http://www.msnbc.msn.com/id/4179618/ns/meet_the_press/t/transcript-feb-th/.
116. "Bremer Will Reject Islam as Source of Law," Associated Press, Feb 16, 2004. See also Bremer, *My Year in Iraq*, 292; Philips, *Losing Iraq*, 186; Chandrasekaran, *Imperial Life at the Emerald City*, 242.
117. But see Feldman and Martinez, "Constitutional Politics and Text in the New Iraq," 919: "[I]t is important not to overstate American influence in shaping the substantive constitutional outcome, particularly regarding the role of Islam. For the most part, the U.S. role was in facilitating, not imposing. . . ." They list Peter Galbraith, *End of Iraq* (New York: Simon & Schuster, 2007), 138–141, and Andrew Arato, "Interim Imposition," *Ethics & International Affairs* 18, no. 3 (2004): 25–50, as overstatements. For another perspective, see Allawi, *The Occupation of Iraq*, 225–226.
118. Feldman, "Imposed Constitutionalism," 877, citing Anthony Shadid, "Debate Begins in Baghdad on Interim Constitution," *Washington Post*, February 1, 2004.
119. Istrabadi, "Reviving Constitutionalism in Iraq," 276–277. Istrabadi stated that the IGC spent weeks considering whether Islam was "the source of legislation," "the principal source of legislation," "a principal source among other principal sources" or "a source among other sources of legislation."
120. Feldman attributes this demand to Bremer's earlier public declarations that the Iraqi constitution would not be Islamic. See Feldman, "Imposed Constitutionalism," 878. However, it was certainly influenced by a similar provision in the Afghan constitution, which was signed into law in January 2004.

121. Istrabadi, "Reviving Constitutionalism in Iraq," 277.
122. Excerpts of the TAL are in Ehrenberg, ed., *The Iraq Papers,* 203–208.
123. Democratic Principles Working Group and Conference of the Iraqi Opposition, *Final Report on the Transition to Democracy in Iraq* (Cobham, Surrey, UK: Democratic Principles Working Group, 2002), 14. The report was written by the Democratic Principles Working Group of the State Department–organized Future of Iraq (FOI) Project, a conference of exiled Iraqi opposition leaders. The FOI became the controversial nonplan because various people pointed to it as evidence that the State Department did postwar planning but was shut out by the Defense Department. Bremer noted that he looked at it but did not consider it as a concrete blueprint for action. Bremer, *My Year in Iraq,* 25. For a contrary view, see Diamond, *Squandered Victory,* 30. Kanan Makiya, an Iraqi exile and principal author of the report *Transition to Democracy,* was profiled in George C. Packer, "Dreaming of Democracy," *New York Times Magazine,* March 2, 2003.
124. A full copy of the letter is unavailable but has been referenced and quoted in several publications. See, for example, Paul Marshall, "Legacy of Liberty: Religious Freedom, Political Freedom and Iraq's New Fundamental Law," *National Review Online,* Feb 20, 2004. Retrieved July 31, 2012, from http://www.nationalreview.com/articles/209578/legacy-liberty/paul-marshall; Feldman, "Imposed Constitutionalism," 876.
125. Ibid.
126. Ibid.
127. Nathan Brown, Transitional Administrative Law: Commentary and Analysis, March 7–8, 2004. Retrieved July 31, 2012, from http://home.gwu.edu/~nbrown/interimiraqiconstitution.html.
128. USCIRF letter addressed to Ambassador L. Paul Bremer on the Iraq Transitional Administrative Law, February 9, 2004. Retrieved May 19, 2011, from http://www.uscirf.gov/index.php?option=com_content&task=view&id=1372&Itemid=1.
129. See Project for the New American Century, *Statement of Principles,* June 3, 1997, http://www.newamericancentury.org/statementofprinciples.htm; *Rebuilding American Defenses: Strategy, Forces and Resources for a New Century,* Sept 2000, http://www.newamericancentury.org/RebuildingAmericasDefenses.pdf; Patrick Tyler, "U.S. Strategy Plan Calls for Insuring No Rivals Develop," *New York Times,* March 8, 1992.
130. See Alan Weisman, *Prince of Darkness, Richard Perle: The Kingdom, the Power and the End of Empire in America* (New York: Union Square Press, 2007), 44.
131. Bremer, *My Year in Iraq,* 294 and 392.
132. Brown, Transitional Administrative Law: Commentary and Analysis; Arato, "Post-Sovereign Constitution-Making," 166. See also Stilt, "Islamic Law," 699,

which argues that the significance of these constitutional provisions can only be understood in relation with substantive laws.

Conclusion

1. Protecting and promoting religious freedom is just one, albeit an important, strand in the persistent narrative of the United States as a "City upon a Hill," tasked with leading humanity out of the wilderness of tyranny and oppression. For examples of this narrative, see Anders Stephanson, *Manifest Destiny: American Expansion and the Empire of Right* (New York: Farrar, Straus and Giroux, 1996); Ernest Tuveson, *Redeemer Nation: The Idea of America's Millennial Role* (Chicago, IL: University of Chicago Press, 1968).
2. The long-held belief was that Catholicism implied a subservient attitude toward a foreign power—the Roman pontiff—hence Catholics were not suitable for freedom-loving, republican institutions. Anti-Catholicism was considered to be the first antiforeign tradition in U.S. history. By 1898, this belief was still common. See, for example, Josiah Strong et al., *Our Country* (New York: Baker & Taylor for the American Home Missionary Society, 1885), in which one of the seven dangers is "Romanism."
3. See Chapter 5 of this book.
4. Cited in Elizabeth Borgwardt, *New Deal for the World* (Cambridge, MA: Harvard University Press, 2005), 280.
5. See Jack Donnelly, "Human Rights: A New Standard of Civilization?," *International Affairs* 74, no. 1 (1998): 1–23; Makau Mutua, "Savages, Victims, and Saviors: The Metaphor of Human Rights," *Harvard International Law Journal* 42 (2001): 201.
6. President George W. Bush, Remarks to a Joint Session of the Philippine Congress, October 18, 2003. Retrieved from http://www.presidency.ucsb.edu/ws/?pid=63501. Bush made the same mistake in comparing Iraq with Japan. See John Dower, "A Warning from History: Don't Expect Democracy in Iraq," *Boston Review* (March 2003). Retrieved January 25, 2013, from http://www.bostonreview.net/BR28.1/dower.html. These historical references bring to the fore the similarities but manage to obscure the differences, although they suggest a persistent mode of thinking. See generally John Dower, *Cultures of War* (New York: W. W. Norton, 2010).
7. The relationship between liberalism and empire has been a subject of recent literature. For a great overview, see Jennifer Pitts, "Political Theory of Empire and Imperialism," *Annual Review of Political Science* 13, no. 1 (May 2010): 211–235. A variant of an empire of liberalism is treated in Michael Ignatieff, *Empire Lite: Nation-Building in Bosnia, Kosovo and Afghanistan* (London: Vintage, 2003). This idea also underlies many democracy and rule-of-law

promotion activities of the United States, the European Union, and many multilateral institutions such as the World Bank.

8. Ruti Teitel, *Humanity's Law* (New York: Oxford University Press, 2011).
9. See, for example, Elizabeth Shakman Hurd, "Believing in Religious Freedom," *The Immanent Frame,* 2012. Retrieved July 25, 2014, from http://blogs.ssrc.org/tif/2012/03/01/believing-in-religious-freedom/ (critiquing the narrow focus on religious belief).
10. For a focus on human rights in general, see Wendy Brown, "The Most We Can Hope For . . . Human Rights and the Politics of Fatalism," *South Atlantic Quarterly* 103, no. 2/3 (Summer 2004): 451–463.

Bibliography

Unpublished Documents/Personal Papers

Bureau of Insular Affairs, Record Group 350.3, National Archives and Records Administration, College Park, Maryland.
Papers of Manley O. Hudson, Harvard Law School Special Collections.
Papers of Charles Kades, Hoover Institution, Stanford University.
Papers of Elihu Root, Manuscript Division, Library of Congress.
Papers of Leonard Wood, Manuscript Division, Library of Congress.

Printed Document Collections

Bacon, Robert, and James Brown Scott, eds. *Military and Colonial Policy of the United States (Addresses and Reports by Elihu Root)*. Cambridge, MA: Harvard University Press, 1916.
Black, Allida, ed. *The Eleanor Roosevelt Papers: The Human Rights Years 1945–1948*, vol. 2. Charlottesville: University of Virginia Press, 2010.
Ehrenberg, John. *The Iraq Papers*. New York, NY: Oxford University Press, 2010.
Hassen, Farrah, United States Department of State. Department of Defense. Office of Reconstruction and Humanitarian Assistance, Future of Iraq Project, and National Security Archive (U.S.). *The Future of Iraq Project*. Washington, DC: U.S. Department of State; George Washington University, National Security Archive, 2002.
Link, Arthur S., ed. *Papers and Addresses of Woodrow Wilson*, 69 vols. Princeton, NJ: Princeton University Press, 1982.
Mantoux, Paul, Arthur S. Link, and Manfred F. Boemeke. *The Deliberations of the Council of Four (March 24–June 28, 1919): Notes of the Official Interpreter*. Princeton, NJ: Princeton University Press, 1992.

Roosevelt, Franklin Delano, and Susan Butler. *My Dear Mr. Stalin: The Complete Correspondence between Franklin D. Roosevelt and Joseph V. Stalin.* New Haven, CT: Yale University Press, 2005.

Roosevelt, Theodore. *Letters of Theodore Roosevelt Accepting the Republican Nomination for President of the United States.* Oyster Bay, NY: Theodore Roosevelt, 1904.

———, Elbing E. Morison, John Morton Blum, and Alfred Dupont Chandler. *The Letters of Theodore Roosevelt. II, The Years of Preparation 1898–1900.* Cambridge, MA: Harvard University Press, 1951.

Wilson, Woodrow, and August Heckscher. *The Politics of Woodrow Wilson, Selections from His Speeches and Writings.* New York: Harper, 1956.

Digital Archives/Electronic Collections

The American Presidency Project, http://www.presidency.ucsb.edu/ws/?pid=55155.

Japan National Diet Library. "Birth of the Constitution of Japan," http://www.ndl.go.jp/constitution/e/index.html.

Moore, Ray, and Donald Robinson, eds. *The Japanese Constitution: A Documentary History of Its Framing and Adoption.* Princeton, NJ: Princeton University Press, 1998 (CD-ROM).

Nixon Presidential Library, The White House Tapes, March 1973, http://www.nixonlibrary.gov/virtuallibrary/tapeexcerpts/index.php.

PBS *Frontline.* "The Lost Year in Iraq," http://www.pbs.org/wgbh/pages/frontline/yeariniraq/.

U.S. Department of State, Bureau of Democracy, Human Rights and Labor. *International Religious Freedom Report 2013,* http://www.state.gov/j/drl/rls/irf/religiousfreedom/index.htm#wrapper.

Oral History

Columbia University Center for Oral History Collection, The Reminiscences of Harold G. Henderson.

The Foreign Affairs Oral History Collection of the Association for Diplomatic Studies and Training, Library of Congress, Interview with Guy E. Coriden Jr., November 18, 1992, http://memory.loc.gov/ammem/collections/diplomacy.

Government Documents

The President

Documentary History of the Truman Presidency, *Creating a Pluralistic Democracy in Japan: The Occupation Government, 1945–1952*. Bethesda, MD: University Publications of America, 1996.

The Public Papers and Addresses of Franklin D. Roosevelt, 1928–1945, 13 vols. New York: Random House/Harper & Bros., 1938–1950.

The Public Papers of the Presidents of the United States: George W. Bush, Book II. Washington, DC: U.S. Government Printing Office, 2005.

United States. President Nixon (1969–1974). *U.S. Foreign Policy for the 1970's: Building for Peace: A Report to the Congress*. Washington, DC: U.S. Government Printing Office, 1971.

———. *U.S. Foreign Policy for the 1970's: The Emerging Structure of Peace: A Report to the Congress*. Washington, DC: U.S. Government Printing Office, 1972.

———. *U.S. Foreign Policy for the 1970s; Shaping a Durable Peace: A Report to the Congress May 3, 1973*. Washington, DC: U.S. Government Printing Office, 1973.

United States. President's Committee on Civil Rights. *To Secure These Rights: The Report of the President's Committee on Civil Rights*. New York: Simon & Schuster, 1947.

United States. White House Office. "The National Security Strategy of the United States of America," 2002.

Wartime Correspondence between President Roosevelt and Pope Pius XII: With an Introduction & Explanatory Notes by Myron C. Taylor. New York: MacMillan, 1947.

Congress

Senate

United States. Congress. Senate. Committee on the Philippines. *Hearings before the Committee on the Philippines of the United States Senate in Relation to Affairs in the Philippine Islands [January 31–June 28, 1902]*. Washington, DC: U.S. Government Printing Office, 1902.

———. *Hearings on Lands Held for Ecclesiastical or Religious Uses in the Philippine Islands*, etc., 56th Cong., 2nd session (1901).

———. Testimony of James F. Byrnes, on Treaties of Peace with Italy, Rumania, Bulgaria and Hungry, *Hearings before the Committee on Foreign Relations*, United States Senate, 80th Congress, 1st Session (1947).

———. Testimony of Henry A. Kissinger, Senate Foreign Relations Committee, *Hearings on Nomination of Henry Kissinger as Secretary of State,* 93rd Congress, 1st sess., Sept 7, 10, 11, and 14, 1973.

———. Consequences of MFN Renewal for China, Hearing before the Senate Foreign Relations Committee, 104th Cong. 2nd sess., June 6, 1996.

———. Hearings on *Religious Persecution in the Middle East: Faces of the Persecuted,* May 1 and June 10, 1997.

———. U.S. Senate Subcommittee on Near Eastern and South Asian Affairs, Foreign Relations Committee. *Hearings on Religious Persecution in the Middle East,* May 1, 1997.

———. *Iraq: Next Steps—What Will an Iraq 5-Year Plan Look Like?,* Hearings before the Senate Foreign Relations Committee, 108th Cong. 1st sess., September 24, 2003.

———. Select Committee on Intelligence. *Report on Whether Public Statements Regarding Iraq by U.S. Government Officials Were Substantiated by Intelligence,* June 5, 2008.

House of Representatives

United States. Congress. House. *Anti-Religious Activities in the Soviet Union and in Eastern Europe,* Hearings before the Subcommittee on Europe, Committee on Foreign Affairs, 1st sess., 89th Congress, May 10–12, 1965.

———. *Report of the Committee on Foreign Affairs. Subcommittee on International Organizations and Movements,* March 27, 1974.

———. *The Communist Exploitation of Religion,* Hearing before the Subcommittee to investigate the administration of the Internal Security Act and Other Internal Security Laws, Committee on the Judiciary, U.S. Senate, 2nd session, 89th Congress, May 6, 1966.

———. *The New Communist Propaganda Line on Religion,* Hearing before the Committee on Un-American Activities, House of Representatives, 1st session, 90th Congress, August 10, 1967.

———. Subcommittee on International Security, International Organizations and Human Rights, Committee on Foreign Affairs. Hearings on *Religious Persecution,* October 28, 1993, and March 9, 1994.

———. Hearings on *Worldwide Persecution of Jews,* February 27, 1996.

———. Hearings on *Victims of Religious Persecution around the World,* June 16, 1998.

———. Subcommittee on African Affairs. Hearings on *Religious Persecution in Sudan,* September 25, 1997.

U.S. Helsinki Commission

United States. Congress. Commission on Security and Cooperation in Europe. 16 vols. *Implementation of the Helsinki Accords: Religious Liberty and Minority Rights in the Soviet Union,* April 27, 1977. Washington, DC: U.S. Government Printing Office, 1977–1981.

Department of State

United States. Department of State. *Department of State Bulletin,* 89 vols. Washington, DC: U.S. Government Printing Office, 1938–1974.

———. *A Treaty of Peace between the United States and Spain. Message from the President of the United States, Transmitting a Treaty of Peace between the United States and Spain, Signed at the City of Paris, on December 10, 1898. Accompanying papers.* Washington, DC: U.S. Government Printing Office, 1899.

———. *Papers Relating to the Foreign Relations of the United States, 1898.* Washington, DC: U.S. Government Printing Office, 1901.

———. *Papers Relating to the Foreign Relations of the United States, 1899.* Washington, DC: U.S. Government Printing Office, 1901.

———. *Papers Relating to the Foreign Relations of the United States, 1900.* Washington, DC: U.S. Government Printing Office, 1902.

———. *Papers Relating to the Foreign Relations of the United States, 1902.* Washington, DC: U.S. Government Printing Office, 1903.

———. *Papers Relating to the Foreign Relations of the United States, 1906.* Washington, DC: U.S. Government Printing Office, 1909.

———. *Papers Relating to the Foreign Relations of the United States, 1911.* Washington, DC: U.S. Government Printing Office, 1913.

———. *Papers Relating to the Foreign Relations of the United States: The Paris Peace Conference, 1919.* Washington, DC: U.S. Government Printing Office, 1942–1947.

———. *A Decade of American Foreign Policy: Basic Documents 1941–1949.* Washington, DC: U.S. Government Printing Office, 1985.

———. *Dumbarton Oaks Documents on International Organization.* Washington, DC: U.S. Government Printing Office, 1944.

———. *Washington Conversations on International Organization, Dumbarton Oaks, 1944.* Washington, DC: U.S. Government Printing Office, 1945.

———, and Harley A. Notter. *Postwar Foreign Policy Preparation, 1939–1945.* Washington, DC: U.S. Government Printing Office, 1949.

———. *Papers Relating to the Foreign Relations of the United States: Paris Peace Conference 1944.* Washington, DC: U.S. Government Printing Office, 1965.

———. *Charter of the United Nations: Report to the President on the Results of the United Nations Conference on International Organization.* Washington, DC: U.S. Government Printing Office, 1945.

———. *The Axis in Defeat: A Collection of Documents on American Policy toward Germany and Japan,* Superintendent of Documents, 1945, Pub. 2423.

———. *Papers Relating to the Foreign Relations of the United States: Paris Peace Conference 1946.* Washington, DC: U.S. Government Printing Office, 1978.

———. *Annual Report, International Religious Freedom 1999, Report Submitted to the Committee on International Relations, U.S. House of Representatives and the Committee on Foreign Relations, United States Senate by the Department of State in Accordance with Section 102 of the International Religious Freedom Act of 1998.* Washington, DC: U.S. Government Printing Office, 2000.

———. Bureau of Democracy, Human Rights. "United States Policies in Support of Religious Freedom: Focus on Christians, Report Consistent with the Omnibus Consolidated Appropriations Act, Fiscal Year 1997, House Report 3610," 1997. Available online at http://purl.fdlp.gov/GPO/gpo11589.

———. Advisory Committee on Religious Freedom. *Final Report of the Advisory Committee on Religious Freedom to the Secretary of State and to the President of the United States.* Washington, DC: Department of State, 1999.

War Department

Dewey, George. *The War with Spain: Operations of the United States Navy on the Asiatic Station: Rreports of Rear-Admiral George Dewey on the Battle of Manila Bay, May 1, 1898, and on the Investment and Fall of Manila, May 1 to August 13, 1898.* Washington, DC: U.S. Government Printing Office, 1900.

United States. Bureau of Insular Affairs. *What Has Been Done in the Philippines. A Record of Practical Accomplishments under Civil Government. . . .* Washington, DC: U.S. Government Printing Office, 1904.

United States. War Department *Five Years of the War Department Following the War with Spain, 1899–1903, As Shown in the Annual Reports of the Secretary of War.* Washington, DC: U.S. Government Printing Office, 1904.

———, and William H. Taft. *Special report of William H. Taft, Secretary of War, to the President, on the Philippines. . . .* Washington, DC: U.S. Government Printing Office, 1908.

———, and United States Philippine Commission (1900–1916). *Lands Held for Ecclesiastical or Religious Uses in the Philippine Islands: Message from the President of the United States Transmitting in Response to Resolution of the Senate of January 26, 1901, a Report from the Secretary of War, with*

Accompanying Papers, Relative to the Lands Held in Mortmain or Otherwise for Ecclesiastical or Religious Uses in the Philippine Islands; also Transmitting Certified Copies of the Acts of the Philippine Commission, Numbers 56 to 68, Inclusive. Washington, DC: U.S. Government Printing Office, 1901.

Philippine Commission and the Moro Province

Governor of the Moro Province. *Annual Report of the Governor of the Province of Moro.* Washington, DC: U.S. Government Printing Office, 1903.

———. *Annual Report of the Governor of the Province of Moro.* Washington, DC: U.S. Government Printing Office, 1904.

———. *Annual Report of the Governor of the Province of Moro.* Washington, DC: U.S. Government Printing Office, 1905.

United States. Philippine Commission (1899–1900), Jacob Gould Schurman, George Dewey, Elwell Stephen Otis, Charles Denby, and Dean C. Worcester. *Report of the Philippine Commission to the President.* Washington, DC: U.S. Government Printing Office, 1900.

———, William Howard Taft, and United States War Department. *Reports of the Taft Philippine Commission: Message from the President of the United States, Transmitting a Report of the Secretary of War, Containing the Reports of the Taft Commission, Its Several Acts of Legislation, and Other Important Information Relating to the Condition and Immediate Wants of the Philippine Islands.* Washington, DC: U.S. Government Printing Office, 1901.

Miscellaneous

Supreme Commander for the Allied Powers Government. *Political Reorientation of Japan.* Washington, DC: U.S. Government Printing Office, 1949.

United States. Adjutant-General's Office. *Correspondence Relating to the War with Spain, 1898–1902.* Washington, DC: U.S. Government Printing Office, 1902.

United States. Department of the Treasury. Bureau of Statistics, Oscar P. Austin, *Colonial Administration, 1800–1900: Methods of Government and Development Adopted by the Principal Colonizing Nations in Their Control of Tropical and Other Colonies and Dependencies.* Washington, DC: U.S. Government Printing Office, 1903.

United States. Office of War Information. *Enemy Japan.* Washington, DC, 1945.

United States Commission on International Religious Freedom, *Iraq: Religion and Reconstruction,* April 28, 2003 http://www.uscirf.gov/index.php?option=com_content&view=article&id=256.

Participant Records and Memoirs

Acheson, Dean G., *Present at the Creation: My Years at the State Department.* New York: W. W. Norton, 1969.

Adams, Brooks. *The Law of Civilization and Decay: An Essay on History.* New York: MacMillan Co., 1895.

Albright, Madeleine. *The Mighty and the Almighty.* New York: HarperCollins, 2006.

al-Istrabadi, Feisal Amin. "Reviving Constitutionalism in Iraq: Key Provisions of the Transitional Administrative Law." *New York Law School Law Review* 50 (2005): 269.

Baker, Ray Stannard. *Woodrow Wilson and World Settlement,* 3 vols. Garden City, NY: Doubleday, 1922.

Baldwin, Simeon E. "Mission of Gov. Taft to the Vatican," *Yale Law Journal* 12 (1902): 1–15.

Ballou, Robert Oleson. *Shinto, the Unconquered Enemy: Japan's Doctrine of Racial Superiority and World Conquest.* New York: Viking Press, 1945.

Benedict, Ruth. *The Chrysanthemum and the Sword: Patterns of Japanese Culture.* Boston, MA: Houghton Mifflin Co., 1946.

Borton, Hugh. "Preparation for the Occupation of Japan." *The Journal of Asian Studies* 25, no. 2 (1966): 203–212.

Bremer, L. Paul III, with Malcolm McConnell. *My Year in Iraq: The Struggle to Build a Future of Hope.* New York: Simon & Schuster, 2006.

Bush, George W., *Decision Points.* New York: Crown Publishers, 2010.

Byrnes, James F., *Speaking Frankly.* New York: Harper, 1947.

Diamond, Larry. "Lessons from Iraq." *Journal of Democracy* 16, no. 1 (2005): 9–23.

———. *Squandered Victory: The American Occupation and the Bungled Effort to Bring Democracy to Iraq.* New York: Times Books, 2005.

Dulles, John Foster. *War or Peace.* New York: Macmillan Company, 1950.

Dyke, Ken R. "Shinto: A Study Prepared by General Headquarters, SCAP, C I & E Section." *Contemporary Religions in Japan* 7, no. 4 (December 1, 1966): 321–360.

Eichelberger, Clark M. *The United Nations Charter: What Was Done at San Francisco.* New York: Harper & Bros., 1945.

Farley, James A. *Jim Farley's Story: The Roosevelt Years.* New York: Whittlesey House, 1948.

Fascell, Dante B. "Did Human Rights Survive Belgrade?" *Foreign Policy* 31 (July 1, 1978): 104–118.

Federal Council of the Churches of Christ in America. Commission on a Just and Durable Peace. *A Righteous Faith for a Just and Durable Peace.* New York: Commission to Study the Bases of a Just and Durable Peace, 1942.

Feith, Douglas G. *War and Decision: Inside the Pentagon at the Dawn of the War on Terrorism.* New York: HarperCollins, 2008.

Feldman, Noah. *After Jihad: America and the Struggle for Islamic Democracy.* New York: Farrar, Straus, and Giroux, 2003.

———. "The Democratic Fatwa: Islam and Democracy in the Realm of Constitutional Politics." *Oklahoma Law Review* 58, no. 1 (2005): 1.

———. "Imposed Constitutionalism." *Connecticut Law Review* 37 (2004): 857.

———. *What We Owe Iraq: War and the Ethics of Nation Building.* Princeton, NJ: Princeton University Press, 2003.

———, and Roman Martinez. "Constitutional Politics and Text in the New Iraq: An Experiment in Islamic Democracy." *Fordham Law Review* 75 (2006): 883.

Finley, John P. "The Commercial Awakening of the Moro and Pagan." *The North American Review* 197, no. 688 (1913): 325–334.

Flynn, Edward Joseph. *You're the Boss: The Practice of American Politics.* New York: Collier Books, 1962.

Forbes, W. Cameron. *The Philippine Islands.* Boston, MA: Houghton Mifflin Co., 1928.

Galbraith, Peter W. *The End of Iraq: How American Incompetence Created a War without End.* New York: Simon & Schuster, 2007.

Goldberg, Arthur. "Human Rights and the Belgrade Meeting." *Hastings Law Journal* 30 (1978): 249–253.

Grayson, Cary T. *Woodrow Wilson: An Intimate Memoir.* New York: Holt, Rinehart, and Winston, 1960.

Grew, Joseph C. *Ten Years in Japan: A Contemporary Record Drawn from the Diaries and Private and Official Papers of Joseph G. Grew, United States Ambassador to Japan, 1932–1942.* New York: Simon & Schuster, 1944.

Holtom, Daniel Clarence. *The National Faith of Japan: A Study in Modern Shinto.* New York: E. P. Dutton, 1938.

———. *The Political Philosophy of Modern Shinto, a Study of the State Religion of Japan.* Tokyo: Asiatic Society of Japan, 1922.

House, Edward M., and Charles Seymour, ed., *What Really Happened in Paris,* New York: Charles Scribner's Sons, 1921.

Hull, Cordell, *The Memoirs of Cordell Hull,* 2 vols. New York: Macmillan, 1948.

Humphrey, John P. *Human Rights and the United Nations: A Great Adventure.* Dobbs Ferry, NY: Transnational Publishers, 1984.

Ito, Hirobumi. *Commentaries on the Constitution of the Empire of Japan,* translated by Baron Miyoji Ito. Westport, CT: Greenwood Press, 1978.

Jennings Bryan, William. *Republic or Empire: The Philippine Question.* Chicago, IL: W. B. Conkey Co., 1900.

Lansing, Robert, *The Peace Negotiations: A Personal Narrative.* Boston, MA: Houghton Mifflin Co., 1921.

Leahy, William D. *I Was There: The Personal Story of the Chief of Staff to Presidents Roosevelt and Truman, Based on His Notes and Diaries Made at the Time.* New York: Whittlesey House, 1950.

LeRoy, James A. *The Americans in the Philippines,* 2 vols. New York: AMS Press, 1970.

Lewis, William Draper. "The Statement of Essential Human Rights by Representatives of the Principal Cultures of the World." *Proceedings of the American Philosophical Society* 89, no. 3 (Oct 11, 1945): 489–494.

Lloyd George, David. *The Truth about the Peace Treaties.* London: Victor Gollancz, 1938.

MacArthur, Douglas. *Reminiscences.* New York: McGraw-Hill, 1964.

Mahan, Alfred. *The Harvest Within: Thoughts on the Life of the Christian.* Boston, MA: Little, Brown & Co., 1909.

Maresca, John J., and Conference on Security and Cooperation in Europe. *To Helsinki: The Conference on Security and Cooperation in Europe, 1973–1975.* Durham, NC: Duke University Press, 1985.

Miller, David Hunter. *The Drafting of the Covenant,* 2 vols. New York: GP Putnam's Sons, 1928.

Morgan, H. Wayne, ed. *Making Peace with Spain: The Diary of Whitelaw Reid.* Austin: University of Texas Press, 1965.

Perkins, Frances. *The Roosevelt I Knew.* New York: Viking Press, 1946.

Robins, Dorothy B. *Experiment in Democracy: The Story of U.S. Citizen Organizations in Forging the Charter of the United Nations.* Glendale, NY: Parkside Press, 1971.

Rosenman, Samuel I. *Working with Roosevelt.* New York: Harper & Bros, 1952.

Rumsfeld, Donald. *Known and Unknown: A Memoir.* New York: Sentinel, 2011.

Shattuck, John. *Freedom on Fire: Human Rights Wars and America's Response.* Cambridge, MA: Harvard University Press, 2009.

Smuts, Jan Christiaan. *The League of Nations; A Practical Suggestion.* London: Hodder and Stoughton, 1918.

Stettinius, Edward R., Thomas M. Campbell, and George C. Herring. *The Diaries of Edward R. Stettinius, Jr., 1943–1946.* New York: New Viewpoints, 1975.

———. "Human Rights in the United Nations Charter." *Annals of the American Academy of Political and Social Science* 243 (January 1, 1946): 1–3.

———. *Roosevelt and the Russians.* Garden City, NY: Doubleday, 1949.

Stewart, Rory. *The Prince of the Marshes: And Other Occupational Hazards of a Year in Iraq.* New York: Houghton Mifflin Harcourt, 2007.

Strong, Josiah. *Expansion under New World Conditions.* New York: The Baker and Taylor Company, 1900.

———. *Our Country: Its Possible Future and Its Present Crisis.* New York: Baker & Taylor for the American Home Missionary Society, 1891.

Twain, Mark. *To the Person Sitting in Darkness.* New York: Anti-Imperialist League of New York, 1901.

Welles, Sumner. *The World of the Four Freedoms.* New York: Columbia University Press, 1943.

Woodard, William P. *The Allied Occupation of Japan 1945–1952 and Japanese Religions.* Leiden: Brill, 1972.

Unpublished Theses/Dissertations

Castañeda, Anna Leah Fidelis Tesoro. "Creating Exceptional Empire: American Liberal Constitutionalism and the Construction of the Constitutional Order of the Philippine Islands, 1898–1935." SJD dissertation, Harvard Law School, 2009.

Coates, Bejamin Allen. "Transatlantic Advocates: American International Law and U.S. Foreign Relations, 1898–1919." PhD dissertation, Columbia University, 2010.

Hirsch, Jordan Chandler. "The Gateway: The Soviet Jewry Movement, the Right to Leave and the Rise of Human Rights on the International Stage." Senior thesis, Columbia University, 2010.

Janson, Michael A. "A Christian Century: Liberal Protestantism, the New Deal and the Origins of Postwar American Politics." PhD dissertation, University of Pennsylvania, 2007.

Klingbeil, Kurt A. "F.D.R. and American Religious Leaders: A Study of President Franklin D. Roosevelt and His Relationship to Selected American Religious Leaders." PhD dissertation, New York University, 1972.

Lindkvist, Linde. "Shrines and Souls: The Reinvention of Religious Liberty and the Genesis of the Universal Declaration of Human Rights." PhD dissertation, Lund University, 2014.

Thompson, Wayne Wray. "Governors of the Moro Province Wood, Bliss, and Pershing in the Southern Philippines, 1903–1913." PhD dissertation, University of California–San Diego, 1975.

Walther, Karine V. "A Door into the Mohammedan World: Islam and U.S. Foreign Policy, 1821–1913." PhD dissertation, Columbia University, 2008.

Secondary Materials

Abou El-Fadl, Khaled. *Islam and the Challenge of Democracy.* Princeton, NJ: Princeton University Press, 2004.

Abrams, Elliott. *The Influence of Faith: Religious Groups and U.S. Foreign Policy.* Lanham, MD: Rowman & Littlefield, 2001.

Adler, Cyrus, Aaron M. Margalith, Cyrus Adler, and American Jewish Committee. *With Firmness in the Right: American Diplomatic Action Affecting Jews, 1840–1945.* New York: The American Jewish Committee, 1946.

Adler, Les K., and Thomas G Paterson. "Red Fascism: The Merger of Nazi Germany and Soviet Russia in the American Image of Totalitarianism, 1930s–1950s." *The American Historical Review* 75, no. 4 (1970).

Alfonso, Oscar M. *Theodore Roosevelt and the Philippines, 1897–1909.* New York: Oriole Editions, 1974.

Alford, William P. "Exporting 'The Pursuit of Happiness.'" *Harvard Law Review* 113, no. 7 (2000): 1677–1715.

Allawi, Ali A. *The Occupation of Iraq: Winning the War, Losing the Peace.* New Haven, CT: Yale University Press, 2008.

Allerfeldt, Kristofer. "Wilsonian Pragmatism? Woodrow Wilson, Japanese Immigration, and the Paris Peace Conference." *Diplomacy and Statecraft* 15, no. 3 (2004): 545–572.

Alvarez, David. "Purely a Business Matter: The Taft Mission to the Vatican." *Diplomatic History* 16, no. 3 (1992): 357–370.

Ambrosius, Lloyd E. *Wilsonian Statecraft: Theory and Practice of Liberal Internationalism during World War I.* Wilmington, DE: SR Books, 1991.

Anderson, Carol Elaine. *Eyes off the Prize: The United Nations and the African American Struggle for Human Rights, 1944–1955.* New York: Cambridge University Press, 2003.

Anghie, Antony. "Colonialism and the Birth of International Institutions: Sovereignty, Economy, and the Mandate System of the League of Nations." *New York University Journal of International Law and Politics* 343 (2002): 513–633.

Annicchino, Pasquale. "The New Guidelines on Freedom of Religion and LGBTI Rights in the External Action of the European Union." *European Human Rights Law Review* 6 (2013): 624–630.

———. "Recent Developments Concerning the Promotion of Freedom of Religion or Belief in Italian Foreign Policy." *Review of Faith and International Affairs* 11, no. 3 (2013): 61–68.

Arato, Andrew. *Constitution Making Under Occupation: The Politics of Imposed Revolution in Iraq.* New York: Columbia University Press, 2009.

———. "Interim Imposition." *Ethics & International Affairs* 18, no. 3 (2004): 25–50.

———. "Post-Sovereign Constitution-Making and Its Pathology in Iraq." *New York Law School Law Review* 51 (2006): 536.

Armitage, David. *The Declaration of Independence: A Global History.* Cambridge, MA: Harvard University Press, 2007.

———, and Jo Guldi. "The Return of the *Longue Duree*: An Anglo-American Perspective." *Annales: Histoire, Sciences Sociales* 69 (2014).

Arnold, James R. *The Moro War: How America Battled a Muslim Insurgency in the Philippine Jungle, 1902–1913.* New York: Bloomsbury Press, 2011.

Babik, Milan. "George D. Herron and the Eschatological Foundations of Woodrow Wilson's Foreign Policy 1917–1919." *Diplomatic History* 35, no. 5 (2011): 837–857.

Bange, Oliver, and Gottfried Niedhart. *Helsinki 1975 and the Transformation of Europe*. New York: Berghahn Books, 2008.

Bass, Gary Jonathan. *Freedom's Battle: The Origins of Humanitarian Intervention*. New York: Alfred A. Knopf, 2008.

Beasley, William G. *The Meiji Restoration*. Stanford, CA: Stanford University Press, 1972.

Beauchamp, Edward Robert, and James M. Vardaman, eds. *Japanese Education Since 1945: A Documentary Study*. Armonk, NY: M. E. Sharpe, 1994.

Beckerman, Gal. *When They Come for Us, We'll Be Gone: The Epic Struggle to Save Soviet Jewry*. New York: Houghton Mifflin Harcourt, 2010.

Beisner, Robert L. *Twelve against Empire; the Anti-Imperialists, 1898–1900*. New York: McGraw-Hill, 1968.

Beitz, Charles. *The Idea of Human Rights*. New York: Oxford University Press, 2009.

Bemis, Samuel Flagg. *A Diplomatic History of the United States*. New York: Holt, Rinehart and Winston, 1965.

Benbow, Mark. *Leading Them to the Promised Land: Woodrow Wilson, Covenant Theology, and the Mexican Revolution, 1913–1915*. Kent, OH: Kent State University Press, 2010.

Bender, Thomas. *Rethinking American History in a Global Age*. Berkeley: University of California Press, 2002.

Bensahel, Nora. *After Saddam: Prewar Planning and the Occupation of Iraq*. Santa Monica, CA: Rand Corporation, 2008.

Bethell, Leslie. *The Cambridge History of Latin America*. Cambridge: Cambridge University Press, 1984.

Bhuta, Nehal. "Two Concepts of Religious Freedom in the European Court of Human Rights." *South Atlantic Quarterly* 113, no. 1 (2014): 10–36.

Billias, George Athan. *American Constitutionalism Heard 'Round the World, 1776–1989: A Global Perspective*. New York: New York University Press, 2009.

Bishop, Donald Gordon. *The Roosevelt-Litvinov Agreements: The American View*. Syracuse, NY: Syracuse University Press, 1965.

Bix, Herbert P. *Hirohito and the Making of Modern Japan*. New York: Harper-Collins, 2001.

Blum, Edward J. *Reforging the White Republic: Race, Religion, and American Nationalism, 1865–1898*. Baton Rouge: Louisiana State University Press, 2005.

Borgwardt, Elizabeth. *A New Deal for the World: America's Vision for Human Rights*. Cambridge, MA: Belknap Press of Harvard University Press, 2005.

Borstelmann, Thomas. *The 1970s: A New Global History from Civil Rights to Economic Inequality.* Princeton, NJ: Princeton University Press, 2012.

Bradley, Gerard V. *Challenges to Religious Liberty in the Twenty-First Century.* Cambridge: Cambridge University Press, 2012.

Brands, Hal W. "Who Saved the Emperor?" *Pacific Historical Review* 75, no. 2 (May 1, 2006): 271–305.

Bronson, Rachel. *Thicker Than Oil: America's Uneasy Partnership with Saudi Arabia.* New York: Oxford University Press, 2006.

Brown, Wendy. "The Most We Can Hope For . . . Human Rights and the Politics of Fatalism." *South Atlantic Quarterly* 103, no. 2/3 (Summer 2004): 451–463.

Burgers, Jan Herman. "The Road to San Francisco: The Revival of the Human Rights Idea in the Twentieth Century." *Human Rights Quarterly* 14 (1992): 447.

Burkman, Thomas W. *Japan and the League of Nations: Empire and World Order, 1914–1938.* Honolulu: University of Hawaii Press, 2008.

Burnett, Christina Duffy, and Burke Marshall. *Foreign in a Domestic Sense: Puerto Rico, American Expansion, and the Constitution.* Durham, NC: Duke University Press, 2001.

Burns, James MacGregor. *Roosevelt: Soldier of Freedom, 1940–1945.* New York: Houghton Mifflin Harcourt, 2002.

Butow, Robert Joseph Charles. *Japan's Decision to Surrender.* Stanford, CA: Stanford University Press, 1954.

Callahan, Michael D. *A Sacred Trust: The League of Nations and Africa, 1929–1946.* Brighton, UK: Sussex Academic Press, 2004.

Canipe, Lee. "Under God and Anti-Communist: How the Pledge of Allegiance Got Religion in Cold War America." *Journal of Church and State* 45, no. 2 (2003): 305.

Carey, Hilary M. *God's Empire: Religion and Colonialism in the British World, c. 1801–1908.* Cambridge: Cambridge University Press, 2011.

Carrington, Paul D. *Spreading America's Word: Stories of Its Lawyer-Missionaries.* New York: Twelve Tables Press, 2005.

Casanova, José. *Public Religions in the Modern World.* Chicago, IL: University of Chicago Press, 1994.

Casey, Steven. *Cautious Crusade: Franklin D. Roosevelt, American Public Opinion, and the War against Nazi Germany.* New York: Oxford University Press, 2001.

Castelli, Elizabeth A. "Praying for the Persecuted Church: US Christian Activism in the Global Arena." *Journal of Human Rights* 4, no. 3 (2005): 321–351.

Chandrasekaran, Rajiv. *Imperial Life in the Emerald City: Inside Iraq's Green Zone.* New York: Knopf, 2006.

Chaplin, Jonathan, and Robert Joustra. *God and Global Order: The Power of Religion in American Foreign Policy.* Waco, TX: Baylor University Press, 2010.

Cleveland, Sarah H. "Norm Internalization and U.S. Economic Sanctions." *Yale Journal of International Law* 26 (2001): 1.

Clymer, Kenton J. *Protestant Missionaries in the Philippines, 1898–1916: An Inquiry into the American Colonial Mentality.* Urbana: University of Illinois Press, 1986.

Cmiel, Kenneth. "The Recent History of Human Rights." In Akira Iriye, Petra Goedde, and William I. Hitchcock, eds., *The Human Rights Revolution: An International History* (pp. 27–52). New York: Oxford University Press, 2012.

Cohen, Theodore, and Herbert Passin. *Remaking Japan: The American Occupation as New Deal.* New York: Free Press, 1987.

Conway, John S. "Myron C. Taylor's Mission to the Vatican, 1940–1950." *Church History* 44, no. 1 (1975): 85–99.

Cooper, John Milton. *Breaking the Heart of the World.* Cambridge: Cambridge University Press, 2001.

———. "A Friend in Power?: Woodrow Wilson and Armenia." In Jay Winter, ed., *America and the Armenian Genocide of 1915* (pp. 103–112). New York: Cambridge University Press, 2003.

———. *Woodrow Wilson: A Biography.* New York: Alfred A. Knopf, 2009.

———, and Woodrow Wilson International Center for Scholars. *Reconsidering Woodrow Wilson: Progressivism, Internationalism, War, and Peace.* Washington, DC: Woodrow Wilson Center Press, and Baltimore, MD: Johns Hopkins University Press, 2008.

Costigliola, Frank. *Roosevelt's Lost Alliances.* Princeton, NJ: Princeton University Press, 2012.

Cronon, E. David. "American Catholics and Mexican Anticlericalism, 1933–1936." *The Mississippi Valley Historical Review* 45, no. 2 (1958): 201–230.

Cunningham, Charles H. "Origin of the Friar Lands Question in the Philippines." *The American Political Science Review* 10, no. 3 (1916): 465–480.

Dallek, Robert. *Franklin D. Roosevelt and American Foreign Policy, 1932–1945: With a New Afterword.* New York: Oxford University Press, 1995.

Danchin, Peter G. "The Emergence and Structure of Religious Freedom in International Law Reconsidered." *Journal of Law and Religion* 23, no. 2 (2007): 455–534.

———. "U.S. Unilateralism and the International Protection of Religious Freedom: The Multilateral Alternative." *The Columbia Journal of Transnational Law* 41 (2002): 33–136.

———, and Elizabeth A. Cole. *Protecting the Human Rights of Religious Minorities in Eastern Europe.* New York: Columbia University Press, 2002.

Dawson, Raymond H. *The Decision to Aid Russia, 1941: Foreign Policy and Domestic Politics.* Chapel Hill: University of North Carolina Press, 1959.

Democratic Principles Working Group and Conference of the Iraqi Opposition. *Final Report on the Transition to Democracy in Iraq: Final Version of the Working Document.* Cobham, Surrey, UK: Democratic Principles Working Group, 2002.

Dezalay, Yves, and Bryant G Garth. *Asian Legal Revivals: Lawyers in the Shadow of Empire.* Chicago, IL: University of Chicago Press, 2010.

Divine, Robert A. *Second Chance: The Triumph of Internationalism in America during World War II.* New York: Atheneum, 1967.

Dobbins, James, Seth G. Jones, Benjamin Runkle, and Siddharth Mohandas. *Occupying Iraq: A History of the Coalition Provisional Authority.* Santa Monica, CA: RAND Corporation, 2009.

Donnelly, Jack. *Universal Human Rights in Theory and Practice,* 2nd ed. Ithaca, NY: Cornell University Press, 2003.

Dower, John W. *Cultures of War: Pearl Harbor / Hiroshima / 9–11 / Iraq.* New York: Pantheon, 1986.

———. *Embracing Defeat: Japan in the Wake of World War II.* New York: W. W. Norton, 2000.

———. *War Without Mercy: Race and Power in the Pacific War.* New York: Random House, 1986.

Drinan, Robert F. *Can God & Caesar Coexist?: Balancing Religious Freedom and International Law.* New Haven, CT: Yale University Press, 2004.

Dudziak, Mary L. *Cold War Civil Rights: Race and the Image of American Democracy.* Princeton, NJ: Princeton University Press, 2000.

Eager, Samuel W., Jr. "Constitutionality of the Proposed Appointment of an Ambassador to the Vatican." *Albany Law Review* 16 (1952): 208.

Eichelberger, Clark Mell. *Organizing for Peace: A Personal History of the Founding of the United Nations.* New York: Harper & Row, 1977.

Escalante, Rene R. *The American Friar Lands Policy: Its Framers, Contexts, and Beneficiaries, 1898–1916.* Manila: De La Salle University Press, 2002.

Evans, Malcolm D. *Religious Liberty and International Law in Europe.* Cambridge: Cambridge University Press, 1997.

Evans, Tony. *U.S. Hegemony and the Project of Universal Human Rights.* Houndmills, England: Macmillan Press, and New York: St. Martin's Press, 1996.

Faber, David. *Munich, 1938: Appeasement and World War II.* New York: Simon & Schuster, 2009.

Farr, Thomas F. *World of Faith and Freedom: Why International Religious Liberty Is Vital to American National Security.* New York: Oxford University Press, 2008.

Farrell, John T. "Background of the 1902 Taft Mission to Rome I." *The Catholic Historical Review* 36, no. 1 (1950): 1–32.

Fassbender, Bardo, Anne Peters, Simone Peter, and Daniel Högger. *The Oxford Handbook of the History of International Law.* Oxford: Oxford University Press, 2012.

Feingold, Henry L. *Bearing Witness: How America and Its Jews Responded to the Holocaust.* Syracuse, NY: Syracuse University Press, 1995.

Feldman, Noah. *Divided by God: America's Church-State Problem—and What We Should Do about It.* New York: Farrar, Straus and Giroux, 2005.

Ferguson, Niall. *Colossus: The Price of America's Empire.* New York: Penguin Press, 2004.

———, Charles S. Maier, Erez Manela, and Daniel J. Sargent. *The Shock of the Global: The 1970s in Perspective.* Cambridge, MA: Harvard University Press, 2010.

Fink, Carole. *Defending the Rights of Others: The Great Powers, the Jews, and International Minority Protection, 1878–1938.* Cambridge; New York: Cambridge University Press, 2004.

———. "The League of Nations and the Minorities Question." *World Affairs* 157, no. 4 (1995): 197–205.

Finn, Richard B. *Winners in Peace: MacArthur, Yoshida, and Postwar Japan.* Berkeley: University of California Press, 1992.

Flynn, George Q. "Franklin Roosevelt and the Vatican: The Myron Taylor Appointment." *The Catholic Historical Review* 58, no. 2 (1972): 171–194.

———. *Roosevelt and Romanism: Catholics and American Diplomacy, 1937–1945.* Westport, CT: Greenwood Press, 1976.

Foner, Eric. *The Story of American Freedom.* New York: W. W. Norton, 1998.

Foster, Elizabeth. *Faith in Empire: Religion, Politics and Colonial Rule in French Senegal, 1880–1940.* Stanford, CA: Stanford University Press, 2013.

Friedman, Murray. *A Second Exodus: The American Movement to Free Soviet Jews.* Hanover, NH: University Press of New England for Brandeis University Press, 1999.

Friedrich, Carl J. *The Impact of American Constitutionalism Abroad.* Boston, MA: Boston University Press, 1967.

Fukuyama, Francis. *The End of History and the Last Man.* New York: Avon Books, 1993.

Gaddis, John Lewis. "A Grand Strategy of Transformation." *Foreign Policy,* issue edited by Robert J. Lieber (2008): 335–342.

Garthoff, Raymond. *Détente and Confrontation.* Washington, DC: Brookings Institution, 1985.

Gelfand, Lawrence E. *The Inquiry: American Preparations for Peace, 1917–1919.* New Haven, CT: Yale University Press, 1963.

Gerstle, Gary. "Race and Nation in the Thought and Politics of Woodrow Wilson." In John Milton Cooper, ed., *Reconsidering Woodrow Wilson: Progressivism, Internationalism, War, and Peace* (pp. 93–123). Baltimore, MD: Johns Hopkins University Press, 2008.

Glendon, Mary Ann. *A World Made New: Eleanor Roosevelt and the Universal Declaration of Human Rights.* New York: Random House, 2001.

Go, Julian. *Patterns of Empire: The British and American Empires, 1688 to the Present.* New York: Cambridge University Press, 2011.

———, and Anne L. Foster, eds. *The American Colonial State in the Philippines: Global Perspectives.* Durham, NC: Duke University Press, 2009.

Goldberg, Paul. *The Final Act: The Dramatic, Revealing Story of the Moscow Helsinki Watch Group.* New York: Morrow, 1988.

Goldstein, Judith, Robert O. Keohane, and Social Science Research Council (U.S.). Committee on Foreign Policy Studies. *Ideas and Foreign Policy: Beliefs, Institutions, and Political Change.* Ithaca, NY: Cornell University Press, 1993.

Golove D. M., and D. J. Hulsebosch. "A Civilized Nation: The Early American Constitution, the Law of Nations, and the Pursuit of International Rrecognition." *New York University Law Review* 85, no. 4 (2010): 932–1066.

Gong, Gerrit W. *The Standard of "Civilization" in International Society.* Oxford: Clarendon Press, 1984.

Gordon, Sarah Barringer. *The Mormon Question: Polygamy and Constitutional Conflict in Nineteenth-Century America.* Chapel Hill: University of North Carolina Press, 2002.

———. *The Spirit of the Law: Religious Voices and the Constitution in Modern America.* Cambridge, MA: Belknap Press of Harvard University Press, 2010.

Gowing, Peter G. *Mandate in Moroland: The American Government of Muslim Filipinos, 1899–1920.* Quezon City: Philippine Center for Advanced Studies, University of the Philippines System, 1977.

Grabill, Joseph L. "Missionary Influence on American Foreign Relations with the Near East, 1914–1923." *The Muslim World* 58, no. 1 (1968): 43–56.

———. *Protestant Diplomacy and the Near East: Missionary Influence on American Policy, 1810–1927.* Minneapolis: University of Minnesota Press, 1971.

Green, Steven K. *The Second Disestablishment: Church and State in Nineteenth-Century America.* New York: Oxford University Press, 2010.

Grzybowski, Kazimierz. "Woodrow Wilson on Law, State, and Society." *George Washington Law Review* 30 (1962): 808–852.

Gunn, T. Jeremy. "American Exceptionalism and Globalist Double Standards: A More Balanced Alternative." *Columbia Journal of Transnational Law* 41 (2002): 137.

———. *Spiritual Weapons: The Cold War and the Forging of an American National Religion.* Westport, CT: Praeger, 2009.

Gustafson, Merlin, and Jerry Rosenberg. "The Faith of Franklin Roosevelt." *Presidential Studies Quarterly* 19, no. 3 (July 1, 1989): 559–566.

Hackett, Rosalind I. J., Mark Silk, Dennis Hoover, and Center for the Study of Religion in Public Life Trinity College. *Religious Persecution as a U.S. Policy*

Issue: Proceedings of a Consultation Held at Trinity College, Hartford, September 26–27, 1999. Center for the Study of Religion in Public Life, Trinity College, Hartford, Connecticut, 2000.

Hamburger, Philip. *Separation of Church and State.* Cambridge, MA: Harvard University Press, 2002.

Handy, Robert T. *Undermined Establishment: Church-State Relations in America, 1880–1920.* Princeton, NJ: Princeton University Press, 1991.

Hanhimäki, Jussi M. "'They Can Write It in Swahili': Kissinger, the Soviets, and the Helsinki Accords, 1973–75." *Journal of Transatlantic Studies* 1, no. 1 (2003): 37–58.

Hardacre, Helen. *Shinto and the State, 1868–1988.* Princeton, NJ: Princeton University Press, 1989.

Harris, Susan K. *God's Arbiters: Americans and the Philippines, 1898–1902.* New York: Oxford University Press, 2011.

Healy, David J. *U.S. Expansionism: The Imperialist Urge in the 1890s.* Madison: University of Wisconsin Press, 1970. http://site.ebrary.com/id/10537626.

Hehir, J. Bryan. *Liberty and Power: A Dialogue on Religion and U.S. Foreign Policy in an Unjust World.* Washington, DC: Brookings Institution Press, 2004.

Hellegers, Dale M. *We, the Japanese People: World War II and the Origins of the Japanese Constitution.* Stanford, CA: Stanford University Press, 2002.

Hendrickson, Kenneth, Jr. "Reluctant Expansionist: Jacob Gould Schurman and the Philippine Question." *Pacific Historical Review* 36, no. 4 (1967): 405–421.

Henkin, Louis. *The International Bill of Rights: The Covenant on Civil and Political Rights.* New York: Columbia University Press, 1981.

———. "U.S. Ratification of Human Rights Conventions: The Ghost of Senator Bricker." *The American Journal of International Law* 89, no. 2 (April 1, 1995): 341–350.

———, and Albert J. Rosenthal. *Constitutionalism and Rights: The Influence of the United States Constitution Abroad.* New York: Columbia University Press, 1990.

Henning, Joseph M. *Outposts of Civilization: Race, Religion, and the Formative Years of American-Japanese Relations.* New York: New York University Press, 2000.

Herring, George C. *From Colony to Superpower: U.S. Foreign Relations since 1776.* New York: Oxford University Press, 2011.

Hertzke, Allen D. *Freeing God's Children: The Unlikely Alliance for Global Human Rights.* Lanham, MD: Rowman & Littlefield, 2006.

———. *The Future of Religious Freedom: Global Challenges.* New York: Oxford University Press, 2013.

Herzog, Jonathan P. *The Spiritual-Industrial Complex: America's Religious Battle against Communism in the Early Cold War.* New York: Oxford University Press, 2011.

Higham, John. *Strangers in the Land; Patterns of American Nativism, 1860–1925.* New Brunswick, NJ: Rutgers University Press, 1955.

Hilderbrand, Robert C. *Dumbarton Oaks: The Origins of the United Nations and the Search for Postwar Security.* Chapel Hill: University of North Carolina Press, 2001.

Hixson, Walter. *The Myth of American Diplomacy: National Identity and American Foreign Policy.* New Haven, CT: Yale University Press, 2008.

Hobsbawm, Eric J. *On Empire: America, War, and Global Supremacy.* New York: Pantheon Books, 2008.

Hofstadter, Richard. *Social Darwinism in American Thought.* New York: G. Braziller, 1959.

Hoganson, Kristin L. *Fighting for American Manhood: How Gender Politics Provoked the Spanish-American and Philippine-American Wars.* New Haven, CT: Yale University Press, 1998.

Holman, Frank Ezekiel. *Story of the "Bricker" Amendment (The First Name).* New York: Committee for Constitutional Government, 1954.

Holmes, Oliver Wendell, and Mark DeWolfe Howe. *The Occasional Speeches of Justice Oliver Wendell Holmes.* Compiled by Mark DeWolfe Howe. Cambridge, MA: Harvard University Press, 1962.

Hoopes, Townsend, and Douglas Brinkley. *FDR and the Creation of the U.N.* New Haven, CT: Yale University Press, 1997.

Horsman, Reginald. *Race and Manifest Destiny: The Origins of American Racial Anglo-Saxonism.* Cambridge, MA: Harvard University Press, 1981.

Howe, Daniel Walker. *What Hath God Wrought: The Transformation of America, 1815–1848.* New York: Oxford University Press, 2007.

Hubbard, James P. *The United States and the End of British Colonial Rule in Africa, 1941–1968.* Jefferson, NC: McFarland, 2011.

Hunt, Lynn. *Inventing Human Rights: A History.* New York: W. W. Norton, 2007.

Hunt, Michael H. *Ideology and U.S. Foreign Policy.* New Haven, CT: Yale University Press, 2009.

Ignatieff, Michael. *Empire Lite: Nation Building in Bosnia, Kosovo and Afghanistan.* London: Vintage, 2003.

———, and Amy Gutmann. *Human Rights as Politics and Idolatry.* Princeton, NJ: Princeton University Press, 2001.

Inboden, William. *Religion and American Foreign Policy, 1945–1960: The Soul of Containment.* New York: Cambridge University Press, 2010.

Inoue, Kyoko. *MacArthur's Japanese Constitution.* Chicago, IL: University of Chicago Press, 1991.

Institute for Peace Research and Security Policy. *OSCE Yearbook 2005: Yearbook on the Organization for Security and Co-operation in Europe.* Baden-Baden: Nomos, 2006.

Iriye, Akira, Petra Goedde, and William Hitchcock. *The Human Rights Revolution: An International History*. Oxford: Oxford University Press, 2012.

Isetti, Ronald. "The Moneychangers of the Temple: FDR, American Civil Religion, and the New Deal." *Presidential Studies Quarterly* 26, no. 3 (1996): 678–693.

Jacobs, Seth. *America's Miracle Man in Vietnam: Ngo Dinh Diem, Religion, Race, and U.S. Intervention in Southeast Asia*. Durham, NC: Duke University Press, 2005.

Jacobson, Matthew Frye. *Barbarian Virtues: The United States Encounters Foreign Peoples at Home and Abroad, 1876–1917*. New York: Hill and Wang, 2000.

James, Stephen Andrew. *Universal Human Rights: Origins and Development*. New York: LFB Scholarly Pub LLC, 2007.

Janowsky, Oscar Isaiah. *The Jews and Minority Rights (1898–1919)*. New York: Columbia University Press, 1933.

Jansen, Marius B. *The Emergence of Meiji Japan*. Cambridge: Cambridge University Press, 1995.

Janssens, Rudolf V. A. *"What Future for Japan?": U.S. Wartime Planning for the Postwar Era, 1942–1945*. Amsterdam: Rodopi, 1995.

Jessup, Philip C. *Elihu Root*. New York: Dodd, Mead & Company, 1938.

Johnson, M. Glen. "The Contributions of Eleanor and Franklin Roosevelt to the Development of International Protection for Human Rights." *Human Rights Quarterly* 9, no. 1 (February 1, 1987): 19–48.

Johnston, Douglas M., Cynthia Sampson, and D.C. Center for Strategic and International Studies Washington. *Religion: The Missing Dimension of Statecraft*. New York: Oxford University Press, 1995.

Kalanges, Kristine. *Religious Liberty in Western and Islamic Law: Toward a World Legal Tradition*. New York: Oxford University Press, 2012.

Kaufman, Natalie Hevener, and David Whiteman. "Opposition to Human Rights Treaties in the United States Senate: The Legacy of the Bricker Amendment." *Human Rights Quarterly* 10, no. 3 (August 1, 1988): 309–337.

Kaufman, Robert Gordon. *Henry M. Jackson: A Life in Politics*. Seattle: University of Washington Press, 2000.

Kawamura, Noriko. "Wilsonian Idealism and Japanese Claims at the Paris Peace Conference." *Pacific Historical Review* 66, no. 4: 503–526.

Kennedy, David. "International Human Rights Movement: Part of the Problem?" *Harvard Human Rights Journal* 15 (2002): 101.

Kennedy, Duncan. *A Critique of Adjudication*. Cambridge, MA: Harvard University Press, 1998.

Kerr, James Edward. *The* Insular *Cases: The Role of the Judiciary in American Expansionism*. Port Washington, NY: Kennikat Press, 1982.

Kertesz, Stephen D. "Human Rights in the Peace Treaties." *Law and Contemporary Problems* 14, no. 4 (1949): 627.

Keys, Barbara. *Reclaiming American Virtue: The Human Rights Revolution of the 1970s.* Cambridge, MA: Harvard University Press, 2014.

Kirby, Dianne, ed. *Religion and the Cold War.* New York: Palgrave, 2013. http://site.ebrary.com/id/10057418.

Kiss, Alexandre Charles, and Mary Frances Dominick. "The International Legal Significance of the Human Rights Provisions of the Helsinki Final Act." *Vanderbilt Journal of Transnational Law* 13 (1980): 293.

Knock, Thomas J. *To End All Wars: Woodrow Wilson and the Quest for a New World Order.* New York: Oxford University Press, 1992.

Koh, Harold Hongju. "Why Do Nations Obey International Law?" *The Yale Law Journal* 106, no. 8 (June 1, 1997): 2599–2659.

Korey, William. *Human Rights and the Helsinki Accord: Focus on U.S. Policy.* New York: Foreign Policy Association, 1983.

———. *NGOs and the Universal Declaration of Human Rights: A Curious Grapevine.* New York: Palgrave, 2001.

———. *The Promises We Keep: Human Rights, the Helsinki Process, and American Foreign Policy.* New York: St. Martin's Press, 1993.

———. "The Story of the Jackson Amendment, 1973–1975." *Midstream: A Jewish Review* 21, no. 3 (March 1975): 3, 11.

———. "The Struggle over Jackson-Mills-Vanik." *The American Jewish Yearbook 1974–1975* (Philadelphia: American Jewish Committee and the Jewish Publication Society of America, 1976), 226.

Kramer, Paul A. *The Blood of Government: Race, Empire, the United States, & the Philippines.* Chapel Hill: University of North Carolina Press, 2006.

———. "Empires, Exceptions, and Anglo-Saxons: Race and Rule between the British and United States Empires, 1880–1910." *Journal of American History* 88, no. 4 (2002): 1315–1353.

———. "Power and Connection: Imperial Histories of the United States in the World." *American Historical Review* 116, no. 5 (2011): 1348–1391.

Krauthammer, Charles. "The Unipolar Moment." *Foreign Affairs* 70, no. 1 (January 1, 1990): 23–33.

LaFeber, Walter. *The New Empire: An Interpretation of American Expansion, 1860–1898.* Ithaca, NY: Published for the American Historical Association by Cornell University Press, 1963.

Lahr, Angela M. *Millennial Dreams and Apocalyptic Nightmares: The Cold War Origins of Political Evangelicalism.* New York: Oxford University Press, 2007.

Lane, Jack C. *Armed Progressive: General Leonard Wood.* San Rafael, CA: Presidio Press, 1978.

Langdell, C. C. "The Status of Our New Territories." *Harvard Law Review* 12, no. 6 (1899): 365–392.
Langer, William L., and S. Everett Gleason. *The Undeclared War, 1940–1941.* New York: Published for the Council on Foreign Relations by Harper, 1953.
Lash, Joseph P. *Eleanor: The Years Alone.* New York: W. W. Norton, 1972.
Lassman, Peter, and Irving Velody. *Max Weber's "Science as a Vocation."* London: Unwyn & Hyman, 1989.
Lauren, Paul Gordon. *The Evolution of International Human Rights: Visions Seen.* Philadelphia: University of Pennsylvania Press, 1998.
Lawson, Gary, and Guy Seidman. *The Constitution of Empire: Territorial Expansion and American Legal History.* New Haven, CT: Yale University Press, 2004.
Lindholm, Tore, W. Cole Durham, Bahia G. Tahzib-Lie, Oslo Coalition on Freedom of Religion or Belief, and Oslo Conference on Freedom of Religion and Belief. *Facilitating Freedom of Religion or Belief: A Deskbook: Published by the Oslo Coalition on Freedom of Religion or Belief in Celebration of the 20th Anniversary of the Declaration on Elimination of All Forms of Intolerance and Discrimination Based on Religion or Belief.* Leiden: Martinus Nijhoff, 2004.
Link, Arthur S. *The Higher Realism of Woodrow Wilson, and Other Essays.* Nashville, TN: Vanderbilt University Press, 1971.
Little, David, John Kelsay, and Abdulaziz Abdulhussein Sachedina. *Human Rights and the Conflict of Cultures: Western and Islamic Perspectives on Religious Liberty.* Columbia: University of South Carolina Press, 1988.
Litwak, Robert. *Détente and the Nixon Doctrine.* New York: Cambridge University Press, 1984.
Lynch, Allen. "Woodrow Wilson and the Principle of National Self-Determination: A Reconsideration." *Review of International Studies* 28, no. 2 (2002): 419–436.
Macartney, C. A. *National States and National Minorities.* New York: Russell & Russell, 1968.
Macklem, Patrick. *The Sovereignty of Human Rights.* Oxford: Oxford University Press, 2015.
MacMillan, Margaret. *Paris 1919: Six Months That Changed the World.* New York: Random House, 2002.
Magee, Malcolm D. *What the World Should Be: Woodrow Wilson and the Crafting of a Faith-Based Foreign Policy.* Waco, TX: Baylor University Press, 2008.
Mahmood, Saba. "Religious Freedom, the Minority Question, and Geopolitics in the Middle East." *Comparative Studies in Society and History* 54, no. 2 (2012): 418–446.
———, and Peter C. Danchin, eds., "Politics of Religious Freedom: Contested Genealogies," Special Issue, *The South Atlantic Quarterly,* 113, no. 1 (2014).

Maier, Charles S. *Among Empires: American Ascendancy and Its Predecessors.* Cambridge, MA: Harvard University Press, 2006.

Majul, Cesar Adib. *Muslims in the Philippines.* Quezon City: Published for the Asian Center by the University of the Philippines Press, 1973.

Manchester, William. *American Caesar: Douglas MacArthur, 1880–1964.* Boston, MA: Little, Brown, 1978.

Manela, Erez. *The Wilsonian Moment: Self-Determination and the International Origins of Anticolonial Nationalism.* Oxford: Oxford University Press, 2007.

March, Andrew F. *Islam and Liberal Citizenship: The Search for an Overlapping Consensus.* Oxford: Oxford University Press, 2009.

Marshall, Louis. *Louis Marshall: Champion of Liberty; Selected Papers and Addresses.* Philadelphia, PA: Jewish Publication Society of America, 1957.

Marshall, Paul A., and Lela Gilbert. *Their Blood Cries Out: The Untold Story of Persecution against Christians in the Modern World.* Dallas, TX: Word Publishing, 1997.

Martin, William. *With God on Our Side.* New York: Broadway Books, 1996.

Martinez, Jenny S. *The Slave Trade and the Origins of International Human Rights Law.* New York: Oxford University Press, 2012.

Masafumi, Okazaki. "Chrysanthemum and Christianity: Education and Religion in Occupied Japan, 1945–1952." *Pacific Historical Review* 79, no. 3 (2010): 393–417.

May, Ernest R., and Angeliki E. Laiou. *The Dumbarton Oaks Conversations and the United Nations, 1944–1994.* Washington, DC: Dumbarton Oaks Research Library and Collection; Distributed by Harvard University Press, 1998.

Mayer, Anne Elizabeth. "Universal versus Islamic Human Rights: A Clash of Cultures or a Clash with a Construct?" *Michigan Journal of International Law* 15, no. 2 (1993): 307–404.

Mazower, Mark. *No Enchanted Palace: The End of Empire and the Ideological Origins of the United Nations.* Princeton, NJ: Princeton University Press, 2009.

———. "The Strange Triumph of Human Rights." *Historical Journal* 47, no. 2 (2004): 379–398.

McCallum, Jack Edward. *Leonard Wood: Rough Rider, Surgeon, Architect of American Imperialism.* New York: New York University Press, 2006.

McCormick, Thomas J. *China Market: America's Quest for Informal Empire, 1893–1901.* Chicago, IL: Quadrangle Books, 1967.

McDougal, Myres S., Harold D. Lasswell, and Longzhi Chen. *Human Rights and World Public Order: The Basic Policies of an International Law of Human Dignity.* New Haven, CT: Yale University Press, 1980.

McNelly, Theodore. *The Origins of Japan's Democratic Constitution.* Lanham, MD: University Press of America, 2000.

Mead, Sidney Earl. *The Lively Experiment: The Shaping of Christianity in America.* New York: Harper & Row, 1963.
Mernissi, Fatima. *Islam and the Fear of the Modern World,* 2nd ed. New York: Basic Books, 2002.
Miller, Stuart Creighton. *Benevolent Assimilation: The American Conquest of the Philippines, 1899–1903.* New Haven, CT: Yale University Press, 1982.
Miller, William Lee. *The First Liberty: America's Foundation in Religious Freedom.* Washington, DC: Georgetown University Press, 2003.
Mockaitis, Thomas R. *The Iraq War: A Documentary and Reference Guide.* Santa Barbara, CA: Greenwood, 2012.
Moore, Ray A. *Soldier of God: MacArthur's Attempt to Christianize Japan.* Portland, ME: MerwinAsia, 2011.
———, and Donald L. Robinson. *Partners for Democracy: Crafting the New Japanese State under MacArthur.* New York: Oxford University Press, 2004.
Morgan, Michael C. "The Seventies and the Rebirth of Human Rights." In Niall Ferguson and Erez Manela, eds., *Shock of the Global.* Cambridge, MA: Harvard University Press, 2011.
Morsink, Johannes. *The Universal Declaration of Human Rights: Origins, Drafting, and Intent.* Philadelphia: University of Pennsylvania Press, 1999.
Mowat, R. B. *Select Treaties and Documents to Illustrate the Development of the Modern European States System, 1815–1916.* Oxford: Clarendon Press, 1916.
Moyn, Samuel. "From Communist to Muslim: European Human Rights, the Cold War and Religious Liberty." *The South Atlantic Quarterly* 113, no. 1 (2014): 63–86.
———. *The Last Utopia: Human Rights in History.* Cambridge, MA: Belknap Press of Harvard University Press, 2010.
Muskie, Edmund S., Kenneth W. Thompson, United States Association of Former Members of Congress, and Atlantic Council of the United States. *The President, the Congress, and Foreign Policy.* Lanham, MD: University Press of America, 1986.
Mutua, Makau. "Savages, Victims, and Saviors: The Metaphor of Human Rights." *Harvard International Law Journal* 42 (2001): 201.
Nakamura, Masanori. *The Japanese Monarchy: Ambassador Joseph Grew and the Making of the "Symbol Emperor System," 1931–1991.* Armonk, NY: M. E. Sharpe, 1992.
Neuhaus, Richard John. *The Naked Public Square: Religion and Democracy in America.* Grand Rapids, MI: W. B. Eerdamns Publishing Company, 1984.
Ninkovich, Frank A. *The United States and Imperialism.* Malden, MA: Blackwell Publishers, 2001.
Nishi, Toshio. *Unconditional Democracy: Education and Politics in Occupied Japan, 1945–1952.* Stanford, CA: Hoover Institution Press, 2004.

Noonan, John Thomas. *The Lustre of Our Country: The American Experience of Religious Freedom.* Berkeley: University of California Press, 1998.

Normand, Roger, and Sarah Zaidi. *Human Rights at the UN: The Political History of Universal Justice.* Bloomington: Indiana University Press, 2008.

Norris, Pippa, and Ronald Inglehart. *Sacred and Secular: Religion and Politics Worldwide.* New York: Cambridge University Press, 2004.

Novak, Michael. *The Rise of the Unmeltable Ethnics.* New York: Macmillan, 1972.

Nugent, Walter T. K. *Habits of Empire: A History of American Expansion.* New York: Alfred A. Knopf, 2008.

Nurser, John. *For All Peoples and All Nations: The Ecumenical Church and Human Rights.* Washington, DC: Georgetown University Press, 2005.

O'Brien, David M., and Yasuo Ōgoshi. *To Dream of Dreams: Religious Freedom and Constitutional Politics in Postwar Japan.* Honolulu: University of Hawaii Press, 1996.

O'Brien, F. William. "General Clark's Nomination as Ambassador to the Vatican: American Reaction." *The Catholic Historical Review* 44, no. 4 (January 1, 1959): 421–439.

Orbach, William W. *The American Movement to Aid Soviet Jews.* Amherst: University of Massachusetts Press, 1979.

Oren, Michael B. *Power, Faith, and Fantasy: America in the Middle East, 1776 to the Present.* New York: W. W. Norton, 2007.

Osgood, Robert Endicott. *Ideals and Self-Interest in America's Foreign Relations: The Great Transformation of the Twentieth Century.* Chicago, IL: University of Chicago Press, 1953.

Parker, Donald Dean. "Church and State in the Philippines, 1896–1906." *The Philippine Social Science Review* 10, no. 4 (November 1938), 354–371.

Paterson, Thomas G., and Stephen G. Rabe, eds. *Imperial Surge: The United States Abroad, the 1890s–Early 1900s.* Lexington, MA: D.C. Heath, 1992.

Payaslian, Simon. *United States Policy toward the Armenian Question and the Armenian Genocide.* New York: Palgrave Macmillan, 2005.

Paz, Moria. "Non-Territorial Ethnic Network and the Making of Human Rights Law: The Case of the Alliance Israelite Universelle." *Interdisciplinary Journal of Human Rights Law* 4 (2010): 1.

Pedersen, Susan. "The Meaning of the Mandates System: An Argument." *Geschichte und Gesellschaft* 32, part 4 (Oct–Dec 2006): 560–582.

Pendergast, William. *The Catholic Voter in American Politics: The Passing of the Democratic Monolith.* Washington, DC: Georgetown University Press, 1999.

Peterson, Christian. *Globalizing Human Rights: Private Citizens, the Soviet Union, and the West.* New York: Routledge, 2012.

Philpott, Daniel. "Religious Freedom and the Undoing of the Westphalian State." *Michigan Journal of International Law* 25, no. 4 (2004): 981.

Pitts, Jennifer. "Political Theory of Empire and Imperialism." *Annual Review of Political Science* 13, no. 1 (May 2010): 211–235.

Plokhy, S. M. *Yalta: The Price of Peace.* New York: Penguin, 2010.

Porter, Andrew. *Religion versus Empire? British Protestant Missionaries and Overseas Expansion, 1700–1914.* Manchester, England: Manchester University Press, 2004.

Potter, Pitman B. "Origin of the System of Mandates under the League of Nations." *American Political Science Review* 16 (1922): 563.

Prendergast, William B. *The Catholic Voter in American Politics: The Passing of the Democratic Monolith.* Washington, DC: Georgetown University Press, 1999.

Preston, Andrew. "Monsters Everywhere: A Genealogy of National Security," Stuart Bernath Lecture. *Diplomatic History* 38, no. 3 (2014): 477–450.

———. *Sword of the Spirit, Shield of Faith: Religion in American War and Diplomacy.* New York: Alfred A. Knopf, 2012.

Price, Willard. *Japan and the Son of Heaven.* New York: Duell, Sloan and Pearce, 1945.

Primus, Richard. *The American Language of Rights.* Cambridge: Cambridge University Press, 1999.

Pringle, Henry F. *The Life and Times of William Howard Taft: A Biography.* New York: Farrar & Rinehart, 1939.

Prucha, Francis Paul. *The Great Father: The United States Government and the American Indians.* Lincoln: University of Nebraska Press, 1984.

Ramet, Sabrina P. *Religious Policy in the Soviet Union.* Cambridge, UK: Cambridge University Press, 1993.

Rana, Aziz. *The Two Faces of American Freedom.* Cambridge, MA: Harvard University Press, 2010.

Randolph, Carman F. "Constitutional Aspects of Annexation." *Harvard Law Review* 12, no. 5 (1898): 291–315.

Reischauer, Edwin Oldfather. *The United States and Japan.* Cambridge, MA: Harvard University Press, 1965.

Reuter, F. T. "William Howard Taft and the Separation of Church and State in the Philippines." *Journal of Church and State* 24, no. 1 (1982): 105–117.

Reuter, Frank T. *Catholic Influence on American Colonial Policies, 1898–1904.* Austin: University of Texas Press, 1967.

Rizal, José. *Noli Me Tangere,* translated with an introduction by Harold Augenbraum. New York: Penguin, 2006.

Robinson, Nehemiah. *The Universal Declaration of Human Rights: Its Origin, Significance, Application, and Interpretation.* New York: Institute of Jewish Affairs, World Jewish Congress, 1958.

Rodgers, Daniel T. *Age of Fracture.* Cambridge, MA: Harvard University Press, 2011.

Rodogno, Davide. *Against Massacre: Humanitarian Interventions in the Ottoman Empire, 1815–1914.* Princeton, NJ: Princeton University Press, 2012.

Roosevelt, Franklin D., and William J. Federer. *The Faith of FDR: From President Franklin Delano Roosevelt's Public Papers, 1933–1945.* St. Louis, MO: Amerisearch, 2006.

Roth, Andrew. *Dilemma in Japan.* Boston, MA: Little, Brown and Company, 1945.

Russell, Ruth B. *A History of the United Nations Charter: The Role of the United States, 1940–1945.* Washington, DC: Brookings Institution, 1958.

Ryan, Halford Ross, ed. *The Inaugural Addresses of Twentieth-Century American Presidents.* Westport, CT: Praeger, 1993.

Saleeby, Najeeb M. *The History of Sulu.* Manila: Bureau of Printing, 1908.

Salman, Michael. *The Embarrassment of Slavery: Controversies over Bondage and Nationalism in the American Colonial Philippines.* Berkeley: University of California Press, 2001.

Sargent, Daniel. "Oasis in the Desert: America's Human Rights Rediscovery." In Jan Eckel and Samuel Moyn, eds., *The Breakthrough: Human Rights in the 1970s.* Philadelphia: University of Pennsylvania Press, 2014.

Schechtman, Joseph B. "Decline of the International Protection of Minority Rights." *The Western Political Quarterly* 4, no. 1 (March 1, 1951): 1–11.

Schlesinger, Stephen C. *Act of Creation: The Founding of the United Nations: A Story of Superpowers, Secret Agents, Wartime Allies and Enemies, and Their Quest for a Peaceful World.* New York: Basic Books, 2003.

Schonberger, Howard B. *Aftermath of War: Americans and the Remaking of Japan, 1945–1952.* Kent, OH: Kent State University Press, 1989.

Schultz, Kevin M. *Tri-Faith America: How Catholics and Jews Held Postwar America to Its Protestant Promise.* New York: Oxford University Press, 2011.

Scolnicov, Anat. *The Right to Religious Freedom in International Law: Between Group Rights and Individual Rights.* London: Routledge, 2011.

Sehat, David. *The Myth of American Religious Freedom.* Oxford: Oxford University Press, 2011.

Sellars, Kirsten. *The Rise and Rise of Human Rights.* Stroud, Gloucestershire: Sutton, 2002.

Sharkey, Heather. *American Evangelicals in Egypt: Missionary Encounters in an Age of Empire.* Princeton, NJ: Princeton University Press, 2008.

Shea, Nina. *In the Lion's Den: A Shocking Account of Persecution and Martyrdom of Christians Today & How We Should Respond.* Nashville, TN: Broadman & Holman Publishers, 1997.

Shibusawa, Naoko. *America's Geisha Ally: Reimagining the Japanese Enemy.* Cambridge, MA: Harvard University Press, 2009.

Shimazu, Naoko. *Japan, Race, and Equality: The Racial Equality Proposal of 1919.* London: Routledge, 1998.

Silbey, David. *A War of Frontier and Empire: The Philippine-American War, 1899–1902*. New York: Hill and Wang, 2007.

Simpson, Alfred William Brian. *Human Rights and the End of Empire: Britain and the Genesis of the European Convention*. Oxford: Oxford University Press, 2004.

Smith, Steven D. *The Rise and Decline of American Religious Freedom*. Cambridge, MA: Harvard University Press, 2014.

Smolin, David M. "Exporting the First Amendment: Evangelism, Proselytism, and the International Religious Freedom Act." *Cumberland Law Review* 31 (2000): 685.

Snyder, Sarah B. *Human Rights Activism and the End of the Cold War: A Transnational History of the Helsinki Network*. New York: Cambridge University Press, 2011.

———. "'Jerry, Don't Go': Domestic Opposition to the 1975 Helsinki Final Act." *Journal of American Studies* 44, no. 1 (2010): 67–81.

Sparrow, Bartholomew H. *The* Insular *Cases and the Emergence of American Empire*. Lawrence: University Press of Kansas, 2006.

Steiner, Henry J., and Philip Alston. *International Human Rights in Context: Law, Politics, Morals: Text and Materials*. Oxford: Clarendon Press, Oxford University Press, 1996.

Stephanson, Anders. *Manifest Destiny: American Expansion and the Empire of Right*. New York: Farrar, Straus and Giroux, 1996.

Stern, Paula. *Water's Edge: Domestic Politics and the Making of American Foreign Policy*. Westport, CT: Greenwood Press, 1979.

Stevens, Jason W. *God-Fearing and Free: A Spiritual History of America's Cold War*. Cambridge, MA: Harvard University Press, 2011.

Stokes, Anson Phelps, and Leo Pfeffer. *Church and State in the United States*. New York: Harper & Row, 1964.

Sullivan, Donna J. "Gender Equality and Religious Freedom: Toward a Framework for Conflict Resolution." *New York University Journal of International Law and Politics* 24 (1991): 795.

Takeda, Kiyoko. *The Dual-Image of the Japanese Emperor*. New York: New York University Press, 1988.

Takemae, Eiji. *The Allied Occupation of Japan*. New York: Continuum International Publishing Group, 2003.

———, Robert Ricketts, and Sebastian Swann. *Inside GHQ: The Allied Occupation of Japan and Its Legacy*. New York: Continuum, 2002.

Teitel, Ruti. *Humanity's Law*. New York: Oxford University Press, 2011.

Thier, J. Alexander. "The Making of a Constitution in Afghanistan." *New York Law School Law Review* 51 (2006): 557.

Thomas, Daniel Charles. *The Helsinki Effect: International Norms, Human Rights, and the Demise of Communism*. Princeton, NJ: Princeton University Press, 2001.

Throntveit Trygve. "The Fable of the Fourteen Points: Woodrow Wilson and National Self-Determination." *Diplomatic History* 35, no. 3 (June 2011): 445–481.

Tibi, Bassam. "Islamic Law/Shari'a, Human Rights, Universal Morality and International Relations." *Human Rights Quarterly* 162 (1994): 277–299.

Tillman, Seth P. *Anglo-American Relations at the Paris Peace Conference of 1919.* Princeton, NJ: Princeton University Press, 1961.

Toft, Monica Duffy, Daniel Philpott, and Timothy Samuel Shah. *God's Century: Resurgent Religion and Global Politics.* New York: W. W. Norton, 2011.

Tompkins, E. Berkeley. *Anti-Imperialism in the United States: The Great Debate, 1890–1920.* Philadelphia: University of Pennsylvania Press, 1970.

Tuveson, Ernest Lee. *Redeemer Nation: The Idea of America's Millennial Role.* Chicago, IL: University of Chicago Press, 1968.

Van Boven, Theo. "The Role of Non-Governmental Organizations in International Human Rights Standard-Setting: A Prerequisite of Democracy." *California Western International Law Journal* 20 (1989): 207.

Waltz, Susan E. "Reclaiming and Rebuilding the History of the Universal Declaration of Human Rights." *Third World Quarterly* 23, no. 3 (2002): 437–448.

Ward, Robert Edward, Yoshikazu Sakamoto, Nihon Gakujutsu Shinkōkai, Joint Committee on Japanese Studies, and Social Science Research Council (U.S.). *Democratizing Japan: The Allied Occupation.* Honolulu: University of Hawaii Press, 1987.

Warren, James. *The Sulu Zone, 1768–1898: The Dynamics of External Trade, Slavery and Ethnicity in the Transformation of a Southeast Asian Maritime State.* Singapore: NUS Press, 2003.

Welles, Benjamin. *Sumner Welles: FDR's Global Strategist: A Biography.* New York: St. Martin's Press, 1997.

Wenger, Andreas, Vojtech Mastny, and Christian Nuenlist, eds. *Origins of the European Security System: The Helsinki Process Revisited, 1965–75.* New York: Routledge, 2008.

Wertheim Stephen. "The League of Nations: A Retreat from International Law?" *Journal of Global History* 7, no. 2 (2012): 210–232.

———. "The League That Wasn't: American Designs for a Legalist-Sanctionist League of Nations and the Intellectual Origins of International Organization, 1914–1920." *Diplomatic History* 35, no. 5 (2011): 797–836.

Williams, Daniel K. *God's Own Party.* New York: Oxford University Press, 2010.

Williams, William Appleman. *The Roots of the Modern American Empire: A Study of the Growth and Shaping of Social Consciousness in a Marketplace Society.* New York: Random House, 1969.

Wilson, Ann Marie. "In the Name of God, Civilization, and Humanity: The United States and the Armenian Massacres of the 1890s." *Le Mouvement Social* 2, no. 227 (2009): 27–44.

Witte, John, and M. Christian Green. "Religious Freedom, Democracy, and International Human Rights." *Emory International Law Review* 23, no. 2 (2009): 583–608.

Wittner, Lawrence S. "MacArthur and the Missionaries: God and Man in Occupied Japan." *Pacific Historical Review* 40, no. 1 (February 1, 1971): 77–98.

Wolf, Thomas P., William D. Pederson, and Byron W. Daynes. *Franklin D. Roosevelt and Congress: The New Deal and Its Aftermath.* Armonk, NY: M. E. Sharpe, 2001.

Wolfe, Robert. *Americans as Proconsuls: United States Military Government in Germany and Japan, 1944–1952.* Carbondale: Southern Illinois University Press, 1984.

Woodward, Bob. *State of Denial: Bush at War.* New York: Simon & Schuster, 2007.

Wright, Quincy. *Mandates under the League of Nations.* Chicago, IL: University of Chicago Press, 1930.

Zietsma, David. "Building the Kingdom of God: Religious Discourse, National Identity and the Good Neighbor Policy, 1930–1938." *Rhetoric & Public Affairs* 11, no. 2 (2008): 179–214.

———. "Sin Has No History: Religion, National Identity and U.S. Intervention, 1937–1941." *Diplomatic History* 31 (2007): 531–565.

Zimmermann, Warren. *First Great Triumph: How Five Americans Made Their Country a World Power.* New York: Farrar, Straus and Giroux, 2002.

Zwierlein, Frederick James. *Theodore Roosevelt and Catholics, 1882–1919.* St. Louis: V. T. Suren; for sale by Art Print Shop, Rochester, NY, 1956.

Websites

About the U.S. Helsinki Commission, http://csce.gov/index.cfm?FuseAction=AboutHelsinkiProcess.OSCE.

Canadian PM announces establishment of the Office of Religious Freedom, February 19, 2013, http://pm.gc.ca/eng/media.asp?category=1&featureId=6&pageId=26&id=5306.

Democratic Party Platform of 1900, http://www.presidency.ucsb.edu/ws/index.php?pid=29587.

Elizabeth Shakman Hurd, "Believing in Religious Freedom," *The Immanent Frame,* 2012, http://blogs.ssrc.org/tif/2012/03/01/believing-in-religious-freedom.

Elizabeth Shakman Hurd, "What's Wrong with Promoting Religious Freedom?," *Foreign Policy,* June 12, 2013, http://mideastafrica.foreignpolicy.com/posts/2013/06/12/whats_wrong_with_promoting_religious_freedom.

Harry S. Truman, Address Recommending aid to Greece and Turkey, March 12, 1947, http://avalon.law.yale.edu/20th_Century/trudoc.asp.

John Dower, "A Warning from History: Don't Expect Democracy in Iraq," *Boston Review* (March 2003), http://www.bostonreview.net/BR28.1/dower.html.

League of Nations Covenant, http://avalon.law.yale.edu/20th_Century/leagcov.asp.

Letter from Harry Truman to Pius XII, August 6, 1947, http://www.presidency.ucsb.edu/ws/?pid=12746.

Pew Research Project on Religion and Public Life, "Religious Hostilities Reach Six-Year High," January 12, 2014, http://www.pewforum.org/files/2014/01/RestrictionsV-full-report.pdf.

Pius XI, Divini Redemptoris (Divine Redeemer), March 19, 1937, http://www.vatican.va/holy_Father/pius_xi/encyclicals/documents/hf_p-xi_enc_19031937_divini-redemptoris_en.html.

President George W. Bush, Remarks to a Joint Session of the Philippine Congress, October 18, 2003, http://www.presidency.ucsb.edu/ws/?pid=63501.

Project for the New American Century, Statement of Principles, June 3, 1997, http://www.newamericancentury.org/statementofprinciples.htm.

Republican Party Platform of 1900, http://www.presidency.ucsb.edu/ws/index.php?pid=29630.

United Nations Declaration of Human Rights, http://www.yale.edu/lawweb/avalon/un/unrights.htm.

Woodrow Wilson's Fourteen Points Speech, http://avalon.law.yale.edu/20th_century/wilson14.asp.

Acknowledgments

This book began at Harvard Law School, a stimulating environment of interdisciplinary learning, and where I had the good fortune to encounter wonderful friends and teachers. Noah Feldman believed in me from the moment I arrived, and he encouraged me to follow the scholarly path as a most suitable pursuit. I learned much about religion and politics and about the relationship between ideals and interests from our conversations. It would be hard to imagine this book without his enthusiasm, confidence, and wisdom. Duncan Kennedy taught me how to think critically about the law. He was an expert and inspiring guide to a theoretical canon that constantly asks one to be mindful of common perceptions. David Armitage generously welcomed me into the world of academic history. I owe him thanks for his unfailing support and for a model of what the life of the mind should be. Their influence on my thinking extends far beyond this work.

I am grateful to the HLS Graduate Program for the institutional support, and for all the fellowships from Harvard Law School, the Edmond J. Safra Center for Ethics, and the Baldy Center for Law and Social Policy at the State University of New York (SUNY) Buffalo Law School. The librarians at HLS and SUNY Buffalo law libraries, especially Terri Saint Amour at HLS, provided indispensable research support and assistance during the writing and revision process.

Many scholars of various disciplines have been generous with their time and comments as they read parts of this work, including Eric Beerbohm, Chris Capozzola, David Foglesong, Rick Garnett, Helen Hardacre, Elizabeth Shakman Hurd, William Inboden, Seth Jacobs, Frances Kamm, Barbara Keys, Erez Manela, Ray Moore, Andrew Preston, and Mikhail Xifaras. Mark Tushnet read and commented on an early version of the manuscript and provided encouragement along the way. Samuel Moyn came to Harvard at a most opportune time: He challenged my arguments and helped me to clarify my claims. I also thank the anonymous reviewers for their careful reading and insightful suggestions on the manuscript. Any remaining mistakes are mine alone.

I have presented different parts of this work at the SJD colloquium at HLS, a seminar at the Edmond J. Safra Center for Ethics; the Religion and Cold War panel of the 2012 Annual Meeting of the Society of Historians of American Foreign Relations; the 2012 Third Roundtable on Law and Religion held at Harvard Law School; the 2013 HLS Institute for Global Law and Policy Workshop held in Doha, Qatar; and in a faculty workshop at the University of Toronto Faculty of Law. I have gained much from the participants in all those venues. Chapter 2 builds upon ideas that were initially developed in "Woodrow Wilson and the Origins of International Religious Freedom," *Journal of the History of International Law* 15, no. 2 (2013): 235–267.

Along the way, I am lucky to have forged many friendships that now span the globe, and they contributed directly and indirectly to this book at its various stages. Ori Aronson, Or Bassok, Shunling Chen, Holger Drössler, Iain Frame, Afroditi Giovanopoulou, Jorge Jacome Gonzalez, Nkatha Kabira, Lisa Kelly, Vishaal Kishore, Jed Kroncke, Jennifer Langlais, Shay Lavie, Saskia Lettmaier, Cheah Wui Ling, Heidi Matthews, Goncalo de Almeida Ribeiro, Nitya Shekar, Adam Shinar, Jennifer Shkabatur, Chris Szabla, Peter Szigeti, and Namita Wahi were all intellectual interlocutors as well as good friends. Holger Drössler and Adam Shinar read many chapters. Lisa Kelly and I debated the work's implications. My compatriots in Cambridge and beyond, Jing Aguda, Dino Aguirre, Peej Bernardo, Cathy Buena, Ryan Castillo, Martin Lacdao, John Molo, Neo Pascual, Chippy del Rosario, Marco Sardillo, Adrian Serojihos, and Peter Pojol, SJ, made the experience fun and memorable.

As this is a first book, I also want to acknowledge the other debts I have incurred in making this journey possible. I learned how to teach from the examples of Mike Klarman from HLS; J. Bryan Hehir, Stanley Hoffmann, and Stephen Rosen from the Department of Government; and my Arabic language teacher Nevenka Korica Sullivan from the Department of Near Eastern Languages and Civilizations. I hope I can provide similar inspiration to my own students. My interest in religion and constitutional law was first nurtured in the classes of my Jesuit mentor Joaquin Bernas, SJ, many years ago at the Ateneo Law School in the Philippines. Father Clem Ignacio took a chance and financially supported my initial legal studies. Tony LaViña gave me valuable opportunities to put theory into practice, including a consulting stint with the Philippine government negotiating team with the Moro Islamic Liberation Front.

Kathleen McDermott, my editor at Harvard University Press, was enthusiastic about the project from the beginning. I am thankful for her support and guidance throughout the publication process.

My close friendships have been such wonderful blessings that one is tempted to think they can only exist either in movies or in one's imagination. But they all shared concretely in my joy, excitement, despair, and heartbreak over the years.

My life is forever enriched by them. Neo Pascual, my best friend of over a decade, kept me sane and hopeful with our chats and summer trips. Cheah Wui Ling made me laugh, mooted my talks, and listened to my rants from across the pond. Nkatha Kabira and I shared a place for three years and a lifetime of happy memories. I have learned a lot from our conversations on law, the postcolonial condition, and life. Adam "Adamee" Shinar has read every single page of this book and patiently engaged with my inchoate thoughts about this project longer than anyone. We've been coauthors, office mates, travel buddies, and best friends—without him the memories of my Harvard years would be impossible.

I dedicate this book to my family—my mom Amy and brother Allan in Manila, and my sister Wei in Los Angeles—each of whom gave unwavering love and much needed emotional and sometimes financial support. Alas, my dad suddenly passed away before I finished writing. He would have understood what was taking me so long to "finish school" had he seen this book.

Last but certainly not least, the great philosopher Søren Kierkegaard's words—"so let us either forget all about Abraham or learn how to be horrified at the monstrous paradox which is the significance of his life, so that we can understand that our time like any other can be glad if it has faith"—sustained me in the years during which this work was completed, and hopefully, in all the years hereafter. *Ad majorem Dei gloriam.*

Index

www.ingramcontent.com/pod-product-compliance
Lightning Source LLC
Chambersburg PA
CBHW021056080326
40727CB00008B/110/J
* 9 7 8 0 6 7 4 2 8 6 0 2 3 *